# The U.S.–Japan Alliance: Past, Present, and Future

# The U.S.–Japan Alliance: Past, Present, and Future

Edited by
Michael J. Green    Patrick M. Cronin

COUNCIL ON FOREIGN RELATIONS PRESS
NEW YORK

The Council on Foreign Relations, Inc., a nonprofit, nonpartisan national membership organization founded in 1921, is dedicated to promoting understanding of international affairs through the free and civil exchange of ideas. The Council's members are dedicated to the belief that America's peace and prosperity are firmly linked to that of the world. From this flows the mission of the Council: to foster America's understanding of its fellow members of the international community, near and far, their peoples, cultures, histories, hopes, quarrels, and ambitions; and thus to serve, protect, and advance America's own global interests through study and debate, private and public.

From time to time books, monographs, and reports written by members of the Council's research staff or others are published as a "Council on Foreign Relations Book." Any work bearing that designation is, in the judgment of the Committee on Studies of the Council's Board of Directors, a responsible treatment of a significant international topic.



*Council on Foreign Relations Books are distributed by Brookings Institution Press (1-800-275-1447). For further information on Council publications, please write the Council on Foreign Relations, 58 East 68th Street, New York, NY 10021, or call the Director of Communications at (212) 434-9400. Or visit our website at www.foreignrelations.org.*



Library of Congress Cataloging-in-Publication Data

The U.S.-Japan Alliance: Past, Present, and Future / edited by Michael J. Green and Patrick M. Cronin

p. cm.
Includes bibliographical references and index.
ISBN 0-87609-249-0
1. United States—Foreign relations—Japan. 2. Japan—Foreign relations—United States. 3. United States—Foreign relations—1989–. 4. National Security—United States—History—20th century. 5. National Security—Japan—History—20th century.
I. Green, Michael J. II. Cronin, Patrick M., 1950–.
III. Title: United States–Japan Alliance.
E183.8.J3U15 1999
1999
327.73052—DC21 99-14009
CIP

# Contents

# Foreword

ONE OF the most significant developments that occurred when I was Secretary of Defense was the completion of the U.S.–Japan Joint Security Declaration in April 1996. While much of the press coverage of President Clinton and Prime Minister Hashimoto's Tokyo summit suggested that the Security Declaration was a reaction to incidents on Okinawa and in the Taiwan Strait, the fact is that we had begun an intensive bilateral dialogue with our Japanese counterparts on the future of the alliance as early as the fall of 1995. Though this dialogue was primarily government-to-government, a great deal of the input on the U.S. side came from experts in the think tank and academic worlds. In meeting various of these scholars to discuss how the administration should proceed in furthering its security relationship with Japan, I was impressed with both the breadth and depth of expertise available concerning the U.S.–Japan alliance. This book brings together some of the best of these scholars' insights into the history, process, and future possibilities for the U.S.–Japan security relationship.

I recommend this volume to any serious student of the U.S.–Japan alliance in government or academia. The scholars and analysts featured here have all had an important impact on the debate over U.S. security policy in Asia, and many will continue to play a role in supporting the alliance into the next century. Readers in Asia will be gratified to know that such expertise informs U.S. thinking about security policy and that there remains a strong intellectual basis for maintaining forward U.S. engagement and presence in the region. Readers in the United States will take note of the evolution of our alliance with Japan and the challenges and opportunities for the future.

One of the early architects of the postwar U.S.–Japan security relationship, Shigeru Yoshida, was said to have warned even at the height of World War II that Japan was incapable of prospering in the future without a close relationship with the United States. The analysis in this book should demonstrate that Yoshida's prescient observation of Japan's interests will also be true for the United States. The United States is an Asia-Pacific power, and its prosperity will depend on a close and cooperative security relationship with Japan.

*William J. Perry*
Secretary of Defense
February 1994–January 1997

# Introductory Note

OVER THE past few years there has been a debate over "reaffirming," "revising," and even "restructuring" the U.S.–Japan alliance, but often missing from this debate has been a full appreciation of exactly how this crucial security relationship works. In this volume, seventeen of the leading experts on the U.S.–Japan alliance bridge that gap, explaining the historical evolution of the alliance; the military, diplomatic, and technological linkages between the United States and Japan; the domestic and international pressures on the security relationship; and the interplay of economic and security relations. The volume's coeditors, Michael Green of the Council on Foreign Relations and Patrick Cronin of the U.S. Institute of Peace, draw on the authors' analyses to recommend an agenda for the alliance that will enhance U.S. interests and overall stability in the Asia-Pacific region.

Despite the rhetoric in U.S. policy of a "strategic partnership" with China and an "alliance" with Russia, in reality the United States can accomplish few of its objectives in Asia without close strategic cooperation with its traditional ally, Japan. This volume explains not only why that is the case, but what must be done to ensure that the U.S.–Japan alliance is ready for future challenges that could emerge in the region. These challenges could come from instability on the Korean Peninsula or in the Taiwan Strait, further economic uncertainty in the region, or the threat from proliferation of weapons of mass destruction. Some of these threats the alliance can manage; others it cannot. Scholars and policymakers considering how the United States can prepare for these contingencies without undermining East Asia's stability will want to read this book closely.

*Lawrence J. Korb*
Maurice R. Greenberg Chair, Director of Studies
Council on Foreign Relations

# Introduction

FROM October 1994 through April 1996, the governments of the United States and Japan undertook an intensive bilateral review of the security relationship in a post–Cold War context. The review, coined "the Nye Initiative" in the media (after then assistant secretary of defense for international security affairs Joseph Nye Jr.), was interrupted by the shocking rape of a young schoolgirl by U.S. servicemen on Okinawa in September 1995 and by Chinese missile demonstrations in the Taiwan Strait in March 1996. These two episodes intensified the public debate over the utility of the U.S.–Japan alliance in Japan and added a new urgency to the two governments' dialogue.

When Prime Minister Ryutaro Hashimoto and President Bill Clinton finally met in April 1996, they codified the results of the Nye Initiative in a Joint Security Declaration. Through that document, the two leaders attempted to demonstrate that the alliance had emerged from the political and security crises of the previous year with even greater political and operational credibility. Specifically, in the Security Declaration the president and the prime minister:

- recognized the continuing importance of the alliance to regional security and stability;
- reaffirmed the importance of maintaining forward U.S. presence in the region at approximately 100,000 troops for the foreseeable future;
- initiated a review of existing Guidelines for Defense Cooperation in order to focus on cooperation in responding to regional contingencies (the existing Guidelines focused more narrowly on the direct defense of Japan);
- agreed on a new Acquisition and Cross-Servicing Agreement;
- agreed to return key U.S. military installations on Okinawa to Japan while maintaining overall U.S. capabilities;
- promised to work together to help China play a constructive role in regional stability.

Throughout the process of the Nye Initiative and the announcement of the Joint Security Declaration, observers questioned whether the exercise was a redefinition or only a reaffirmation of the U.S.–Japan alliance. On one side, critics of the status quo who wanted Japan to do more in regional defense (or who wanted fewer U.S. forces on Japanese soil) argued that the redefinition was insufficient. On the other side, critics who feared that Japan was doing *too much* warned that the treaty had been essentially rewritten by the Security Declaration—that the redefinition had gone too far (this was particularly true of the Chinese reaction). For their part, Prime Minister Hashimoto and President Clinton avoided the term *redefinition* altogether and claimed in the Security Declaration only that they had reaffirmed the fundamental importance of the bilateral alliance.

Redefinition or reaffirmation? In July 1994, when the Security Declaration was still in the concept stage, we published a monograph proposing an agenda for bilateral dialogue entitled "Redefining the U.S.–Japan Alliance." That title took on far more import in Japan than either of us intended—in fact, in retrospect, it appears to have introduced the concept of redefinition into the rhetoric of the debate over the role of the alliance.[1] Our intention in the monograph was to propose a proactive agenda for strengthening U.S.–Japan security cooperation, not a reinterpretation or rewriting of the Security Treaty. However, after some reflection, we decided that the ensuing debate over redefinition versus reaffirmation was actually important. We also decided that the answer to the question of how much has, will, or should change in the alliance required a detailed assessment beyond one short monograph.

To begin the process, the Johns Hopkins University Paul H. Nitze School of Advanced International Studies, the Institute for National Strategic Studies at the National Defense University, and the Institute for Defense Analyses jointly sponsored a conference in December 1995 under the title "The U.S.–Japan Alliance: Past, Present, and Future." Scholars and policy analysts were invited from the United States and Japan to present a series of historical papers and policy prescriptions on key elements in the alliance relationship. At the end of the conference, senior scholars and policymakers who had participated urged greater dissemination of the findings, and the majority of participants in the conference agreed to collaborate in the production of an edited volume featuring the revised and updated versions of best papers and presentations. This book is the result.

In editing the authors' contributions and preparing our own conclusions and recommendations, we realized that the book might also be useful as a comprehensive "owner's manual" on the alliance. With this in mind, we have organized the book into four sections: the strategic environment, the military bond, the politics of the alliance, and economics, technology, and security. With the help of Emily Metzgar, Rollie Lal, and Yoshiko Tanaka, we also created a chronology and annotated appendices to help students of the alliance use this book as a portal to further research and inquiry.

The authors of the chapters are policymakers, historians, international relations theorists, economists, and policy analysts. All were actively engaged in the policy and scholarly debate that generated the April 1996 Joint Security Declaration and its subsequent implementation. All agree on the importance of maintaining and strengthening the U.S.–Japan alliance, but have different ideas on how to proceed. All have intimate understanding of the politics, history, and process of U.S.–Japan security cooperation, though none purports to represent official positions or anyone other than themselves. This volume highlights the research and policy prescriptions of the American participants in the debate. It is the hope of the authors that a subsequent volume will feature essays from both sides of the Pacific.

From the eclectic group of security and Japan experts contributing to this volume emerge five consistent themes. First, all of the authors—whether critics of the status quo or not—begin with the fundamental premise that the U.S.–Japan alliance is critical to the maintenance of U.S. interests and stability in the Asia-Pacific region. In fact, most of the arguments here are based on assessments of self-interest and not idealism. The United States and Japan are indeed bound by common values related to democracy, an open economic system, and human rights, but the description of the real "glue" of the alliance in these pages focuses on military and political cooperation in a fundamentally competitive and unpredictable world. It is important for political leaders to articulate the ideals that motivate our bilateral security cooperation, but ultimately, common security interests will determine the endurance of the alliance.

A second theme that emerges in these pages is that the alliance is still not a fully functioning military alliance. From technology cooperation to military planning, the U.S.–Japan alliance is in many areas a pale comparison to NATO or the U.S.–Republic of Korea (ROK) alliance. The reasons for these gaps in the relationship have much to do with the legacy of the Pacific War in regional and domestic Japanese politics. There is also a good amount of "old think" on the U.S. side. As a political alliance, the U.S.–Japan security relationship was a huge success during the Cold War. It helped to contain and complicate Soviet expansion in the Far East, and it contributed to political stability and economic growth in the region. As Sheila Smith argues in her chapter, the United States and Japan gradually established a basis for military cooperation throughout this period, but the impact was once again political for the most part—legitimizing Japan's security policy and rearmament at home and in the region. Smith and other authors point out that the credibility of the alliance now depends on translating that political legitimacy back into real military interoperability and readiness between U.S. and Japanese forces. The April 1996 summit began that process, but there is much to be completed.

Incrementalism is a third theme that appears throughout the chapters in this book. Whether in the evolution of military cooperation, the building of a domestic political consensus in Japan on bilateral security cooperation, or the management of technological collaboration—Japan has moved forward, but only in small steps and with plenty of careful looking over the shoulder for regional reactions and domestic political support. The authors are somewhat divided on whether or not this incrementalism is a good thing. On the one hand, predictability is an important ingredient in regional stability. On the other hand, "too little, too late" from Japan in a regional crisis could have devastating consequences for the bilateral security relationship. As several of the historical essays in the book indicate, change in Japanese security policy has often come in reaction to crises in domestic politics, regional balances of power, or U.S. security policy. The challenge for Washington, then, is to maintain progress in bilateral security cooperation without having to rely on a crisis to move forward. To some extent, the 1995–96 Nye Initiative demonstrated an ability for self-initiated enhancement of security cooperation, but even that exercise was propelled forward by the incidents on Okinawa and in the Taiwan Strait.

A fourth theme, particularly evident in the chapters by Robert Manning and James Przystup, is that the U.S.–Japan alliance is an increasingly important variable in Asia's fluid regional security environment. There has always been a regional dimension to U.S.–Japan security cooperation, of course, but during the Cold War Japan's political alignment with the United States and military capabilities for self-defense were most important in the more static context of containing Soviet political and military expansion. The dynamics of East Asia's post–Cold War security environment are far more fluid, and thus subtle changes in Japan's security cooperation with the United States have a far greater impact on security calculations made throughout the region—particularly in Beijing. In a sense, this new dynamic is a check on those who argue for abandoning the incremental approach to bilateral security cooperation. Washington and Tokyo are under long-term pressure to realign U.S. forces in Japan without undermining faith in U.S. staying power and to enhance regional security cooperation without threatening China or upsetting South Korea. Absent a crisis, incrementalism seems almost unavoidable.

The fifth theme is that the security policymaking process in both the United States and Japan is becoming more fluid and pluralistic. The good news in these pages is that support for the alliance has expanded in both countries and that the traditional opponents of the alliance (trade hawks, left-wing socialists, and revisionists) are increasingly marginalized. At the same time, the participants in the security debate in Japan have proliferated and the influence of the defense policy elite in the Liberal Democratic Party (LDP) and the government has weakened. As Lee Howell points out, continued political realignment will only add greater uncertainty to management of the alliance relationship. In the United States, meanwhile, the voices against overseas presence and forward engagement are eerily quiet at present. However, as Richard Samuels and Christopher Twomey indicate in their chapter, the theoretical basis for new variations on the alliance is being prepared in anticipation of future fiscal or security challenges to the status quo. In both countries, the "anti" versus "pro" U.S.–Japan alliance debate could be replaced by what the Japanese call *"Soron Sansei, Kakuron Hantai"*—agreement with the overall principle, but profound disagreement on the specifics.

The editors reexamine these themes in the conclusion of the book. The main text is divided into four sections. The first section, The Strategic Environment, establishes the theoretical and policy framework for the subsequent case studies. In chapter 1, "The Eagle Eyes the Pacific: American Foreign Policy Options in East Asia after the Cold War," Richard Samuels and Christopher Twomey outline the United States' strategic options in Asia as (1) maintaining the status quo, (2) severing alliances and abandoning bases abroad while developing more long-range capabilities, (3) finding a new ally, and (4) reconfiguring the U.S.–Japan alliance. The Samuels-Twomey prescriptions lay out the policy choices clearly and form a useful contextual starting point for the chapters that follow (though we do disagree with some of their specific prescriptions for reconfiguring the alliance). The chapter is particularly important for setting up the trade-offs that policymakers face between using the alliance to shape the regional security environment and maintaining political support for the alliance at home. "Symmetry" and "fairness" are irrelevant to the former task (if not downright harmful), but could be indispensable to the latter task.

In chapters 2 and 3, James Przystup and Robert Manning examine the constraints placed on bilateral cooperation by regional security concerns and the ability of bilateral security cooperation in turn to shape the regional environment. In "China, Japan, and the United States," Przystup places East Asia's critical trilateral relationship in historical perspective. He concludes that history teaches us that the United States and Japan cannot force China to act against its perceived interests, but that the U.S.–Japan alliance does provide instruments for creating an international environment that will lead Beijing to see integration as a matter of Chinese national interests. Manning's "Waiting for Godot? Northeast Asian Future Shock and the U.S.–Japan Alliance" examines the future role of the U.S.–Japan alliance in shaping the regional security environment and concludes that events such as the transformation of the Korean Peninsula will only lead to greater uncertainty and hedging in regional security politics. He points to the Sino–Russian entente as a warning sign that hedging—including the reaffirmation of the U.S.–Japan alliance—may be prudent but carries risks. He argues that the great powers must act now to establish a new equilibrium rather than place their faith in multilateral institutions such as the Association of Southeast Asian Nations (ASEAN) Regional Forum. His chapter suggests that the U.S.–Japan alliance can underpin that new equilibrium by demonstrating both resolve and self-restraint.

The second section of the book, the Military Bond, gets down to the nuts and bolts of defense cooperation between the United States and Japan. In "The Evolution of Military Cooperation in the U.S.–Japan Alliance," Sheila Smith explains that U.S.–Japan military cooperation began late in the alliance relationship. Without an integrated command or joint strategy, Washington and Tokyo had to establish military cooperation through formulas such as the nonbinding Defense Guidelines of 1978 and the division of roles and missions in the 1980s. Smith argues that this general approach is still appropriate for defining military cooperation, but warns that it will become more difficult if the United States and Japan begin considering cooperation in areas beyond the defense of Japan or contingencies on the Korean Peninsula. She notes that the 1997 revision of the Defense Guidelines sends the United States and Japan into just such uncharted waters and that the success of the new Guidelines will depend on Tokyo's ability to define visible missions for the Japanese Self-Defense Forces that are still consistent with the Japanese constitution. In "Managing the New U.S.–Japan Security Alliance: Enhancing Structures and Mechanisms to Address Post–Cold War Requirements," Paul Giarra and Akihisa Nagashima explain the unique bureaucratic and political arrangements that have replaced a combined command structure between the United States and Japan. They note that the new levels of military cooperation envisioned in the 1997 Defense Guidelines and new pressure for joint utilization of bases will tax the traditional system, and that it may be time to consider the establishment of joint staffing, if not an actual combined command structure. While direct military-to-military planning is a more recent dimension of the overall U.S.–Japan security relationship, the stationing of U.S. forces in Japan has always been at the core of the alliance. In "U.S. Bases in Japan: Historical Background and Innovative Approaches to Maintaining Strategic Presence," Paul Giarra explains the history and purpose of the U.S. military presence in Japan and argues that absent U.S. bases, the alliance and Asian stability itself would not survive. At the same time, he recognizes the likelihood of increasing domestic political pressure on U.S. bases in Japan, and advocates expanded joint bilateral use of bases and other steps to improve efficiency and public support. Anne Dixon turns to the newest arena for U.S.–Japan security cooperation in "Can Eagles and Cranes Flock Together? U.S. and Japanese Approaches to Multilateral Security after the Cold War." Dixon delineates the differences in U.S. and Japanese approaches to peacekeeping operations and multilateral dialogue, as well as the inherent limits to multilateralism, but concludes that there is enough overlap to make this an important outlet for bilateral cooperation. She argues that both nations may find a useful division of roles and missions between conflict termination (the U.S. role) and humanitarian or economic recovery (the Japanese role) under the multilateral flag of the United Nations. The second section concludes with an examination of U.S.–Japan theater missile defense cooperation by Patrick Cronin, Paul Giarra, and Michael Green.

The third section explores the most vexing and complex aspect of alliance relations—the domestic political processes. Thomas Berger sets the historical context in "Alliance Politics and Japan's Postwar Culture of Antimilitarism." Berger explains that the security relationship provided stability for an uneasy coalition of conservative forces in Japan by limiting difficult decisions over how far to remilitarize. At the same time, the alliance polarized the left and right in Japan, reflecting the global divisions of the Cold War. As the center broadened its consensus around the alliance and the extreme right and left contracted, a new postwar culture of antimilitarism took root in the norms and structures of bilateral security cooperation. Lee Howell picks up the story in the 1990s in "The Alliance and Post–Cold War Political Realignment in Japan." Howell explains how new electoral rules, new parties, and growing local political influence will increase the debate over Japan's right of collective self-defense and U.S. bases on Okinawa, even as general support for the alliance has taken root.

The fourth and final section of the book, Economics, Technology and Security, dissects the aspect of the U.S.–Japan alliance that has animated scholars the most in recent decades. In "Economics and Security: A Conceptual Framework," Mike Mochizuki outlines the theoretical traditions behind this analysis. Mochizuki distinguishes between the liberalist tradition, which maintains that economic relations would increase interdependence between the United States and Japan, and the realist tradition, which maintains that pursuit of relative gains would increase friction between the United States and Japan. He argues that the realist perspective on economic growth is too alarmist at present to describe international relations in East Asia, but he does see certain negative security implications from growing regional economic integration. In terms of the U.S.–Japan alliance, these negative implications are (1) growing regional suspicion of Japan's international extension of *keiretsu* business groupings, and (2) growing U.S. frustration with its inability to penetrate the Japanese keiretsu in third Asian markets. In his policy recommendations, Mochizuki argues against explicit linkage of U.S. trade and security policies toward Japan (wondering whether the U.S. government would be capable of doing so even if desirable), but maintains that pressure must be kept up to maintain access to Japanese markets and technology so that private sector frustration in the United States does not undermine the alliance.

Laura Stone's chapter builds on Mochizuki's theoretical framework to offer more specific historical and policy treatment of the trade-offs between economics and security in the U.S.–Japan alliance. In "Whither Trade and Security? A Historical Perspective," Stone explains how the evolution of trade friction began to have a spillover effect on the security relationship by the end of the Cold War. She concludes, however, that Japan's slower economic performance and new trade friction with China in the decades after the end of the Cold War may help to insulate the alliance from economic problems once again.

While Mochizuki and Stone reach different conclusions about the degree to which bilateral trade and investment shape security relations, there is one area where trade, technology, and security clearly do intersect and that is the area of defense production. In "U.S.–Japan Armaments Cooperation," Gregg Rubinstein provides historical evidence for the important impact of weapons sales and development on bilateral security ties. He concludes that autonomy in weapons production is growing increasingly difficult for Japan, and that this will only lead to greater integration with the United States if the U.S. side takes a more flexible posture toward technology transfers and joint programs. Michael Chinworth's chapter, "The Technology Factor in U.S.–Japan Security Relations," focuses on the increasing relevance of Japan's strength in dual-use technologies to bilateral defense cooperation. Chinworth lays out a range of policy options based on the premise that the U.S. government's leverage on Japan and on the Japanese government's ability to deliver commercial technology are both limited. He concludes that a lower-profile approach to hands-on bilateral R&D is the most effective mechanism for achieving a balance of technological and security interests between the United States and Japan.

These four sections and fourteen chapters provide the analytical baseline for the editors' conclusion and recommendations at the end of the book. We believe that the mix of historical, regional, and domestic political influences behind the current alliance structure leads to an optimistic future for bilateral security relations and to fairly clear choices for policy. The authors may not agree with our recommendations, though we do base them on the solid empirical work they have done for the book. Readers also will want to reach their own conclusions.

This project was completed with the help of five important people: Andrew Bacevich, formerly at SAIS (now at Boston University), who helped to initiate the endeavor, and Emily Metzgar and Rollie Lal at National Defense University (NDU), who helped to bring the final manuscript to press. Thanks are also due to Akihisa Nagashima at the Council on Foreign Relations for his coordinating role and to Yoshiko Tanaka for work on the appendices.

## Note

1. See Daniel Williams, "Rebuilding Military Ties to Tokyo," *Washington Post*, February 19, 1995; or *Sankei Shimbun*, February 22, 1995.

# I

# The Strategic Environment

# 1

# The Eagle Eyes the Pacific: American Foreign Policy Options in East Asia after the Cold War

RICHARD J. SAMUELS AND CHRISTOPHER P. TWOMEY

WITH THE end of the Cold War, the institutions of international security in Europe and the grand strategies of its principal states have undergone fundamental changes. Comparable changes have yet to reach Asia. While NATO is both evolving into a collective security organization has moved the East–West divide eastward by some 500 miles, the centerpiece of international security in East Asia, the U.S.–Japan alliance, has not been altered in any way. To the contrary, Japanese and American alliance managers have reaffirmed it in its present form. For the past fifty years the United States has sought to prevent the spread of communism in Asia (often at great cost), and in particular to stem the influence of the Soviet Union. With the disintegration of communism as an ideology and the Soviet Union as a state, this purpose can no longer motivate American policy in the region. And yet, despite the withering away of its primary mission, the U.S. strategy and the concomitant architecture it erected to implement that strategy remain unchanged.

It is now time to step back and assess anew reasons for U.S. strategic engagement in the region. With its primary adversary vanquished, and with the nations of the region enriched and increasingly democratic, the United States must reconsider its interests and the full range of policies it might pursue to secure them. In the final analysis, retention of the current alliance structure, albeit with some adjustment, is advisable. But this conclusion is not preordained by the legacy of the Cold War. It should be arrived at through a thorough "bottom-up" assessment of regional dynamics and U.S. interests.

## Beginning from First Principles: Identifying U.S. Interests

The United States has a great many security interests at stake in Asia. Foremost among these are the following, in approximate order of importance:[1]

1. *Preserving stability among the great powers.* This policy is justified on simple grounds of security. The last time there was a great power war in Asia, the United States was drawn in. The last two times there was a great power war in Europe, the United States was drawn in. All three wars were costly, and American policy should be aimed at preventing such conflicts in the future.
2. *Preserving the safety of the sea-lanes of communication (SLOCs) throughout East and Southeast Asia.* The United States trades more with East Asia than with any other region in the world. Preservation of the SLOCs is vital if the United States is to participate in the prosperity of the world's (once, and possibly once again) fastest-growing region. It also ensures that U.S. ships have the right of free passage to other areas of vital national interest, such as the Middle East.
3. *Maintaining an American leadership role in regional and global institutions.* The ability of the United States to project power to a region that welcomes it is connected directly to regime formation. A legitimate and welcomed U.S. constabulary role ensures that the United States retains a place at the table (likely the head) where the rules of commerce are determined and the coordination of foreign policies occurs.[2]
4. *Peaceful resolution of the division of the Korean Peninsula on Seoul's terms.* The security of our South Korean ally is important because (1) it enhances U.S. credibility as a reliable ally, (2) the freedom and security of other democracies enhances our own, (3) a second Korean war would likely involve weapons of mass destruction, and finally, (4) the regime in the North has proven to be one of the most reckless in the region. Were it to control the peninsula, the Northeast Asian balance would shift in dangerous ways.

5. *Peaceful resolution of the Chinese–Taiwanese conflict that upholds democracy and economic freedom.* Like Korea, Taiwan has implications for U.S. credibility and maintaining the democratic peace. Taiwanese democracy is the only Chinese democracy in the world, an example that helps refute claims that authoritarianism is a necessary part of Chinese political culture. Finally, Taiwan has strategic significance, as it sits astride important Asian SLOCs.
6. *Avoiding the proliferation of weapons of mass destruction (WMD).* Nuclear weapons programs in South Asia make us acutely aware of the dangers of further proliferation. In the wrong hands, weapons of mass destruction threaten the ability of the United States to provide aid to friendly states and military support to allies, to secure natural resources, and to undertake other kinds of unilateral action in its national interest. Nuclear weapons proliferation raises the cost of conflict and is a direct security threat to the continental United States.
7. *Ensuring the independence of Indochina and Southeast Asia.* It is in the interests of the United States to prevent hegemonism in Asia. Indochina and Southeast Asia sit astride some of the most traveled, and congested, SLOCs in the world. We have gone to war over this region twice before in this century.

Identifying these interests is only a beginning. There are a variety of strategies the United States might pursue to achieve its goals. Choosing among strategies requires three steps: first, identifying them; second, determining if they do indeed protect American interests; and third, assessing their costs.

## Strategies to Be Avoided

Neither isolationism nor multilateralism—supported by some in the public debate today—will achieve the American goals laid out above.

### ISOLATIONISM

Isolationism (sometimes referred to as "restraint") is enjoying a resurgence among academics, policy analysts, and some politicians.[3] Proponents of this strategy argue that in the post–Cold War world, the United States is already secure, and could be more prosperous at no real security cost if it spent less on defense. Forward deployment in Asia is expensive and exposes U.S. troops to the risk of being caught in an Asian cross fire. Scholars supporting restraint posit two core U.S. interests: security and prosperity. The crux of their argument is the expectation that the Asian balance of power will be smoothly obtained. However, this strategy construes U.S. security too narrowly, underestimates the full costs of prosperity, and overstates the ease with which stable balances of power can be achieved. Due to these shortcomings, a strategy of isolation, or "restraint," would not effectively defend the interests outlined above.

Even evaluated on its own terms, this strategy is flawed. Proponents agree that if U.S. security is to be attained, aggressors must be deterred. But they suggest that such balancing will occur smoothly—for example, China will adjust to a Japanese defense buildup at low or zero cost to the United States, or a unified Korea will not threaten Japan (or vice versa). Such outcomes seem untenable in the face of historical evidence that balancing often is accompanied by substantial conflict and violence.[4] Indeed, when one of the great powers stays out of such balancing activity—their prescription for the United States—the level of violence might rise even higher.[5] Kenneth Waltz warns that the process of balancing can be quite dangerous: multipolar systems are more conflict prone than bipolar ones because in the former, nations have incentives to free-ride in alliances, thus avoiding their role in balancing.[6] It is true that the balance of power must eventually prevail, as it is that wars eventually end. Both these truisms overlook the more pressing questions of "how long until then?" and "at what cost?"

A U.S. withdrawal to continental North America would jeopardize several of the interests listed above. It risks sparking great power conflict and may accelerate the rise of a new hegemon. The most likely conflict is that between China and Japan (two of the biggest economies in the world), although Korean–Chinese, Korean–Japanese, and Russo–Japanese tensions are also likely to be stimulated. It is not likely that the United States would stand aside.

If, in the absence of an alliance with the United States, Japan chose to aggressively balance against China, the region would face a dangerously destabilizing arms race. Korea and much of Southeast Asia would be forced to take sides. For Japan to truly compete in such a race, it would have to acquire nuclear weapons, a dangerous and destabilizing step that, in Harrison's words, "would only provoke a more belligerent posture on the part of both China and Russia."[7] Moreover, while bilateral relations in which both sides possess secure second strikes are considered stable, that would certainly not be the situation were Japan to announce its development and possession of nuclear weapons. The same forces that lead China and Japan into an adversarial relationship in the first place might well push them to the brink of war. From a U.S. perspective, this would be disastrous, for several reasons:

- War between two of America's largest trading partners would be devastating to the U.S. economy.
- U.S. involvement would be difficult to avoid in a war between a former ally and a former enemy.
- War between a nuclear power and a threshold nuclear power would push the nuclear envelope in new and disconcerting ways.
- War between the two would be a(nother) humanitarian disaster.
- Nuclearization in Japan would press both Koreas to do the same, and perhaps pressure other Asian nations to follow suit.

Even if China and Japan did not go to war, a Cold War between the two great powers could impose high costs on the region, and indeed the globe, if the last simmering conflict between two giants on the world scene has taught us anything. At a minimum, the remarkable (and hard-earned) domestic political stability in Japan would further unravel, creating even greater uncertainties for its foreign policy and its evolving role as provider of global public goods. These are all negative outcomes for the United States. By maintaining a close alliance with Japan—one providing nuclear guarantees and serving as a more neutral guarantor of the stability in the region—the United States can prevent this outcome.

On the other hand, if Japan bandwagons in the face of Chinese economic growth and military expansion, the United States will face a number of unpalatable risks:

- A non–status quo China could hunger for additional appeasement, à la Munich.
- A closer relationship with Japan would provide China with substantial additional economic as well as political-military power, certainly threatening Taiwan, probably Southeast Asia (e.g., the Spratly Islands), and possibly Indochina.
- Korea, reunified or not, would be squeezed between two giants. If U.S. troops were there, they would be surrounded. If not, then Korea would be.
- Aggression would have paid off.

Clearly, these are all negative outcomes from a U.S. perspective. By demonstrating to China that the regional status quo can be positive sum, and by providing Japan with the wherewithal to resist Chinese demands—either through strong alliance with the United States or through one of the other mechanisms outlined below—this possible future can be avoided.

Of course, it is possible that China and Japan would adjust comfortably to sharing influence in the region, resolving their disputes peacefully, and avoiding tension. Sadly, history does not suggest that this is likely. Levels of mistrust (both popular and elite) between Japan and China have not receded.[8] Moreover, even with the U.S. cork in the Japanese military bottle, Japanese—and Chinese—military budgets are expanding to record levels. Finally, whereas we recognize this outcome to be a possibility, we also recognize that it is only one of many contingencies for which the United States must be prepared.

If the United States is not engaged actively in the region, then a number of other interests will also go undefended (aside from the issue of great power conflict). It is far less likely that Japan would stand between China and Taiwan than that the United States would do so. Similarly, while Japan has a profound interest in peaceful commerce in the South China Sea, it may choose not to defend it and thereby to provide the public good of safe commerce for the other states in the region. Japanese debates over the wisdom of confronting Saddam Hussein in the Gulf War suggest that Japan may instead choose to pay a premium to reroute its commerce, if such an option were available. Moreover, since a unified Korea is as likely to be a security concern vis-à-vis-Japan as vis-à-vis China, neither regional great power may strongly encourage that process to move forward.

Achieving *these* goals requires, first and foremost, a U.S. military presence in the region. This conclusion is not based on paternalistic reasoning: it is not that we can secure these goals better than can Asian countries. It is simply that Asian countries will not necessarily find it in their interest to defend them. Japan may prefer a divided Korea, or China may risk violence in absorbing Taiwan. The independence of Indochina may be considered a mixed blessing for both China and Japan. In these cases, U.S. interests are not shared universally; it would therefore help considerably if the United States could continue to pursue them from within the region. The "Viable Strategies" considered below allow for this through a variety of mechanisms.

## MULTILATERALISM

Multilateralism comprises two strategies: a formal alliance structure and a collective security arrangement. Neither will provide adequately for American interests in the next few decades.

The first strategy looks to the example of NATO and suggests that American interests in East Asia can best be pursued through a tight, formal, militarized alliance aimed against the threatening power or powers. This alliance might be referred to as the "Pacific Treaty Organization" ("PaTO"). This form of multilateralism, rooted firmly in the traditions of *realpolitik,* would rely primarily on the threat or use of military power. To the extent it mirrors NATO, a PaTO would require creation of a multinational military force. Military alliances require specific enemies. In practice, the power that such an alliance would be aimed against would likely be China.

This strategy has several shortcomings. First, it is not yet clear that China is a threat that needs to be contained. Chinese domestic politics and its economic transformation are both extremely fluid. It is not in the U.S. interest to contribute to Chinese fears of encirclement, a strategy that certainly would worsen the prospects for peace. Second, even if we judged China to be a threat, creating this type of alliance would be difficult. We would need to assume a willingness on the part of Japan, Korea, and/or the Association of Southeast Asian Nations (ASEAN) to participate in a containment policy. Each would be an extremely unlikely partner. In post–World War II Europe, the threat posed by the Soviet Union was relatively clear-cut, making countervailing alliances such as NATO easier to arrange. Today in Asia, the threat posed by China is uncertain and varies across nations. Securing broad agreement on the parameters for a PaTO would be a daunting task. Third, incorporating the most avid potential partner, Taiwan, would be particularly galling to China. It would also destroy anything that remains of value in the American policy of constructive ambiguity on the Chinese reunification issue. A fourth problem is that this strategy might discourage the independence of mid-sized states. States not in the PaTO would feel a need to choose sides in the conflict, and some might opt for China. While it is difficult to foresee such a move by Australia or New Zealand, states on the Korean Peninsula, or in Indochina, might choose differently. Such a polarization is not in American interests. Finally, the United States alone has sufficient capability to oppose China, if that is necessary. It need not inflame Chinese nationalist passions vis-à-vis its neighbors and thereby ensure political and military instability in the region.

The second variant of a possible multilateral U.S. strategy in Asia would look more like the European example of the Conference on Security and Cooperation in Europe (CSCE). A CSC*A* might build upon the ASEAN Regional Forum (ARF) or other nascent institutional fora. It would aim to create an inclusive security community with primary emphasis on established traditions in international law. The threat of force would remain the ultimate arbiter of disputes, but a CSCA would sanction violence based on transgression of predetermined legal norms that would apply to all members, in contrast to the PaTO's reliance on ad hoc, power-based calculations. It is attractive for a number of reasons: it enhances transparency, it builds confidence among members, and it integrates rising powers like China peacefully. Moreover, from the particular perspective of the United States, a CSCA might deliver disproportionate advantages to states with "soft power" resources.

There are, however, a number of problems: first, it is difficult to imagine such an international regime working effectively, especially in the short run. No historian of the Cold War in Europe gives the CSCE credit for keeping the peace there. After all, the CSCE coexisted with NATO; it did not substitute for a military alliance. History offers an earlier lesson as well. The League of Nations, another example of a collective security organization, proved impotent at the first instance of great power aggression. There is no reason to think that a CSCA would be any more successful at resolving conflicts of interest among the great powers, although we can imagine that norms of trust and consultation resulting from interactions within such a regime could serve to ameliorate the most pointed divisions between states.

Second, like the League of Nations, the CSCE was built upon several key points of consensus. For example, members agreed to shelve territorial disputes and no state questioned the right of others to be present at the table. Such agreement is hard to imagine in the contemporary Asian context, for territorial disputes between Japan and China (Senkakus/Diaoyutai), Japan and Korea (Takeshima/Tokdo), Japan and Russia (Southern Kuriles/Northern Territories), and China and the ASEAN states (the Spratlys) are the nub of extant regional security concerns. These concerns also apply to the sovereignty of key players such as the Democratic People's Republic of Korea (DPRK) and Taiwan. If consensus could be achieved on some of these issues, then U.S. interests would be well served indeed. However, proposing a collective security arrangement that presupposes the resolution of such issues is not a strategy for getting the region to that point. Nor, it must be noted, is the transition from the status quo to one of multilateral security necessarily easy. To the contrary, it is likely to be very destabilizing and dangerous.

Finally, pertinent to any thoughtful evaluation of U.S. options is the notion that international institutions are likely to strengthen over time, as norms for cooperation evolve and transform the behavior of member states.[9] Whatever we might think of its long-term possibilities, in the *short term* a collective security strategy is an unlikely vehicle for achieving U.S. interests.

## Viable Strategies Exist

If neither isolationism nor multilateralism in either of its two forms seems likely to serve American interests, there are other strategies that will. We see four possibilities: (1) maintenance of the status quo, (2) a more "balanced" alliance, (3) creation of a stand-off military option, and (4) a shift to alternative allies.

### ACCEPT THE RISKS OF A FRAGILE STATUS QUO

The status quo—built around the U.S.–Japan alliance as the central axis—is an inexpensive and effective way to achieve U.S. security objectives. It requires that no new forces be deployed and that no new bases be built. Certainly a status quo of this sort is less threatening to other regional powers than sudden change. Each of the states in the region has expressed comfort with the U.S. presence—the Japanese because it protects them from North Korea and/or China and China because it contains Japan. The alliance allows the United States to remain in the thick of (and to affect) great power relations in the Northwest Pacific.

There are substantial problems, however, dating from the 1970s. Throughout much of the Cold War, the United States provided regional public goods in the form of a stable political and military environment, open markets, and access to the world's most abundant technology base. U.S. politicians and the American public could hardly have failed to notice that Japan grew richer relative to the United States, in the process becoming the second largest economy in the world and America's most formidable economic competitor. Japanese producers have enjoyed the advantage of competing head-to-head with U.S. firms in the United States and third markets, while being effectively protected in a sanctuary market at home. Shifts in Japan's relative economic and technological strength, combined with its "cheap ride" on U.S. security guarantees, has had a corrosive effect on the overall relationship. Japan's reluctance to assume a greater share of the responsibility for creating collective goods in science, technology, and security, combined with its staggering global and bilateral trade surpluses, makes the alliance seem unfair to many Americans.[10] While the Japanese recession of the 1990s has helped to dull the most pointed attacks on the relationship (indeed, it contributed to an excessive American triumphalism), what remains are economic asymmetries in direct investment and bilateral trade—which are available for political exploitation.[11]

Meanwhile, the threat of monolithic communism, like the U.S.S.R. itself, has disappeared. With nothing left to stand *against*, it became unclear what the alliance stood *for*. Through the "Guidelines for U.S.–Japan Defense Cooperation" promulgated in September 1997, alliance managers hoped to stimulate the Japanese public to pay greater attention to security issues and to ensure a forward base for U.S. troops after the reunification of Korea. They have succeeded to some extent, but their success is mitigated by the public demands of some political leaders for the removal of U.S. troops from the archipelago.[12] Promises of an expanded Japanese security role which would be more reciprocal and balanced, while enhancing mutual trust, remain unfulfilled. The Japanese foreign minister announced that "the new 'Guidelines' will not change the U.S.–Japan Security Treaty nor its related rights and obligations nor the fundamental framework of the United States–Japan alliance relationship."[13] Japan is still "planned out" in U.S. military contingency plans. In short, the revised Guidelines are well-meaning, but they do little to ensure significant Japanese contributions in the case of a conflict that threatens Japanese and U.S. interests.[14] Americans will likely respond to Japanese recalcitrance with renewed and vigorous resentment.

In a strictly military sense, fairness has limited relevance to the ability of this to achieve American interests at a low direct cost. However, the political costs of this strategy may be higher. Should it come to conflict, Americans will wonder why their rich ally cannot assist the U.S. military more, and the Japanese will question why they are being asked to play a role in a conflict that appears more important to Washington than Tokyo. Both are good questions. Unless the elites in both capitals find answers to these concerns, the alliance will remain fragile.

In short, while overdue attention has been paid in recent years to strengthening the alliance, and while the alliance provides the United States with a (subsidized) foot in the regional door, it is not without its own political, economic, and technological costs. The current U.S.–Japan alliance is essentially unchanged from that of fifteen years ago, and neither the Japanese nor the American public has focused publicly on the need for a new alliance architecture. Thus, while the status quo may serve to provide the United States the wherewithal to defend its regional interests, there are reasons to question whether it can survive a serious test.

## RECONFIGURE THE ALLIANCE

Sometimes referred to as the "overt linkage" option, this approach accepts that the U.S.–Japan alliance is the most effective mechanism for realizing U.S. interests (including regional stability) in Asia.[15] But it is based upon the view that the United States needs (and deserves) a better (more symmetrical) deal. The primary American interest, the avoidance of either great power conflict or hegemony, should be Japan's primary interest as well. Even if U.S. costs are less than they might otherwise be, it is politically unsustainable (if not morally inappropriate) for the United States to bear the bulk of the burden to achieve this.[16]

With the end of the Cold War, it is no longer necessary or desirable for the United States to trade off its political-military and techno-economic interests. Instead of offering Japan security guarantees *and* (effectively) unlimited access to advanced technology and its domestic market, the United States ought to offer security guarantees, technology, and market access in the context of reciprocal access to Japanese technology and the Japanese market. In short, this view advocates overt linkage of military, economic, and technological security, correcting Japan's "cheap ride" on U.S. security guarantees. The ability of Japan to exploit the security relationship for economic and technological gain should be reduced. U.S. firms should have the same unintermediated access to sell and invest in the Japanese market that Japanese firms enjoy in the United States. As late as 1998, nearly a decade after the burst of the Japanese economic "bubble," and despite promises of "Big Bang" economic deregulation, bilateral trade and investment were nearly as imbalanced as ever. One way to move closer to this access would be to implement a free-trade agreement between the United States and Japan. This would likely attract support on both sides of the Pacific, and would call attention to the benefits of the overall relationship. Since the Japanese already have effectively free access to the U.S. market, U.S. interests could only be served from a better articulated set of bilateral rules of trade and investment.[17]

In short (and at a minimum), the American public will expect Japan to pay the full costs (and assume fuller risks) necessary to preserve regional peace and security—including well-defined (and publicly supported) roles and missions in the event of a regional military crisis. Even after the promulgation of the Guidelines in September 1997 the Japanese government did not commit publicly to applying the alliance to the Asia-Pacific region.[18] Nor did Japan put into law regulations that would fully expedite the provisions of supplies and rear-area support—something Japan did for the United States in both the Korean and Vietnam wars. Addressing these shortcomings will ensure that vital Japanese domestic political support will be more likely forthcoming in the event of a crisis.

Finally, as a component of a post–Cold War strategy that must be more sea- and air-based than heretofore, it would seem prudent to withdraw the U.S. Marines from Okinawa. Although nominally comprising a division, the current deployment includes only a regiment of troops (approximately one third of a division). It is unlikely that such a small group of ground forces would have a material effect on the outcome of conflict on the Asian landmass. Such a step has three collateral benefits: (1) reassuring the Chinese that the United States does not intend to become involved in another land war in Asia, (2) demonstrating to the Japanese that the United States is confident that Japan can defend itself, and (3) eliminating the long-festering irritant that disposed Japanese public opinion strongly against the American military. The role of the Okinawa-based U.S. Marines today is primarily to enhance the credibility of the alliance and provide for a Korean contingency. Concern that moving the marines from Okinawa would undermine this credibility is met by the fact that what is most needed in a Korean contingency is additional tactical intelligence assets (AWACS or JSTARS) and additional heavy long-range artillery, not light infantry. Deploying either of the former at the same time the marines are relocated would actually bolster U.S. credibility without increasing substantially the base structure on the peninsula. Taking the steps we have enunciated above—in particular, those aimed at "selling" the alliance to the Japanese people—will do more than small deployment of American forces.[19]

The key advantage of this strategy over the status quo is that it explicitly addresses the issue of public support in both countries, thus strengthening the relationship for the long term. Americans will not resent the relative economic losses in our relationship with Japan, and the Japanese will recognize through the behavior and public statements of their government the nature and scope of their commitments to the alliance, as well as the true costs of national security.

Achieving this option will by no means be easy. The issues discussed above have long plagued U.S.–Japanese relations, but there are grounds for optimism today. During the Cold War the United States depended heavily on its Japanese bases to deter Soviet expansion in the Pacific. Today, Washington has other options, and this should strengthen our position when bargaining with Tokyo. Similarly, during the Cold War Japan could contribute little to the alliance: thus, its lack of commitment was less problematic. Today, however, the potential Japanese contribution is substantial. This means ensuring domestic support for a more active Japanese role will be vital, and American measures that ease this, as mentioned above, will be even more welcomed. The end of the Cold War has increased both the need for and the value of a more "balanced" alliance.

## THE "ALLY-FREE" OPTION: CONSTRUCT A STANDOFF FORCE

In the event this rebalancing proves elusive, there are two alternatives available to the United States. The first takes advantage of America's substantial technological prowess. The United States could elect to sever its Asian alliances and abandon its bases abroad, yet retain the ability to intervene in Asian contingencies. To do so it would need to develop a long-range military force that would frequently deploy to the region from the continental United States, Hawaii, Alaska, Guam, and Diego Garcia. The United States would need to make clear its intent to defend its interests in the region, and it would need to develop the military force to make this intent credible. Retaining such a long-range power projection capability would be expensive (and potentially destabilizing), but it is possible within the existing technological envelope.

This strategy would require a substantial change in the composition of American military forces. In particular, increased prepositioning of forces afloat would allow the United States to rapidly insert ground forces.[20] Strategic air forces and carrier-based air forces would have to substitute for shorter range, ground-based tactical aircraft. (Ground-based tactical air power can deliver ordinance less expensively at a given level of accuracy than can strategic or carrier air power.) Also, the number of carrier battle groups that we maintain would have to be increased. The Pentagon estimates that it takes five carriers in the inventory to keep one on station in the Mediterranean Sea. In contrast, it only takes 1.7 to keep one on station in the Western Pacific.[21] Having a home port in Yokosuka, Japan, saves a substantial amount of transit time, making trips for maintenance, shore leave, resupply, and so forth all the much quicker. A standoff force strategy would sacrifice such savings.

It would also require the expensive development of new weaponry. Long-range strike aircraft, more capable carrier-based aircraft, arsenal ships (a recent proposal by the U.S. Navy for large ships serving as missile launchers with minimal crew requirements), more varied types of long-range cruise missiles, and "smarter" ordinance would all have to be developed. None would be cheap.

Pursuing such a strategy would also likely raise the human cost to the United States in the event of hostilities. Credibility comes at a price. One way of buying it is to station "trip-wire" forces in the line of possible conflict as the United States did in Europe and Korea during the Cold War. Absent that, credibility must be earned. Establishing a reputation for defending one's interests may require several demonstrations of will, something that would be extremely difficult to sell to the American public.

Cost concerns and public acceptance aside, this strategy seems well placed with regard to defending American interests. Most of the conflicts the United States hopes to deter would be fought at sea. Due to the high vulnerability of very expensive naval assets to well-targeted munitions, the United States can easily play a role here. It was much easier for the Seventh Fleet to step between China and Taiwan in 1996 than it would have been for the United States to stop the border conflict between China and Vietnam eighteen years before.

With regard to ground conflicts that run counter to U.S. interests—most likely a Korean War and a Chinese expansion into Indochina—the United States would have to rely primarily on air power. In most Korean scenarios, this would be more than enough. In Indochina, air power would be useful, but perhaps not as dominant (i.e., the Chinese would have more margin for losses against the Vietnamese than do the North Koreans against the South Koreans).

Since this strategy commits the United States to no entangling alliances, America need not worry about damaging the cohesion of any alliance through actions taken or left undone. Nonetheless, as long as the interests identified above accurately reflect the calculations of U.S. strategists, U.S. intervention—even "selective engagement"[22]—seems as likely as ever. The advantage of this "ally-free" option over the status quo is thus fairly marginal.

A final disadvantage to consider is the effect on the size of the Japanese military. To the extent that Japan currently depends on the United States to provide for its security, removing the cork from the Japanese bottle would allow Tokyo to take matters into its own hands. It would have to increase military spending substantially, setting into motion spirals of arms races and security dilemmas, which may work against American interests.

## FIND A NEW FRIEND

The final option for a United States weary of the recalcitrance of its Japanese ally, and seeking to avoid the high costs of the standoff strategy, is to try to find another ally, one willing to provide substantial basing and other support. This would allow the United States to retain a presence directly in the region, enhancing its credibility as a "player" in East Asian security affairs. It would also make better use of our current military assets.

Through the judicious selection of this ally, Washington might be able to achieve some of its goals directly (i.e., those pertaining to independence of Southeast Asia and Indochina and the peaceful settlements of the two divided nations in the region, Korea and China). Over the last 25 years, the United States has been forced to leave both Vietnam and the Philippines. Now it is conceivable that those countries might invite the United States back. Taiwan would certainly welcome a closer military relationship with Washington. Australia has enough territory for substantial bases and seems willing to consider this possibility, although it sits only at the periphery of the East Asian region.

Depending on the precise location of Washington's new security partner, both costs and benefits are likely to accrue. A shift southward for the Seventh Fleet would help maintain open SLOCs and would help ensure an independent Indochina and Southeast Asia. But it would also take U.S. forces away from the likely hub of great power conflict in the Northwestern Pacific. This strategy, like the standoff one, would pull the cork out of the Japanese bottle.

Finally, there is the simple effect that such a major change in deployment would have on the countries in the region. The current pattern of bilateral alliances is familiar to all. Governments throughout the region's capitals have considered the American relationship with Japan and have *all* found it to be constructive.[23] Unanimous support for such a contentious issue as the deployment of force abroad in the anarchic world of international security is rare. It seems unlikely that any other possible basing location could secure such sweeping support.

## Choosing an American Strategy for the 21st Century

Each of the latter three options outlined above has its attractions and difficulties, as does the status quo. Washington cannot pick and choose among them by itself. It must consult with the regional powers to secure their support. If Japan is not willing to move toward a reconfigured, more "balanced" alliance, and especially if the preferences expressed by political leaders such as Hosokawa, Hatoyama, and Kan are more widely embraced, then the United States should consult with other regional players to more fully consider the "Find a New Friend" option. Once that is done, choosing between that strategy and the status quo can be more objectively considered. If both these seem unpalatable, the United States retains the expensive "Standoff Force" option. In the interim, we will be very fortunate indeed if the fragile status quo of the U.S.–Japan alliance is not tested.

## Notes

1. Our list of interests summarizes most of what the United States *says* it wants to do: see the "Nye Report" a.k.a. Department of Defense, Office of International Security Affairs, "United States Security Strategy for the East Asia–Pacific Region," Washington, D.C., February 1995. It is also consistent with those interests put forth in Mike M. Mochizuki, "American Economic and Security Interests in Japan," a working paper for the second meeting of the study group on "American Interests in Asia: Economic and Security Priorities," sponsored by the Economic Strategy Institute, Washington, D.C., November 14, 1996.

2. On the utility of military power in securing economic concessions, even from allies, see Robert Gilpin, "The Politics of Transnational Economic Relations," in Robert Keohane and Joseph Nye, Jr., eds., *Transnational Relations and World Politics* (Cambridge, MA: Harvard University Press, 1971), pp. 48–69. On international economic regimes and the distribution of power, see Stephen D. Krasner, *Structural Conflict: The Third World Against Global Liberalism* (Berkeley, CA: University of California Press, 1985). For application of this point to post–Cold War U.S. foreign policy, see Samuel P. Huntington, "Why International Primacy Matters," *International Security* 17, no. 4 (Spring 1993).

3. The fullest post–Cold War expression of this view is Eric A. Nordlinger, *Isolationism Reconfigured: American Foreign Policy for a New Century* (Princeton, NJ: Princeton University Press, 1995). This is also developed in Eugene Gholz, Daryl Press, and Harvey Sapolsky, "Come Home America: The Strategy of Restraint in the Face of Temptation," *International Security* 21, 4(Spring 1997). For an offshore balancing variant, see Christopher Layne, "The Unipolar Illusion: Why New Great Powers Will Rise," *International Security* 17, no. 4 (Spring 1993): 45–51.

4. "Throughout its history of more than four hundred years the policy of the balance of power succeeded in preventing any one state from gaining universal domination . . . Yet universal domination by any one state was prevented only at the price of warfare, which from 1648 to 1815 was virtually continuous and in the twentieth century has twice engulfed practically the whole world." Hans Morgenthau and William Thompson, *Politics Among Nations: The Struggle for Power and Peace*, 6th ed. (New York: McGraw-Hill, 1985), p. 222. Also see Paul Schroeder, "Historical Reality vs. Neo-Realist Theory," *International Security* 19, no. 1 (Summer 1994): 108–48.

5. Here the example of pre–WWI Britain is apposite. Had Britain been less equivocal in the July Crisis, it is possible that Germany would have been less reckless.

6. Kenneth Waltz, *Theory of International Politics* (New York: McGraw-Hill, 1979).

7. Selig Harrison, *Japan's Nuclear Future: The Plutonium Debate and East Asian Security* (Washington, D.C.: Carnegie Endowment for International Peace, 1996), p. 26.

8. Poll results in both countries bear this out. See Benjamin Kang Lim, *Reuters Newswire,* February 15, 1997.

9. See Robert Axelrod, *The Evolution of Cooperation* (New York: Basic Books, 1984); also, Robert O. Keohane notes that the initial creation of an institution is difficult relative to its perpetuation, in *After Hegemony: Cooperation and Discord in the World Economy* (Princeton, NJ: Princeton University Press, 1984). Finally, Stephen Krasner notes the self-reinforcing positive feedback characteristic of institutions, in "Sovereignty: An Institutional Perspective," *Comparative Political Studies* 21, no. 1 (April 1988): 80–86.

10. See the National Research Council, ed., *Maximizing U.S. Interests in Science and Technology Relations with Japan,* Report of the Defense Task Force, (Washington, D.C.: National Academy Press, 1995).

11. For an account that shares our concerns, see Bruce Stokes and James J. Shinn, eds., *The Tests of War and the Strains of Peace: The U.S.–Japan Security Relationship* (New York: Council on Foreign Relations, 1998).

12. This position was first staked out by Yukio Hatoyama and Naoto Kan when they established the Democratic Party of Japan in October 1996. They have since toned down their call for the removal of U.S. forces from Japan and now focus on "adjustment", in the form of "consolidation, reduction, and relocation of U.S. military bases on Okinawa." (This is from the DPJ web page: http://www.dpj.or.jp/english/policies.html#foreign.) In a provocative article published in *Foreign Affairs* (July/August 1998), former Prime Minister Hosokawa Motohiro went much further, arguing that current host nation support of $5b/year is "a burden to Japanese taxpayers [that] hangs like a darkening cloud over the future of the alliance" (p. 5). He claimed that the U.S. Navy is not responsible for protecting Japanese commercial shipping, but argued that the United States ought to continue to provide a nuclear umbrella for Japan, "so long as it does not wish to see Japan withdraw from the NPT and develop its own nuclear deterrent" (p. 5). While he would maintain the alliance by permitting U.S. naval forces to use Yokosuka and Sasebo (after their return to Japan), he called upon the Japanese government to refuse to renew its agreement to support U.S. troops when it is due for renewal in 2000.

13. "Obuchi Interviewed on Defense Guidelines," *Tokyo Shukan Daiyamondo* (November 8, 1997): pp. 94–97, FBIS-EAS-97-314, November 12, 1997.

14. See Eric Heginbotham and Richard J. Samuels, "Mercantile Realism and Japanese Foreign Policy," *International Security* (Spring 1998) for a fuller critique of the Guidelines.

15. For a similar argument, see Committee on Japan Defense Task Force, ed., *Maximizing U.S. Interests in Science and Technology Relations with Japan*

(Washington, D.C.: National Academy Press, 1995). For one that accepts our diagnosis, but that eschews our "realist" preferences for a more "liberal" approach to reconfiguring the alliance, see Mike M. Mochizuki and Michael O'Hanlon, "A Liberal Vision for the U.S.–Japan Alliance," *Survival* (Summer 1998).

16. Annual SOFA contributions of $5 billion do little to defray the costs of maintaining the military force structure necessary for the United States to project power into the region. A small American carrier battle group can cost upwards of $20 billion to procure. A conflict in the Pacific would require a half dozen or so such groups.

17. See the thoughtful and clear-eyed argument by Kurt Tong, "Revolutionizing America's Japan Policy," *Foreign Policy*, no. 105 (Winter 1996–97): 107–24.

18. Japanese statements on the Guidelines repeatedly insist that the phrase "situation in areas surrounding Japan" (the key revision in the new Guidelines) is "situational," rather than geographical. (For instance, see "Obuchi Interviewed on Defense Guidelines," *Tokyo Shukan Daiyamondo* (November 8, 1997): 94–97, FBIS-EAS-97-314, November 12, 1997; "LDP, Partners Disagree on Scope of Defense Guidelines," *Kyodo*, 0857GMT (October 3, 1997), FBIS-EAS-97-276, October 6, 1997; Hideto Fujiwara, "MOFA Official Visits PRC, Gives Briefing on Guidelines," *Asahi Shimbun* (October 9, 1997), Morning Edition, p. 3, FBIS-EAS-97-282, October 14, 1997.) This paradoxical exclusion of geography from the understanding of the phrase grates not only on American ears in translation. An anonymous senior JDA official, complaining of these contortions, stated, "no matter how it is written, it ends up being tautological." (See "Article Says New Guidelines Contain 'Various Problems.'" *Asahi Shimbun* (September 25, 1997), Morning Edition, p. 2, FBIS-EAS-97-268, September 26, 1997).

19. For a detailed evaluation of the Okinawa-based marines, see Mike M. Mochizuki and Michael O'Hanlon, "The Marines Should Come Home," *The Brookings Review* (Spring 1996).

20. Currently, we maintain enough prepositioned equipment afloat to equip one marine division and a heavy army brigade. In addition, we have enough amphibious assault ships to deploy approximately another one and a half marine divisions. See Secretary of Defense William Perry, *Annual Report to the President and Congress* (Washington, D.C.: U.S. Government Printing Office, March 1996), pp. 162, 193–97.

21. Figures from Navy presentation at "General James H. Doolittle Workshop: The Future of Naval Aviation," Security Studies at MIT, April 24, 1996.

22. For a good definition of this term, see Barry R. Posen and Andrew L. Ross, "Competing Visions for U.S. Grand Strategy," *International Security* 21, no. 3 (Winter 1996–97): 5–53.

23. This is the position taken, at least privately, by even North Korean and Chinese senior officials.

# 2

# China, Japan, and the United States

JAMES PRZYSTUP

CHINA'S emergence as a great power will be one of the defining events of the 21st century. Given its size, economic dynamism, and military potential, how China integrates itself into the international system, or fails to do so, will both shape the geopolitical landscape of East Asia and define the very nature of the now emerging post–Cold War international order. Vital economic and strategic interests of the United States and Japan are, and will be, at stake in this process. For governments in Washington and Tokyo, the challenge will be to create an international environment that will incline Beijing to see integration as a matter of China's own national interest.

Collectively, the United States and Japan have the policy instruments necessary to perform this task. Success cannot be taken for granted, however. To understand why, it is necessary to look at the role China has played in the U.S.–Japan relationship over the course of the twentieth century. It is hoped that this century's first four decades will not be a prologue to the future, but for the United States and Japan, history should not be overlooked as they address 21st-century China.

## 1895–1941: The United States, China, and the Open Door

One hundred years ago, imperial China was recovering from defeat in the Sino–Japanese War of 1894–95. In a war precipitated by competing Japanese and Chinese interests on the Korean Peninsula, a modernizing

Japan had shocked the world with the speed of its victory. In the Treaty of Shimonoseki, Japan laid claim to Taiwan and the Liaotung Peninsula in Southern Manchuria. Although the United States had found the war deplorable, the conflict was not perceived to endanger U.S. policy in Asia.

Internally, the defeat moved many in China to embrace the same modernization process on which Japan had embarked at the outset of the Meiji restoration. At the same time, modernization produced its own reaction, which manifested itself in the Boxer Rebellion of 1900. China's defeat also set off a scramble for territorial and economic concessions among the imperialist powers. China's inability to resist soon raised concerns over its future integrity.

Three years later, in 1898, the United States defeated Spain and in 1899 annexed the Philippines, drawing American interests and attention closer to developments on the mainland of Asia. Concern over the possible effect of China's dismemberment on America's traditional commercial interests in China led to the Open Door Notes of 1899 and 1900. The initial note called on the imperialist powers to preserve equality of commercial opportunity within their spheres of influence. The second note, issued during the Boxer Rebellion, called on the powers to respect China's "territorial and administrative integrity."

John Hay's Open Door Notes represented a unilateral diplomatic initiative on the part of the United States. Implementation, however, depended not on willingness to use force to support the Open Door, but on the complex interaction between American moral suasion and the self-interest of the imperial powers to avoid entanglements in Asia at a time of growing uncertainty in Europe. Originally conceived of as a measure to avoid positive action, within a decade the Open Door policy was considered a cardinal principle of American diplomacy.[1] Upholding the Open Door in China was argued to be "part of the price" the United States had to pay for its "new found greatness."[2]

Together, the Open Door Notes served as the basis for U.S. policy toward China through mid-century. In essence, since the beginning of the twentieth century, American policy toward China and East Asia has focused on a series on interlocking objectives: freedom of the seas and access to markets, equality of commercial opportunity, preservation of China's territorial and administrative integrity, and prevention of any one power from dominating the region to the exclusion of the United States. Though tactics have differed—balance of power, multilateralism, and alliances—the strategic objectives have been pursued with remarkable consistency.

## Theodore Roosevelt, Japan, and China

Early in the new century, Russia's expansion into Asia appeared to pose the greatest challenge to China's territorial integrity. Moscow's designs on Northern Manchuria raised alarms in Tokyo and Washington. Unable and unwilling to contest Russian expansion in Asia, the United States stood on diplomacy to uphold the Open Door in Manchuria. Japan acted. The result was the Russo–Japanese War of 1904 and 1905.

Despite victories at Port Arthur and Tsushima, the war threatened to bankrupt Japan. At Portsmouth, New Hampshire, Roosevelt intervened to terminate the war on terms favorable to Japan, for as Roosevelt wrote, "Japan is playing our game."[3] As a result, the Treaty of Portsmouth established Japan as a power on the mainland of Asia, with recognized interests in Korea and Manchuria.

Under Roosevelt, American policy lent support to Japan's expansion on the Asian mainland. The Taft-Katsura Agreement of 1905 recognized Japan's protectorate over Korea. The "gentleman's agreement" of 1907 worked to restrict Japanese immigration to the United States, a side effect of which was to redirect it elsewhere, to Korea, Manchuria, and South America. Finally, the Root-Takahira agreement of 1908 committed both governments to mutual respect of their territorial possessions in the Asia-Pacific region and to support equality of commercial opportunity in China as well as China's independence and territorial integrity.

Roosevelt's approach to Asia policy is well reflected in his call for a narrow, national interest–based strategy toward Japan. "To get good results from any policy toward Japan," he argued, "it is necessary to have a coherent plan for treaty affairs in Manchuria, affairs in the Philippines, affairs about immigration to the Pacific Slope."[4] Roosevelt's views of China, the Open Door, and Japanese activities in Manchuria reflect a similar realism.

While praising the Open Door and still hopeful of its future, Roosevelt noted that it "completely disappeared as soon as a powerful nation determined to disregard it, and is willing to run the risk of war rather than forego its intentions."[5] He argued that Japan's actions in Manchuria, where it still faced a hostile Russia, should be judged "on the actual facts of the case, and not by mere study of treaties."[6] Roosevelt dismissed American willingness to resort to war to challenge Japan. Likewise, he dismissed any help from an alliance with China. Given its "absolute military helplessness," China represented "not an additional strength . . . but an additional obligation."[7]

## The Open Door: From Theory to Practice

There were, however, different views of China. In contrast to Roosevelt's caution toward China, others were optimistic with regard to China's future and America's share in it. An article in the magazine *The World Today* described China as "standing on the threshold of her career . . . at the parting of the ways." China needed only to be "gently directed and wisely led."[8] That optimism suggested different policy choices and directions.

Even as a weakened China struggled to forestall the demands of the imperial powers, internally a process of reform and rejuvenation gathered momentum. China's awakening at long last appeared at hand. At the same time, Americans took pride in the Open Door and their disinterested approach to China. Further, many diplomats and journalists argued that the Chinese recognized the United States as a champion of China's sovereignty and territorial integrity. Under American tutelage, China would naturally develop along American lines. A contemporary author argued that, "If China is to be like America in certain ways how can she avoid approximating us in all?" Indeed, he concluded that "the possibilities in a China imbued with Western ideas . . . are enormous."[9]

Roosevelt's Asia policy did not long survive his administration. As Tokyo continued to expand Japanese rights and interests in Korea, Manchuria, and the coastal provinces of China, the successor Taft administration came to see Japan as the major threat to China's territorial integrity and the Open Door. During his trip to Asia in 1907, Taft saw Japan as determined to secure a position of dominance in China's affairs and the need for the United States to "assert with considerable stiffness its determination to insist on the Open Door policy."[10] As Secretary of State Philander Knox wrote with regard to the Open Door, the objective was to "reduce theory to practice."[11]

In contrast to Roosevelt's realism, Secretary of State Philander Knox could find no reason why Japan needed Manchuria more than China "who own it now or why it is any more vital to them than it is to China." As for defending the Open Door, while recognizing that the United States was not prepared to go to war for it, he was not prepared to prejudice America's position by admitting that "we would not, under any circumstances, go to war." The best policy would be to stand firm and "to continue to bring Japan's policy in China to the level of ours . . . than to lower ours to the level of hers."[12]

The disposition to protect China from Japan's encroachments produced the Manchurian Railway Neutralization Plan of 1909. American officials grew concerned that both Russia and Japan were intent on expanding their rights of railroad administration in Manchuria to include political jurisdiction over cities along their respective rail lines, thus detaching them from Chinese sovereignty and putting China's territorial integrity at risk. To prevent this threat of dismemberment, the United States proposed that an international consortium be formed to finance China's purchase of both Russian and Japanese railways in Manchuria.

The objective of the Neutralization Plan was to isolate Japan. Success depended on the cooperation of the European powers, including Great Britain and Russia. It failed in large part because the assumption of shared U.S.–European commercial interests in China failed to provide sufficient grounds for diplomatic cooperation in the Far East, which remained peripheral to Europe's immediate political concerns and diplomatic maneuverings.

State Department officials laid the major blame for the failure of the Neutralization Plan on the existence of the Anglo–Japanese Alliance which, in their view, gave Japan diplomatic leverage against the United States in China. As the United States continued to assume a higher-profile diplomatic role in China, weakening or breaking the alliance became a long-term objective in Washington policy circles. That goal was realized in 1921 when the Anglo–Japanese Alliance was terminated and a new multilateral system to deal with issues of China, Asian security, and naval competition was put in place at the Washington Conference.

## China and the Washington Conference

Turmoil beset China in the years following the 1911 Revolution. Political unity was short-lived under the republic that replaced the Manchu dynasty in 1912. By the end of the decade, political power was divided between a northern government in Beijing, largely a collection of former warlords with diplomatic recognition, and a pseudo government in Canton led by Dr. Sun Yat-sen and his Nationalist Party. Fearing the consequences of China's disintegration and the dangers arising from another scramble for concessions, the great powers looked for ways to cooperate to keep China together.

Out of Anglo-American efforts to come to grips with a series of complex problems—including budget pressures for postwar naval reduction; China; the continued existence of the Anglo–Japanese Alliance; and an incipient U.S.–Japan naval rivalry—the United States launched the Washington Conference in 1921. The results of the conference, a Four-Power Treaty on the Pacific, a Five-Power Treaty on Naval Limitations, and a Nine-Power Treaty on China, established a multilateral cooperative framework for managing the problems of East Asia.

At Washington, Japan traded the certainties of the Anglo–Japanese Alliance, the cornerstone of its diplomacy since 1902, for assurances of international cooperation to protect its special interests in Manchuria and China. At the same time, the Nine-Power Treaty enshrined the Open Door's respect for China's territorial and administrative integrity and committed the signatories to "refrain from taking advantage of conditions in China to seek special rights and privileges."[13]

China came to Washington determined to end the diplomacy of imperialism. For close to a century, the European powers and Japan, through a series of treaties, had extracted territorial concessions and special privileges that compromised China's sovereignty. What China secured at Washington was a promise by the powers to convene a tariff conference and to establish a commission on extraterritoriality. Beijing's failure to secure tariff autonomy and put an end to extraterritoriality fueled the forces of Chinese nationalism, contributing to breakdown of authority, warlordism, and ultimately civil war. Increasingly hostile, antiforeign Chinese nationalism demanded immediate revision of the treaty system and posed a challenge to the cooperative structure of the Washington Conference system.

For Tokyo, the weakness of the governing authority in China posed a threat to Japan's special interests on the mainland, particularly in Manchuria. Yet, through the middle of the decade, Japan remained committed to the international cooperation embodied in the Washington Conference system as the most effective means to protect its interests in China.

Ultimately, however, the force of Chinese nationalism fractured this cooperative structure. Demands for treaty revision and threats of termination or abrogation intensified. First the United Kingdom, then the United States broke ranks with the Washington concert of powers, taking unilateral steps to accommodate China's demands on treaty revision. In Japan, this unilateralism and lack of responsiveness to Chinese threats to treaty rights governing Japanese interests called into question the benefits of international cooperation in China. By the end of the decade, Tokyo too had shifted from cooperation to its own assertive unilateralism, and ultimately to intervention in Manchuria.

## Prescriptions for the Present and Future

Looking backward, it is clear that China played a major role in the evolution of the U.S.–Japan relationship in the early years of this century. By the mid-1930s, China-related issues served to define a relationship of divergent, if not adversarial, national interests between Tokyo and Washington. If the United States and Japan are to be successful in coming to grips with the challenges China will present in the coming century, it is perhaps useful to look for policy insights that may be gleaned from the estrangement in the Pacific which ultimately led to Pearl Harbor.

The starting point should be recognition in both Washington and Tokyo of the need for a clear definition and understanding of the two countries' respective national interests toward China. This is fundamental. As Theodore Roosevelt cogently argued, a coherent and well-integrated strategy is essential for success in Asia. For both the United States and Japan, the overarching strategic goal of American and Japanese national policies in the coming century should be China's own integration into the international system.

The lessons of the past underscore the risks of unilateralism. Close and almost continuous consultation on tactical questions relating to individual policy decisions is essential. Without such coordination, tactical differences risk misunderstanding and strategic separation. Both the Manchurian Neutralization Plan and the breakdown of the Washington Conference system testify to the dangers of unilateralism. While the current U.S.–Japan alliance relationship has served to structure policy dialogue and consultation, continuation of the alliance cannot be taken for granted.

In retrospect, the termination of the Anglo–Japanese Alliance in 1921 opened the door to Japanese unilateralism later in the decade. Multilateralism, as embodied in the Washington Conference treaties, proved an insufficient means of protecting Japan's interests in China. For over four decades since the end of the Second World War, the U.S.–Japan alliance has served to defend Japan and to protect its interests in Asia. At the same time, the alliance has served as the foundation of U.S. presence and influence in the region.

Counterintuitive though it may seem, the alliance in today's post-Soviet world is more central to the collective national interests of both countries than it ever was during the Cold War. The U.S. ability to project power and to meet its security commitments to Japan, the Republic of Korea, and other Asian allies and friends is related directly to the presence of forward deployed U.S. air, naval, and land forces in Japan. For the United States, the alliance is a cornerstone of its integrated Japan, regional, and global strategies. For Japan, Northeast Asia remains a dangerous and potentially volatile region, despite the demise of the Soviet Union. It is a region in which the forces of history remain strong, one in which Japan lacks natural friends.

These national interest–based strategic realities must be squarely faced. The alliance remains the sine qua non of both U.S. and Japanese security interests in Asia. This is not to deny the diplomatic value of reassurance gained through security dialogues and multilateral security fora, such as the Association of Southeast Asian Nations (ASEAN) Regional Forum (ARF). Such institutions can complement the alliance, but they can never replace it.

Nevertheless, in the post–Cold War world, there is much intellectual confusion regarding the continuing relevance of Cold War instruments, such as the alliance, and the very nature of security. Multilateralism has become fashionable. Multilateral security fora, such as the ARF, are now seen as emerging security structures. This is a dangerous trend. To the extent that modern multilateralism contributes to a belief that alliances are passé, it is a security delusion. Neither country should harbor any illusions when it comes to security. The alliance is irreplaceable.

## China, the United States, and Japan: Into the Next Century

Predictions about where China is going, what China will become, and what it might mean for the international community are traditionally a risky business. A brief review of twentieth-century history only underscores this fact concerning China.

Early in the twentieth century, many political leaders, diplomats, and journalists considered China an awakening giant, the nation of the future in Asia. In 1905, one American magazine, *The Independent*, predicted that China would become "the greatest military power in the world" within the next quarter century.[14] In 1908, Theodore Roosevelt portrayed China's wakening as one of the "great events of our age."[15] Roosevelt's characterization reflected widespread American optimism toward China, its future, and the future of American relations with China.

The Chinese Revolution of 1911 and the collapse of the Qing dynasty only served to reinforce that optimism. In the United States, China's revolution was portrayed as a contemporary version of America's own. Americans saw the "new ideals" which they assumed to have taken root in China as broadly representing the "American spirit of democracy, human rights, fair play and equal opportunity."[16] One journalist observed that republican China was "extending her hand across the Pacific to grasp ours," asking the United States "to teach her how to be free and happy and strong."[17]

Events did not develop as expected. For China, this century has been marked by interference and competition among the imperial powers;

warlordism, civil war, and the triumph of Chiang Kai-shek and the Kuomintang in the 1920s; the Japanese invasion, civil war, and the Communist Revolution in the 1930s and 1940s; as well as the disasters of Maoism, the Great Leap Forward in the 1950s and the Cultural Revolution of the late 1960s.

China's road to the 21st century began in the late 1970s. Following the death of Mao Tse-tung and the fall of the Gang of Four, Deng Xiaoping emerged as China's paramount leader. Seeking to recover from the economic ravages of Maoism, Deng launched China on an economic reform program in 1978. The Four Modernizations, as Deng's strategy came to be known, focused on agriculture, industry, science and technology, and the military, with the objective of creating a modern China by the year 2000. Modernization of China's military was last among Deng's priorities. However, following a strategic review in the early 1990s, efforts to modernize the People's Liberation Army have been stepped up with an emphasis on the acquisition of power projection capabilities and advanced weaponry.

In contrast with the disintegrating China of a hundred years ago, China today stands as an emerging great power. It is also a polity with a long history of wrongs suffered at the hands of the imperial powers, and thus is sensitive on issues related to sovereignty. In terms of both theory and hard geopolitical realities, how China integrates itself into the international system, or fails to do so, will be among the defining issues of international relations for the first quarter of the 21st century.

Since 1980, China's growth rate has averaged close to 9 percent. Should growth continue at relatively similar rates, many economists are now projecting that at some point in the first quarter of the 21st century China will have the world's largest economy measured in GDP terms. While China's ultimate national objectives are open to debate, success in its modernization strategy will require access to international markets, finance, and technologies. In this regard, the United States and Japan are, and will be, central to the success of China's modernization strategy. Success will also require a stable international and regional environment to facilitate China's growth and development.

To enhance stability in Asia, since the late 1980s China has normalized relations with a number of its neighbors—Singapore, Indonesia, South Korea, and Vietnam—all countries with which Beijing has had a troubled history. Over North Korea's strong objections, China joined with the United States and the Republic of Korea to support the simultaneous entry of both Koreas into the United Nations. In the early 1990s, Beijing moved away from its long-standing support for the Khmer Rouge to embrace the Paris Peace Accords which ended the civil war in Cambodia. China also abstained in the U.N. Security Council vote that authorized the use of all possible means to expel Iraq from Kuwait, thus paving the way for the United States–led victory in the Gulf War.

China, however, has also demonstrated a willingness to use force to advance its interests. In 1979, Deng Xiaoping used the People's Liberation Army (PLA) to teach Vietnam a lesson following Hanoi's invasion of Khmer Rouge–ruled Cambodia, then a Chinese client state. Similarly, China has used force to advance territorial claims on its periphery. In 1975, the PLA was employed to evict Vietnam from the Paracel Islands, and in 1995 to stake a claim against the Philippines in the South China Sea.

Beijing has also demonstrated a willingness to use force for purposes of political intimidation. In July 1995 and in March 1996, China conducted a series of large-scale military exercises in South China and in international waters near Taiwan in an attempt to influence the results of Taiwan's legislative and presidential elections. These exercises included test firings of nuclear-capable missiles.

China's Communist Party remains the sole source of political orthodoxy and authority. Yet, among all but the party's most faithful, ideological commitment has almost disappeared. Political fervor has been replaced by an overwhelming focus on material success, a by-product of Deng's economic reforms. Once the source of a dynamic ideology, the Communist Party is now increasingly viewed as the source of nepotism and privilege. China's commitment to communism is now being replaced by a dangerous political cynicism and a surging nationalism, particularly among China's younger generations. This nationalism has been most recently manifested in support of China's claims to sovereignty over the Senkaku Islands in the East China Sea.

At the global level, China has demonstrated an interest in greater international integration. Beijing has made entry into the World Trade Organization (WTO) a major foreign policy objective. However, it has also demonstrated an unwillingness to compromise on conditions of membership, insisting that China join on its terms as a developing country. If China, which is a major trading nation with one of the world's most dynamic economies, were to remain outside the WTO and play by its own rules, it would pose a major threat to the international trading order. That order would soon become dysfunctional if China, using the leverage of its market, opted to set its own rules of business and terms of trade.

Beijing has also signed the Nuclear Nonproliferation Treaty and the Nuclear Test Ban Treaty. And it has repeatedly offered assurances of its intent to respect the international Missile Technology Control Regime.

Yet China appears determined to continue its nuclear assistance programs and missile sales to Iran and Pakistan. Such programs put vital United States and Japanese security interests in South Asia and the Persian Gulf at risk.

Strategic ambiguity may not be China's strategy, but the ambiguity of its conduct does raise fundamental questions about the nature of China as an emerging great power and its relationship to the international system and to the United States and Japan. What kind of a power is China? Is it a revolutionary or revisionist power seeking to transform the very nature of the international system? Is it an assertive, but basically status quo power? Is it a global ideological and military adversary like the former Soviet Union? Is it Germany of the 1890s, a rising expansionist power prepared to challenge elements of the status quo? Is it Gaullist France, using cultural nationalism and independence to restore national purpose, while remaining a status quo power?

There are, of course, no appropriate historical models. Reality is always much more complex. China's conduct will be neither black nor white, but some shade of gray. It will undoubtedly be, often simultaneously, both cooperative and assertive on a wide range of issues. It will undoubtedly seek to shape to its own advantage the terms and conditions of its engagement with the world. This will make life difficult for political leaders and policymakers in Washington and Tokyo.

## Coming to Grips with China: Interests and Issues

The United States and Japan share an overarching strategic interest in international stability and in the smooth functioning of an open trading order. These interests will be significantly influenced by China's integration into the international economic order. The United States and Japan also share an interest in China's own internal stability, for a China that is unable to meet the economic needs and political aspirations of its people would threaten Asia's peace and prosperity. Finally, the United States and Japan share an interest in Asia's stability and in the peaceful resolution of its territorial disputes.

At the same time, the forces of geography and history are immutable. Geographic propinquity establishes distinctive relations between countries and shapes the evolution of their policies. Much like American relations with Mexico or Canada, what happens in China affects Japan most immediately. In the early decades of this century, political instability in China profoundly affected Japanese interests on the Asian mainland; and in Japan's emerging democracy of the 1920s, China policy was a matter of intense political debate. As noted earlier, following the collapse of the Washington Conference system, Tokyo moved from multilateral diplomacy to aggressive unilateralism in Northern China and Manchuria.

For Japan, stability in China is paramount. Since normalization of relations with China in 1972, Japanese political leaders have used economic aid, trade, and investment to encourage China toward foreign policy moderation and greater openness. Economic engagement remains the centerpiece of Japan's strategy toward China. Set against the background of Japan's recent economic stagnation, however, the cumulative effect of two decades of double-digit economic growth in China has raised questions in Tokyo concerning balance in Sino–Japanese relations. There are also concerns about the implications of China's ongoing military modernization program, its lack of transparency, and its growing assertiveness.

In the case of Japan's relations with China, the reality of geography is suffused with the legacy of the 1930s and the Second World War, Japan's postwar constitution, and political pacifism. These forces have inclined Japan toward a more circumspect approach to China. In contrast, the American policy is often assertive and direct. These stylistic differences, if not recognized for what they are, could lead to political friction between Tokyo and Washington even as they pursue similar goals with respect to China. At the same time, China-related contingencies could pose difficult policy and strategic choices for political leaders in Washington and Tokyo.

Against this background, the following discussion focuses on a number of China-related issues which could affect the U.S.–Japan relationship and their respective relations with Beijing. The issues highlighted are by no means exhaustive and are meant to be illustrative only.

## WORLD TRADE ORGANIZATION

As major trading powers, the United States and Japan share an interest in China's entry into the WTO and its acceptance of international legal standards that affect commerce such as patents, copyrights, and intellectual property protection. Such integration corresponds to China's own long-term commercial and economic interests. Indeed, the continued success of China's modernization strategy will depend largely on such rule-based integration. Difficult negotiations with Beijing and much hard bargaining lie ahead. Successful integration will require close coordination among the United States, Japan, and the European Union.

However, WTO membership will require Beijing to further open its market. This, in turn, could put at risk inefficient state-owned enterprises that employ millions of Chinese. Should Beijing judge the economic and political costs to be excessive, it could be tempted to use the lure of the China market to its advantage. Beijing could use political favoritism to set off a dangerous competitive dynamic in the China market. Inevitably, this would involve American and Japanese companies, and eventually this could affect political relations between Washington and Tokyo.

## HUMAN RIGHTS AND NONPROLIFERATION

China remains a one-party state with a repressive human rights record. Given the strong U.S. commitment to political freedom, unilateral initiatives in the form of economic sanctions have had strong political appeal in Washington. However, the Clinton administration's early attempts to link trade and human rights were considered counterproductive in Tokyo. At the same time, future Tiananmen tragedies cannot be ruled out as pressures for reform build inside China. In 1989, Japan followed the U.S. lead in adopting economic sanctions against Beijing, but it also worked quietly behind the scenes to lift them. Japan's proximity to the mainland, its large economic stake, and its interest in China's internal stability will make it difficult for Tokyo to sustain economic sanctions over an extended period of time.

U.S. law mandates unilateral economic sanctions in response to nuclear proliferation. The United States is unique in this legal mandate. Should China continue to sell nuclear technology to Pakistan and Iran, it will remain a political target for economic sanctions. Japan's readiness to move toward sanctions is changing as evidenced by its suspension of yen loans in response to China's nuclear testing. This reflects a more assertive and less defensive attitude toward China on the part of Japan's political leaders. But pressure from the United States to join in unilateral economic sanctions could complicate relations between Washington and Tokyo and expose political fault lines.

## ASIAN SECURITY

The most challenging issue will be the shaping of East Asia's security order. Despite Asia's end-of-century prosperity, stability remains fragile and long-term security problematic. For both the United States and Japan, their respective abilities to manage relations with China will define the nature of Asia's security environment for the first quarter of the next century. To a large extent, Asia's defining security challenges center on China, its territorial claims, its civil war legacies, its growing military might, and its long-term strategic interests. All may involve the U.S.–Japan alliance. All have the potential to test its enduring strength.

## TAIWAN AND THE SOUTH CHINA SEA

A decision by China to blockade or use force against Taiwan to prevent what it considers a bid for independence would trigger a crisis in Sino–American relations. Reaction by the United States in the form of military intervention to defend historic interests in freedom of the seas or to protect Taiwan could trigger a similar crisis in the alliance. This would be particularly true if the United States employed air and naval units based in Japan. Such actions would immediately raise constitutional issues in Japan and cause domestic political turmoil. Failure to support the United States would strain, if not shatter, the alliance. Yet support for the United States would rupture ties with Beijing and put Japan's own security at risk. The challenge for U.S. and Japanese diplomacy will be to prevent such a contingency from arising.

## THE KOREAN PENINSULA

Beijing has consolidated relations with Seoul while maintaining fraternal ties with Pyongyang. In effect, China has positioned itself to play a pivotal role in the unification process. This position could give Beijing leverage with regard to the future of U.S. forces in a unified Korea. Indeed, China's price for supporting unification may be the withdrawal of U.S. forces from Korea. This would bring China's policy into closer alignment with its principled opposition to the deployment of forces on foreign soil. Should China act in such a manner, the results would directly affect the U.S. military presence in Japan, particularly on Okinawa, and bring pressure to bear on the U.S.–Japan alliance. Korean unification, when it occurs, will transform the Asian security environment.

## CHINA, THE ALLIANCE, AND U.S.–JAPAN DEFENSE COOPERATION

During the Cold War, Beijing followed a two-track approach to the U.S.–Japan alliance—formal and principled opposition with informal acceptance and tolerance. For China, the alliance served as a key factor in Asia's regional security equation, in large part by constraining Japan.

Chinese views of the alliance, however, began to change as relations with Washington deteriorated at the end of the Cold War and the United States emerged as the world's single superpower. In Beijing, foreign and defense policy analysts began to speculate about America's intentions toward China, many seeing in the Clinton administration's early, disjointed policies signs of deliberate attempts to weaken or contain China. Against this background, efforts to restructure the U.S.–Japan alliance and the evolving security debate in Japan combined to heighten Chinese concerns.

During the Cold War, the primary purpose of the U.S.–Japan alliance was to contain the Soviet Union and, if necessary, to defend Japan. The collapse of the Soviet Union shifted American concerns in Asia to broader issues affecting regional stability and security. Initially these concerns focused on the Korean Peninsula and on the question of Japanese support for U.S. military action in the event of a Korean contingency. In the wake of Japan's belated response to the Persian Gulf War, it was feared that a similar halting response to a contingency involving the United States on the peninsula, an area of immediate security interest to Japan, would shatter the alliance. Thus, Washington moved to expand the operational dimension of the alliance, shifting its emphasis from Article V of the U.S.–Japan Security Treaty to Article VI, matters affecting "peace and security in the Far East" (see Appendix 2).

At the April 1996 bilateral summit in Tokyo, President Clinton and Prime Minister Hashimoto reaffirmed the continuing relevance of the alliance in the 21st century. The two leaders issued a Joint Declaration on the alliance, and the prime minister also committed his government to review Japan's Defense Policy Guidelines (see Appendix 3). China reacted strongly to what it perceived to be a broadening of the scope of the alliance in the Joint Declaration's reference to shared U.S.–Japan interests in a "peaceful resolution of problems in the region" (see Appendix 5). Beijing interpreted this as a reference to Taiwan, which it views as an internal affair of China. In the same vein, China viewed Tokyo's commitment to review Japan's Defense Policy Guidelines as evidence of a joint effort to expand Japan's military role within the existing alliance structure. Previously Beijing had voiced similar concerns with respect to Japan's decision to participate in international peacekeeping efforts.

Four months later, the Japan Defense Agency released the 1996 Defense White Paper. The document noted that China's defense spending grew 11 percent in 1995, the eighth consecutive year it had exceeded 10 percent, and, as originally reported by the Japanese news service Kyodo, went on to warn that "the situation must be watched with caution in terms of promotion of nuclear weapons and modernization of the navy and air forces, expansion of naval activity and heightened tension in the Taiwan Strait as seen in the military drill near Taiwan."[18] The Kyodo report reflected official Japanese concerns with China that had first surfaced during the 1995 revision of the National Defense Program Outline (see Appendix 6a and 6b). The reference to "caution," however, does not appear in the White Paper text published in English by the *Japan Times*.[19]

Japan's growing security concerns about the strategic uncertainties posed by China are also reflected in the ongoing debate over the development and deployment of a Theater Missile Defense (TMD) system. In the aftermath of the Gulf War, TMD was initially suggested by the United States as a means of protecting American forces forward deployed in Japan against ballistic missile attack. Japan's own vulnerability to ballistic missile attack was exposed in 1992, when North Korea test-fired the Nodong 1—a missile capable of reaching parts of Japan.

China, however, has viewed the TMD debate from a different perspective. Seeing TMD as a threat to its nuclear deterrent as well as a defensive shield behind which Japan could develop its own offensive nuclear capabilities, China made clear its opposition to TMD deployment in Japan. The implication that China was actively targeting Japan and U.S. forces stationed there came as a shock to many Japanese. Beijing's reaction to the TMD debate has only served to increase Japanese uncertainties about China.

## Dealing with China: Strategies

Having reviewed the interests and issues affecting Sino–American and Sino–Japanese relations, we need to address questions of fundamental strategy. Can strategies be found that will accommodate and advance the interests of the United States, Japan, and China? How policymakers view China will significantly influence their choice of strategies for dealing with it. Is China today a threat to the interests of the United States and Japan? Or does it represent a more complex and ambiguous phenomenon? If so, how should one deal with a country that is both assertive and cooperative?

If China is viewed as a threat, a containment strategy must be considered as one way of dealing with the problem. Containment worked against the Soviet Union because in the late 1940s it was perceived to be a direct and immediate threat to the security interests of the United States and its allies in Europe and Asia. Despite China's growing military might, its often assertive behavior, and occasional challenges to internationally accepted norms, a Soviet-like threat perception of China is neither immediate nor shared as a political consensus in the United States, in Japan, or across Asia.

At this time, it is highly unlikely that Japan or America's other allies in the region, much less the European Union, are prepared to join in a concerted containment strategy aimed at China. Indeed, they have voiced their apprehension that actions taken in Washington could cause them to be confronted with difficult choices, and they have cautioned against prejudging the outcome. Moreover, national rivalries among American allies in Asia point to the difficulty of drawing a cordon sanitaire around China.

Containment against Moscow also worked because Stalin's economic policies had set the Soviet Union on a course of autarky in the 1930s. As a result, at the end of the Second World War, U.S. and allied economic interests in the Soviet Union were insignificant. Moscow's decision to reject the Marshall Plan and to close the Eastern bloc economies to foreign participation in postwar recovery ensured that Western economic interests remained insignificant throughout the Cold War.

Unlike the Soviet Union, China today is a major force and market in the international economy. Also unlike the Soviet Union, significant American and Japanese economic interests are engaged in China. In the ten-year span from 1985 to 1995, Japan's two-way trade with China grew from $19 billion to $57.9 billion.[20] From 1992 through 1995, Japan's exports to China nearly doubled from $11.9 billion to $21.9 billion.[21] Over the same ten-year span, U.S. two-way trade with China grew from $7.7 billion[22] to $57.3 billion.[23] In 1995, American exports to China totaled $11.8 billion.[24] Likewise, from 1983 through 1994, American and Japanese companies invested more than $15 billion in China.[25] Meanwhile, Japan's foreign assistance to China, including grant aid, technical cooperation, and official development assistance (ODA) loans, has amounted to $9.3 billion over the period 1979 to 1994.[26]

This mix of aid, trade, and investment has spurred China's growth, while increasing the degree of interdependence. In Washington and Tokyo, commercial ties can also serve to constrain government policy choices on a wide range of economic, political, and security issues. This reality was highlighted in the early years of the Clinton administration when the White House attempted to link renewal of China's most-favored-nation (MFN) trading status to an improvement in its human rights record. Resistance in the American business community was particularly strong and played a significant role in President Clinton's 1994 decision to reverse course and move away from linkage.

The demonstrated clout of the business community inside the White House also resonated in Beijing. By the autumn of 1993, China began reciting to the United States the arguments of the American business community on the importance of the China market to American prosperity. Indeed, Beijing's growing confidence in its economic power, and in turn the political leverage of its market, promises to complicate cooperation on policy issues in Washington and Tokyo.

Illustrative of China's willingness to use political favors in its marketplace was the 1996 decision to favor Airbus over Boeing in the award of a contract. This was done to express Beijing's displeasure over America's stand on human rights issues. Should Beijing continue such a course, it could result in political strain among Western countries, who are strategic allies but also commercial competitors in China's market. Indeed, France, Germany, and Japan have been particularly diffident on human rights issues in their high-level meetings with China's leadership.

Yet, without clear priorities among various American interests in China and without a clear understanding of the steps the United States is prepared to take if China acts against American interests, strategies of engagement and dialogue will not be effective in advancing those interests. For example, Chinese missiles are shipped to Iran and Pakistan along with nuclear technology; intellectual property rights continue to be violated; and China has used its military muscle in the South China Sea and against Taiwan. All are against American and Japanese interests. Beijing's persistence in such actions raises questions about current American strategies and, more fundamentally, about whether there is a basis for a productive relationship with China.

Hans Morgenthau often remarked that good foreign policy is good common sense, and that good common sense generally makes good foreign policy.[27] Such observations provide a starting point for building a constructive 21st-century relationship with China. Common sense dictates that despite very real and significant differences on a number of issues, the United States, Japan, and China do share some common interests.

First, there is a shared interest in the stability of the Asia-Pacific region. For Americans, the dollar value of trade with Asia has long surpassed that of U.S. trade with Europe. In 1994, American exports to Asia grew at a rate of 16.2 percent to exceed $153 billion. The booming countries of the Asia-Pacific region purchased over $45 billion more from U.S. exporters than the fifteen nations of the European Union and almost $30 billion more than Europe as a whole.[28] Meanwhile, Japan's two-way trade with the region totaled $343.6 billion in 1995.[29] In the five-year period from 1991 to 1995, Japanese exports to Asia nearly doubled, growing from $113.2 billion[30] to $202.3 billion.[31] Thus, the prosperity and economic well-being of countless Americans and Japanese are intimately tied to the future of Asia.

Likewise, stability in Asia is essential if China's modernization strategy is to succeed. In 1995, China's two-way trade with the region approached $167 billion, accounting for close to 60 percent of China's total two-way trade. At the same time, Asia's booming economies provide China with a major source of investment capital. In 1995, foreign direct investment in China totaled over $91 billion; of this, more than 70 percent came from Asian countries.[32] In brief, these figures highlight the importance of a secure and prosperous Asia to China's own economic development.

Since the 1970s, stability in Asia has been based on a tacit, shared understanding of the region's security structure—a structure with its origins in the U.S.–Japan security alliance and a continuing U.S. security commitment to the region. There is no question that this once-shared strategic understanding has been strained by events of the mid-1990s, and it is imperative that Washington and Beijing move expeditiously to reconfirm this central tenet of Asia's stability and security, while at the same time coming to grips with China's growing influence and power in the region.

As great trading nations, the United States, Japan, and China share a common interest in a rule-based international economic system. For China to develop a 21st-century economy, Beijing will have to move toward such a system. For the United States and the international community as well, China's entry into the WTO should be a top priority. Beijing's acceptance and observance of international norms will only strengthen the international trading system. Failure to do so will put that order and China's own future at risk.

A successful strategy toward China should be based on and build from these shared interests. At various times in recent years, the American strategic objective toward China has been defined as the integration of China into the international community. This formulation implies that China is a passive actor, which it is not. Given its population, resources, economic dynamism, and military potential, China is certain to play a role in shaping the nature of the 21st-century international system. The U.S. objective should be to create conditions that will lead Beijing to see acceptance and observance of international norms as in its own economic, political, and security interests.

Morgenthau would also caution against treating China as either enemy or friend. This requires, however, that American and Japanese political leaders and policymakers define and prioritize respective interests toward China. Choices have to be made, and leadership does matter. Morgenthau's argument dictates that the United States and Japan must quietly, but firmly, communicate those interests and priorities to Beijing and indicate the price willing to be paid to protect and advance those interests and priorities.

Actions must consistently support declared interests. Not doing so undercuts credibility and raises questions of intent and resolve. The Clinton administration's ill-fated effort to link MFN to human rights questions is a case in point. Likewise, Japan's decision in 1991 to link future ODA decisions with the nature of recipients' political and military behavior has not been applied consistently to China. Indeed, in 1994, Tokyo announced that annual ODA disbursements for China would increase in the three-year period after 1996. Similarly, while Japan did act in May 1995 to suspend aid in response to China's nuclear testing, the suspension came only in the grant aid category; the more significant yen loan package was not affected. While never seeking to paint China into a corner, the United States and Japan must be prepared to respond resolutely if China acts against the stated interests of either.

Dealing with China requires an understanding of limits. The history of the twentieth century has repeatedly demonstrated that neither the United States nor Japan can force China to act against its perceived interests. What the United States and Japan can do is to communicate interests clearly and coordinate approaches with like-minded democracies with the intent of creating an international environment in which China, in the pursuit of its interests, will be inclined to do the right thing. Should that strategy prove untenable, it will, nevertheless, have laid a firm foundation for a different approach.

## Notes

1. Archibald Carey Coolidge, *The United States as a World Power* (New York: Macmillan, 1908), p. 183.
2. *Outlook* 97 (January 14, 1911): 59–60.
3. Richard W. Leopold, *The Growth of American Foreign Policy* (New York: Alfred A. Knopf, 1962), p. 221.
4. Roosevelt to T.R. Jr., December 5, 1910. Morison, *Letters* 7: 178.
5. Roosevelt to Taft, December 22, 1910. *Taft Papers.*
6. Roosevelt to Taft, December 8, 1910. *Taft Papers.*
7. Roosevelt to Taft, December 22, 1910. *Taft Papers.*
8. "The Chinese Awakening," *The World Today* 17 (September 1909): 978.

9. Joseph King Goodrich, *The Coming China* (Chicago: A.C. McClurg, 1911), p. 110.
10. Taft to Root, October 10, 1907. *Taft Papers.*
11. Knox's suggested but unsent reply to TR, December 22, 1910. *Taft Papers.*
12. Ibid.
13. Leopold, p. 434.
14. "The Awakening of China," *The Independent* 57 (20 April 1905): 916.
15. Theodore Roosevelt, "The Awakening China," *Outlook* 90 (28 November 1908): 666.
16. William T. Ellis, "China in Revolution," *Outlook* 99 (28 October 1991): 461.
17. "Recognition at Last," *The Independent* 74 (May 8, 1913): 1009–10.
18. Kyodo Report, July 19, 1996; FBIS-EA 96–140, July 19, 1996.
19. *Defense of Japan 1996*, p. 45.
20. *Japan Statistical Yearbook 1997*, Statistics Bureau, Management and Coordination Agency, Government of Japan. Pp. 412, 414.
21. Ibid., p. 412.
22. *U.S. Foreign Trade Highlights 1989*, Office of Trade and Economic Analysis, International Trade Administration, U.S. Department of Commerce. pp. 35, 40.
23. *U.S. Foreign Trade Highlights 1995*, Office of Trade and Economic Analysis, International Trade Administration, U.S. Department of Commerce. pp. 18, 22.
24. Ibid., p. 18.
25. *The Chinese Economy: Fighting Inflation, Deepening Reforms* (Washington, D.C.: World Bank, 1996) p. 108.
26. *Asia's Global Power: China–Japan Relations in the 21st Century* (Commonwealth of Australia), 1996, p. 67.
27. Author's notes from classes with Dr. Morgenthau at the University of Chicago.
28. John T. Dori, "As U.S. Exports to Asia Boom, So Does Creation of American Jobs," *F.Y.I. 70/95.* The Heritage Foundation, November 15, 1995, p. 1.
29. *Japan Statistical Yearbook 1997*, Statistics Bureau, Management and Coordination Agency, Government of Japan. Pp. 412–15.
30. *Japan Statistical Yearbook 1986*, Statistics Bureau, Management and Coordination Agency, Government of Japan. Pp. 410–11.
31. *Japan Statistical Yearbook 1987*, Statistics Bureau, Management and Coordination Agency, Government of Japan. Pp. 412–13.
32. *China Country Commercial Guide 1996–1997*, U.S. Embassy Beijing, August 1996. Appendix D, viii–94, viii–95.

# 3

# Waiting for Godot? Northeast Asian Future Shock and the U.S.–Japan Alliance

**ROBERT A. MANNING**

As it approaches the 21st century, the Asia-Pacific security environment is a lot like the old joke about Richard Wagner's music: not as bad as it sounds. Even before the region was beset with what now appear to be economic turbulence and a protracted, deep recession, its security dynamics were in flux, punctuated by episodic political and military skirmishes that may variously be interpreted as harbingers of confrontation among newly buoyant, competing nationalisms beginning to bump up against each other or, more charitably, as growing pains of maturing powers feeling their way toward a new balance. In either case, recent developments are a reflection of a lag in the Asia Pacific's relatively static international relations and its still remarkable economic dynamism. Certainly, seven years after the demise of the Soviet Union, East Asia did not inspire confidence that a buoyant new Pacific community was taking shape, or even that linear projections of its stability or economic dynamism were safe assumptions.

One need not look much further than the specter in March 1996 of China lobbing nuclear-capable M-9 missiles twenty miles from Kaohsiung, the third largest container port in the world, while two U.S. aircraft carrier task forces steamed into the East China Sea, to conjecture that the Asia-Pacific region may be less secure now than it was in 1990. North Korean development of intermediate-range, three-stage missiles lobbed over Japan also underscores the ease with which regional conflict could erupt. Other recent developments—a Korea–Japan row over

Takeshima/Tokdo Island, Sino-Japanese tensions over the disputed Senkaku Islands and other issues, North Korea's drift toward implosion, political upheaval in Indonesia and turmoil in Malaysia—similarly suggest that the region's relative calm in the two decades following the Vietnam War may be yielding to a new turbulence. These events follow a confrontation over conflicting claims (and Chinese assertiveness) to the Spratly Islands in the South China Sea in 1995, one that has resurfaced intermittently, most recently, in renewed dispute over Chinese construction on Philippines-claimed Mischief Reef.

## New Economic Malaise

The most traumatic development is the sudden shift from the much vaunted Asia-Pacific economic miracle to the Asian malaise as the economy of Japan, the world's second-largest economy, is mired in protracted stagnation and financial tumult, while the economies of South Korea, Thailand, Malaysia, the Philippines, and most of all Indonesia seek to reform their way out of recession from the shock produced in late 1997. At that time a volatile mix of currency misalignments, untransparent, weak financial systems—flaws in the "Asian model"—and a bit of investor panic plunged the region into economic recession and disarray.

For most of the past two decades, virtually all discussions about Asian security were premised on the perpetuation of the dynamic economic growth that had come to characterize the Asia-Pacific region. Certainly, the underlying assumption of the emergence of Japan as a major power, and of late the premise of the rise of a modernized China as a dominant regional and major global force, and of the Association of Southeast Asian Nations (ASEAN) as an international voice, were all an outgrowth of that economic dynamism. As well, the region's heightened importance to American global interests was—if not a shift from a Europe-centered world economy to a Pacific-centered one—a reflection of the growing weight of that economic prowess.[1]

The impact of this new reality in the Pacific is difficult to fully assess. As of late 1998 it was still a rolling crisis, with fear that Indonesia might unravel and fragment politically, in a twin political-economic crisis, and uncertainty about whether Japan's economic crisis would deepen further. But it is possible to disaggregate the problem into four categories: the directly affected (Thailand, South Korea, Indonesia, Malaysia), those caught in the cross-currents (Hong Kong, Philippines), the insulated by nonconvertible currencies but marginally affected and potentially victimized (China, India), and Japan.

Overall, it appears that the deep Asian recession is at least a three-to-five-year problem (dating from June 1997) and in some cases more of a five-to-seven-year predicament. Certainly Japan has the wherewithal to regain a path to growth by the year 2000. Similarly, Thailand and South Korea appear on a course to stabilize and resume a trajectory of growth by 2000–2001. But Indonesia may be a longer-term problem with no stable government likely before late 1999, and little progress on how to clear the books on $84 billion in corporate debt, which is key to restoring financial flows. China, whose exports and foreign direct investment began to ebb in 1998, is a wild card that could slip into recession, and if so, into political turmoil in the foreseeable future.

Certainly, it is fair to say that the notion of "Asian values" and the Asian "development state" model of growth that was a source of pride if not cockiness, has been seriously tarnished. At the same time the triumphalist notion of a future of unfettered free markets has also been called into question. The economic crisis has been a humbling experience for a region that had known only greater expectations and modernizing societies for more than a generation. It has also exposed the immaturity and limited utility of fledgling regional institutions—ASEAN, Asia-Pacific Economic Cooperation (APEC), the ASEAN Regional Forum (ARF)—as the United States and the International Monetary Fund have been the dominant actors in managing the crisis. However, many of the characteristics that led to the region's success—high savings rates, emphasis on education, hard work, prudent fiscal and monetary policies—are cause for optimism that after structural reforms in the 1998–2000 period, East Asian economies will reemerge as competitive tigers.

One can begin to discern some of the impact on security dynamics fallout from the new economic realities of the region. Certainly, we are entering a period when virtually all the major actors in East Asia will be more inward focused and absorbed with managing their domestic problems into the 21st century. One obvious consequence is the deferral and slowdown of military modernization that has been a feature across the region. This can be measured in canceled weapons systems procurement, from AWACS in Korea to F-18 fighterjets in Thailand, and in Japan's first reduction in defense spending in recent memory.[2] The object of paramount regional concern, the direction of a newly powerful China, appears a bit less intimidating, as China's energies are focused on the difficult second wave of economic reforms—privatizing state-owned enterprises, reforming a deeply troubled banking system, and dismantling the iron rice bowl writ large—in an unfavorable regional economic climate. Nonetheless, with the rise of China and

Japan as multidimensional great powers, we are witnessing a kind of slow-motion generational leadership change (e.g., China, Indonesia, Vietnam, North Korea) and assertive nationalisms across East Asia playing out in uncertain ways. Moreover, the region is in the process of defining its post–Cold War interests and trying to fashion institutions to safeguard its economic growth and ameliorate security concerns as it reclaims its pre-modern role as a central actor on the world stage. Beyond the two major rising powers, the prospect of a unified Korea, 70 million strong, and an enlarged ASEAN, stretching from Burma to the Philippines, with some 500 million people, also reflects an East Asia coming of age. For the near term, however, the crisis in Indonesia, conflict in Cambodia, and an unresolved legitimacy question in Burma are among the factors leaving a dark cloud over ASEAN's future.

Against this backdrop, the East Asian security environment has an unsettled, fluid sense of anticipation, with impending change on the Korean Peninsula and tensions over Taiwan looming as loci of the most likely conflicts. Both also hold the potential for near-term strategic shocks that could redefine geopolitics in the region. Epochal change has been occurring so incrementally that the magnitude of change unfolding is being discounted, even as all regional actors brace for it.

By and large, Asia-Pacific actors are pursuing increasingly sophisticated hedging strategies in response to China's growing economic and geopolitical weight, persistent fears of a fading U.S. balancing role, and in some cases, perceptions of a new Japanese role. This is reflected in continuing military modernization across the board (though in varying degrees) in East Asia, in new alignments such as the December 1995 Australia-Indonesia Security Accord, in the expansion and increasingly independent posture of ASEAN, perhaps most consequentially, by the new coziness of Sino–Russian relations, and new dynamics in Japanese-Russian relations.

Asians tend to make calculations based on long-term trends. The region's economic and political dynamism has been underpinned by an informal security system comprised principally of the U.S. forward deployed presence and network of bilateral alliances, the keystone of which is the U.S.–Japan alliance, but also treaty alliances with South Korea, the Philippines, Thailand, and Australia, and security ties extending to other ASEAN states. East Asia's prosperity has depended on access to the relatively open U.S. market. Now, the *relative* decline of the importance of the U.S. market (e.g., a diminishing percentage of East Asian total exports), in contrast to what has been until recently explosive intra-Asian trade and investment and the downsizing of the U.S. military, and set against the emergence of a more self-directed

Japan and, most dramatically in continental Asia, China, has begun to alter the equation. Intra-Asian (about 45 percent of total Asian trade, 70 percent of Asian investment) and trans-Pacific trade (U.S.–East Asian trade was over $520 billion in 1997) and investment has grown exponentially (the former faster than the latter). One consequence of the Asian financial meltdown is that U.S. companies are increasing their presence in the region, hunting for bargains amid bankrupt firms, privatized financial sectors, and sold-off pieces of Asian conglomerates. This rise of geoeconomics must be considered an important integrative factor, one mitigating if not reshaping the security calculus of regional actors.

Casting the largest shadow of uncertainty is a China with what appears an expansive definition of the Middle Kingdom and a large, understandable sense of grievance. This is manifested in its territorial definitions of surrounding waters (e.g., 1992 People's Congress law on national sovereignty) and recent provocations in the South and East China Seas, and has stoked fears about China's intentions. After more than twelve years of double-digit economic growth, continued efforts to modernize a largely antiquated military with a doctrine, structure, and air and sea capabilities increasingly aimed as power projection in local conflicts, and a more assertive diplomatic posture, the emergence of China as a dominant regional and major global power is the principal political optic in East Asia. Nonetheless, the sense of China reclaiming its pre-Modern historic role is at present more one of anticipation than reality. China remains a society in the throes of massive transformation whose outcome is uncertain.

The China question has begun to eclipse what at the end of the Cold War could be viewed as the "three concerns" that preoccupied thinking about Asian security: the new role of China, the emerging role of Japan, and the concern about a contracting U.S. role. Nonetheless, there remains much anxiety in the Asia-Pacific predicament, expressed by what the Chinese might call the three paradoxes.

1. The region is still more prosperous and peaceful than at any time in the recent past, yet haunted by its past and uneasy about the future.
2. Apart from the North Korean threat and tensions on the peninsula and in China–Taiwan relations, there are no immediate security threats, or even overtly adversarial relations, yet the region features the world's largest military forces, most of whom continue to steadily increase their military capabilities even as the United States and Russia and Europe reduce theirs.

3. In an age when regional economic integration is rapidly increasing and instantaneous global flows of capital and information have eroded the very concept of sovereignty, long-standing territorial disputes are becoming more prominent expressions of national identity.

## Burden of History

For all the concern about the future, to a substantial degree, the Asian security environment is shaped by the burden of historic legacies that are being brought into sharp relief by burgeoning nationalisms. The success of the 1997–98 best-seller *The Rape of Nanking* underscores the volatility of Japan's history in the pathology of Sino–Japanese and Korean–Japanese relations. The two most probable sources of large-scale armed conflict, a divided and heavily armed Korean Peninsula and China–Taiwan, are both legacies of the Cold War. It is not difficult to imagine that looming in the minds of many Asia-Pacific actors is a remembrance of things past—the precolonial Chinese tributary system, which some fear Beijing may be seeking to recreate, albeit a 21st-century version. Perhaps the most enduring, neuralgic example of history shaping regional perceptions is Japan's persistent inability to fully come to terms with its past. This problem of whitewashing a brutal imperial past continues to be a factor, particularly in Chinese and Korean nationalism, and plagues Sino–Japanese relations and Sino–Korean relations. More generally, the stigma of the past impedes Japan's evolution toward what Ichiro Ozawa has called "a normal nation," both in terms of forging a domestic consensus for a new global role and in regard to regional acceptance of a more assertive Japanese political-military role. Japan has recently taken important steps toward addressing the past, in unprecedented apologies during the October 1998 visit of Korean President Kim Dae Jung, and in similar acts during Jiang Zemin's November 1998 visit to Japan.

Another burden of history is that in the converse of the situation in Europe and the Helsinki process, which sanctified Europe's borders, few nations in Asia would be comfortable if their current borders were made final. Indeed, though there has been substantial movement toward clarifying them, particularly with Russia, India, and Vietnam, virtually all of China's borders in some measure lack clear definition. Apart from the South and East China Sea disputes, there is the Northern territories problem impeding Russian–Japanese relations, and a host of minor disputes among the ASEAN states. This problem is rarely considered in frequent calls for an "Asian OSCE."

## KOREA SHOCK

In a remarkable reversal of fortune from the past, when strategic competition among the surrounding major powers has determined the fate of Korea, it is the approaching reunification of Korea, whether peaceful or not, that will likely be a strategic shock to the already tentative balance in East Asia. The behavior of the key major powers, particularly that of China and the United States, may affect the pace and manner in which Korea is transformed. But reunification will be decided principally by actions and decisions of the two Koreas and may well occur in unanticipated ways.

Four years after the October 1994 U.S.–North Korea "Agreed Framework," successful in freezing North Korea's *known* nuclear weapons program, the accord has yet to seriously reduce tensions, the conventional military threat, or advance North–South reconciliation. Moreover, U.S. intelligence reports that Pyongyang may be constructing new secret nuclear facilities along with the development of two new intermediate-range missiles, the No Dong and Taepo Dong, suggest that military tensions may be on the increase—and the "Agreed Framework" may be short-lived.

For all its urgency and implications, North Korea's nuclear weapons program was but a symptom of the larger Korea problem, not the source of it. If Pyongyang's nuclear weapons program disappeared overnight, the heavily armed Korean Peninsula would still remain one of the world's most volatile flashpoints. Even a significantly degraded Democratic People's Republic of Korea (DPRK) military can still cause unacceptable damage to the greater Seoul area with its 11,000 forward-deployed artillery tubes, Scuds, No Dongs and Taepo Dongs, and chemical weapons within 100 km of the demilitarized zone (DMZ). Moreover, unusual troop movements at times over the past several years may have further reduced an already narrow warning time.

This situation is further complicated by the continued deterioration of North Korea as reflected in the floods and structural damage to its agriculture, food shortages, and seven years of net negative economic growth averaging about –5 percent annually.[3] In official statements, its foreign investment laws, and the creation of the Rajin-Sonbong free trade, there is ample evidence that Pyongyang recognizes the need to open and reform its economy. Yet the fear that Chinese-type reforms would undermine its ruling myths (Kim-Il-Sungism) and political control has precluded the DPRK from substantially restructuring what in economic terms may be the most distorted economy in the world.

Instead, North Korea appears to be pursuing a "muddle-through" strategy, experimenting at the margins with economic opening, and forced by the severity of its famine and economic decline to allow decentralized economic activity. In short, it will accept some aid and investment, but on carefully controlled terms.

Pyongyang's inability to systematically open and reform its economy on more than an experimental basis undercuts the logic of the nuclear deal. The inherent assumption of the Agreed Framework was that with the right mix of incentives, Pyongyang could be persuaded to make the least bad choice in a spectrum of very bad options, and would trade its ultimate insurance policy, its nuclear weapons program, for security assurances and a new economic and political engagement with the United States, South Korea, and Japan. The nuclear accord thus suggested, in effect, the first phase of a bailout for a failing state. The implicit premises of the deal were: on the North Korean side, the need for security assurances, economic aid, trade, and investment to revive its moribund economy as key to its survival; and on the U.S.–Republic of Korea–Japan side, the desire to avoid a war or a collapse and achieve a "soft landing" and gradual reunification process.

As the situation has unfolded, the unstated premise of the nuclear deal appears highly questionable, even as the accord has, on its own terms, been remarkably successful. The nuclear program is frozen; most of the fuel rods have been canned. The Korean Peninsula Energy Development Organization (KEDO) has reached detailed agreements with the DPRK, allowing it to begin the process of building two light-water reactors (LWRs). But there has been an absence of substantive progress in North–South reconciliation, in U.S.–North Korean relations, or Japanese–North Korean relations. There have been no further deals curbing missiles and chemical weapons or reducing force levels; nor have there been confidence-building measures such as pulling forces back from the DMZ. Instead, there are continued tensions on the peninsula growing out of various DPRK provocations (e.g., sending troops into the DMZ and test-firing Taepo Dong missiles over Japan in August 1998) and the underlying residual distrust between the United States and DPRK, and the mutual suspicion and competition between the North and the South.

With the election of Kim Dae Jung in South Korea, there was some indication that we might enter a new phase in the diplomacy of the Korean Peninsula. The economic crisis, which made Seoul appear less intimidating to Pyongyang, combined with the new, less vindictive, more enlightened approach by South Korean President Kim Dae Jung, separating economics from politics and pursuing a clear vision of a gradual multistage process of confederation, raise the prospects that

North Korean desperation may propel it into a meaningful North–South reconciliation process. But this will be a protracted affair during which the North will seek to sustain a political climate conducive to large-scale global charity to ameliorate massive food shortages, estimated at some 1.2 million tons annually.

## DRIFTING TOWARD CONFLICT?

The source of this diplomatic stagnation and drift toward confrontation is the DPRK's failure to embark on a course of radical economic reform and its strategic focus on advancing relations with the United States while marginalizing the Republic of Korea (ROK). From Pyongyang's perspective this is a rational strategy, but it has proved, and will continue to prove, counterproductive. In both Washington and Seoul, political realities render it difficult to build the nuclear accord into a larger political bargain. The United States is in the odd position of maintaining an economic embargo against the DPRK while Pyongyang is now the third-largest U.S. aid recipient in Asia, receiving more than $140 million in food alone by 1998.[4] Congressional skepticism over North Korea has grown in light of DPRK provocations, putting at risk U.S. funds for KEDO. The absence of a larger strategy beyond the nuclear accord has allowed the DPRK to set the diplomatic agenda since 1993. This has in turn fostered new levels of distrust in U.S.–ROK relations.

The net result is that despite its success in addressing the nuclear problem the Agreed Framework is likely to prove unsustainable unless it is embedded in a larger policy of North–South reconciliation. Absent progress in realizing the December 1991 North–South Reconciliation and Cooperation Accords, or any alternative framework for tension reduction and North–South cooperation, it is at best problematic that the ROK parliament will authorize more than small initial portions of the required $3–$4 billion.

The bottom line is that the idea of a soft landing and gradual reunification process appears increasingly problematic. The "soft landing" concept requires a rejuvenated DPRK economy of which there now appears little prospect. This does not mean, as some U.S. analysts and officials have suggested, that the DPRK is on the brink of collapse.[5] Its tightly controlled system, its international emergency aid, and China's moves to keep the DPRK afloat, all suggest the Kim regime may be far more resilient than many analysts believe.[6] Nonetheless, absent systematic, radical economic reform, its moribund economy will continue to decline, and at some point over the next decade or less, implosion of the regime and/or the state is not an improbable scenario.

The increasing danger is that if Pyongyang continues its slide toward oblivion some precipitous internal development will lead the political-military elite to conclude that absorption looms ahead and thus there is nothing to lose by initiating some desperate limited military action designed not to take and hold territory but to "sue for peace," to obtain better terms of reunification. This is most troubling in the worst-case scenario, where Pyongyang might mate a nuclear weapon with one of its missiles. The risk, however, is one of miscalculation or overreaction on either side.

Whether a peaceful or violent implosion occurs—and there is a possibility of "no landing," perpetuating the current regime in the near to mid term—it will almost certainly have a large impact on the U.S. forward deployed force presence in East Asia. It is difficult to envision a sustained U.S. military presence in Korea after there is a stable, unified Korea, though a treaty alliance, and a small residual logistics group as in Singapore, may endure in some form. If there is violent conflict in the process in a manner that discredits U.S. credibility, such a worst-case scenario could be destabilizing to the region and transform hedging strategies into new strategic competition among China, Japan, the United States, and Korea.

## THE TAIWAN FACTOR

Like the denouement in Korea, the Taiwan problem holds the potential to alter the East Asian balance. This was foreshadowed in the March 1996 Taiwan Strait crisis, when the People's Republic of China (PRC) fired nuclear-capable M-9 missiles and conducted live-fire exercises off Taiwan while two U.S. aircraft carrier task forces deployed in the East China Sea "monitored" activities. China's message was unmistakable: formal Taiwanese independence was unacceptable and would trigger a military response. For the United States, a cross-strait military conflict is almost certainly a lose-lose proposition. If the United States did not come to Taipei's aid in the event of an invasion, it would raise profound doubts in the minds of allies as to the credibility of the U.S. security umbrella. Yet a U.S. military response would force choices polarizing East Asia and put its alliances at risk.

Taiwan's military modernization—its $11.2 billion defense budget is roughly the size of the defense expenditures of all ASEAN states combined—has directly impacted PRC modernization. With 150 F-16s and 60 Mirage fighters, Taiwan will have one of the most modern air forces in the world. In addition, the U.S. and Lafayette frigates, and perhaps new submarines, offer significant naval capabilities. In response, Beijing has begun to acquire at least 72 Su-27 fighters, and perhaps as many as 75 more under co-production from Russia. More recently, during his December 1996 visit to Moscow, Premier Li Peng finalized a deal to purchase two Sovremenny-class missile-carrying destroyers for $400 million each. These ships were developed in 1980 by the Soviets to counter Aegis-class cruisers, and the Chinese People's Liberation Army (PLA) Navy likely sees such hardware as necessary if it is planning to counter U.S. aircraft carrier task forces in the future. In addition, there are reports that Beijing is negotiating to buy 50 Sukhoi Su-30MK multi-role fighters.[7]

Cross-strait tensions have abated, but in no small measure as a by-product of improvements in Sino–American relations. Taiwan's quest for a larger international role persists and is a source of tension that could erupt as both sides maneuver for position. But for both Beijing and Taipei, the issue is driven largely by domestic politics, and will continue to ebb and flow. The renewal of cross-strait dialogue in 1998 suggests new incentives on both sides are likely to lead to progress on technical issues, and perhaps later political questions. Sovereignty is a particularly neuralgic and popular issue as a new generation displays increased national assertiveness. No Chinese leader could permit Taiwan to become formally an independent state and survive politically.

Yet democracy in Taiwan changes the old assumptions. President Lee Teng-hui ruled out independence in his May 1996 inaugural address. But Taipei's quest for more international political space, its desire for recognition of Taiwanese identity and success, is a new constant. It was not coincidence that Taipei's foreign minister mysteriously appeared in the Ukraine en route from a trip to Central America in August 1995, for example. It was Lee Teng-hui's private visit to the United States in June 1995 that began the downward spiral in cross-strait relations and pushed Sino–American relations to the brink.

The carefully crafted formulations of the past quarter century have served all three parties well. All have prospered under the political fictions engendered by President Richard M. Nixon's 1971 opening to China and the three Sino–American communiqués that have set the framework of U.S.–China relations. The 1972 communiqué carefully obscured Sino–American differences. In that document, the United States acknowledged that "Chinese on both sides of the straits agree there is but one China." The 1978 communiqué established diplomatic relations with Beijing, and "derecognized" Taiwan. Since 1978, the United States has had only "unofficial" economic, political, and cultural ties to Taiwan, and support for Taiwan's defense efforts have been governed by our Taiwan Relations Act (TRA). The 1982 joint communiqué purported to set quantitative and qualitative limits on United States arms sales to Taiwan.

The three communiqués may remain an adequate framework, but new interpretations are needed to underpin cross-strait equilibrium. The danger is that some may not recognize what should be obvious: a return to the status quo ante is not possible. So long as Washington and Beijing operate under the old assumptions, continued tension, periodic confrontation, and the risk of miscalculation will be almost inevitable. Difficult as it may be to achieve, nothing less than a new set of understandings between China and Taiwan—and expectations of both about the U.S. role—will create a stable equilibrium between the two. Until such a new cross-strait bargain occurs, U.S.–China relations will be bedeviled by the Taiwan issue.

Discussion of a resolution of the Taiwan problem is beyond the scope of this chapter, but a few points should be noted. First, until a decent interval (roughly 2010) after the reversion of Hong Kong to PRC sovereignty, no offer on the ultimate status of Taiwan will be credible in Taipei. The character of the regime in Beijing will be an important factor in determining what form of association between the mainland and Taiwan will be tenable. In the interim, a quid pro quo in which Taipei concedes the "One China" principle of sovereignty, and Beijing permits Taipei de jure political autonomy in the United Nations system, is possible.[8]

Unlike the Korean case, the Taiwan problem does not involve a failing state. Indeed, it involves two of the most dynamic economies in the world moving economically toward integrating into a "Greater China." The large and growing trade and investment of Taiwan in the mainland—over 20 percent of Taiwan's trade, and some $30 billion in investment—provides both sides a large stake in finding some accommodation.

## THE CHINA FACTOR

The March 1996 Taiwan episode highlighted the reality overshadowing all other aspects of the Asian predicament: a China looming ever larger with more than its share of historical grievances. The immediate possibility of a U.S.–China confrontation and the longer-term question of coping with China—as a military power, economic competitor, major energy importer, and polluter—pose broad challenges to the region and special concerns for managing the transformation of the Korean Peninsula. In the recent flare-up over the Senkaku/Diaoyu Islands and the 1995 episode over the Spratly Islands in the South China Sea, China's national assertiveness has become a dominant regional concern.

China's emergence is of particular concern because it occurs at a moment of fluidity in the international system of relations. Indeed, it is perhaps the paramount single challenge to the post–Cold War system of relations. In the case of Northeast Asia, where there are no collective security structures, multilateral institutions, or even firm alliances outside the U.S network of bilateral alliances, economically dynamic states are modernizing their respective military forces. It is, for example, the first time in modern history that China and Japan have emerged as major economic and geopolitical actors at the same time. Festering territorial and resource disputes overlaid with historic "score settling" suggest an environment where relatively small incidents can unexpectedly flare into major conflagrations.

Resource concerns, mixed with or instead of nationalism, may be a factor in Chinese behavior. A 1978 U.N. study indicated oil and gas may lie beneath the offshore waters of the Senkaku/Diaoyu Islands. It should be recalled that China became a net oil importer at the end of 1993, and energy is a major preoccupation of Chinese planners. China currently needs some 600,000 barrels of imported oil a day. According to APEC estimates, its requirements for imported oil may reach 3 million barrels a day by 2010, roughly half the production of Saudi Arabia. While resource scarcity projections are notoriously unreliable and fail to reflect new technological breakthroughs or new energy discoveries, these are nonetheless problems Beijing can hardly afford to ignore. However, a radical shift from key player in energy demand growth to a net reduction in Asian energy demand resulting from the economic recession and most current projections suggests that ample supplies at prices in the range they have been ($15 to $20 per barrel) are likely for the foreseeable future (e.g., to about 2010). Another underexamined trend is Chinese (and East Asia's generally) growing dependence on Persian Gulf oil, the geopolitical implications of which remain unclear.

Energy security concerns dovetail nicely with revisionist historical claims. Even after China had in 1995 pledged to base claims on the Law of the Sea, last May it announced that the area of sea under Chinese jurisdiction had expanded from 370,000 sq. km. to about 3 million. China achieved this by the 200-mile economic zone as not simply 200 miles from its shores, but to include the Paracel archipelago, a creative interpretation of the Law of the Sea. Thus, like the South China Sea dispute, the Senkaku/Diaoyuti issue is part and parcel of expansive definitions of Chinese sovereignty.

One measure of the level of anxiety in East Asia is that the nations of the region have surpassed Europe in military spending. One motivating factor behind the military buildup in the region is the Law of the Sea

Treaty, which gave countries 200-mile Exclusive Economic Zones (EEZ) to protect. Thus, ASEAN states in particular have been modernizing air and naval forces: Malaysia's acquisition of 28 Hawks, 8 F-18Ds, 18 Mig-29s, and missile frigates; Singapore's F-16s and E2Cs; Indonesia's purchase of former East German ships; and Thailand's F-16s. In the past several years, Singapore's acquisition of F-16s and Indonesia's acquisition of submarines seem to be triggering a cycle of escalation in military capabilities. As discussed above, this cycle of modernization appears to be on hold as ASEAN economies recover economically.

Japan continues to modernize its forces, with the largest naval fleet in the Pacific apart from that of the United States, including four new AWACS, Aegis cruisers, and submarines, increasing satellite and reconnaissance capabilities, and although it is for civilian nuclear power, a growing stockpile of plutonium. The reality of Japan has fed into historic Korean fears, and this is reflected in South Korea's military modernization. Rather than focusing on the overland threat from North Korea, Seoul is acquiring 100 long-range fighters, surveillance aircraft, submarines, and destroyer-class ships, and is even planning to acquire an aircraft carrier.[9]

And, of course, China's purchase of Su-27s, some of which are based on Hainan Island and all of which are based in the southern region, its building of a military base on Woody Island in the Paracels as well as acquiring 24 Mig-31 Foxhound interceptors, its development of air refueling capabilities, naval modernization, and rapid deployment/local war doctrine all point in one direction. Against the background of China's expansive 1992 sovereignty law, and its historic pattern of using military force, Beijing's resistance to efforts to elevate the Indonesian-sponsored South China Sea workshops to official diplomacy is an issue of concern. China's pro forma participation in nascent security dialogues while impeding serious attempts at preventive diplomacy, and its long history as a unitary actor, suggest that nascent efforts to forge meaningful regional security mechanisms are unlikely to yield productive results.

It is worth noting that in the debate over multilateral security mechanisms throughout the 1990s, the one occasion in Asian history when a multilateral system was erected—the Washington Conference in the 1920s—failed. Moreover, at that time, the Anglo–Japanese bilateral treaty was ended, to be replaced by the Washington Conference system. Serious consideration of multilateral security institutions to replace the essentially bilateral relations that make up the status quo now would be wise to carefully study the efforts earlier this century.

The question of stability in Northeast Asia in some measure revolves around what role China will play in the world: that of a revisionist power or that of a major power and steward of the international system. The problem is that it may not be possible to attain a clear judgment about China: Beijing is likely to display elements of both roles, as it does presently, cooperating in some areas, acting hegemonistic, or as a "spoiler," in others. In any event, the outcome will have a significant impact on U.S.–China and Sino–Japanese relations as well as on the U.S.–Japan alliance. The answers to this question are closely related to the unresolved issue of the political character of a post-Deng China.

The release of a China Defense White Paper by Beijing's State Council in late July 1998, however, begins to offer a glimpse into China's intentions. Consider the White Paper's description of what it counts as factors threatening peace: "Hegemonism and power politics [whom could they be thinking of?] remain the main forces of threats to world peace and stability . . . the enlargement of military blocs and the strengthening of military alliances have added factors of instability to international security; some countries by relying on their military advantages pose military threats to other countries."

Still more pointed language is in a section on Taiwan. "Directly or indirectly incorporating the Taiwan Straits into the security and cooperation sphere of any country or military alliance," says the report, "is an infringement upon and interference in China's sovereignty." This language is particularly interesting; for example, Beijing's view of Taiwan as an internal matter. The Taiwan Strait is an international body of water.

The United States is never named directly. But there can be little doubt that China is expressing its objections to a world order dominated by the United States as a single superpower, and indeed, to the very idea of deterrence basic to strategy. In particular, Beijing's rebuff of military alliances is a thinly veiled rejection of both the expansion of the North Atlantic Treaty Organization and the recently strengthened U.S.–Japan alliance, the cornerstone of U.S. policy toward East Asia. The 1996 renewal of the U.S.–Japan alliance, cemented at the Clinton-Hashimoto summit, has been a continuing source of friction in China's discussions with both the United States and Japan. Beijing tends to view the U.S.–Japan alliance as an instrument of containment. But at the heart of its concern is its fear that the alliance is an obstacle to the reunification of Taiwan with the mainland, at least on Beijing's terms.

This official Chinese view is the diametric opposite of long-standing U.S. policy. In a 1995 strategy paper, the Pentagon stressed that keeping 100,000 U.S. troops in East Asia was the measure of America's commitment to it. The importance of the U.S. military presence in the region as the cornerstone of stability was further underscored in a new East Asia strategy review, which the Defense Department released in the fall of

1998. Thus, China has presented a competing vision of the future, one that, if pursued as operational Chinese policy, may be incompatible with U.S. and Japanese interests.

What Beijing is hinting at in its White Paper is eventually displacing the United States as the preeminent power in Asia. In its 5,000 years of civilization, China has experienced only two types of security systems in Asia. Until the nineteenth century, there was the tributary system: the region revolved around the Middle Kingdom, with countries paying it a loose fealty. "Mutual trust" and "dialogue" and "cooperation" take on interesting meanings in that context. More recently, China has been the victim of foreign invasion by Japan and the West. Beijing obviously prefers the former system, albeit a 21st-century version.

The irony here is that many in the region (including the Clinton administration) have been advocating what I call "mindless multilateralism," the notion that simply assembling governments and holding a dialogue on security, as exemplified by the ASEAN Regional Forum, amounts to a new security architecture. Clinton has called such efforts "overlapping plates of armor," complementing U.S. bilateral arrangements. China has cleverly seized on this vague rhetoric of multilateral dialogue and cooperation, taking the idea of multilateralism as an end in itself, rather than a means, to its logical conclusion to make the case against Cold War–origin alliances.

This is in contrast to successful institutions of collective defense such as NATO, which were clearly defined as a means to a clearly defined end. The difference is a clear sense of purpose. Multilateral institutions may be key to the future of Asian security. But to be effective they must have a clear and commonly understood purpose and embody the political commitment of the major players involved.

Whether China, as it evolves into a multidimensional great power, will pursue such a course or find ways to accommodate the United States as a Pacific power may hinge on the outcome of its historic change. China is in the midst of unprecedented transformations in every respect thus far, except that of its political system, which unlike its economic reform, demographic and social change, and cultural norms, has remained static, controlled by a small elite hierarchy. China faces some enormous challenges in the period ahead as it seeks to consolidate a post-Deng leadership. These include redefining relations between Beijing and the regions of China; reforming state industries, and perhaps the weakest financial system in Asia; reducing the coastal-interior disparity in economic growth and incomes; and moving beyond its widespread corruption to more of a rule-of-law system. How it meets these challenges will affect the legitimacy of the Communist

Party, and that legitimacy issue will increase the role of nationalism in China's foreign relations.

There are four alternative futures toward which China could evolve, each with its own implications for East Asia. The best-case outcome is a China that continues its long march of reform toward some type of constitutionalism, or a rule-of-law-based system with Chinese characteristics. Another possible direction in which some current trends point is a renewed authoritarianism facilitated by nationalist appeal. The third alternative is degeneration to a loose coalition of regional neo-warlords. The final possibility is a variant of the first two, what Robert Scalapino has dubbed "authoritarian pluralism," incorporating some aspects of rule of law, with an authoritarian, collectivist state.

## Northeast Asia: Looming Strategic Competition?

Regardless of which outcome occurs, there will be some measure of nationalism inherent in China's international behavior. Even if it is democratic, popular nationalism may be an unwieldy force. One may recall a young democracy a century ago, declaring its dominance over an entire hemisphere: the Monroe Doctrine. But a more accountable regime in China would certainly have a significant impact on U.S. and Japanese policies toward Beijing. It is important to note that virtually all the disputes that have triggered fears concerning Chinese behavior have involved territory either historically Chinese or part of a suzerainty system—Hong Kong, Taiwan, or Tibet, for example—severed by Western imperial powers over the past 150 years, a brief moment in Chinese history.

It is useful to examine briefly the three key bilateral relationships (U.S.–China, U.S.–Japan, and Sino–Japanese) that determine the northeast Asian balance in light of the "Whither China" question. Sino–Russian relations have also become a new factor in the equation. Some analysts have begun to speak of a triangular relationship among the United States, Japan, and China, but this can be misleading. All three relationships have varying degrees of impact on the quality of each other, but there is not a zero-sum strategic triangle in the sense that the U.S.–U.S.S.R.–China triangle shaped strategic reality in the last two decades of the Cold War. And over the next decade, the U.S.–Japan alliance will almost certainly remain the linchpin of stability in East Asia.

In the near term, the still troubled U.S.–China relationship will for the most part be the largest external determinant of the other two relationships, and may itself be impacted by the transformation of Korea. Because of two roughly simultaneous events—the Tiananmen massacre on June 4, 1989, and the demise of the U.S.S.R.—the U.S.–China relationship has been devoid of a strategic rationale for the first time in half a century. At the same time, China has become increasingly assertive. It is enmeshed in the world, but not systematically integrated into the world system. This makes for a large collection of difficult issues, the cumulative impact of which has led to a cycle of mutual recrimination and tension in Sino–American relations.

The Taiwan issue, although it is the most explosive, is but one of the many landmines impeding U.S.–China relations. There are lingering human rights concerns, which find expression each June in the debate over renewing China's most-favored-nation (MFN) trade status. There is a burgeoning trade agenda reflected in China's growing trade surplus, projected at nearly $57 billion in 1998, and friction over the terms of China's entry into the World Trade Organization (WTO). Moreover, there are a host of missile and nuclear proliferation issues in Southwest Asia. Any of these mines is capable of being detonated at any given moment. Indeed, the Taiwan episode brought to a head a downward spiral in Sino–American relations, a relationship that has been without a center of gravity since June 4, 1989.

Unless and until the United States and China reach a new strategic understanding on key issues, the relationship will continue to be highly volatile. One potentially positive result of the Taiwan crisis was that from late 1996, there appeared to be a mutual stepping back from the brink and moves to foster a new dynamic in the relationship. This was evident in a series of events that began with a visit by China's senior foreign policy adviser Liu Huaqiu to Washington in April 1997, where he met with Anthony Lake, Clinton's national security adviser to the October 1997 Jiang-Clinton summit. The tenor of the renewed momentum in U.S.–China relations was set by then Secretary of State Warren Christopher in a speech at Fudan University in Shanghai the previous year. He said that "our strategy is to support a China that not only abides by international rules, but plays an active and responsible role in setting them."[10] This trajectory accelerated when Christopher went to China and Clinton gave a policy speech in Australia, then met with President Jiang Zemin around the APEC summit in Manila in November 1996. The public diplomacy was peppered with phrases such as a "new era of cooperation," and at the 1997 Jiang-Clinton summit of "seeking to build a constructive strategic partnership." This rhetorical shift, though still largely a debasing of language, is a step forward from the false choice of "engagement" or "containment," terms that have dominated discussions of China over the past four years. But the new emphasis on cooperation, important because for the first time it acknowledges China as a major power, is still trapped in a Cold War state of mind: China is either friend or enemy; engagement and cooperation, or containment and isolation. In fact, the reality is neither black nor white, but some shade of gray, and will continue to be ambiguous over the coming decade.

Nonetheless, the exchange of summits, with Clinton's visit in June 1998, suggests a new seriousness on both sides and atmospherics that could set the stage for a more stable U.S.–China relationship. A durable new Sino–American bargain would have to find a tolerable balance on what I call the "Six Burdens": a new PRC–Taiwan understanding, China's role in South Asia, curbing China's support for Iran's military buildup in the Persian Gulf, linking China's nuclear modernization to the next stage of the U.S.–Russian build-down, China's reaching terms of accession to the World Trade Organization (WTO), and—not least—U.S.–PRC understanding of their roles in Northeast Asia.

Altering the political psychology of Sino–American relations is a significant part of the problem. A dangerous cycle of recrimination has developed, where the United States accuses China of breaching international norms, or of acting as an aggressive "rogue state"; and China views each U.S. action as part of a "containment" strategy designed to keep China weak and divided. One need only glance at the officially sanctioned Chinese best-seller *The China That Can Say No* to get a glimpse of the problem. There is a psychology of victimization, rooted in its historical experience, shaping Chinese perceptions. In this century, China has suffered at every turning point. At Versailles after World War I, Chinese interests were not accommodated, although China contributed to the Allied victory. At Yalta, after World War II, again Chinese interests were not taken into account despite its suffering and its major role in Japan's defeat. And finally, at the end of the Cold War, despite an anti-Soviet entente that facilitated the U.S.S.R.'s demise, Beijing was not rewarded, but rather became the target of a search in some quarters for a new global adversary.

Similarly, in each discrete issue—opposition to the year 2000 Olympics in Beijing, democracy in Hong Kong, arms sales to Taiwan, WTO membership, U.S. normalization with Vietnam—China sees not independent issues or interest group politics. Instead, each separate act is seen as part of a concerted strategy to contain China, to keep it weak and divided. Only a protracted process of rebuilding Sino–American ties based on a new balance of interests will overcome such a pathology.

## Sino–Japanese Relations

While different from the dynamics of U.S.–China relations, Sino–Japanese relations have also been profoundly troubled. Though dependent in large measure on U.S–China and U.S.–Japan relations, over time Sino–Japanese relations will become the independent variable in determining East Asian stability. Much like Franco–German relations are to European stability, the degree to which China and Japan come to terms and accommodate each other's core interests will likely be key to shaping the Asia-Pacific security environment by the second quarter of the 21st century.

Since China and Japan normalized relations in 1972, memory has been a major factor shaping the political psychology of their relationship. The relationship has been characterized by a duality of economic and political cooperation but mutual fears of economic and strategic competition. The dynamic has been one of Japanese war guilt mixed with something of a superiority complex on the one side, and Chinese suspicion and distrust on the other. China could use the war guilt as a lever to manipulate the relationship. Until very recently Beijing has used that lever quite effectively. Japan's principal concern was about stability in China and fostering mutually beneficial economic growth. Thus, it is not surprising that Japanese official aid, much of it in the form of yen loans, totals some $30 billion. Nor that Sino–Japanese trade mushroomed to nearly $62 billion by the end of 1997.

Yet Japan's inability to honestly confront its past—as, say, Germany has done in Europe—remains a major source of insecurity in China and elsewhere in East Asia. This was displayed in dramatic fashion in 1995 during many controversies that marked the fiftieth anniversary of the end of the war, particularly the issue of "comfort women," forced prostitution to service Japanese soldiers. Rarely does a year go by when a World War II generation Japanese cabinet minister does not make an embarrassing remark that either distorts the past or seeks to justify Japanese colonial behavior, often forcing him to resign.

During the Cold War, however, overriding concern about the Soviet Union submerged China's abiding fears, however far-fetched, of resurgent Japanese militarism. Indeed, in the late 1970s and early 1980s China was informally aligned with the United States and Japan. Beijing encouraged the strengthening of the U.S.–Japan alliance. China seemed unconcerned as Japan modernized air and naval forces, as this took place under the U.S.–Japan umbrella. In fact, when the United States returned Okinawa to Japanese sovereignty in 1972, and included the Senkakus under Japanese administration, China did not press the matter. Beijing and Tokyo had agreed to defer the issue indefinitely when they restored relations the previous year.

The combination of the Cold War, China's top priority of economic modernization, and Japan's hopes of penetrating the China market made for a relatively stable relationship well into the 1980s. By the latter half of the 1980s, however, several developments began to alter Chinese views of Japan. In the aftermath of the 1985 Plaza Accord, which overnight doubled Japan's wealth, Japan appeared as an emerging financial superpower. At the same time a debate over whether the United States was in decline became a hot intellectual topic, while the emergence of Mikhail Gorbachev and a collapsing Soviet Union sparked China's intellectuals to rethink the Japan question.

Against this background, Japanese military capabilities that had been viewed favorably as a counterweight to Moscow began to look rather different. A turning point came in 1987, when Japan's defense budget exceeded the symbolic 1 percent of GNP limit it had put as a benchmark. Suddenly Chinese commentaries began to decry Japan's defense expenditures and more closely analyze the "roles and missions" it was assigned in the U.S–Japan security alliance. Chinese analysts began to argue that Japan, having become a major economic power, would inevitably become a major military power as well. Beijing was casting a wary eye on Tokyo even as it cashed the steady flow of aid checks.

For its part, even after the June 4, 1989, Tiananmen massacre, Japan sought to minimize the Group of Seven (G-7) response. Indeed, it was then Prime Minister Noburo Takeshita who announced at the 1992 G–7 that Japan would resume a major yen loan suspended after Tiananmen. The World War II generation dominating the bureaucracy, and the Liberal Democratic Party (LDP) continued the attitude of assuaging guilt with a continuing aid flow.

Things began to change in Japan around 1993. As a new postwar generation began to rise in the ranks of government, politics, and business, it saw China in a different light. A decade of double-digit economic growth led the World Bank to suggest China might already be the world's third-largest economy. At the same time, the opaque Chinese military budget was also growing by double digits annually. And politically, China began to act more assertively. In 1992, the Chinese parliament passed a national sovereignty law making broad territorial claims in the South and East China Seas. In particular, its claims on the potentially oil rich Spratly Islands, claimed by China, Taiwan, Vietnam, the Philippines, Malaysia, and Brunei, triggered an unexpected powerful reaction from the ASEAN nations. But the South China Sea question was but one manifestation of a China filled with historical grievances beginning to define itself in an expansive manner.

Suddenly China appeared less a very large, struggling developing nation and more an economic competitor, one with nuclear weapons and a burgeoning conventional military arsenal—an emerging major power with a rather large historical chip on its shoulder. A turning point came in early 1995 when Japan for the first time cut off a small amount of grant aid to China in response to Beijing's nuclear testing. As efforts to extend the Nuclear Nonproliferation Treaty (NPT), and to reach a comprehensive Test Ban Treaty gathered steam, Beijing was defying a moratorium on testing which the other nuclear powers were honoring, although France later broke from the pack. Japanese diplomats had been warning China not to conduct any nuclear detonations, but were met with testy responses from a China seeking to modernize its modest nuclear arsenal.

At the same time, for China, pushing the war guilt button suddenly failed to get the desired response from Japan. A new generation not yet born when the travesties China decries occurred and that has little interest in China meant that Beijing was losing control over the Japan relationship. At the same time, beginning in 1994, the United States and Japan, both concerned about a newly assertive China, began a process of reaffirming their security alliance. This culminated in the Clinton-Hashimoto summit in April 1996. Hashimoto pledged a more active Japanese defense role, including active contingency planning for regional crises, and potentially more active cooperation with the United States in a regional conflict. This appeared to push the boundaries of current interpretations of Article 9 in Japan's peace constitution.

This shoring up of an alliance that had appeared wobbly since the end of the Cold War was viewed in Beijing as more evidence of containment. "If Japan's self-defense forces further build up armaments," warned Chinese Foreign Ministry spokesman Shen Goufang, "it is bound to cause concern and vigilance among other Asian nations." He added, "We urge Japan to move with caution."

It must be noted that, despite recent controversy between Washington and Tokyo over the Senkakus, the U.S. position is less ambiguous than that portrayed in much of the Japanese press. The United States recognized Japan's administration of the Senkakus when Okinawa reverted to Japanese sovereignty in 1972, but takes no position on the conflicting Chinese and Japanese territorial claims. Washington has, however, made it clear to Tokyo that Article 5, the Defense of Japan, does apply if a conflict were to occur over the Senkakus.

## Conclusion: Great Powers in Northeast Asia

What does all this add up to? In the behavior of all the major powers, hedging strategies are evident. The reaffirmation of the U.S.–Japan alliance at the Clinton-Hashimoto summit in April 1996 was in no small measure a reflection of mutual concerns over China's future role. Indeed, the remarkable recent progress in Japanese–Russian relations must also be viewed in this light. One can only speculate as to whether the renewed security partnership would have been as warmly embraced in Japan had the summit occurred prior to the March 1996 Taiwan Strait crisis.

By the same token, the newfound Sino–Russian amity—including Moscow's willingness to help speed up Beijing's military modernization—reflects hedging strategies by both Eurasian nuclear powers that could, if present trends continue, evolve into antagonistic new post–Cold War alignments. It was probably more than coincidence that only weeks before Li Peng became the first foreign leader to meet Yeltsin since his surgery, NATO decided to take up the issue of expansion next July. Similarly, China's diplomacy—which also saw President Jiang Zemin bolster ties to India in November 1996—is in no small measure a hedge against worst-case fears in regard to the reaffirmation of the U.S.–Japan alliance. Amid concerns about U.S. global preeminence, both Moscow and Beijing are seeking counterweights.

Certainly, there are other factors driving these two historic rivals toward a new marriage of convenience, or more accurately, an affair on the rebound. For Beijing, cementing peace along its nearly 4,000-mile borders with Russia and the former Soviet Republics is a high priority. So is obtaining relatively cheap military technology for its modernization efforts, and diversifying its trading partners. Meanwhile, Russia is desperate to sell what competitive industrial goods it can; military hardware and a nuclear power plant are important hard currency earners. On the strategic side, firming up stability along its borders is also of importance to Moscow.

At the same time, it would be a mistake to take at face value proclamations of a new "strategic partnership." If there were any doubts about lingering Russian suspicion of China, they were erased by Defense Minister Rodionov in his speech on the day of Li's arrival arguing that China was among the countries posing a military threat to Moscow! Whatever the limits of friendship, Li and Yeltsin did not miss the opportunity to blast the United States for acting like a single superpower, calling for a future with a more equal multipolar world, "not divided into leaders and those who are led."

For the United States and its allies, the Sino–Russian entente should serve as an early warning signal. NATO expansion on the Russian side, U.S. policies in East Asia on the other, and the stance of both Beijing and Moscow on the prospect of U.S. development of strategic missile defenses all reflect downside geopolitical trends.

China and Russia are wary of U.S. plans for ballistic missile defenses. Neither has a legitimate complaint against much needed U.S. theater missile defenses such as Patriot or PAC-3 systems. But concerns over development of potentially strategically capable systems, such as THAAD and Navy's Upper Tier, must be carefully evaluated. If Chinese or Russian strategists believe that systems able to neutralize their nuclear deterrents will be deployed, the result may be not only an end to the post–Cold War nuclear build-down, but a nuclear buildup, at least by still modest Chinese nuclear forces. While China is improving its missile capabilities and building smaller, more accurate warheads, and may deploy multiple warheads on missiles, there is no evidence yet that it plans to increase its total number of warheads.

The irony of all this is the circular logic of what appears to be the new strategic competition. For the United States and Japan, expanding NATO and reaffirming the U.S.–Japan alliance are both hedging strategies against Russia's experiment going awry and the uncertainty of China's emerging role. Such an impulse to safeguard against uncertainty is not imprudent. The problem is that what we are witnessing is a defensive, reactive foreign policy on the part of each of the three great powers. History, unfortunately, is littered with such chain reactions by major powers to new powers and unfamiliar geopolitical realities.

This is the danger inherent in the new Asia-Pacific security environment. Scenario-spinners can easily concoct a host of possibilities. Chinese and Korean Japanophobia could lead to a continental–rimland polarization in Northeast Asia between a Sino–Korean entente on the one hand and a U.S.–Japan alliance on the other. One can also envision a real or virtual nuclear arms race among a unified Korea, Japan, and China. Even in Southeast Asia, instability in Indonesia, a revival of tensions between Indonesia and Malaysia, or conflict over the Spratly Islands are all within the realm of the thinkable.

The challenge to the United States and other actors in the Asia Pacific is to begin to define a new equilibrium in the region. Most pressing is to establish a stable triangular relationship among the U.S.–China, U.S.–Japan, and Sino–Japanese relationships. The key is to determine how China fits into the security architecture of the region. Henry Kissinger has used the term *balance of dissatisfactions,* where the minimal requirements of each nation are taken into account and a complement of balance of power and concert of power define a system of international relations. Such a vision suggests it might be wise to cautiously explore a new approach to security in order to gradually move beyond the reality of the U.S. guaranteed system and the vagaries of the ASEAN Regional Forum. But for the moment, questions about Asian security appear to be far more numerous than their answers.

## Notes

1. For a good overview of the economic crisis, see the *Economist*, "Frozen Miracle: A Survey of East Asian Economies," March 7, 1998, and the United States Institute of Peace, Asian economic *Crisis Report*, April 1998.
2. See Steven Lee Holmes, "Asian Turmoil Putting Brakes on Arms Race," *New York Times*, January 13, 1998, p. 1.
3. For a comprehensive, if pessimistic critique of the DPRK, see Marcus Noland, "The North Korean Economy," in Joint U.S.-Korean Academic Studies, vol 6, 1996, Korean Economic Institute (KEI) pp. 127–78. Noland's analysis suggests sweeping reform under the current regime is highly improbable. See also, Noland and Gordon Flake, "Evaluation of the Rajin-Sonbong Economic and Trade Zone," KEI, September 1996.
4. See Robert A. Manning and James Przystup, "Starve North Korea or Save It: Right Now We Are Doing Both," *Washington Post*, June 23, 1996. The aid is $2 million for MIA cooperation, $8 million for emergency food aid, $23 million for KEDO, and an additional $15 million to $20 million to can the fuel rods.
5. See Larry A. Niksch, "The Prospect of Relations between the United States and North Korea," paper for the Annual Symposium of the Korea National Defense University, August 22, 1996, for a detailed discussion of the "collapse theory."
6. See John Burton, "Beijing Moves to Bolster N. Korea with Aid Offer," *Financial Times*, July 16, 1996. See also Steve Glain, "China Pushes North Korea Commerce," *Wall Street Journal*, September 16, 1996.
7. See "China Expands Reach With Russian Destroyers," *Jane's Defence Weekly*, January 15, 1997, p. 5.
8. Taiwan might, on a divided nation basis, for example, be permitted membership in the World Bank, IMF, WHO, IAEA, up to and including U.N. observer or full member. The example of the two Koreas in one model, or that of the Ukraine and other Soviet republics under the old USSR, is another legal precedent.
9. See Barbara Opall, "South Korean Arms Raise Japanese Ire," *Defense News*, November 25, 1996, p. 1.
10. See Warren Christopher, speech before the Asia Society in New York, May 16, 1996.

# II

# The Military Bond

# 4

# The Evolution of Military Cooperation in the U.S.–Japan Alliance

SHEILA A. SMITH

WHILE THE U.S.–Japan alliance has been an integral part of the architecture of international politics since 1952, military cooperation between the United States and Japan did not begin until late in the Cold War. The relationship between the American and Japanese militaries has grown into the framework set out in the bilateral Security Treaty revised in 1960.[1] The bilateral Security Treaty offers an implicit description of how the two national militaries should work together. One of these articles, Article V, commits the United States to assisting Japan should it be threatened or attacked. Article VI provides for Japanese cooperation with the United States in providing for the "peace and stability of the Far East," that is, for the provision of bases and facilities for the U.S. military on Japanese territory.[2] These two articles focus on military cooperation seem overly restrictive given the new challenges facing the United States and Japan today.

In contrast to the more integrated military operations presumed in other U.S. Cold War alliances, such as NATO and the U.S.–Republic of Korea (ROK) alliance, cooperation between American and Japanese militaries at the end of the Cold War remained limited to specific missions. There was no joint strategy in which the United States and Japan agreed to act jointly to contend with conflicts outside the parameters of Japan's defense. Moreover, there was no joint command structure between the Self-Defense Forces (SDF) and U.S. military forces stationed in Japan, even for the limited mission of Japan's national defense. By the end of the Cold War, however, the two countries had devised an acceptable division of labor for their respective militaries that came to be known as the roles and missions approach to security collaboration. This formula for considering how the SDF and U.S. forces would operate jointly allowed both governments to balance the need for coordination between their two militaries, while reserving the autonomy of national decision-making processes over their use.

Today, there is a great deal more interest in Washington in exploring the potential for military cooperation with Japan; in Japan there is concern that the changes in the Asia-Pacific region will impinge directly on Tokyo's own security interests, a concern combined with an awareness that the mechanisms for security cooperation developed over the course of the Cold War could be sorely tested should regional conflict arise. The issue for contemporary policymakers is whether or not the two militaries can extend cooperation to new missions, missions that were not considered during the Cold War. The military division of labor that designated specific roles and missions for the SDF complemented U.S. military strategy, which was directed toward containment of Soviet forces in northeast Asia. Today, the U.S. military must consider a more uncertain array of objectives, putting new demands on the alliance. Both the pace and evolution of military cooperation between the United States and Japan in the past reveals that future collaboration will likely make the roles and missions formula the appropriate basis for considering broadened collaboration. The question now is what roles and what missions are most suitable for Japan's SDF.

The process of devising an acceptable formula for considering military cooperation in the U.S.–Japan alliance indicates areas in which future efforts should be focused. While there may be some divergence between the United States and Japan about the utility of the use of force in the resolution of international conflicts, there is little doubt that should a conflict emerge in the Asia-Pacific region, the means and mechanisms for cooperation are already in place. The division of military labor that developed incrementally between the United States and Japan indicates the disparate roles assigned to the two militaries in the implementation of policy. The United States and Japan have divergent fields of vision regarding their respective security interests. American interests are global, and U.S. military strategy reveals the extent to which Washington is willing to commit its military to considering future global challenges.

Tokyo's security interests, in contrast, are tied more closely to the Asia-Pacific region, yet there is great caution about using the SDF to cope with potential challenges. As an instrument of state policy, the SDF continues to have only a limited role beyond Japanese territory. At issue is not simply the utility of military force in coping with international politics, but also the desire to constrain the military's role and influence over the making of national policy. The evolution of military cooperation within the U.S.–Japan alliance suggests that efforts to redefine the mechanisms of security cooperation in the wake of the Cold War must focus on specific missions and allow for decisions about the participation of the Self-Defense Forces to be handled on a case-by-case basis with the full support of the Japanese public.

## Japan's Role in U.S. Strategy

As an ally of the United States, Japan's primary mechanism for coping with international changes that impinge upon its security has been through collaboration with the United States. Since 1952, the U.S.–Japan alliance has provided the context within which Japan developed its postwar security policy, and as U.S. strategy unfolded over the course of the Cold War, Japan's role in that strategy expanded. Japan's contribution in the early years of the Cold War was in the form of bases for U.S. forces, but by the end of the Cold War the SDF had been included in U.S. regional operations and Tokyo had expanded its participation in the economic and technological fronts of the Western Cold War coalition.

For much of the Cold War, however, Japan's military was excluded from the bilateral security dialogue. Until Japan regained its economic strength, there was little interest in promoting operational coordination between American and Japanese militaries. The bilateral Security Treaty forged during the Korean War was focused primarily on the terms of continuing the American military presence on Japanese territory.[3] At the end of the American occupation of Japan, 260,000 U.S. military personnel remained in Japan with their bases and facilities covering 1,352 square kilometers. The most significant U.S. military bases in the early years of the Cold War were those located on Okinawa, which remained under U.S. administration until 1972. These U.S. bases in Japan served as an operational support base for combat operations in both the Korean and Vietnam wars.

While Japan's military played almost no role in the implementation of U.S. Cold War strategy during the early years, the U.S. military played a significant role in the development of the SDF. Occupation authorities issued the order for the formation of the National Police Reserve, a ground force that was to become Japan's Ground Self-

Defense Force (GSDF). Also during the Occupation, U.S. military and coast guard officials served as advisors on the creation of a coastal defense force that later emerged as Japan's navy, the Maritime Self-Defense Force (MSDF).[4] Finally, the creation of a third military force, an independent Air Self-Defense Force (ASDF), was the most prominent legacy of the American military's influence over Japan's postwar military. Equipment for these new forces came initially from the United States, and subsequent modernization efforts were based on licensed production agreements with the United States.[5]

The U.S. military also played a key role in the operational training of the SDF. The United States provided Japan's defense while the SDF was still a nascent force. Once a skeletal force had been deployed, the United States handed over responsibility for national defense missions. After the United States withdrew its ground forces from Japan at the conclusion of the Korean War, the U.S. Army continued to maintain logistical and supply units there, units later utilized during the Vietnam War. By the early 1970s, most U.S. Army bases were either closed or turned over to other U.S. services. The Army presence in Japan has been minimal ever since.

The U.S. Navy and Air Force continued to assist their Japanese counterparts in air and coastal defenses for much longer. In 1967, the two air forces decided on a division of labor that transferred operational responsibility for Japan's air defenses to the ASDF while the U.S. Air Force concentrated on air missions beyond Japanese territory.[6] U.S. fighter interceptors were deployed in northern Japan, however, and the U.S. Air Force retained operational control over Japanese airspace to the south from bases in the Ryukyu Islands until those islands reverted to Japanese sovereignty in the early 1970s.

Naval operations between the two countries were always considered essentially joint operations. Nonetheless, the scope of operations for the Japanese Maritime Self-Defense Force was limited primarily by their capability. Coastal defense operations began early, and the MSDF moved to antisubmarine missions by the late 1960s. Joint training and exercises between the MSDF and the U.S. Navy were often held "over the horizon" in open waters, out of sight of domestic critics who worried about what role the SDF was playing in U.S. regional strategy.[7]

While the provision of bases for U.S. forces in Japan remained key to U.S. strategic aims in the region, Washington did look to Japan to contribute militarily to the American regional strategy in new ways as Japan's military capabilities improved. A fundamental shift in U.S. strategy in the late 1960s and early 1970s transformed U.S. expectations of Japan. As U.S. global military deployments were reorganized away from the two-and-a-half war scenario of a global conflict with the communist bloc to a one-and-a-half war organization of conventional forces, the implications for Asia were significant. U.S. troop reductions in the region in the wake of the Vietnam War implied American withdrawal from immediate engagement in Asia. The U.S. and Japanese governments negotiated a major consolidation of U.S. military facilities and bases in Japan, and the number of U.S. military personnel stationed there dropped precipitously in the wake of Vietnam. The U.S. Air Force and Navy retained major airfields and ports, however. Nevertheless, the Seventh Fleet in particular relied heavily on access to Japanese ports and ship repair services to maintain its forward presence. In 1974 the U.S. Navy decided to make Yokosuka Naval Base the home port for the USS *Midway*, the only U.S. aircraft carrier with home port overseas.

Japan, like other American allies at the time, was encouraged to increase its efforts to provide for its own defense. In the words of then President Nixon, Japan was expected to assume "primary responsibility" for its own defense.[8] During negotiations over the reversion of Okinawa to Japanese control, Japan's political leaders began their effort to "raise Japan's defense consciousness." They tried to assuage Washington's fears about its political commitment to allow the U.S. military use of Japanese bases by stating that the security of South Korea and Taiwan were directly linked to Japan's security interests.[9] While this phase of readjustment of U.S. global military deployments did not promote a noticeable change in Japan's own national defense policy, it did signal Washington's new attention to the need for greater military burden sharing—something that had been absent in the early Cold War years.

The intensification of U.S.–Soviet military competition in the 1980s, a phase often referred to in Tokyo as the "new Cold War," brought the Japanese military to the forefront of superpower strategic interaction for the first time. With the changes in Soviet strategic deployment patterns,[10] the United States sought to upgrade its conventional forces in the Northwest Pacific. U.S. military bases in Japan were an important component of maintenance of a constant, visible American presence in the Northwest Pacific. As such, U.S. air and naval deployments to Japanese bases were upgraded throughout the 1980s. Japan's naval and air capabilities were also critical to the emerging U.S. strategy. Japan's geographic position was advantageous as it straddled the exits used by the Soviet Pacific Fleet from its coastal bases to the Pacific Ocean. The strategic importance of this location provided justification for SDF deployments. Their developments raised the aggregate balance of military forces in this region. SDF operations thus became a part of the calculus of regional East Asian force balance, and more than just part of Japan's basic defense needs.[11]

Over the course of four decades, Japan's role in U.S. Cold War strategy was transformed from that of a rear basing area for combat operations in the Korean and Vietnam wars to that of a participant in the regional military balance of forces between the United States and the former Soviet Union. Two major trends are visible throughout that period. First, as the U.S. military's physical presence diminished on the main island, its composition changed coincident to the ebb and flow of the strategic competition between the Soviet Union and the United States. Second, Japan's economic growth and the rehabilitation of its military increased Tokyo's value to the United States in the effort to compete with the Soviet Union. Japan's role in American strategy during the latter part of the Cold War reflected the growing capability of the SDF, as well as the need to respond to improvements in Soviet naval and air deployments in the Pacific.

Beyond the military capabilities of the SDF, however, American policymakers also considered Japan's economic and technological strengths when calculating the ability of the West to contend with the Soviet Union. While the SDF joined the front line of the military competition between the United States and the USSR in the Pacific, Japan's political leaders began to engage in security cooperation with the United States, which included participation in discussion about contending with Soviet Intermediate-Range Nuclear Force (INF) deployments, initiating defense technology cooperation, and committing to the joint research and development of nuclear missile defense systems considered within the Strategic Defense Initiative (SDI).

## The Rehabilitation of the Military in Postwar Japan

While changes in U.S. strategy have often prompted new policy initiatives within the bilateral alliance, the capacity for the Japanese government to respond to these changes has often been hindered by a lack of policy mechanisms for implementing new kinds of security cooperation. Japan essentially had to re-craft its state institutions for making national security policy in the postwar era and had to develop a new policymaking process consistent with the broader aims of enhancing the democratic process in Japan. Not only did Japan have a reformed military, but the postwar reorganization of state institutions required a vigilant civilian role in the policymaking process. Even today, the United States and Japan continue to work on mechanisms for cooperation requiring that domestic strictures on the SDF be relaxed. Domestic constraints affecting contemporary deliberations are an indication of how slow and careful the process of incorporating the SDF into national policymaking has been.

The need to maintain visible strictures on the scope of SDF operations remains central to attempts to design new policies for alliance cooperation, and the decision-making process prior to policy change has consistently evoked debate over the import of the constitution. Political debates throughout the postwar period have focused on the government's interpretation of the constitution, and under the rule of the Liberal Democratic Party (LDP), the gradual rehabilitation of the military and its mission of self-defense could only proceed as fast as the opposition parties allowed. Abandoned early in the postwar era was the notion that Japan would participate in "collective defense" efforts, and therefore, the U.S.–Japan alliance has continued to provide only for U.S. military assistance in the case of aggression against Japan.

Even within the realm of self-defense the activities of Japan's SDF have been circumscribed. While the nascent military force assembled under the direction of the Supreme Commander of the Allied Powers (SCAP) assumed its place as a national military with the passage of the 1954 Self-Defense Force Law, every effort was made to ensure that the potential influence of the military be contained within the civilian authorities of the state. Japan's democracy was being tested by the rearmament process, and there were many who agreed with the Japan Socialist Party (JSP) that the formation of the SDF was in violation of the postwar constitution.[12]

During deliberations over the laws that outlined the organization and goals of the administrative agencies that would oversee Japan's national defense policy, much attention was given to outlining the ways in which the Japanese military would be subject to civilian authority.[13] The bureaucracy charged with managing the military and with considering Japan's long-term defense needs was demoted to the status of "agency" rather than "ministry," and was placed under the supervision of the prime minister's office. This new agency was meant to be the administrative structure for a new postwar military, and it was charged with peace-time administration of the policymaking process.[14] Moreover, the SDF was given no privileges beyond those assigned to other civil servants, and the state was given no means by which to oblige citizens to serve. The Japan Defense Agency (JDA) in its initial years was populated primarily by individuals seconded from other, stronger bureaucracies in the Japanese government. Furthermore, a cabinet-level body, the National Defense Council (later called the National Security

Council), was created to oversee and judge JDA's policy recommendations (see Giarra and Nagashima, chapter 5 in this volume).

Creating mechanisms for ensuring civilian oversight of the security planning process was only the first step. Ensuring that these new institutional arrangements would produce an effective policymaking process took time. The postwar Japanese military's mission of "exclusive self defense" was set out clearly in the Self-Defense Force Law, but the requirements for maintaining this defense posture were not quite so clear. The problem was in defining the parameters of defense. In Diet deliberations leading to the passage of the SDF Law, it was obvious that definition of those parameters was going to be problematic. Japan's military was perceived to be a different sort of military—one that engaged not in offensive military operations, but one that instead provided only territorial defense.[15] Once the SDF was established, JDA devised four defense buildup plans with U.S. assistance. The plans were designed to achieve first a skeletal force and then the necessary force required by Japan to meet external threat.[16] Japan's rearmament program was based on the premise of a local and limited conflict between the United States and the communist powers in the Asian region—a region in which Japan would be involved only peripherally.[17]

While Japan's military capability was being restored, the issue of the operational radius of the SDF was addressed only in hypothetical terms. Early on, the government described the relationship between the United States and Japan as that of "sword and shield," implying that as long as Japan managed to create the capability to defend its own territory the U.S. military would cope with operations beyond. In keeping with the notion that the SDF was to remain a defensive force, certain types of weapons systems were eliminated from consideration because they would have given Japan a reach beyond that was considered appropriate for defensive purposes.[18] The geographical bounds of the defense mission were initially satisfactory, but over time, and in the face of growing military deployments by Japan's neighbors, the question of what satisfied this basic need for territorial defense became more problematic. The kind of operations to be required of the SDF were of concern to JDA planners, but in public debates, operational concerns and requirements were superseded by insistence on a geographically confined radius for the SDF in order to conform with the demand for identifiable limits on their operations.

By the early 1970s, in the face of the fiscal constraints imposed by the oil crisis and the growing concerns of the opposition political parties about the seemingly unending rearmament process, Japan's political leaders announced that the process of rearmament was complete. The government shifted the aim of Japan's procurement to that of maintenance of a "standard defense force" (*kibanteki boeiryoku*) posture for peacetime. The contradiction between past arguments within the Defense Agency that Japan needed to match the military capability deployed by potential regional adversaries and the political desire for constraining expansion of Japan's capability was resolved in the mid-1970s with the National Defense Program Outline (NDPO). For planning purposes, JDA determined that Japan would prepare itself for "small and limited-scale aggression," which was the most likely scenario in an era of declining superpower tensions, and would focus on maintaining current force levels while developing the necessary mechanisms for expanding the "standard defense force" should crisis or conflict emerge. Moreover, responding to opposition party demands that a brake on Japan's military capability be clearly visible, the cabinet also sought to mollify government critics by announcing that Japan would spend no more than 1 percent of its GNP on defense.

The effort to balance the demands of military planning with the desire for ensuring the viability of the new mechanisms of civilian control seemed to focus solely on the JDA itself, and less political attention was devoted to enhancing the policymaking process beyond the administrative bureaucracy. Civilian control was interpreted narrowly in the early years of the agency's existence when there were reports of ruffled feathers as the civilian members within the agency sought to ensure they were in charge of policy.

The policy process outside the Defense Agency took longer to develop. While the institutional constraints on the military were in place early in the postwar period, the actual engagement of the prime minister and his cabinet in the making of national defense policy was called into question when in 1965 a supposedly secret planning document prepared by the Self-Defense Forces was revealed in the Diet.[19] The *Mitsuya Kenkyu* (or "Three Arrows Study") reviewed the options available to the SDF should a conflict erupt on the Korean Peninsula, concluding that joint operations between American and Japanese militaries were the best means of defending Japan.

While today this may seem an innocuous conclusion for Japan's military planners to have drawn, it was explosive in terms of the political differences of the time between the LDP government and the opposition parties, most notably the JSP. First, the JSP charged that civilian authorities had no knowledge of this sort of exercise nor of the content of the study's conclusions. These accusations resonated deeply in postwar politics. Since the JSP adamantly refused to acknowledge the constitutionality of the SDF, this precluded the possibility of any type of intra-party dialogue over the content of policy. Instead, the JSP focused its attacks on the lack of legitimacy of the postwar military, and the failings of the LDP to monitor its activities. Despite the fact that all militaries must consider their defense needs by conducting contingency plans, the Japanese government failed to argue that this was part of the SDF's responsibility. Prime Minister Eisaku Sato reportedly was privately shocked at the import of the SDF plan, and the most damaging implication for the efficacy of postwar civilian control was the references made by the SDF to the need for considering legal measures required for operations in case of a conflict. This was considered as an intrusion into the realm of civil authority, and suggested to the JSP critics that the government had not successfully implemented civilian oversight of the SDF.

The second aspect of the *Mitsuya Kenkyu* that had long-term consequences was that the SDF's argument for joint operations with the U.S. military was deemed as evidence that the aspirations of the postwar military exceeded constitutional limits. In reality, the text of the study released to the Diet revealed the absence of dialogue or coordination of SDF operations with those of the U.S. military. Nonetheless, the controversy generated by the Diet debate over *Mitsuya Kenkyu* made any attempt to create mechanisms for military coordination anathema to Japan's political leadership, and the incident reinforced the government's tendency to divorce Japan's own defense requirements from a discussion of the implementation of alliance cooperation in national policy debates. Repercussions from the *Mitsuya Kenkyu* scandal froze any attempt to coordinate these two aspects of Japan's security policy for over a decade.

The issue of whether or not the government was creating a policy-making process that incorporated guarantees of civilian oversight of the military remained pertinent to opposition party complaints. During the early 1970s, when SDF's long-term goals were reviewed, the LDP was charged with violating the principle of civilian control in its procurement of new fighter aircraft.[20] In negotiating the 1976 National Defense Program Outline (NDPO), the call for greater transparency and accountability in the military planning process was also an issue, and, in an effort to clarify the role played by the military, the director general of the Defense Agency made public JDA's planning process for assessing Japan's defense needs. Revealing the way in which the JDA developed its plans was one aspect of enhancing civilian authority; another was revitalizing the National Defense Council's role in reviewing policy choices. Bringing crucial debates into the public arena was a task supported by then director general Michita Sakata,[21] who in fact went further than his JSP critics by arguing that true civilian control could only be achieved by legislative deliberations about the substance and aims of Japan's security policy.

Over time, the way in which Japan's defense policy was made became less of an issue as the government became more responsive to concerns about the policymaking process. As civilian institutions demonstrated their influence over the process by the mid-1970s, the SDF became less of an object of public hostility. The legitimacy of the military had been contested in the early postwar years, but by the mid-1970s, after considerable public debate about the National Defense Program Outline, a consensus was reached recognizing the need for a national defense capability. It was only after the Liberal Democratic Party moved in the direction of creating greater transparency in the policy planning process that this became possible, however. Satisfying opposition parties and the public that civilian institutions were in control of the security policymaking process was a necessary first step toward gaining national confidence in the new, postwar security planning mechanisms.

The Japanese government had to create a policy planning process that provided for the country's defense needs while satisfying domestic critics; the process had to be in compliance with the spirit of the constitution and firmly under civilian control. Without this kind of foundation, there was little hope of serious consideration of military cooperation within the U.S.–Japan alliance. Linking Japan's national military planning to greater coordination with the United States was impossible for more than a decade after the 1960 Security Treaty was revised. Once the NDPO was on its way to being national policy, Sakata moved quickly to engage the American government in discussions about how the basis of Japan's national defense planning, that is, joint operations between the Japanese and American militaries, would be achieved.

## U.S.–Japan Military Cooperation: A Carefully Negotiated Division of Labor

The relatively late incorporation of Japan's military into U.S. regional strategy was due to two separate sets of factors. The first was the role assigned to Japan in the evolving American strategy. There is little evidence that U.S. military planners sought to enhance the SDF role in its regional strategy. The aggregate benefits of Japan's participation in the

Cold War were significant, and the specific benefits the United States derived from Japan's provision of military bases were crucial to the implementation of American strategic goals. Japan's rearmament was necessary, but operational cooperation between the United States and Japanese militaries for much of the Cold War was seen as a means of strengthening Japan's ability to cope with its own defense needs. By the late 1970s, however, this view had changed somewhat, and the United States was more receptive to Japanese initiatives to review the mechanisms for coordination between the two national militaries. The second set of influences on the development of bilateral military cooperation is related to the complex process of defining an acceptable place for the postwar military in national policy. Over the course of the postwar period, Japan's security planning process has revolved around the contentious domestic issue of defining the purpose of the SDF as well as containment of the military's institutional influence in national policy formulation. It was not until the national policymaking process had gained greater domestic support that the Japanese government could move in the direction of creating a policy dialogue with the U.S. government to establish procedures and goals for cooperation between the two militaries.

The assumption behind Japan's military planning was that U.S. forces would assist Japan in case of a conflict. The preponderant U.S. military presence in and around Japan during the early decades of the Cold War seemed evidence enough that the U.S. military would be there to assist in any situation that might threaten Japan's security. While Japan's uniformed planners seemed to have appreciated the need for direct coordination of missions between the United States and Japan, the Diet debacle over the *Mitsuya Kenkyu* had erased all political incentives for pursuing this aspect of military planning. The U.S. withdrawal of forces from the Pacific region in the wake of Vietnam suggested, however, that the capacity of the U.S. military to allocate resources to Japan's defense was diminishing. The evolution of Japan's policymaking process coincided with heightened concern about long-term American intentions in the region.

The opportunity was ripe for focusing on building mechanisms of coordination between the two militaries, and the director general of the JDA instigated a bilateral dialogue on coordinating military operations. As a result of this overture by the Japanese government, officials from both the United States and Japan engaged in a study of the requirements of their respective militaries under the provisions of the bilateral security treaty. In 1978, the two governments announced their conclusions in the form of the Guidelines for U.S.–Japan Defense Cooperation.[22] In keeping with the notion that Japan could use its military only for the purpose of territorial defense, the Guidelines focused on Article V of the treaty, which provides for American assistance in Japan's defense. The Guidelines also included provisions for investigating potential cooperation in providing for the "peace and stability of the Far East," otherwise known as Article VI cooperation.

Establishment of these Guidelines set in motion a process of joint military studies and exercises based on the notion of functional integration of operations between the two militaries. Moving away from a strictly geographical division of labor restricting SDF operations on Japanese territory and U.S. military operations beyond, the requirements for joint operations suggested that while the SDF retained a focus on operations strictly for the defense of Japan, there were ways in which the operations of the two militaries would need to be coordinated if this concept was ever put to the test.

Implementation of the 1978 Guidelines focused on joint studies and exercises between the two militaries, and the roles and missions approach to coordinating operations within the alliance began to show the impact of some of the restrictions imposed upon the SDF. Four sets of joint studies were pursued over the course of the 1980s: U.S.–Japan joint operations, sea-lane defense, wartime support, and interoperability. The basic starting point for the two militaries was their operational overlap in the defense of Japan. This first study began in December 1978. The final report was made in December 1984, and the results were submitted to both the prime minister and the chairman of the Joint Staff Council for approval. The commander of the U.S. forces in Japan signed the plan. While the contents of the study remain classified, some aspects of the plan were publicly reported,[23] and many analysts realized that this outline of Japan's defense needs was based on a simple and unrealistic scenario—a conflict that involved Japan only. A more likely scenario is one in which Japan is involved in a war with a simultaneous outbreak elsewhere and which spreads to involve Japan. In such a case, availability of the necessary degree of U.S. military assistance is questionable, and the priority assigned to assisting Japan could be less if Washington had to respond in the context of a wider conflict.[24]

Beyond the joint operations required for the defense of Japan, the most controversial study was on sea-lane defense. This study was initiated in May 1981 after Prime Minister Suzuki's announcement that Japan would assume responsibility for the defense of sea-lanes up to 1,000 miles from Japan. After a meeting of U.S. and Japanese officials in August 1982, the two governments agreed to launch a study on the joint operational requirements of this mission within the constraining limitation of the scenario of an attack against Japan.[25] The issue raised by this study was just how "joint" U.S. and Japanese military operations would be. Whereas Japan's MSDF had considered sea-lane defenses since the early 1970s, it had done so based on the needs of Japan's defense and on the unlikely scenario of a small-scale and limited invasion of Japan. But the U.S.–Japan dialogue about the division of military roles and missions suggested a different sort of enterprise: one in which Japan would work with the United States in case of a conflict and would cover the geographic area within 1,000 miles of its territory. Again the scenario of this sort of military cooperation was at issue. In the study, the JDA continued to frame discussions in terms of the Japan-only scenario, thereby sidestepping the political question of whether the SDF had the right to engage in collective military efforts. The U.S. approach was revealed at a meeting between the American secretary of defense and the director general of the JDA in 1982 when the U.S. secretary explicitly noted that Japan's assumption of the sea-lane mission would allow for U.S. military operations to be concentrated elsewhere.[26]

Other problems emerged in consideration of later studies, and the 1978 provision for exploring cooperation between the two militaries in case of a regional conflict based on Article VI cooperation made little headway. Defense Agency officials were hesitant to pursue this avenue of cooperation, mostly because their mandate was to provide only for the defense of Japan. Whereas a study committing Japan to participation in regional contingencies was problematic, joint exercises between the SDF and U.S. militaries provided a means for giving the SDF a better sense of the operational objectives and requirements of the United States in just such a scenario. Exercises between the two militaries expanded over the course of the 1980s. Whereas naval cooperation had been a facet of the alliance since the early years of the Cold War, the MSDF began to participate in U.S.-led exercises incorporating other allies in the region—the Rim of the Pacific exercise.[27]

Joint exercises between American and Japanese air forces were a departure from the past, however. The lack of a joint command structure for air operations was a fundamental problem, and while they had worked out a division of operations in 1967, changes in the regional military balance and in the operational requirements for air defense since then required a much closer relationship than in the past. The ASDF's lack of combat experience also impinged upon its readiness particularly in the face of the more advanced fighter units deployed by the Soviet Union in the late 1970s. Exercises between the U.S. Air Force and the

ASDF concentrated on tactical fighter operations, air defense operations, and command and control exercises.

The GSDF initiated joint exercises with the U.S. Army in 1981. While the initial emphasis was on U.S. support of operations for the Hokkaido front, the two ground forces expanded joint training to include command post exercises that incorporated other branches of the SDF, thus leading to greater coordination through the Japanese Joint Staff Council. By the end of the Cold War, deliberations for overall joint training exercises had moved from the individual services to the Joint Staff and with U.S. military guidance, a review of the gaps in logistical interdependence among Japan's Ground, Maritime, and Air Self Defense Forces was conducted.

Moreover, the implementation of military cooperation instigated by the 1978 Guidelines enhanced the coordination of different agencies within the Japanese government engaged in various aspects of cooperation with the United States, thereby creating a forum for collaboration between the Defense Agency and another powerful bureaucracy, the Ministry of Foreign Affairs. Deliberations over the Guidelines allowed the operational requirements of the SDF to be incorporated into the political deliberations, and the U.S. military's operational goals and experience added weight to the notion that the operational requirements were as important as the political concerns involved in determining Japan's roles and missions.

The success of the roles and missions formula for approaching military cooperation in the U.S.–Japan alliance was due to two factors. First, the role Japan's military played in the implementation of U.S. strategic aims during the Cold War had to be limited to specific operations that could be construed as being required for Japan's defense. Second, the postwar proscription on the mission of Japan's military made it impossible to relinquish national control over their use.

The Cold War context of this evolution of military cooperation between the United States and Japan both hindered and helped the alliance dialogue. In the early years of the Cold War, there was greater concern within Japan that the alliance would inevitably involve Japan in a war, and the resistance to the notion of joint military planning stemmed from deep divisions over the U.S. goals. In terms of operational cooperation between the U.S. and Japanese militaries, however, U.S. forward deployments not only contributed to Japan's own defense needs, but the presence of U.S. forces in the region was certain. When U.S. forces were reduced in the 1970s, Japanese policymakers realized for the first time the need for a direct dialogue over how military cooperation outlined in the bilateral treaty would be implemented. Now in the wake of the Cold War, the mechanisms for military coordination within the alliance remain. How the two militaries can adjust the roles and missions formula to cope with new contingencies, and for much less predictable ones, needs to be examined.

## Now That the Cold War is Over . . .

New avenues must be explored in the wake of the Cold War. The current attempt by Washington and Tokyo to redefine the U.S.–Japan alliance is, at the core, an attempt to review and amend the mechanisms of security cooperation developed over the course of the Cold War. The 1991 Gulf War raised the specter of just how challenging the prospect of maintaining security cooperation between the United States and its Cold War allies might be in the aftermath of U.S.–Soviet rivalry. The call for Tokyo to go beyond being a "checkbook power" prompted national debate in Japan about how to make a greater contribution to collective efforts to address security challenges. While there is widespread support for the notion that the time has come for Japan to play a greater role in international collaboration in the security realm, the prescriptions for the means by which Japan can accomplish this vary.

Despite a number of efforts to demonstrate Japan's new interest in expanding its cooperation beyond the narrow confines of national defense, the focal point of bilateral attention remains the issue of the role of the SDF in implementing the terms of alliance cooperation. Expectations of Japan during the Gulf War also indicated that, beyond the limited realm of bilateral military cooperation in the Asia-Pacific region, the United States was exploring the potential for expanding military cooperation with Japan beyond regional contingencies. Financial contributions to Desert Storm were quickly forthcoming, but the government's attempt to generate domestic legislation that would allow the SDF to play a role in the multinational coalition force in the Gulf suggested that the limits imposed by domestic politics over the role and purpose of the SDF remained a significant barrier to expanding joint military operations.[23] The question of whether the SDF would have been welcome in the U.S.-led military coalition remains unanswered. The Gulf War did, however, force Japan to begin rethinking the implications of domestic restrictions on the SDF in the post–Cold War era. It was clear that Japan was expected to play a bigger, more visible role in the provision of common security interests around the globe.

There is still considerable reluctance within Japan to assign the SDF full responsibility for fulfilling this role, and while the government sought to expand its legislative mandate for sending the SDF to U.N.-sponsored multinational efforts such as the Gulf, public debate focused on alternative means such as humanitarian relief and aid spending. The end of the Cold War has already prompted a review of the restrictions on the Japanese military that derive from past governments' interpretations of the Japanese constitution. One of Japan's major newspapers actively sought to encourage national debate over the need for Article IX as well as other restraints on the postwar military such as the interpretation that the constitution restrained Japan from entering "collective defense" arrangements. Such issues are being reexamined. The passage of the Peacekeeping Operation (PKO) Law in 1992 allowed the SDF to participate in selected U.N. peacekeeping operations, but restrictions on the kinds of missions, on the armament allowed the SDF, and on the conditions of withdrawing the Japanese military reinforce the idea that national control over the use of the SDF will be a priority in any policy initiative. The Ministry of Foreign Affairs has approved and guided SDF participation in a number of peacekeeping missions, including Mozambique, Somalia, the Golan Heights, and most recently Honduras, but the review of the freeze imposed on the PKO Law by reticent legislators in 1992 has yet to take place.[29]

Nonetheless, this new mission for the SDF has found its way into the ongoing review of the premises of Japan's security planning. First up for review was the 1976 NDPO, and the transformation of the international environment in the late 1980s instigated what many thought was a long-overdue look at the goals and conditions under which the SDF would provide for national defense. A new defense program outline was issued in 1995 incorporating the gains from military coordination within the U.S.–Japan alliance over the course of the 1980s. It also went further to note the demands placed on the SDF by its new peacekeeping mission. Missing from the 1995 NDPO is the awkward and restricting premise that the SDF will plan solely for a "small and limited scale attack." Gone, too, is the notion that national defense planning is separate from military coordination between U.S. and Japanese military forces. To integrate the accomplishments of the studies and exercises conducted between the two militaries, and to explore the mechanisms through which the United States and Japan could expand their cooperation in regional and global security forums were the primary goals revealed in the 1995 statement of Japan's future security goals.

What remains to be done, however, is to move beyond the Cold War framework for considering the scope of U.S.–Japan military cooperation. While the 1978 Guidelines for U.S.-Japan Defense Cooperation brought the two national militaries together for the first time to formally consider the operational overlap required by their joint mission of the defense of Japan, the process of policy coordination that took place within the alliance over the last decade of the Cold War did not make much progress in looking at joint operations beyond the narrow confines of the mission of Japan's defense. The restrictions on the Defense Agency were clear, and many JDA planners felt that they had no institutional mandate for going beyond the defense mission. It was also clear that the drafters of the 1978 Guidelines provided for the future when they inserted a reference to cooperation that would "provide for the peace and security of the Far East," or security cooperation mandated by Article VI of the bilateral treaty. Washington and Tokyo began reviewing the Guidelines based on the April 1996 Clinton-Hashimoto summit. An interim report was issued in June 1997 and a final report in September 1997 outlining how the two militaries might respond if a war or military confrontation emerged in the Asia-Pacific region.

While the new Guidelines are deliberately vague on which scenario they would cover, the most familiar scenario for joint collaboration is conflict on the Korean Peninsula. Here the legacy of Cold War military collaboration between the U.S. and Japanese militaries is evident. This was the scenario that instigated the *Mitsuya Kenkyu* scandal in the mid-1960s, and it is the scenario for which U.S. military planners have the clearest mandate and strategy for military operations. There is a definitive treaty commitment for U.S. military action in case of an attack on South Korea, one conflict scenario Japanese leaders would support. Some time ago they acknowledged that they would not hesitate to offer support for U.S. forces if war broke out. U.S. bases in Japan and the military forces stationed in and around Japan, would be directly engaged in a Korean conflict, and the Japanese government has all but publicly stated that it would allow the United States unlimited use of these facilities in the case of such a conflict.

Even here, in a conflict where one can expect the United States and Japan to have little disagreement over goals or the means of implementing them, there remains a great deal of uncertainty about what sort of role Japan's military might play and about whether the United States could count on the Japanese government to allow the SDF to give logistical or rear area support to the U.S. military. Questions such as whether the SDF would be allowed to help evacuate Japanese personnel from Korea, or whether the U.S. military would be allowed to use SDF bases in the case of war, were cleared up by the Defense Guidelines review, but real preparedness still requires legislative authority in Japan and a credible mechanism for bilateral training and coordination. This mechanism will have to include not only the Ministry of Foreign Affairs and the JDA, but other relevant ministries (such as transport) as well. Under Prime Minister Hashimoto these other bureaucracies were brought into the process, but it is not certain whether future cabinets will be as focused on security. Domestic legislation has yet to be drafted to cope with this sort of situation, and while bureaucrats in both the Ministry of Foreign Affairs and the Defense Agency grapple with the legal issues that could be raised by such a conflict, there is still some skepticism within the U.S. government about whether Tokyo would have the political will to act quickly and in concert with the United States, even in such a seemingly clear-cut case of this common security interest.

Perhaps the most critical task ahead for U.S. and Japanese policymakers is thinking through how the mechanisms of alliance cooperation, cautiously crafted within the relatively static international environment of the Cold War, can be designed to keep pace with the rapid changes already evident in the post–Cold War era. Beyond the relatively predictable scenario on the Korean Peninsula, some of the greatest challenges facing the alliance focus only implicitly on potentially divisive questions with regard to the use of force. While both countries support the efforts of the ASEAN Regional Forum (ARF) to develop a dialogue on regional security collaboration incorporating China, there remains considerable ambiguity concerning how the United States and Japan might craft a joint policy for coping with China. Calibrating a common response to China will be a challenge for Tokyo and Washington, and the notion of how to respond—even if through a demonstration of joint military cooperation—to a test of the alliance's cohesion needs to be considered.

Military cooperation between the United States and Japan in operations that do not involve a combat role for the SDF is also possible beyond the Asia-Pacific region. Japan's selective participation in U.N.-sponsored peacekeeping efforts has opened up the possibility of using the SDF for roles that can conform to the continued desire by the Japanese public that its military not engage in combat. Since the end of the Cold War, a notable taboo on the use of the SDF was lifted when the Japanese government decided to deploy them overseas, first for cleanup operations in the Strait of Hormuz after the Gulf War, and then for their first peacekeeping mission to Cambodia to participate in the U.N. Transition Authority in Cambodia.

Potential for exploring collaboration between the American and Japanese militaries remains great as long as a direct combat role for the SDF is absent, and as long as the Japanese military is encased within bilateral or multilateral forums. The U.S.–Japan alliance has provided the framework within which Japan's military has been and rebuilt, and this framework has also allowed Japan to loosen restrictions on their use, albeit slowly and cautiously. The key to the future success of U.S.–Japan security cooperation lies in identifying missions that allow Japan to continue to subscribe to its policy of military restraint in keeping with the spirit of the constitution, while at the same time providing a visible and viable role for the SDF in providing for common security concerns.

## Notes

1. See Appendix 2.
2. The revised treaty signed in 1960 included two separate provisions that set forth the terms of U.S.–Japan security cooperation. Article V reads, "Each party recognizes that an armed attack against either Party in the territories under the administration of Japan would be dangerous to its own peace and safety and declares that it would act to meet the common danger in accordance with its constitutional provisions and processes." Article VI states, "For the purposes of contributing to the security of Japan and the maintenance of international peace and security in the Far East, the United States of America is granted the use by its land, air, and naval forces of facilities and areas in Japan."

   In terms of implementing military cooperation, Article V suggested the need for joint operations between the Japanese and U.S. militaries for the defense of Japan while Article VI provided for the provision of bases and facilities for the U.S. military as a means of providing for the peace and stability of the region.
3. From the beginning of the Cold War, however, the strategic value of the U.S. alliance with Japan was based not only on its geographic proximity to the Asian mainland, but also on its economic and political orientation toward the U.S.-led Cold War coalition. Japan's increasing industrial capacity furnished the U.S. military with material support that fit well with early notions by U.S. military planners in the office of the Joint Chief of Staff that Japan could serve U.S. strategic interests as "Asia's arsenal."

   For the documents that outlined U.S. strategic thinking in the immediate postwar years, see Thomas H. Etzold and John Lewis Gaddis, *Containment: Documents on American Policy and Strategy, 1945–1950* (New York: Columbia University Press, 1978), pp. 226–69. See also Yonosuke Nagai and Akira Iriye, *The Origins of the Cold War in Asia* (New York: Columbia University Press, 1977), and Robert A. Pollard, *The Economic Origins of the Cold War, 1945–1950* (New York: Columbia University Press, 1985), chap. 8.
4. For a thorough examination of the role played by the U.S. military in reshaping Japan's postwar navy, see James Auer, *The Postwar Rearmament*

*of Japanese Maritime Forces, 1945–71* (New York: Praeger, 1973). A Japanese planning group, comprised of officers from the Imperial Japanese Navy, also discussed the naval requirements of postwar Japan. Although the minutes of the *Y-Iinkai* [the Y Committee] remain classified, the deliberations of this Committee are discussed in *Saigunbi no Kiseki* [The Tracks of Rearmament] (Tokyo: Yomiuri Shimbunsha, 1981), and in a volume prepared by the historians of the Japanese Defense Agency, *Boeicho Shishitsu Hensan no Sengo Boei no Ayumi: Keisatsu Yobitai kara Jietai e* [The Historians of the Defense Agency's Account of the Evolution of Japan's Postwar Defense: From the National Police Reserve to the Self Defense Force] (Tokyo: Asagumo Shimbunsha, 1988–89).

5. The extension of this type of cooperation to joint production of the FSX and to joint research on a theater missile defense system reveals the maturation of this aspect of alliance cooperation. For a comprehensive treatment of defense technology arrangements between the United States and Japan, see the chapters in this volume by Chinworth and Rubinstein. See also Michael J. Green, *Arming Japan: Defense Production, Alliance Politics, and the Postwar Search for Autonomy* (New York: Columbia University Press, 1995).

6. In 1959, the commander of the U.S. Fifth Air Force and the chief of staff of the Japanese ASDF concluded an agreement that outlined how the U.S. and Japanese air forces would independently conduct operations pertinent to Japan's air defense. From 1963–65, the U.S. 5th Air Force conducted a study on air defense operations in Japan that became the basis for consolidating U.S. deployments there, and led to the official transfer of full responsibility for Japan's air defense to the ASDF. See Tomohisa Sakanaka, "Jieitai no Jittai" in Asahi Shimbun Anzen Hosho Chosakai, eds. *Nihon no Jieiryoku* (Tokyo: Asahi Shimbunsha, 1967).

7. Numerous accusations of the existence of joint operational plans between the U.S. military and the SDF filled Diet debate over Japan's national defense planning in the 1960s. For a full account of Japan Socialist Party concerns and their discussions with the LDP in the Diet, see Hiroshi Matsukawa and Saburo Ienaga, editors, *Nichibei Anpo Joyaku Taiseishi, vol. 3, 1961–68* (Tokyo: Sanseido, 1970).

8. Richard Nixon laid out what was later to become known as the Guam Doctrine, or Nixon Doctrine, in an article published in the October 1967 issue of *Foreign Affairs*, prior to his election. This was not adopted as the basis of U.S. foreign policy toward Asia until 1969. For insight into how this applied to U.S. policy toward Japan, see Henry Kissinger, *The White House Years* (Boston: Little, Brown, 1979), chap. 7.

9. Prime Minister Eisaku Sato made this public commitment at a press conference in Washington after his meeting with President Nixon in 1968. The prime minister's statement was ambiguous in wording, and many U.S. negotiators saw it as an overstatement of Japan's position designed to mollify the U.S. public and gain U.S. government agreement to return Oki-

nawa to Japan. See I.M. Destler et al., *Managing an Alliance: The Politics of U.S.–Japan Relations* (Washington, DC: Brookings Institution, 1976).

10. For a comprehensive analysis of the trends in Soviet deployments in the Asia-Pacific region and the implications for the region, see Richard Solomon and Kosaka Masataka, eds., *The Soviet Far East Military Build-Up: Nuclear Dilemmas and Asian Security* (Dover, MA: Auburn House, 1986).

11. Hokkaido had been a major region of concentration of Japanese ground and air forces throughout the postwar period, but it was not until the early 1980s that it was made the locus of Japan's defense strategy. Attention to growing Soviet military deployments in the Far East made the notion of a Soviet attack on Hokkaido plausible. Japan's "Northern Strategy" had been in the making for some time, but the deployment of new surface-to-ship missiles by the GSDF in the mid-1980s increased the strategic impact of Japan's military deployments. Moreover, this new ability to affect the U.S.–Soviet military balance in the Northwest Pacific by Japan's own ground forces revealed the extent to which Japan's own services were basing their long-term plans on a notion of integrated operations between the U.S. and Japanese militaries. See Shigeki Nishimura, "Thinking about Japan's Defense: A Global Approach to the Northern Forward Strategy," in *Shin Boei Ronshu*, 12, No. 1 (July 1984).

12. For an excellent study of how the early political deliberations in Japan over the creation of the SDF and the alliance with the United States in the Cold War shaped the postwar political landscape against the nationalism of the past, see Hideo Otake, *Saigunbi to Nashyonarizumu: Hoshu, Riberaru, Shakai Minshushugisha no Boeikan* [Rearmament and Nationalism: The Defense Views of Conservatives, Liberals and Socialists] (Tokyo: Chuko Shinsho, 1988).

13. Two laws govern the administration of Japan's military: The Defense Agency Establishment Law and the Self Defense Force Law. For an account of the government deliberations on the drafting of these laws, see Yoji Kato, *Shiryoku - Jieitaishi: Keisatsu Yobitai kara Konnichi made* [A Personal History of the Self Defense Force: From the National Police Reserve to Today] (Tokyo: Seiji Gepposha, 1979).

14. The Defense Agency Establishment Law also gave the Agency responsibility for managing the U.S. military stationed in Japan.

15. When asked in Diet deliberations whether or not the SDF was a military, the government suggested that it was not a traditional military. On 22 December 1954, the director general of the Defense Agency answered the question in this way: "Is the Self Defense Force a military? The Self Defense Force has the mission of resisting an invasion from a foreign country, and if you call this kind of thing a military, then it is possible to call the Self Defense Force a military. But [the SDF] is not [a military] in the sense of having a variety of capabilities as that would violate the constitution."

Testimony presented in the Lower House Budget Committee of the Diet, December 22, 1954. *Boei Handobukku, Heisei 2-nen,* pp. 416–17.

16. Indeed, in the first four defense buildup plans, the notion of a "necessary defense capability" *(shoyo boeiryoku)* was based on the analysis of the threat posed to Japan by surrounding countries, and as the former Soviet Union upgraded its military deployments in the Soviet Far East, the military capability that could potentially threaten Japan became increasingly sophisticated. Matching this capability was deemed impossible, and moreover, the effort to modernize the SDF's front line equipment had to conform to the political demands that Japan's military strength remain limited.

17. A local conflict was the premise of Japan's defense planning since the 1960s, and even in the 1976 NDPO the goal of SDF planning was to meet a "small and limited scale" invasion only.

18. Over time, a number of specific weapons systems were declared out of bounds. Again, the distinction sought in debates between the ruling party and its opposition critics was that between offensive and defense weapons. In keeping with the government's interpretation of the constitution, Japan's military would be dedicated exclusively to the mission of defending Japan. In the nuclear era, this seemed anachronistic, but nonetheless, the exclusion of certain types of weapons systems was achieved.

    The first type of weapon that the government clearly thought would be in violation of the defense mission was the intercontinental ballistic missile. Another was the long-range strategic bomber. Finally, as late as the 1980s, after some internal debate, JDA stated that an offensive aircraft carrier would not be in keeping with the SDF's mission. The difference between an offensive and a defensive aircraft carrier may seem unclear to outside observers, but in the context of the debate in Japan, an acceptable aircraft carrier for the SDF might be a Harrier-based carrier such as the British deploy.

19. The *Mitsuya Kenkyu,* officially known as the 1963 Joint Staff Defense Study (Joint Staff Document 3, No. 30–38), was a major military study conducted between February and June 1963. The study was organized under the auspices of the Joint Staff Council, and 84 mid-level military officers from the three Self-Defense Forces participated. The text of the Diet debates and the documents presented by Haruo Okada and other JSP members can be found in the *Kokkai Gijiryoku* [National Diet Record], 1965. The debates took place in the Lower House Budget Committee on February 10, March 3–4, March 10, March 19, and May 31 . In addition, a special subcommittee was formed to investigate the *Mitsuya* case.

20. The issue postponed Diet approval of the national budget for three weeks until the speaker of the lower house, Naka Funada, intervened. The government then met opposition party criticism that it had overstepped the proper procedures of civilian control over policies related to the Defense Agency by proposing "Measures for Strengthening Civilian Control"

which were then approved by the Cabinet. See National Defense Council and Cabinet Decision, October 9, 1972.

21. Sakata is widely credited with the success of Japanese government efforts to engage in a public debate over the legitimacy and the aims of Japan's national defense planning that created the consensus underpinning the NDPO. One of his first policies after becoming the director general of the Defense Agency in 1975 was to establish a panel of nongovernment experts to advise the Agency on issues related to Japan's defense. This group of advisors was named the *Boei o Kangaeru Kai,* the Committee to Consider Japan's Defense Needs, and its members were respected members of industry, the media, and academia.

22. The Guidelines for U.S.–Japan Defense Cooperation were drafted by the Subcommittee on Defense Cooperation of the U.S.–Japan Security Consultative Committee (SCC). A complete text of the Guidelines can be found in *Nihon no Boei, Showa 54-nen* (Tokyo: Okurasho Insatsukyoku, 1979), p. 267, or in *The Defense of Japan* (Tokyo: *Japan Times,* 1984), p. 278. See Appendix 3.

23. In case of a conflict, the following supplementary military forces would be required from the United States: *(a)* U.S. naval air forces would respond immediately, and within one month, ground forces would be sent to Japan; *(b)* initially 2 naval task forces would be needed; and *(c)* about 20 squadrons (480 aircraft) of tactical air forces would be sent from the U.S. mainland. This was reported in the *Yomiuri Shimbun,* May 11, 1982, and later cited in the *Boei Nenkan–1989,* p. 42.

24. It was not until nearly a decade later that this sort of broader conflict scenario became the basis of U.S.–Japan military coordination revealing the Japanese government's sensitivity to the political opposition that might arise within Japan if it became known that the Defense Agency was sanctioning U.S.–Japan military planning premised on a systemwide Cold War conflict.

25. Over the course of the three-year study, various aspects of the study were reported in the Japanese press. For a synopsis of the study, see *Ajia no Anzen Hosho, 1987–88,* pp. 84–85.

26. One analyst made it clear that "this sort of notion was not in keeping with Japan's notion of defense, which based on its constitutional interpretation does not allow participation in collective defense efforts. Resolving this perception gap remains a major issue [in U.S.–Japan military collaboration]. The joint study on sea-lane defense remained the model form of how to respond in the case of an attack on Japan, and because of this, this continues to be a latent problem [for the alliance]." Quoted from "Nichibei Boei Kyoroku to Yokushi Mondai," *Boei Nenkan–1989,* p. 44.

27. When the Ohira Cabinet agreed to MSDF participation in RimPac exercises in December 1979, the opposition parties challenged the government on the grounds that this constituted participation in a collective security mechanism prohibited by the government's interpretation of the constitu-

tion. In response, however, the government argued that this "was not the type of exercise designed to defend any particular country premised on the use of force for collective defense; rather, it was simply a means for improving tactical expertise" and "therefore, did not constitute a contradiction of past Japanese government policy." See "Nichibei Boei Kyoryoku to Yokushi Mondai," *Boei Nenkan–1989*, p. 48.

28. For an analysis of the domestic political debate instigated by the Gulf War, see Masaru Tamamoto, "Trial of an Ideal: Japan's Debate over the Gulf Crisis," *World Policy Journal* 8, no. 1 (Winter 1990–91): 89–106.

29. For a description of Japanese participation in various U.N. peacekeeping activities, see chapter 7 in this volume.

# 5

# Managing the New U.S.–Japan Security Alliance: Enhancing Structures and Mechanisms to Address Post–Cold War Requirements

PAUL S. GIARRA AND AKIHISA NAGASHIMA

OVER THE last several years, tremendous strides have been made in preparing the U.S.–Japan security relationship for the routines and requirements of the 21st century. Outside events and global political realities have combined to motivate a far-reaching reaffirmation of the alliance, thereby boosting its deliberate, carefully organized modernization. This process has taken Japan's constitution and self-restrained security policies as its guide, with the principle of reinforcing the Mutual Security Treaty as its organizing basis. The Defense Guidelines review,[1] the redefinition of alliance roles and missions, has gone further still, carefully expanding Japan's focus and responsibilities in an incremental, calibrated approach.

These are remarkable achievements. The Defense Guidelines review has established new, expanded limits of legitimate security cooperation, in essence, additional Japanese rear area support for American operations, concentrating on logistical, materiel, and base and facilities contributions. With somewhat more certainty than before possible, Japan for the first time at least has the option of being counted "in" if there were a serious crisis in East Asia. However, difficult as they have been to achieve, these are the easier aspects of alliance transformation.

Now comes the hard part: translating sometimes subtle political guidance and tentative public legitimacy for additional Japanese responsibility into an objectively enhanced security relationship.[2]

So far, the Defense Guidelines review does not address by what means and to what extent the alliance will have to transform its "business operations." If this putative post–Cold War alliance is to operate effectively, it will have to become a partnership that, within clearly defined political constraints, can achieve something as an *alliance,* not as the sum of its individual parts. To do so, new structures and processes will have to be invented and implemented for the control and execution of political and military planning, coordination, and decision-making.

This necessary transformation inevitably will be strong medicine for what has been up to now a rather diffident alliance. Expectations of change have been raised very high by the promise of the review, but the difficulties in fulfilling them will be enormous. This is a separate proposition entirely from the other new, specifically military, changes that will be required, for example, improved, realistic operational cooperation and enhanced combined (U.S.–Japan) command arrangements. In effect, this prescription amounts to improved bilateral "civilian control" of a rather enhanced, more complex alliance security relationship. Without the utmost care, this strong dose might kill the patient.

## The Cold War Structure of Bilateral Consultations

The Security Treaty (the Treaty of Mutual Cooperation and Security between Japan and the United States)[3] established a number of sophisticated, institutionalized, somewhat stylized controlling structures, including the most important bilateral fora for discussing the political and military affairs of the relationship security. It is these political dialogues that have dealt with the Cold War requirements of the alliance. Notable by its absence, however, was any semblance of effective command integration, as well as the ability to coordinate complex, timely decisions regarding regional security.

Only two of these political structures, one directly subordinate to the other, have been explicitly chartered to make them credibly effective in dealing with the broader issues of the alliance. They are the now reinvigorated, ministerial-level Security Consultative Committee (SCC) and the more detail oriented Security Sub-Committee (SSC) at the assistant secretary–director general level. Each includes the requisite authoritative panoply of American interagency representatives and their Japanese counterparts to discuss regional and global security issues and the character of the alliance. They are set up to deal with matters beyond those specifically dealing with the issues raised by U.S. bases and the daily routines of U.S. forces in Japan. On the U.S. side they originate and are led from Washington. From these structures emanate the vision and authority that has brought the process of change this far.

## THE SECURITY CONSULTATIVE COMMITTEE[4]

The SCC was established under Article IV of the 1960 "Treaty of Mutual Cooperation and Security Between the United States of America and Japan." The original arrangement established the U.S. principals in the forum as the American ambassador to Japan and the commander in chief, U.S. Pacific Command (USCINCPAC); and the Japanese principals as the minister of foreign affairs (MOFA) and the director general of the Japan Defense Agency (JDA). In 1990, at the request of the Japanese government, the principal U.S. representatives were elevated to parallel their Japanese counterparts, and now are the secretary of state and the secretary of defense. It was some time before the revamped SCC finally met, in September 1995 at the Waldorf Astoria Hotel in New York, with all four principals present for the first time. (Given its balanced composition, this new ministerial arrangement is referred to colloquially as the "2+2.") Since the meeting in New York, the "2+2" has met frequently on matters of bilateral defense policy, consulting on the activities of U.S. forces, and discussing regional security issues of mutual concern. It is from the "2+2" that recommendations on security cooperation are made to the president and prime minister. The reinvigorated SCC chartered functional groups, notably the Sub-Committee on Defense Cooperation (SDC) to work out the details of the Defense Guidelines review and the Special Action Committee on Okinawa (SACO) to carry out the relocation of Futenma Marine Corps Air Station on Okinawa.[5] Both groups comprised the same assistant secretary and director general representatives as made up the SCC's Security Sub-Committee (SSC).

## THE SECURITY SUB-COMMITTEE OF THE SCC[6]

The SCC's Security Sub-Committee was established concurrently with the SCC to recommend the SCC's agenda and to address bilateral security issues at the working level. The principals on the U.S. side are the assistant secretary of defense for International Security Affairs (whose security brief effectively puts him at the head of the American side) and the assistant secretary of state for East Asian and Pacific Affairs. The Japanese principals are the director general of the North American Affairs

Bureau of the Ministry of Foreign Affairs (who leads the Japanese delegation) and the director general of the Japan Defense Agency's Defense Policy Bureau. The forum meets routinely, and is the political-military workhorse of the alliance. It has chartered a number of working-level groups that have met frequently on security issues of mutual concern or interest. A notable example is the Theater Missile Defense Working Group, that has been exploring the potential for bilateral cooperation on theater missile defense. In recent years the importance of the SSC has grown, especially when the SCC did not convene. The complementary "Mini-SSC" subgroup, at the deputy assistant secretary level, has been the engine powering the working-level discussions of the alliance.

## Shortcomings of the Cold War Structure

By definition and design these (i.e., SCC/SSC) consultations have been inherently limited. They have reflected the aspirations and capacities of the security relationship itself, in which planning, consultation, and decision-making have been consciously and effectively circumscribed since the origins of the modern bilateral relationship in 1951. By definition, neither the SCC nor the SSC could be very much more ambitious or effective than the alliance itself, which was satisfied with passive consultation and never aspired to active decision-making.

Of course, the alliance has operated fairly effectively under these circumstances, but it did so in the Cold War context by virtually unilateral American proxy, not by deliberate alliance action. There are a number of long-standing reasons for this anachronism, virtually all of which still exist. American expectations of Japanese capabilities and contributions have been uniformly very low. Compounded by a consistent American preference, both for freedom of U.S. action when operating from Japan and for minimizing Japan's role as a matter of regional practicality if not postwar principle, low expectations have resulted in a resigned, albeit occasionally troubled, hands-off U.S. approach to the lack of active Japanese involvement in the security alliance. Japan's reluctance to become entangled in either American or her own external security responsibilities drove the trend to downplay the alliance's potential for affirmative bilateral action, reflecting Japan's consciously self-constrained security policies. Japan assumed the role of landlord—generally hospitable, but occasionally intent on enforcing the terms of the lease, and always retaining the ultimate authority on legitimate use of the premises.

During the Cold War, if Japan were to become involved in an external conflict, presumably it would do so because of a peripheral attack on Japanese territory, but even then the extent of Japanese involvement would have been minimal, and the clear preference was avoidance rather than participation. One way to ensure that understatement remained a constant defining factor of the alliance was to set the technical threshold for security cooperation extraordinarily high. Official bilateral "prior consultation" would ensue only in the most extreme emergencies, and then merely to elicit formal Japanese permission for American operations from Japanese bases in what would have been a global war scenario. Anything less—the Vietnam War, for instance—evoked a blind eye toward even obvious U.S. operations, and thereby plausible deniability from Tokyo. Accordingly, by the strict, working definition such tacit approval did not involve the alliance per se. Daily cooperation was severely circumscribed, and reasonably effective only at sea (out of sight, out of mind), thereby accounting for the particularly close professional relationship between the U.S. Navy and the Japan Maritime Self-Defense Force (MSDF).[7]

The net result has been an alliance of "balanced asymmetry" that worked best when its disparate parts did not come in contact. The United States provided the strategic guarantees of the "nuclear umbrella," power projection forces, and a context for the alliance of regional and global engagement. Japan provided for its own defense (albeit without even a coherent mechanism for incorporating American forces into its own territorial operations), bases in Japan for American forces, and financial host nation support. By design, combined U.S.–Japanese planning, coordination, and decision-making were structurally precluded.

Until now, the alliance has been a political arrangement, not a military pact by any traditional measure. In a sense, the unique bureaucratic and political structures of the alliance existed primarily to replace and compensate for the lack of a combined alliance command structure, reflecting Tokyo's arms-length approach to tangible security cooperation with the United States. Planning and structures that would support and implement real cooperation could be dispensed with because there was no expectation of alliance military operations. From this perspective, the SCC and the SSC have fulfilled the purposes for which they were designed—political discussions that served to institutionalize alliance constraints. These fora became very effective consultative mechanisms, but were never designed for active control of the alliance.

These daily strictures of the alliance were rather more definitive and consciously applied than perhaps met the eye, imbuing the security relationship with a character of restraint and distance. The structures and functions of the Cold War bilateral alliance dialogue were not designed to produce strong, affirmative action or effective bilateral cooperation. Resources of the dialogue were sized and shaped to fit the requirements of the time, reflecting politically the same ambivalence as did the lack of operational cooperation. Generally superficial dialogue typically avoided objectively difficult or bilaterally contentious subjects whenever possible, such as the potential threat to stability inherent in China's rise, or some of the more difficult aspects of weapons acquisition and defense technology cooperation. Repetitive, inconclusive agendas held little prospect for effective problem solving (quite by design). Discussions over the years often took on the attributes of the lowest common denominator—Japanese domestic politics and diplomatic reticence. The absence of substantive consultation thereby effectively, and satisfactorily, precluded Japan's involvement in security matters beyond its own territorial defense and enabled Tokyo to disavow involvement concerning American operations, if not presence. This suited Japanese national policies which the United States was prepared to accommodate.

With such minimalist expectations, the alliance of the Cold War period was not designed to fight. Its unspoken charter was to keep the United States present in Japan in particular, and in East Asia and the Pacific more generally. This was a point of singular clarity on which Tokyo and Washington could agree. It was a paper alliance that could be, and was, run virtually from desktops and filing cabinets. Under these circumstances, just a few American desk officers—no more than a dozen, and led by the Japan Desks at OSD/ISA and State—could, with not much more than the phones on their desks, coordinate the political machinery of the security relationship with their U.S. colleagues and Japanese interlocutors.

This inauspicious heritage notwithstanding, the Persian Gulf War and the 1994 North Korean nuclear crisis have done much to raise strategic expectations of Japan, which in any case had been shifting inexorably since the end of the Cold War toward greater Japanese responsibility. These crises exemplify the traditional dependence of the alliance upon external pressure to promote change or get things done, whether that pressure is internally derived from United States demands or externally applied by the intrusion of real-world circumstances.

Since the Gulf War, one of the factors motivating the changes now under way has been the destabilizing effect of the alliance not being able to cooperate more realistically. The presumption was that without tighter coordination, Washington and Tokyo would continue the perceived drifting apart that characterized the earlier part of the decade. The resulting schism would be especially acute in a crisis, particularly in Japan's own backyard, and might be the death of the alliance.

Internally in the alliance, motivation for change was caused by the dawning realization at higher levels in both the United States and Japan, leading up to and especially during the 1994 North Korean nuclear crisis, that Japan might not be able to participate effectively. Coming generally on the heels of Tokyo's inability to play more than a monetary role during the Persian Gulf War, this recognition emerged for the first time as a practical matter, rather than as a hypothetical point in a postulated anti-Soviet Cold War scenario. In Northeast Asia, the political and proximate stakes for Japan were inescapably higher, but the capability to respond effectively to a serious Korean crisis in 1994 was no greater than that demonstrated during Operation Desert Storm.

Externally, Asian observers in particular became increasingly concerned that Washington and Tokyo would be unable to bridge the gap between expectations and capabilities. With Korea as the realistic scenario, the ramifications for Asians became the fatal weakening if not dissolution of the U.S.–Japan security relationship and Japan subsequently emerging as a new factor in Asian security.

For once, instead of constraining the alliance, bilateral political discussions slowly transformed themselves into a forum for evolutionary change. Key milestones were the 1994 North Korean nuclear crisis, the 1994–95 Nye Initiative to revamp the security relationship, the 1995 Okinawa rape crisis, and the April 1996 Tokyo Security Declaration.[8] Since then, the Defense Guidelines review has established the practical and political extent to which expectations of greater Japanese responsibility could and should be met. The Guidelines review was chartered to establish new benchmarks for what would be considered legitimate alliance security cooperation. The review, intrinsically political, was designed to be an inherently public process. Transparency and public acceptance were key objectives from the outset.

In addition, the successful crafting of an Acquisition and Cross Servicing Agreement (ACSA), first applied only to peacetime training and peacekeeping operations, and later upgraded to include contingency support, represents an integrative watershed for the alliance. For the first time, there now exists an embryonic agreement to regularize logistical cooperation between U.S. forces and the Japan Self-Defense Forces (SDF). This amounts to the beginnings of much more realistic bilateral cooperation. Logistics are the sinews of military operations, and thereby were selected as the focus of Defense Guidelines cooperation, in which Japan would provide not just limited operational support for regional contingencies (which has attracted by far the most public and media attention) but, more important, enhanced rear area logistical, materiel, and bases and facilities support for U.S. operations.

## Implications of the Agreement on Defense Guidelines

With real-world domestic and regional strictures in mind, Japan's role has been redefined to incorporate an incremental but quite substantive expansion of responsibilities. The bilateral security relationship's new responsibilities require far more than a political declaration to make them effective, however. Extensive Japanese legal and administrative changes will be required. Alliance structures for planning, coordination, and decision-making will have to be revamped. The process of change must incorporate the rather extensive implications of the new agreement on Defense Guidelines. Its proceedings will continue to be fundamentally public, and its outcomes will have to adhere to rather strict political guidance. Very large devils dwell in these details.

Ideally, the revised Defense Guidelines have institutionalized a number of key new principles. The political implications of these principles are profound.

For the first time, accepting that external stability is important to its own security, Japan takes active responsibility for regional security beyond its borders. What the Guidelines provide is the outline and framework for the legitimacy of the bilateral defense cooperation not only for the defense of Japan but also in the "areas surrounding Japan."

Japan will provide active support for U.S. forces—not just permission for the American use of bases. In the past, Japan's contribution was essentially limited to permitting American operations from bases in Japan, definitely in case of a direct attack on Japan, but also, only potentially, in scenarios in which Japan had not been attacked.

During the Cold War, the threshold for bilateral consultation was set too high to have ever occurred.[9] Since the end of the Cold War, the threshold of bilateral decision-making, planning, and coordination has been drastically lowered. Given the Defense Guidelines potential for instilling intrinsic cooperation virtually on a daily basis, "prior consultation" and joint decision-making should take place continuously. The very nature of alliance security consultation will have to be redefined.

By reaffirmation, the new Guidelines also define the continuing limits of bilateral cooperation. Japan will preserve the peace clause of its present constitution, forego the exercise of the right of collective self-defense, and maintain neither nuclear weapons nor power projection capability. Preserving the asymmetric distribution of responsibilities in the alliance, these later roles remain reserved to the United States, but Japan will be able to make much larger, indirect contributions to them.

Specific agreements in the review require the United States and Japan to:

- conduct bilateral (military-to-military) defense planning;
- conduct mutual cooperation planning (policy–political coordination);
- develop a comprehensive (national) mechanism involving not only the U.S. Forces Japan (USFJ) and SDF but other government agen-

cies to ensure the effectiveness of bilateral work (meaning the government of Japan [GOJ] will establish an organization coordinating various GOJ agencies' relevant works to facilitate the bilateral works listed above—this organization was established by a GOJ Cabinet decision in October 1997 and already has begun working);

- establish under normal circumstances a bilateral coordination mechanism involving the relevant agencies of the two countries in order to harmonize respective activities in case of an attack against Japan and in situations in areas surrounding Japan, and to ensure appropriate bilateral cooperation;
- establish a common standard of preparation of cooperative measures for the defense of Japan and in situations in areas surrounding Japan "so that they may select common readiness stages by mutual agreement" (akin to preplanned political and military "rules of engagement");
- establish common procedures related to operations, intelligence, logistics, and so forth for the defense of Japan and in situations in areas surrounding Japan.

The Defense Guidelines did not derive from a specific scenario, such as a Korean contingency or a Taiwan crisis. However, the easiest way to gauge the practical ramifications of the Guidelines agreement is to consider the range of requirements derived from what might happen on the Korean Peninsula. Korea is the closest, if not the most stressful, foreseeable regional scenario, and incorporates virtually every aspect of proposed alliance cooperation.

The implications of the Guidelines should not be limited to this situation, however. Enhanced cooperation in the more traditional defense of Japan presents its own major requirements, and the prospect of global cooperation in peacekeeping and humanitarian and disaster relief operations provides potentially very significant opportunities and obligations.

## New Requirements

The doctrinal commitments described above illustrate how the character of bilateral consultation is about to change—will have to change if the premises of the Defense Guidelines review are to be realized—from stylized and contrived cooperation to rather more realistic, timely, and pragmatic active Japanese contributions. After years of bottom-up maneuvering, we find ourselves propelled forward on a fast-moving road, pressured to change from the top down and from the outside in, with a number of key summit meetings having culminated in the review of the Defense Guidelines. Despite the consciously limiting emphasis on Japanese support for U.S. military operations, however, in a fundamentally political alliance, the political discomfort of Japanese participation in external defense operations, and thereby the requirements for extensive political dialogue, will remain extraordinarily high. It will take dealing with this endemic discomfort through expanded coordination and dialogue to cement more tangible cooperation.

Planning and coordination are the two pillars supporting effective decision-making. Given that future circumstances will be characterized by cooperation—and therefore decision-making, which is much more complex—new coordination structures will have to be much more robust. Both the United States and Japan will require more effective planning and coordination structures to support pragmatic, well-informed decision-making.

There are real-world, certifiable consequences of not instituting enhancements to current coordination mechanisms. For example, the attempt to provide U.S. airlift support for Japan's Ground Self-Defense Forces' (GSDF) humanitarian relief mission to Goma, Zaire, during the Rwanda refugee crisis in 1994 failed in part because old alliance structures were insufficient to coordinate the mission's complex political and operational requirements.

The Defense Guidelines review amounts to a charter of heightened political expectations. With the end of the Cold War came expectations for new levels of cooperation, and the Defense Guidelines review is the articulated response to expectations since then.

So far, the agreements of the Defense Guidelines review are intangible. Having defined the outlines of legitimate security cooperation in principle, now the alliance will have to develop the practical political, legal, administrative, diplomatic, and consultative wherewithal to deal effectively with the newly legitimate requirements and responsibilities of the alliance. This is where the heavy lifting will occur, in transforming the alliance into a practical extension of proactive bilateral security policies. The Diet process of passing enabling legislation is now underway. Highlighted by public statements of support from the secretary of defense and the secretary of state, it will grant new, transforming authority.

To capitalize on this new authority, the alliance will have to incorporate into its operations predictable expanded requirements for planning, coordination, and decision-making. The consultative processes will have to transform themselves, enhancing and extrapolating their capacities and capabilities without collapsing under the weight of newly expanded requirements. Unchanged, the current SCC/SSC process is not sufficient to achieve these changes, or to manage the expanded requirements of an enhanced alliance. As a fundamentally political dialogue, however, it is perfectly suited to what will remain a basically political alliance.

## An Illustrative Scenario: Refueling American Aerial Tanker Aircraft at Kadena Air Base

Illustrative scenarios have been consistently successful in outlining new alliance requirements since 1991. They can be utilized here as well to help visualize how to embellish the SCC/SSC process, which is the political heart of the security dialogue. It is this structural center of the alliance that must deal with the frequency and complexity of politically guided planning and politically charged coordination. The SCC/SSC will have to generate decision-making of drastically increased political and operational significance if the alliance is to evolve successfully. The SCC/SSC are of the proper configuration for the task at hand, but currently do not have the resources or the reach to control the amplified political strategic workings of the alliance which are an unprecedented factor.

Assessing a representative scenario can illustrate what the political requirements might be, differentiating between technical or military requirements on the one hand and their political aspects on the other. The objective is to resolve transcendent alliance political issues in such a way as to make technical, military, and rear area infrastructure support possible in the first place. Political discussions will continue to clear the path ahead, like a plow's blade through heavy snow.

*The mission:* a long-range U.S. Air Force (USAF) mission will either originate from or pass by Kadena Air Base on Okinawa. This mission requires in-flight refueling by USAF aerial tankers operating from Kadena. The USAF tanker aircraft will have to be fueled at Kadena in preparation for the mission. The requirement to fuel the tanker aircraft is passed by the Commander of the Fifth Air Force up and down through operational channels, as well as up the political chain of command. The decision is made in the U.S. government that this is a situation covered by the new latitude of the Defense Guidelines, and that it is appropriate to ask for assistance from the GOJ.

*The assignment for the alliance:* establish structures and procedures in advance that will have enabled politically guided military-to-military planning for operations such as this one that have regional or global implications; coordinate effectively and with little advance notification the political details of the proposed operation, reaching bilateral consensus that this is a legitimate opportunity for cooperation; and generate a positive political decision between Tokyo and Washington that effectively reaches all the way down to the Japanese and American personnel working together at Kadena Air Base.

Under Cold War circumstances, this proposed Japanese assistance would have been out of the question, or ineffective, because it came in extremis, without prior planning. More typically, Japan would have—on extraordinarily short notice, in the midst of a grave emergency—considered an American request for permission to operate from Japanese bases. It would be the prime minister's role, along with the foreign minister and minister of state for defense, to deliver an affirmative reply; and that would be the extent of Japan's role. But short of a Third World War, the entire proposed mission would be up to the United States—the operation itself, the planning, the ground support and logistics—in this case providing American fuel, fuel trucks, and equipment operators to refuel USAF aircraft at Kadena Air Base.

Given the provisional legitimacy afforded by the Defense Guidelines, however, it would be theoretically possible for Japan to consider a proactive role in the posited Kadena scenario. Now, it is possible to anticipate the time when Japan might contribute to the U.S. effort, depending upon the strategic, operational, and political particulars. Much would depend upon the strategic and political background and purposes of the mission, and the outcome of political-military coordination at the time of the crisis. This qualifying dependence dictates and underscores the continuing political ramifications of the request; the inferred requirements highlight the sort of new bilateral planning, coordination, and decision-making capabilities that will have to be established.

First, cooperation would have been made possible in the first place by intensive, politically derived military-to-military planning, which would have not only anticipated the possibility of the particular support requirement, but prepared for the myriad technical details as well. For example, if Japan were to be asked to provide fuel for the USAF aerial tankers at Kadena, with very short advance notice, Japanese fuel trucks with the correct grade of fuel, the appropriate hose fittings, and the required quantity of fuel would have to arrive at a precisely specified time beneath the wing of the correct KC-10. The Japanese fuel truck operators would have to be prepared to function in close coordination with the USAF line crews servicing the tanker aircraft.

Second, a myriad number of issues would have to be coordinated. With the request will come a flurry of questions that must be answered by the political coordination process, for political consumption in Japan. Like a newspaper editor instead of just a landlord, the GOJ would expect the United States to explain the full details, the "who, why, what, where, when, and how" of the mission. This will take place in the SCC/SSC process, in which the pending requirements for coordinating details and reaching into the heart of national bureaucratic structures for solutions will have far outstripped the few assets apportioned to it. Depending on the scenario, from a mid-air refueling of routine C-5 Galaxy logistics missions en route to Australia to support for B-52s on the way to launch missile attacks in the Persian Gulf, the internal political ramifications for the alliance could be relatively simple or extremely complex.

Third, timely and resilient decision-making mechanisms, both national and bilateral, will have to be capable of responding effectively in order to provide active operational, and potentially strategic, control of alliance operations.

## Implementing the Defense Guidelines Review: What Must Come Next for the Alliance

The accomplishments of the U.S.–Japan review of Defense Guidelines are a great breakthrough; however, just as in a more typical military campaign, a breakthrough is successful only if one can capitalize on it. Next must come two major efforts.

*The first major effort* will be a continuing exercise in civilian control, making sure the alliance treats the evolution of the security relationship as a purposefully public and political effort. This means that the process should not revert to the old style of surreptitious bureaucratic and military planning. This would have the effect of delaminating what has been by design a carefully layered, three-tiered process—public-political/policy-bureaucratic/military-technical—intended to tie the military planning and operational outcome directly and explicitly, from the earliest stages, to the political process of authorizing new limits while accepting current constraints.

This means that American and Japanese politicians must come to be actively involved in the debate over security, and participate closely in the formulation of enabling legislation. This is necessary to sustain and review the process of alliance maturation. Otherwise the attempt to transform the alliance will revert to an exercise in cynical force-building for the Self-Defense Forces, thereby losing much of its punch and increasing the chances that it will become counterproductive and gather opposition instead of support.

In this regard, internal transparency is as important as the more highly touted external, regional transparency. The opportunity for the Diet to assert itself will come in the process of debating enabling legislation. Such legislation is crucial in order to implement the specifics of the Defense Guidelines review.[10] Predictably, however, the propensity will be for the Diet not to play a formative, or even constructive, role.

The American legislative branch has an important role to play as well. The U.S. Congress must satisfy itself that the strategic implications and consequences of the redefinition of the bilateral U.S.–Japan security relationship are acceptable and appropriate to broader U.S. interests and strategic principles. Rebuilding the congressional dialogue with Japanese counterparts, fallen on hard times in recent years, will help to stimulate political thought about the alliance in both countries, an outcome of great benefit to the security relationship and the broader bilateral connection as well. So far, however, Congress has largely ignored the process.

*The second major effort* will determine how far the Defense Guidelines will go—whether the alliance will be transformed fundamentally, or simply change by exception and solely for the purpose of planning for a Korean contingency. The minimalist view holds that all that is necessary is the ability to plan for a Korean contingency. Accepting this shortsightedness would define the utility of the bilateral security relationship as extending no further than Korean unification.

On the contrary, however, the implications of the Guidelines review could amount to a much more fundamental change in the security relationship. Of course, it is necessary to plan for and anticipate the requirements a Korean contingency would impose. But being able to cooperate in specific high-intensity scenarios, and to achieve the even more consequential transforming effect more broadly throughout the alliance as well, requires daily practice, on a global basis, of those cooperative functions newly defined as legitimate by the Guidelines. This means that those missions deliberately included in the Guidelines because they entail virtually all of the Guidelines' targeted capabilities—peacekeeping, humanitarian and disaster relief, and noncombatant evacuation operations—must be taken up politically and operationally as new alliance functions and incorporated into routine operations of the bilateral security relationship. This is important for three reasons.

First, the tendency in both Washington and Tokyo has been to set aside these low-intensity missions as an excursion from the security relationship, an independent Japanese responsibility instead of an opportunity for alliance cooperation. This unfortunate lapse in alliance doctrine has tended to encourage divergence between the two sides, rather than combining political and military resources. Exercising the authority for global cooperation in these mission areas will not only redress this lapse, but also strengthen alliance solidarity in politically useful and acceptable endeavors such as peacekeeping and humanitarian and disaster relief. This is just the sort of demonstration needed to enhance political credibility.

Second, the routine conduct of these relatively high probability, low intensity operations on a global basis amounts to invaluable practice for much more stressful and totally unprecedented high-intensity regional contingency operations. Coordinated peacekeeping operations and disaster and humanitarian relief missions, sometimes with Japanese and American units together in the field, sometimes with more distant support provided for one by the other, entail most of those military functions common to much more intense, more traditional missions, and would prepare for the higher-end missions. They include many of the same requirements that Japan and the United States would expect to coordinate in a Korean scenario, such as intelligence support, logistics cooperation, self-protection, materiel support, and communications interoperability. As U.S. Navy Admiral Charles Larson, then commander in chief of the U.S. Pacific Command, said of the diversion of U.S. Marine Corps III MEF forces to Bangladesh for a humanitarian relief mission on the way back to Japan from the Persian Gulf after Operation Desert Storm: "Deploying these forces for this humanitarian relief mission was the same as deploying them in combat."

Third, this sort of bilateral coordination in low-threat situations would exercise the same political structures and coordination procedures necessary in a crisis. The scale of operations might be different, but the decision-making process would be the same. Not only is the practice necessary, but it provides a priceless opportunity to test new arrangements for planning, coordination, and decision-making in advance, before the stakes are too high. Practice makes perfect, and the bugs can be worked out. Plans successfully tested in areas like intelligence sharing, logistics, and communications will turn out to be real confidence-builders. Finding out under fire that the new system has shortcomings and defects is not a viable alternative. This is especially important in light of the third major effort.

*The third major effort* of the alliance will be to institute realistic mechanisms for active political coordination and control. Conducting these low-intensity operations with some frequency can transform the alliance, and institutionalize political progress practically and operationally. Constant routine is what it will take to transform the alliance as a whole, not just carefully prepared but fragile crisis planning set aside "on the shelf" for major operations. It will take capitalizing on the breakthrough of the Defense Guidelines review in this way to transform the attitudes, assumptions, and practices imbued over almost fifty years. Constant feedback will test the design for the legislative, structural, and policy changes necessary to make the concept of active Japanese rear area support for American regional operations a reality.

The alternative is to prepare for a serious contingency in the abstract, but American commanders know that complex operations do not work without extensive practice. Ambitious operational plans shelved until a crisis erupts do not convince friends or allies that much has changed. Real change, and credible deterrence, will require more wide-ranging embellishments to the ability to plan, coordinate, and decide the newly legitimate, operational business of the security relationship.

An added advantage of exercising the alliance more broadly is that, by underscoring the emphasis on bilateral coordination in the pursuit of global responsibility, it undercuts the argument from North Korea, China, and others that the Guidelines review is scenario, and thereby country, specific. Effective planning, coordination, and decision-making structures may establish the political and geographic boundaries of potential bilateral cooperation. They may provide a range of preplanned and emerging options for decision-makers. But their diversity by nature preserves the national prerogatives of both Japan and the United States. There is no commitment in advance, no automatic response envisioned. Rather, the process so far has expanded the viable options for national civilian and military decision-makers. This is precisely why effective coordination is so important at the time of decision, and why many more resources than are now available must be assigned to this function.

## New Structures

How best to institute the new agreements and responsibilities embodied in the review of the Defense Guidelines, exercise new capabilities, and strengthen the all-important political structures of the alliance? What will ensure that effective political and civilian guidance continues to control a technical and operational military process? To achieve these goals, the Security Treaty–chartered SCC/SSC process must be carefully, thoughtfully, and extensively embellished. New bilateral planning structures that compensate for the lack of a combined U.S.–Japan command system will have to be created. This structure will have to be more responsive and accountable to civilian control than present arrangements permit. There are several major structural implications for alliance managers.

First, because of American regional and global responsibilities and interests, bilateral planning, coordination, and decision-making will have more than a Japan-centered focus. The explicit extension of the alliance's responsibilities to the region and beyond supersedes the capacities and authority of the commander of USFJ, the American sub-unified command in Japan headquartered at Yokota Air Base on the outskirts of Tokyo. This means that the commander in chief of the U.S. Pacific Command (CINCPAC) and the Joint Staff will have to be far more directly involved in the coordination process than ever before, dictating an unprecedented assumption of responsibility by CINCPAC and the Joint Staff, rather than a further delegation of responsibility to USFJ.

Second, some sort of supercharged coordination mechanism will have to be set up to carry out the orders of the SCC process, especially important in an alliance that will continue to be fundamentally political. The SCC structure, led by the office of the Secretary of Defense and the Department of State, is the appropriate forum for an expanded alliance security dialogue. It will be necessary, however, to significantly expand its capacity.

One way to achieve this is to establish an alliance secretariat subordinate to the SSC. The Japan–U.S. Treaty Organization (JUSTO) would consist of diplomats, civilian defense officials, and military officers from both countries. They would be assigned and organized along functional lines paralleling the new requirements highlighted by the Guidelines' decisions for expanded alliance responsibility—such as transportation, logistics, materiel planning, operations, and communications. Reflecting the structure of the SCC/SSC, the JUSTO secretariat would draw upon the expertise and functional and regional responsibilities of the Office of the Secretary of Defense, the Joint Staff, CINCPAC, USFJ, and the four military services on the American side. On the Japanese side, it would include representatives from the Japan Defense Agency, the Ministry of Foreign Affairs, the Joint Staff Council, and the three Self-Defense Forces—Ground, Maritime, and Air. Representatives from the U.S. National Security Council and Japan's newly established interagency coordination council might also be included.

The JUSTO secretariat would be led by representatives from the United States and Japan, subordinate to the assistant secretaries and directors general who make up the SSC. To be most effective, this organization would be an extension of the working-level process. On the U.S. side, the secretariat would report to the deputy assistant secretaries responsible for the U.S.–Japan security relationship, in effect amounting to an expansion of the capacity of the American desk officers and Japanese division directors traditionally tasked with running the alliance.

No location is optimum. Given U.S. emphasis on regional and global responsibilities, and to facilitate travel to either capital, the JUSTO secretariat could be co-located with CINCPAC at Camp Smith in Hawaii. A more likely and politically acceptable alternative would be to locate JUSTO in the Japan Defense Agency headquarters in Tokyo or in the Joint Staff Office Command Center.

Drawing upon appropriate national resources, the JUSTO secretariat would have three major political responsibilities, acting together to complement, coordinate, and connect, but not supplant, national and military command structures. It would direct and integrate the process of bilateral political and military planning. It would coordinate national responses to real-world operations. And the JUSTO secretariat would facilitate alliance decision-making with political and strategic recommendations.

Finally, the JUSTO secretariat would coordinate the bilateral decision-making process that will require timely, well-informed feedback to the policy and operational apparatus of the alliance. The SCC/SSC principals are the right officials to make major alliance decisions when necessary, although decision-making should be pushed to the lowest level possible. The JUSTO secretariat also would provide enhanced technical support for more frequent decision-making and contact between the principal leaders of the alliance by instituting a high-technology "2+2" structure, including innovations such as encrypted video-teleconferencing that facilitate active deliberations at great distance.

## The Alternative: Reverting to Type

Achieving the benefits of the Defense Guidelines will tax the imagination and resources of both Japan and the United States. The Defense Guidelines are a two-edged sword, however: there are real consequences for failure to move beyond this agreement in principle. Along with the prospect of active assistance from Japan comes the requirement for thoroughgoing American consultation with an ally, one that for the first time is being asked to share accountable responsibility for potentially wide-ranging American operations.

When the time comes for alliance action, its success will depend not just upon Japanese acquiescence, but upon assistance as well. The processes of planning, coordination, and decision-making will have to function smoothly. If the structure and the process of coordination and decision-making are not sufficiently supple, odds are that operations dependent upon bilateral cooperation will be delayed or derailed. If that is the case, then the price for bilateral cooperation will be too high.

If the current structures are not successfully revamped, then the end result would be relatively decreased American flexibility. In any foreseeable future scenario, given the choice between active assistance and accustomed flexibility, American commanders and political leaders would more likely opt for unilateral flexibility rather than bilateral cooperation. The end result would be to return to the status quo ante, cutting Japan out of the process of coordination and increased responsibility in international security affairs, reverting instead to the old-alliance routine of the [ally's] "blind eye" toward unilateral American actions. This would undermine the whole point of the movement—since the beginning of the decade—toward more cooperation and responsibility on the part of Tokyo. Failure would be unsettling for the alliance and by extension for the region, which had earlier noted the destabilizing effect of the alliance not being able to operate more effectively.

## Conclusion

Both of these initiatives—a maturation of Japan's public, political decision-making on security issues, and the fundamental revamping of the essential processes and practices of the security alliance—will present even more of a challenge for the alliance than did the political process that led to the agreement on the principles of the Defense Guidelines.

This second Guidelines review, eminently successful, points to much more work, rather than marking the conclusion of a process. Ultimate success depends on close political control of defense policy by defense officials, diplomats, and military commanders, not an abrupt hand-off of alliance planning responsibilities to technicians and operators. The evolutionary change of the alliance will continue to depend upon Diet and congressional approval for its legitimacy. Continued cooperation of both policymakers and parliamentarians will be necessary to shepherd the agreement toward a real facsimile of what has been agreed upon so far.

## Notes

1. Promulgated by the Joint Statement of the U.S.–Japan Security Consultative Committee, "Completion of the Review of the Guidelines for U.S.–Japan Defense Cooperation," New York, September 23, 1997. See Appendix 3 for the full text.
2. Paul S. Giarra, "Point of Choice, Point of Departure," *Japan Quarterly* 44, no. 1 (January–March 1997): 16–29.

3. See Appendix 2 for the full text of the Security Treaty.
4. See the Report on the Security Relationship Between the United States and Japan, March 1, 1995, Submitted in Compliance with Section 1325 of the FY 95 Defense Authorization Act.
5. See Appendix 4 for the full text of the SACO Final Report.
6. See the Report on the Security Relationship, March 1, 1995.
7. For details of the postwar naval cooperation between U.S. Navy and Japan Maritime Self Defense Force, see Naoyuki Agawa and James E. Auer, "Historical Implications of U.S.–Japan Naval Cooperation," paper presented for a workshop on Restructuring U.S.–Japan Security Relations, co-sponsored by the Okazaki Institute, The Policy Study Group, and the Pacific Forum CSIS (Washington, D.C., April 29–30, 1996).
8. See Appendix 5 for the full text of the U.S.–Japan Joint Declaration on Security: Alliance for the Twenty-first Century.
9. According to the exchange of notes between Prime Minister Nobusuke Kishi and Secretary of State Christian Herter on January 19, 1960, concerning the implementation of Article VI of the Mutual Security Treaty ("For the purpose of contributing to the security of Japan and the maintenance of international peace and security in the Far East, the United States of America is granted the use by its land, air and naval forces of facilities and areas in Japan."), Tokyo would expect the United States to consult with the government of Japan in case of major changes in the deployment into Japan of United States armed forces, major changes in their equipment, and the use of facilities and areas in Japan as bases for military combat operations to be undertaken from Japan other than those conducted under Article V of the said Treaty.
10. For the details about the role of Japan's political leadership, see Michael J. Green and Akihisa Nagashima, "Shingaidorain Hoseibi: Yatto 'Ippo' wo Fumidashita [The Legislation of the Guidelines: 'One Step' Forward at Last]," *This Is Yomiuri* (June 1998): 212–19.

# 6

# U.S. Bases in Japan: Historical Background and Innovative Approaches to Maintaining Strategic Presence

PAUL S. GIARRA

THE U.S.–JAPAN Mutual Security Treaty (see Appendix 2) provides in Article VI that "[f]or the purpose of contributing to the security of Japan and the maintenance of international peace and security in the Far East, the United States of America is granted the use by its land, air and naval forces of facilities and areas in Japan." These American bases define the implicit bargain of the bilateral alliance, and are far more valuable strategically and as a political anchor than the highly touted and more publicly appreciated financial host nation support provided by the Japanese government.

As a unique Japanese contribution, provided in kind rather than cash, bases for U.S. forces in Japan exemplify what might be called the balanced asymmetry of the bilateral security relationship. The United States provides the nuclear umbrella of strategic deterrence, offensive power projection, and global intelligence, surveillance, and command and control. Japan, in turn, offers host nation support, complementary forces for its own defense, and bases for American forces.

These bases, in any reasonable calculus, are essential to the current and future security equation of the region. They are vital to the defense of Japan, to the security and stability of East Asia, and to American security and political and economic strategy both in East Asia and globally. The value and indispensability of these Japanese bases—they represent, aside from the fixed-in-place U.S. forces in South Korea, the last major concentrations of U.S. military power between Guam and the Persian Gulf—balance the powerful American contributions to the security relationship, and they give substance to Japan's role as an alliance partner.

Compared to U.S. bases in Korea, provided for the specific purpose of forestalling North Korean aggression, bases in Japan provide strategically irreplaceable flexibility and numerous options for U.S. military commanders. This is especially important in light of the demise of virtually all the rest of U.S. postwar base structure on the East Asian littoral. These bases are central to the U.S. strategy of national commitment, forward deployment, and regional engagement. They are also the most important element in Japan's burden-sharing contribution to the bilateral alliance. After all, American taxpayers usually fund U.S. military operations, and they could do so in this case.[1] Only Japan, however, can provide the bases. Compared to the financial host nation support paid by Japan, even at its current level of more than $5 billion a year, bases for U.S. forces in Japan are far more valuable in supporting American forward presence and military operations throughout the region.

On Okinawa, however, and at airfields in the crowded Kanto Plain, around Tokyo in particular, U.S. operations have become subject to vexing local political pressure from surrounding communities. This pressure has permeated into Japanese national politics, and calls from opposition political parties are growing for an alliance without bases. This has had a corrosive, restrictive effect, psychological and practical, on the bilateral relationship and on American sustainability, posing an essential introspective question for the alliance: how can this pressure be relieved, debilitating operational constraints avoided, and the strategic value of the installations preserved? Doing so will require the transformation of the bases so that they are perceived by Japan in a fundamentally different way.

First, the bases must be understood in Japan to be directly essential to the nation's own security. Tokyo will have to internalize and reflect the conclusion that Japanese interests will be put at risk if the usefulness or viability of the bases is allowed to erode. Far too often the bases are construed or described as being important only to the United States, thereby skewing the discussion. Their role in the defense of Japan, especially their effect on regional stability and international security, is often misunderstood, minimized, or overlooked, in both Japan and the United States. This erroneous, minimalist calculation will not change until Tokyo can acknowledge and take credit for the indirect but essential regional role Japan plays in providing these bases and tangibly supporting the United States (and the United Nations) in other ways for the purposes of deterrence, crisis response, regional stability, and international security.[2]

Second, the installations will have to make positive contributions to municipal and prefectural economic development, and there will have to be a clear matching local perception. This should be possible to a limited but important extent, especially on Okinawa, where civil economic development has not completely overshadowed the effects of local U.S. expenditures. Opening the bases and integrating them with the civil economic infrastructure is one way to enhance their perceived value, both locally and in Tokyo. Combined with traditional methods of close attention to local base relations and domestic politics, this approach will help to preserve the bases over the long term.

Third, the bases should be integrated into Self-Defense Force (SDF) operations and plans, with SDF units stationed in what are now exclusively American enclaves. There are several advantages to this approach. Most important, it would reverse the tendency of SDF officers and Japanese Defense Agency (JDA) officials to dismiss issues surrounding exclusive United States installations as exclusively American problems. Approaches to solving operational and community relations problems at integrated bases—such as Yokosuka Naval Base, Sasebo Naval Base, and Misawa Air Base—are much more effective because responsibility is shared in a more fundamental way. Furthermore, more general integration of bases would re-instill emphasis on bilateral interoperability and the effectiveness of the alliance, instead of the current general practice of geographic and operational segregation. (There are, of course, notable examples of operational integration, especially between the U.S. Navy and the Japanese Maritime Self-Defense Force [MSDF] submarine forces, and between P-3 squadrons of each nation, but these are exceptions that prove the general rule. This is the result of having chosen early on to keep separate command and control functions, and not establish a combined command like those in NATO or in Korea.)

Fourth, the Okinawan base issue in particular is a stalking horse of the future of American presence in East Asia and the western Pacific. Combined populist Japanese domestic impulse and American isolationist tendencies will put great pressure on the political wherewithal necessary to continue to pay the financial and political costs necessary to support effective forward defense as a basic national security strategy in Asia.

The base "footprint" on Okinawa can and should be further reduced, in a careful and deliberate process. Some steps can be taken right away, given the requisite imagination and political determination to reorient forces. Most will have to wait until Korea is reunited. In doing so, however, it is imperative that forces and capabilities relocated from Okinawa should move northward to Japan's main islands, not eastward to Guam, Hawaii, or the continental United States. Moving U.S. forces east instead of north would be a double blow, reducing Japan's contribution to an asymmetric alliance and undercutting American resolve.

The history of the U.S.–Japan relationship involves base consolidations, reversions, accommodations, and realignment on both sides as American requirements have waxed and waned. The end of the Cold War has brought changed attitudes and presumptions about the bases and the problems they cause for Japanese communities. Recent events on Okinawa have focused more attention than ever before on these issues; some say that the scrutiny has put the security relationship itself at risk.

How the United States and Japan resolve these problems will affect the health and viability of the security relationship and America's long-term military presence in Asia and the Pacific. Two basic objectives remain foremost—maintaining American forces in geographically strategic locations, and preserving the nature and extent of Japanese contributions that preserve the bilateral alliance.

## U.S. Bases, Strategic Context, and Current Circumstances

As part of a larger whole, Okinawan base issues impact on much larger concerns. With the United States and Japan at an important crossroads for base issues, the Okinawan bases are significant enough, both politically and with respect to U.S. military capabilities concentrated there, to affect the much broader question of the future of American presence. Despite progress made by the bilateral Special Action Committee on Okinawa (SACO), traditional approaches hold little prospect for anything more than a temporary patching-over of fundamental problems on Okinawa, or throughout Japan. Given the current formula of incremental returns of base property to Okinawan landowners, rising expectations there for the closure of U.S. bases are unlikely to be fulfilled without a substantially different calculus in both Naha (the prefectural capital) and Tokyo. For the foreseeable future, U.S. commanders on Okinawa will remain under political siege. Without a reorienting and redressing of the concerns of

Okinawans, Japanese and American policymakers alike will be hard pressed to give appropriate attention to other major issues in the security relationship. Unconventional solutions, however, not only could mitigate Okinawan concerns but have broad applicability to bilateral base issues throughout Japan.

## The Legal Basis of American Bases in Japan

Literally and figuratively, the American bases in Japan are a legacy of World War II. In August 1945, U.S. and Allied forces occupied Imperial Japanese Army and Navy bases on the four main islands—Hokkaido, Honshu, Shikoku, and Kyushu—and on Okinawa. On Okinawa, more than elsewhere, in addition to occupying existing bases, U.S. forces constructed extensive facilities on property taken from local landowners, rents for which are paid to the owners by the Japanese government.

As in Europe, in Japan the massive postwar American presence diminished only slowly. Any consideration of large-scale withdrawals ended with the onset of the Korean War and the militarization of Cold War containment. The provision of bases was made a Japanese national responsibility with the normalization of relations that marked the end of the occupation of Japan's main islands, by the Security Treaty signed in 1951, and by the 1954 Status of Forces Agreement (SOFA), which governed their use and Japan's obligations to U.S. forces. Japan's responsibilities were further ratified and updated by revisions of each of these agreements in 1960, including the Mutual Security Treaty, signed on January 19, 1960, which updated, and made permanent, the 1951 defense pact. Article VI of the Security Treaty allows U.S. forces to use facilities and areas in Japan for maintaining regional peace and security.

> "For the purposes of contributing to the security of Japan and the maintenance of international peace and stability in the Far East, the United States is granted the use by its land, air, and naval forces of facilities in Japan. The use of these facilities and areas . . . shall be governed by a separate agreement" [i.e., the Status of Forces Agreement (SOFA)]

Unlike in mainland Japan, the Okinawan base complex was administered as part of an American occupation, which ended in 1972 with the drawdown of U.S. military involvement in Vietnam. In the years before that reversion, Tokyo pressed to have virtually all U.S. ground forces eliminated from mainland Japanese bases. In a natural process, most U.S. ground forces consolidated and relocated on Okinawa, where U.S. control made such actions relatively easy. The legacy of that process is the current concentration of U.S. forces on Okinawa.

Base consolidations and reductions in the U.S. presence occurred periodically during the Cold War, generally paralleling the state of international and bilateral relations. Today U.S. forces are generally concentrated in five locations: Misawa in northern Honshu, the Kanto plain base complex, Iwakuni Air Base in western Honshu, Sasebo Naval Base in Kyushu, and the Okinawa base complex.

## Major U.S. Forces in Japan[3]

THE KANTO PLAIN BASE COMPLEX

Yokota Air Base
- COMUSJAPAN Headquarters
- Fifth Air Force Headquarters
- 374th Airlift Wing
- Logistics/Transport Hub

Yokosuka Naval Base
- Seventh Fleet Flagship (USS *Blue Ridge*)
  - Commander, seventh Fleet
- USS *Kitty Hawk* Carrier Battle Group
  - Commander, Carrier Striking Force, Seventh Fleet
- Ten surface combatants (cruisers, destroyers, frigates)
- Commander, U.S. Naval Forces, Japan
- Commander, Submarine Group 7
- Ship Repair Facility, Yokosuka

Atsugi Air Base
- Commander, Fleet Air Western Pacific
- Carrier Air Wing Five (USS *Kitty Hawk* Air Wing)
- Light Helicopter Anti-Submarine Squadron 51

Kamiseya Communications Facility
- Commander, Patrol Wing One
- Headquarters, Seventh Fleet Maritime Patrol Aircraft Task Force
- Headquarters, Fifth Fleet Maritime Patrol Aircraft Task Force

Yokohama
- Headquarters, Military Sealift Command, Far East
- Yokohama Military Port
- Sagami Army Depot

Camp Zama
- Headquarters, U.S. Army, Japan Ninth Theater Army Area Command (TAACOM)
- I (U.S.) Corps (Forward) Liaison Detachment
- Seventeenth Army Support Group (ASG)
- Army Medical Department Activity Japan (MEDDACJAPAN)

Camp Fuji
USMC live firing area

## SASEBO

Sasebo Naval Base
Amphibious Ready Group (ARG) Bravo
4 amphibious ships
2 minesweepers

## MISAWA

Misawa Air Base
Thirty-fifth Fighter Wing (USAF)
36 F-16 aircraft
Fleet Electronic Reconnaissance Detachment (Navy)
2 EP-3 aircraft
Misawa Air Patrol Group (Navy)
6–7 P-3C aircraft

## IWAKUNI

Iwakuni Marine Corps Air Station
Marine Air Group 12 (MAG 12)
USMC F/A-18, EA-6B, and C-130 aircraft

In accordance with the SACO Final Report of December 2, 1996, transfer of 14 AV-8 aircraft from Iwakuni Air Base to the United States has been completed.

## THE OKINAWA BASE COMPLEX

Camp Zukeran
Marine Corps Base Camp S.D. Butler
Headquarters, Marine Corps Bases Okinawa
First Marine Aircraft Wing (1 MAW) Headquarters
Twelfth Marine Regiment (Artillery)

In accordance with the SACO Final Report of December 2, 1996, U.S. housing areas in Camp Zukeran will be consolidated, and portions of the land in housing areas there will be returned, with the intention to finish the process by the end of March 2008 (approx. 83 ha/206 acres at Camp Zukeran).

Camp Courtney
Headquarters, Third Marine Expeditionary Force (III MEF)
Headquarters, Third Marine Division (–)
Headquarters, Thirty-first Marine Expeditionary Unit (31 MEU)
Camp McTureous
USMC housing facility
Camp Kuwae
U.S. Naval Hospital

Now a jointly used facility agreed under Article 2 paragraph 4(a) of the SOFA. The new Yomitan town office is being built within Camp Kuwae.

In accordance with the SACO Final Report of December 2, 1996, most of Camp Kuwae (approximately 99 ha/245 acres) will be returned, with the intention to finish the process by the end of March 2008 after the Naval Hospital is relocated to Camp Zukeran and remaining facilities there are relocated to either Camp Zukeran or other U.S. facilities and areas in Okinawa.

In accordance with the SACO Final Report of December 2, 1996, U.S. housing areas in Camp Kuwae will be consolidated, and portions of the land in housing areas there will be returned, with the intention to finish the process by the end of March 2008 (approximately 35 ha/85 acres at Camp Kuwae will be returned through housing consolidation. That land amount is included in the above entry).

Tengan Pier
U.S. Navy ordnance handling facility
Futenma Marine Corps Air Station
Marine Air Group 36 (MAG 36)
CH-53, CH-46, AH-1, and UH-1 helicopters

The December 1996 SACO Final Report announced that this facility would be returned by the United States to Japan within the next five to seven years, after adequate replacement facilities are completed and operational.

In accordance with the SACO Final Report of December 2, 1996, 12 KC-130 aircraft currently based at Futenma Air Station will be transferred to Iwakuni Air Base after adequate facilities are provided.

Kadena Air Base
Eighteenth Wing
54 F-15 aircraft
E-3 AWACS
KC-135 aerial refueling aircraft
353 Special Operations Group (SOG) C-130 aircraft
Okinawa Air Patrol Group (Navy)
6–7 P-3C aircraft

Kadena Ammunition Storage Area
USAF and USMC
Ammunition storage facility
Army Oil Storage Facility
Fuel storage
Camp Shields
USAF and Navy barracks
Construction equipment repair facility
Yomitan Auxiliary Airfield
USMC training facility
Electromagnetic buffer zone for Sobe Communications Site and Torii Station
Former site of parachute training
Runway no longer used by fixed wing aircraft

Now a jointly used facility agreed under Article 2 paragraph 4(a) of SOFA. Within the airfield boundary, an exercise park, including a baseball field, and a village office have been built.

In accordance with the SACO Final Report of December 2, 1996, Yomitan Auxiliary Airfield (approximately 191 ha/471 acres) will be returned, with the intention to finish the process by the end of March 2001 after the parachute drop training is relocated to Ie Jima Auxiliary Airfield and Sobe Communications Site is relocated.

Torii Station
First Battalion, First Special Forces Group, U.S. Army (Airborne)
Tenth Army Area Support Group
Communications site
Senaha Communication Station

In accordance with the SACO Final Report of December 2, 1996, Senaha Communication Station will be returned (approximately 61 ha/151 acres), with the intention to finish the process by the end of March 2001 after the antenna facilities and associated support facilities are relocated to Torii Communication Station. However, the microwave tower portion (approximately 0.1 ha/0.3 acres) will be retained.

Sobe Communication Site
U.S. Navy communications facility

In accordance with the SACO Final Report of December 2, 1996, Sobe Communications Site will be returned (approximately 53 ha/132 acres), with the intention to finish the process by the end of March 2001 after the antenna facilities and associated support facilities are relocated to Camp Hansen.

Makiminato Service Area
USMC logistics base
Third Force Service Support Group
In accordance with the SACO Final Report of December 2, 1996, land adjacent to Route 58 will be returned (approximately 3 ha/8 acres) in order to widen the Route, after the facilities that will be affected by the return are relocated within the remaining Makiminato Service Area.

Naha Military Port
U.S. Army Logistics Command facility
Embarkation point for combat-loading of III MEF equipment
The return of Naha military Port, agreed upon at the 15th Security Consultative Committee meeting more than twenty years ago, has been stymied by the lack of a suitable alternative on Okinawa.
In accordance with the SACO Final Report of December 2, 1996, the United States and Japan will jointly continue best efforts to accelerate the return of Naha Port (approximately 57 ha/140 acres) in connection with its relocation to the Urasoe Pier area (approximately 35 ha/87 acres).

Camp Schwab
Fourth Marine Regiment (Infantry)
Live firing and amphibious training exercises
The December 2, 1996 SACO Final Report proposed a sea-based facility that would replace Futenma Air Station in the waters off Camp Schwab.

Henoko Ordnance Depot
USMC ammunition storage
Adjacent to Camp Schwab

Camp Hansen
Fourth Marine Regiment (Infantry)
Artillery live fire exercises

Gimbaru Training Area
USMC training facility
Helicopter operations and amphibious training exercises
In accordance with the SACO Final Report of December 2, 1996, Gimbaru Training Area will be returned (approximately 60 ha/149 acres), with the intention to finish the process by the end of March 1998 after the helicopter landing zone is relocated to Kin Blue Beach Training Area, and the other facilities are relocated to Camp Hansen.

Kin Blue Beach
USMC training facility
Ship-to-shore movement training

Kin Red Beach
USMC training facility
Embarkation training
White Beach
Commander, Amphibious Group One (U.S. Navy)
Seventh Fleet Commander of Amphibious Ready Groups (ARGs) permanently stationed in Japan and deploying from the United States
Naval support facility and piers
Awase Communication Site
U.S. Navy communications facility
Northern Training Area

In accordance with the SACO Final Report of December 2, 1996, the major portion of the Northern Training Area will be returned (approximately 3,987 ha/9,852 acres), and the U.S. will release joint use of certain reservoirs (approximately 159 ha/393 acres) with the intention to finish the process by the end of March 2003 under the following conditions:

Provide land area (approximately 38 ha/93 acres) and water area (approximately 121 ha/298 acres) with the intention to finish the process by the end of March 1998 in order to ensure access from the remaining Northern Training Area to the ocean.

In accordance with the SACO Final Report of December 2, 1996, helicopter landing zones will be relocated from the areas to be returned to the remaining Northern Training Area.

Aha Training Area
USMC training facility
Temporary facility agreed under Article 2 paragraph 4(b) of the United States and Japan SOFA.
Surrounded by the Northern Training Area

In accordance with the SACO Final Report of December 2, 1996, the United States will release joint use of Aha Training Area (approximately 480 ha/1,185 acres) and release U.S. joint use of the water area (approximately 7,895/19,509 acres) with the intention to finish the process by the end of March 1998 after land and water access areas from the Northern Training Area to the ocean are provided.

Ie Jima Auxiliary Airfield
USMC training facility
AV-8 Harrier aircraft take-off and landing exercises, and parachute training
Okuma Rest Center
USAF recreation facility

The use of the bases is not unrestricted. Japan reserves the right to veto major American deployments into the country, operations from it, and major changes in U.S. equipment there. In an exchange of notes dated January 19, 1960, the day the Mutual Security Treaty was signed, Japan stipulated and the United States confirmed that

> concerning the implementation of Article VI [of the Mutual Security Treaty, i.e., operations not directly in the defense of Japan]: Major changes of the deployment into Japan of United States armed forces, major changes in their equipment, and the use of facilities and areas in Japan as bases for military combat operations to be undertaken from Japan other than those conducted under Article V of the said Treaty, shall be the subjects of prior consultation with the Government of Japan.[4]

The seven U.S. bases on the mainland (Yokota Air Base, Camp Zama, Yokosuka Naval Base, Sasebo Naval Base) and on Okinawa (Kadena Air Base, Futenma Marine Corps Air Station, White Beach) are also U.N. Command installations. Like strictly American facilities, these bases are supported by a U.N. Status of Forces Agreement (SOFA) with the government of Japan. It is significant that, unlike other U.S. bases in Japan, they can be used, without consultation with Japan, to support U.N. forces in Korea in the event of renewed hostilities there.[5] Troops from several countries of the original 1950–53 U.N. Command also have access to these facilities, and occasionally exercise that right. This exceptional legal status is based on the continued existence of the U.N. Command (Forward) in Korea, the future of which is often debated without reference to U.N. bases in Japan.

## Focus on Okinawa

On both Okinawa and in mainland Japan, without the overshadowing influence of the Cold War, base issues will increase in complexity and contentiousness. As mainland Japanese politics increasingly devolve to the local level, Diet members representing communities near bases find it more difficult to entreat mayors and governors to be patient or to cooperate for the sake of national security and bilateral relations. Decades of spectacular growth have both reduced the local economic benefits of the installations in relative terms and placed a higher premium on prime real estate taken up by U.S. military facilities.

Encroachment is a serious concern. Schools and houses have crowded in on facilities, especially air bases, denying them the buffer zones which, like fences, make for good neighbors. Young Americans, impoverished by the rise of the yen, often cannot afford to shop or eat off base, raising frustration levels and precluding the long-term advantages of friendly young American faces mixing with curious and hospitable Japanese. The generation of local elected officials who worked out practical solutions throughout Japan during the Cold War is passing from the scene.

Nowhere have base issues been more intensely debated than on Okinawa. Okinawa, the scene of the only ground combat on populated Japanese territory during World War II, was the focus of the biggest base issue of all—the reversion of the Ryukyus to Japanese sovereignty in 1972—and currently supports the densest concentration of U.S. forces in Japan.

Today, the situation on Okinawa is complicated by a number of factors, symptomatic of the complex relationship between Okinawa and the rest of Japan. The first is the minimal Okinawan cultural affinity with the rest of Japan, a land of ostensible homogeneity. Another is resentment over Japanese military excesses during the 1945 battle for Okinawa. Finally, there is a sense of continuing disproportional sacrifice, beginning with horrific civilian casualties during the war, and persisting because Okinawa supports a much higher fraction of U.S. forces than does the rest of Japan. (Almost 20 percent of the main island was taken up by U.S. military facilities before the process of reductions administered by SACO.)

The pressure on U.S. bases on Okinawa intensified with the election of Governor Masahide Ota, a political independent and university professor turned politician. His election marked the end of Liberal Democratic Party (LDP) control of the Okinawan Diet delegation, and it exemplifies the trend toward more populist pressures on U.S. bases throughout Japan. Although not anti-American, the governor is a dedicated pacifist, opposed equally to U.S. forces and their Self Defense Force counterparts. He has seized upon perceptions of grievance and long-term neglect by Tokyo of Japan's poorest prefecture to rally support for his program to reduce and eliminate U.S. bases on Okinawa. He has combined this campaign with demands for increased financial assistance for Okinawan development from the government of Japan. Ota's political influence gained a dramatic boost when a young Okinawan schoolgirl was raped by three American servicemen in September 1995.

Okinawans like Governor Ota have a profound and evenhanded aversion to both Japanese and American military forces. But beyond that lie three uniquely Okinawan ideological convictions: that the prefecture has been victimized by both the government of Japan and the U.S. military; that U.S. bases impede Okinawa's prospects for sharing in Japan's prosperity; and that the removal of U.S. bases is necessary for the prefecture's economic development.

The Okinawan ideological intent to close all U.S. bases has, since September 1995, struck a resonant chord throughout Japan, captured the attention of the Japanese media, and shaken the very foundations of the security relationship. In response, both nations pledged to make progress toward significant base consolidation on Okinawa. As a direct result, SACO was established in November 1995 to define a process by which the United States would be able to return Futenma Marine Corps Air Station (MCAS) to Japan in return for an alternative facility on Okinawa. By the time of the April 1996 Clinton-Hashimoto summit in Tokyo, the SACO had announced a provisional plan to relocate Futenma MCAS and return the land to its original owners. Although a number of other issues had been resolved and significant acreage returned to Japanese control as of the final SACO report in November 1996, the Futenma reversion process itself has bogged down over the Okinawa prefectural government's refusal to endorse a militarily viable relocation.

Instead of resolution and relaxed tensions, pressure continues on the Okinawan bases. Under Governor Ota, the prefectural government has proposed a plan to phase out the U.S. presence on Okinawa by 2015. Delegations from Okinawa and from Japanese political parties continued to visit Washington to consult on the subject and to press the issue in Congress, in the executive branch, and with the U.S. military. Governor Ota lost his reelection bid in November 1998, and the new LDP Government in Naha pursued a more flexible approach with Tokyo. Still, the pressure for action on the bases remains.

By March 1997, the holders of some 3,000 (of a total of 30,000) leases for land taken for use by U.S. facilities on Okinawa were refusing to renew them upon expiration in May. Only a hundred were actual Okinawan landowners; the rest were political activists from elsewhere in Japan, who had divided up original plots into "postage stamp" holdings of a few square meters each. In April 1997, the Diet approved Prime Minister Hashimoto's unilateral decision to force renewal of the leases. The situation had become consequential enough to force the central government to strengthen its rights of eminent domain. The continuing contretemps over leases has also seriously curtailed other important security discussions, such as the review of the Defense Guidelines (designed to redefine Japan's security contributions from simply granting permission for American actions to more active, albeit rear area, logistical and infrastructure support).

## What Is at Stake?

For the United States, American forces in Japan and on Okinawa are emblematic of the American determination to preserve the advantages and political leverage that come from keeping its military forces forward deployed. Basing U.S. forces in Japan keeps American defensive boundaries on the Asian littoral instead of in the Eastern Pacific. Strategically, the United States cannot afford to withdraw significant forces from Okinawa, for which no realistic and viable alternative exists. American influence and political and security policy in Asia depend on these forces remaining where they are. To agree to remove or reduce these forces would put American credibility at significant risk.

Claims that the utility—and thus the indispensability—of marine and air forces have lessened are not realistic. This applies especially to assertions that they could easily be withdrawn to Hawaii or the West Coast of the United States, to be flown back to the region in time of crisis. In addition to their combat potential, these forces are important place-holders. They are, in effect, indicators as well as determinants of the U.S. security stake in the region. Because of their forward location, they have an important deterrent influence on the delicate strategic and psychological balance in and around Japan.

Furthermore, it is quite clear that the other nations of the region want the United States to remain fully engaged, to preserve regional stability, to retain the balance of power, or to provide Tokyo with a nonmilitary option for Japanese security. Even Beijing, perhaps with the most to gain from an American reduction or withdrawal, is at least ambivalent about the U.S. presence, and more often than not has been quietly supportive.

As a practical matter, it would be almost impossible to relocate major U.S. units elsewhere. Not only are strategic locations unavailable and available locations misplaced, but the cost of a major move would be astronomical, and not borne lightly by either government.

Withdrawal of these forces would do more than complicate the local strategic situation, causing consternation throughout the region and necessitating recalculation of the American role. Their departure also would make much more problematic any subsequent political decision to reintroduce them for deterrence or crisis response in the region. Like aircraft carriers, which are easy to employ because they can move without political complications, forward-deployed forces of all kinds are relatively simple to use in a crisis, because they are already engaged in active defense.

Also unrealistic is the notion that if the marines were to withdraw eastward, marine and navy forces, which would then be separated by an ocean, could still be expected to operate effectively together. Emphasis on navy–marine reciprocity—maritime jointness—was strengthened significantly by the emergence of post–Cold War naval doctrine. The new maritime strategy places renewed priority on power projection "from the sea." The Okinawan bases are part of a scheme of coordinated navy–marine corps forward deployment; they are now more important to the Marine Corps than they were, not less so.

Furthermore, few civilians can appreciate the importance or extent of military contingency plans. Bases on Okinawa, which may seem underutilized on a normal day, in a crisis would overflow with troops, equipment, and materiel. Based on normal peacetime patterns, uninformed estimates of their operational utility, which fail to take account of real crisis requirements, produce woefully inadequate descriptions of the continued value of the bases and facilities in question.

## THE U.S. MARINES

These conclusions are particularly applicable to the marine garrison on Okinawa, which is currently under the most pressure. These marines are essential to the security of the United States. They are the anchor of the nation's security in East Asia—ready, mobile, powerful, self-sustaining, and flexible both politically and operationally. They are a credible force, and credibility deters aggression. Whether sea-based, air-transported, engaged in amphibious assault, or in garrison, they are emblematic of the American commitment to the defense of Japan, regional security, and Asian stability.

The Nye Initiative—the bilateral discussions in 1994–95 that reasserted the primacy of the alliance—underscored the commitment of the United States and the credibility of the U.S.–Japan alliance by arresting the perceptions of imminent troop reductions, which otherwise would have signaled withdrawal and disengagement. Failing to do so would have empowered Beijing and disillusioned the region. Likewise, future reductions in Japan-based marine forces would negate the bilateral progress in the U.S.–Japan security dialogue and the regional political and diplomatic successes of 1994–96 which underscored both the stability and the continuity of U.S. leadership.

Forward deployment in Japan amplifies the political and military impact of the marines. With an amphibious ready group based at Sasebo, they are only days away from crisis spots by sea; by air they are only hours away. Transporting the same force from Hawaii or the continental United States could take weeks by sea and days by air, especially if more than one contingency were under way.

Important, too, is the fact that forward deployed marines are the first line of defense. Their immediate use is implicit in their forward deployment. As a result they can respond without delay to either crisis or domestic political debate, projecting power, forcing entry, and enabling the flow of reinforcements. The early stages of the 1991 Persian Gulf crisis offered a powerful example of such strategic benefits: marines from Okinawa (as well as elsewhere) were quickly in place to deter Iraq from attacking into Saudi Arabia.

But perhaps most important, these forward deployed marines are *convincing*. The same marines today are preventing the renewal of the kind of strategic vacuum in the South China Sea that followed the U.S. withdrawal from the Philippines. The relative calm of the Senkaku Islands dispute—in contrast to the Spratlys in 1994—can be attributed to the presence of U.S. forces nearby.[6]

Only the marines are sufficiently self-sustaining and flexible enough to respond to demands of broad geographic and functional diversity without dependence upon established facilities and extensive logistical support ashore. However, that expeditionary capacity comes at a price. The marines depend on self-contained, organizational balance. Because marine formations organize, deploy, and operate as complete entities, redeploying even one element of the ground-air-combat support team away from Japan would impose significant operational and readiness penalties. Helicopters have to be close to the infantry because they train together to operate together, as must artillery units. This also makes redeployment within Japan difficult, because relatively large formations would have to shift location together.

Marines are also assigned a major wartime role, as theater ready reserve and crisis response assets. In that connection, the marine expeditionary force in the Pacific (III MEF) is crucial with respect to the Korean Peninsula. Its amphibious capabilities complicate North Korean planning and increase the effectiveness of the U.S. deterrent in Northeast Asia. On the other hand, reductions to III MEF or its relocation, let alone demobilization, would encourage recklessness in Pyongyang. No American president, in fact, is likely to propose such reductions while the potential for war on the Korean Peninsula is near present levels, or while the misreading of strategic American intentions might have such significant regional ramifications.

## JAPANESE INTERESTS

What is at stake for Japan? U.S. forces in Japan are critical to that nation's defense as well. Support, or lack thereof, of the Japanese government for the American bases has important ramifications for the security of Japan and for the bilateral relationship. Most broadly, Tokyo benefits from the global missions assigned to U.S. forces based in Japan. In fact, Japanese support is vital to their ability to operate as far away as, for instance, the Persian Gulf. This animates Japan's foreign policy, and tends to align U.S. policies and actions with Japanese interests. They reinforce each other, to Japan's benefit.

At the regional level, deterrence on the Korean Peninsula and stable relations with China are the two most important elements of Tokyo's security policy, and both are underscored by the U.S. military forces based in Japan. The expeditionary forces among them would also participate in evacuation and other humanitarian operations of importance to Japan. Defense Guideline initiatives are building on this basis for bilateral cooperation. If, on the other hand, Japan could not sustain sufficient public support to cope with peacetime basing requirements, it is unlikely that it would countenance the arrival of the massive reinforcements that would be necessary for a regional contingency—or the defense of the nation.

Finally, other Asian countries are gauging Japan's ability to support the alliance with the United States. They understand the potentially dramatic implications of Tokyo's failure to overcome domestic roadblocks. Ironically, they seem more willing to acknowledge the broad-ranging implications for both Japan and the region of a change in the status or location of marines on Okinawa than do the Japanese.

Policymakers in both countries, under siege on Okinawa base issues particularly, are being distracted from other important matters. If this condition endures much longer, it is likely to damage Japan's credibility as an alliance partner. On the other hand, an actual diminution of Japan's political commitment to U.S. bases would directly challenge the alliance, by undermining Tokyo's major contribution to it.

## Imaginative Compromise

These strategic parameters account for the long-standing and pragmatic U.S. policy of incremental base consolidation and land reversion. By that approach, the United States will continue to look for ways to return use of property to its original owners; strategic considerations, however, must come first. This constraint on the U.S. side has in practice meant limiting changes to "footprint, not forces." Given local circumstances, there is not nearly enough flexibility in this entirely appropriate but circumscribed policy to fulfill Okinawan expectations.

Present approaches alone will not overcome the obstacles to progress that exist on Okinawa and in Tokyo and Washington. Too many practical considerations stand in the way of continuing incremental land reversion. Furthermore, such conventional solutions can provide only minimal adjustments before they seriously reduce the strategic value of the bases. Nor will they satisfy Okinawan ideological or political demands. Consequently, a number of obstacles make an unconventional approach advisable.

First, Okinawan circumstances are not solely ideological. Practical local obstacles have forestalled real progress on important land and base issues for years. There is no consensus among Okinawans on the bases; since the employment of Okinawans on U.S. bases is not inconsequential, there is even a sizable, largely silent constituency in favor of the status quo. With their members' livelihoods at stake, the base employees' unions want the installations to remain, and they did not participate in major demonstrations against the United States in the fall of 1995.

Second, rents for base lands paid to Okinawan landowners are very significant to the recipients, especially when the land has little intrinsic value. Owners of otherwise worthless land depend upon these payments, sometimes exclusively, and they do not want the land returned. Even when the property does have value, there is seldom consensus on its future use among the hundreds of landowners of large tracts. These resist return as well, since rent received is better than the certain impasse that would follow reversion. The former Makiminato housing area is a case in point: U.S. buildings were razed and the land returned, but disagreement among Okinawan owners has forestalled development for more than a decade.

Third, there is a U.S. requirement that the return of functional facilities must be contingent upon provision of a suitable replacement by the government of Japan. This is the case, for instance, at Naha Military Port, for which no natural alternative exists on the island. Just north of Naha, in Urasoe, plans are under way for an artificial harbor, but there is little support for military relocation there.

These local but important factors strengthen the case for an unconventional approach. Indeed, the inherent contradiction between Okinawan practical motivations and the political and military realities, and the conflict between local ideology and regional strategy, can be resolved by imaginative compromise. The basis for such compromise is in the significant store of natural goodwill that endures on Okinawa. It is significant that the marines held a day of reflection there after the September 1995 rape incident, and that the October 1995 demonstrations against U.S. bases did not call for an end to the Security Treaty. More to the point, on two occasions Okinawan demonstrators prevented the burning of an American flag by protesters from the mainland.

There is room for compromise, given sufficient imagination and certain fundamentally positive political preconditions. First, the security relationship has to be kept healthy enough to withstand the inevitable strains of working out solutions. Second, the Japanese government must accept and subscribe to the fact that U.S. bases and troops must remain. Third, while the SACO produced acceptable short-term results and generated credibility for subsequent measures, its one-year term was not nearly long enough to provide real solutions; the process of resolution must be extended considerably. Fourth, Japan's central government will have to work out its presently ambivalent relationship with Okinawa, which only came under Japanese rule in 1879. Finally, there are no cheap solutions: the bill will include prodigious effort, time, and, most significantly, capital—most of which must come from the Japanese.

## Integration of the Bases

It is possible to sketch a new, unconventional approach to what Japan and the United States might undertake to advance their shared goals. In the long run, American bases can no longer remain the exclusive enclaves they have been. They must be made more generally relevant to the mainland Japanese, the Okinawans, and the government of Japan. These bases have to be seen locally less as the problem and more as the solution, with respect, for example, to development plans and economic expansion. As a general prescription for future base relations, this suggestion is not commonplace, but neither is it radical. There are examples of effective combined civil-military use of bases in both the United States and Japan; Hickam Air Force Base in Hawaii and Misawa Air Base in northern Japan are among them. Actually, Misawa is a tri-use base, shared by the Japanese Air Self-Defense Force (JASDF), the U.S. Navy and Air Force, and Japanese domestic airlines.

The concept of shared access is most applicable to airfields and port facilities, where runways and pier space can be shared. It is especially plausible in cases where large facilities, such as Naha Military Port, must be maintained for surge operations during periods of crisis or war but are underutilized the rest of the time. During normal operations in peacetime, their basic facilities should be made available for commercial operations. Civilian access would have to be structured carefully so that military planners and commanders could depend upon unfettered use of the facilities during intensified military operations. Nevertheless, there is no reason why Kadena Air Base, for instance, could not host a considerable number of civilian flights, or why Futenma could not have become a regional air cargo hub while remaining a U.S. Marine Corps air station. As a port facility (though not as an industrial park), Naha Military Port can be the focus for greatly expanded maritime traffic in and out of Okinawa. That concept is both a complement and a viable alternative to other Okinawan development schemes. It might be pursued before much more time and effort are invested in relocating the U.S. port facility at Naha to the new artificial harbor at Urasoe.

American bases in Japan also have become too exclusive in the strictly military sense. Interoperability between the U.S. military and the Japan Self-Defense Forces is often touted, but seldom practiced. U.S. forces and the SDF rarely operate next to one another, let alone together. In the past, when Japan was relearning how to organize and operate its military after World War II, SDF training in the United States was far more common, and the practice of assigning counterparts for American officers was widespread. The present segregation precludes the advantage of the SDF and U.S. forces getting to know one another, both professionally and socially. The marines, for whom there is no direct counterpart in the SDF, are especially isolated. The Ground Self-Defense Force is more likely to identify with the U.S. Army instead.

A policy of sharing facilities has advantages for both countries. A significant SDF permanent presence on U.S. installations would give Japan's uniformed military services, and the Japan Defense Agency (JDA) and the Ministry of Foreign Affairs as well, a sense of ownership of U.S. facilities that they otherwise see as expendable, both politically and operationally. The United States should in return expect routine reciprocal privileges for U.S. forces on SDF bases. This would enable much more effective planning for surge operations during periods of crisis or conflict. It is easy to imagine the potential for increased bilateral doctrinal cooperation, training opportunities, and commonality of maintenance, repair, and supply.

Crisis and wartime roles for bases will have to be explained more fully to the public, to the prefectural government, and to the government of Japan. Currently, for example, Okinawan assertions about the reduced utility of Futenma and Naha Port go unchallenged. Without a more effective public argument for the crucial role these and other similar facilities play during crisis and war, nothing will mitigate the growing consensus that they are expendable. It should be possible to make the public case without compromising war plans or other critical information.

U.S. facilities that can revert to SDF custody should be handed over without delay. This applies particularly to Okinawa's training areas. If the Japanese government is prepared to guarantee the preservation of these tracts and satisfactory access for training purposes to U.S. forces, there is no reason why they cannot be removed from the U.S. books, in addition to the significant acreage already returned in the SACO process.

Consolidation and reversion plans that make sense and are already recognized as acceptable need to be accelerated. The U.S. communications facility at Hansa is a good example of how delays in Japanese funding can hold up the relocation and reversion of U.S. facilities. Funding for the relocation of Hansa's antennas would quickly solve the issue of Yomitan Auxiliary Airfield, which otherwise cannot be released for development because of the potential for electro-magnetic interference (EMI) with U.S. military communications.

Marine artillery training could be relocated to Korea, as well as elsewhere in Japan. Korea is where the marines are most likely to fight, and the Seoul government can help to relieve pressure on Okinawa. Doing so would remind the Japanese government that although Japan's security relationship with the United States is an exclusive one, there are other allies in the region who are prepared to cooperate. Equally, air traffic control restrictions that impede the flow of civilian flights are a point of contention, but they can be revised. Peacetime military aircraft operating and training areas and airfield operating procedures could accommodate civilian aircraft much more readily than at present. If Japan Air Self-Defense Force restrictions at Naha Airport cause delays for civilian airliners there, then their operations must be made more flexible.

As for U.S. Air Force assets, some units at Kadena Air Base, such as reconnaissance aircraft, might be relocated fairly easily to other U.S. air bases in Japan; not all of these units are an integral part of the operations of the Eighteenth Wing. Also, the Special Forces battalion at Torii Station can be relocated to a U.S. Marine Corps base, or even elsewhere in Japan. It is very important, however, that the "First of the First" remain in theater, forward deployed and co-located with the C-130s of the USAF 353 Special Operations Group (353 SOG). As a package, both could be relocated to southern Honshu, in order to consolidate C-130 support at Iwakuni Air Base where other Okinawa-based C-130s are being moved from Futenma MCAS.

Some observers, Japanese and American, insist that the fewer marines on Okinawa the better. Modernization and technological advances may promote the trend toward fewer troops in any given unit, but fewer Americans does not necessarily equate to a better environment. Presently, many marine units and individual marines rotate to Okinawa only for short tours, generally six months to a year. Marines deploying for these short periods, without their families, feel they have little investment in good community relations, and their behavior is not the same. A better solution might be to make a larger fraction of marine unit assignments to Okinawa permanent. Individual marines would come to Okinawa for longer tours, two or three years, rotating as replacements to units continuously assigned to the island. Their families would accompany them.

Of course, this would mean a net increase in the total number of American "military" personnel (for this purpose, dependents count as marines). More family housing would be required, but quality of life would improve for Americans and Okinawans alike. The political and financial costs to Washington and Tokyo, including more realistic local housing and cost-of-living allowances for U.S. service members, would be more than offset by the benefits of stability, the influence of family socialization, improvement in troop morale and behavior, and benefits to community relations. The U.S. Marine Corps could keep the same number of marines forward deployed, with less disruption to the rest of the force structure. Local military command and management continuity on Okinawa would be improved, and previously rotating units would become available for other essential missions, such as crisis response and standing Joint Task Force duties.

Whatever the eventual number of U.S. forces on Okinawa, there must be a better screening process for U.S. service members assigned there. The standard overseas screening regimen is not sufficient to reduce the likelihood of off-duty misconduct. There is precedent for this in the way troops were screened for duty in Berlin. The more rigorous "Berlin Screen" recognized the unacceptable consequences of infractions there, and distinguished between troops eligible for duty in Germany in general, and those who could serve in Berlin.

Command attention is essential in this regard, and the marine commandant has decided to increase the seniority of the III MEF commander to lieutenant general (three-star) rank. This is an effective practical step, but should be complemented by the detailing of a marine general officer to concentrate exclusively on community relations. This might facilitate imaginative solutions to difficult problems, and thereby defuse long-standing animosities. This officer might start by implementing the very benign recommendations of the 1996 Shimada Commission chartered by Prime Minister Hashimoto, such as the replanting by U.S. forces of areas denuded by artillery fire. Another Shimada Commission proposal would permit the transiting of base facilities by students on their way to school. Even the Soviets allowed Americans such privileges in Berlin. The Shimada Commission's recommendations include:

- U.S. soldiers planting saplings in barren training areas;
- Enhancement of community relations;

- Traffic passage through American bases;
- Examination of the possibility of returning some restricted coastal waters;
- Use of on-base freshwater sources for local communities.

## Conclusion

There is pressure on U.S. bases throughout Japan, not just on Okinawa. Ideological pressure may not be as significant a factor to the north, but encroachment, noise, and a diminished public sense of military requirements are problems everywhere. While local economic development is not generally an issue elsewhere in Japan, integration of U.S. bases with the SDF and with local economies would give Japan a verifiable stake in their longevity and preserve them for the long term. On the Kanto Plain, for example, Yokota Air Base could be developed as a major civil air cargo hub for Tokyo while preserving its basic logistical functions and vital surge capacity for the U.S. Air Force. Civil access to Atsugi Air Base could help relieve some of the severe pressure directed at that combined SDF–U.S. forces base.

Mayor Richard Gordon of Olongapo City in the Philippines proved what could be done to develop military facilities after the United States departs. However, in retrospect, there was no reason that Subic Bay economic development could not have taken place with the United States as a full partner. American bases in Subic Bay could have been part of the solution, rather than the problem, for local industrial development. Mayor Gordon was always a strong supporter of the U.S. military presence in Subic Bay. Most likely he would have preferred to carry out his plans with the U.S. military, rather than after the bases closed. Innovative solutions might have made the difference in the Philippine Senate's final vote on the U.S. bases. We need to learn from our departure from the Philippines, so that what happened there does not occur in Japan.

Neither the United States nor Japan can afford to overlook any solution that would strengthen the U.S.–Japan security relationship. Base issues are matters that can never be perfectly resolved, but innovative approaches can overcome ideological barriers and remove practical obstacles. We must make the attempt to preserve the stabilizing U.S. presence that is vital to both nations' international interests.

## Notes

1. Japan's annual host nation support contributions to the United States currently amount to more than $5 billion, including the approximately $1 bil-

lion yearly average for the Facilities Improvement Program. This accounts for approximately 70 percent of the nonsalary costs for U.S. forces in Japan.

2. "The use of facilities and areas by the U.S. armed forces under the Unified Command of the United Nations established pursuant to the Security Council Resolution of July 7, 1950, and their status in Japan are governed by arrangements made pursuant to the Treaty of Mutual Cooperation and Security." Security Treaty Exchange of Notes, January 19, 1960.
3. Report on the Security Relationship Between the United States and Japan, March 1, 1995, Submitted in Compliance with Section 1325 of the FY 95 Defense Authorization Act, and the Special Action Committee on Okinawa (SACO) Final Report, December 2, 1996 (expanded and updated to show changes through September 1, 1998). Note: Minor facilities are not listed.
4. Exchange of notes between Nobusuke Kishi, Prime Minister of Japan, and Christian A. Herter, Secretary of State of the United States of America, January 19, 1960.
5. "U.S. Forces Command Briefing," February 22, 1996.
6. For a discussion of these South China Sea issues, see Henry J. Kenny, "The South China Sea: A Dangerous Ground," *Naval War College Review* (Summer 1996), esp. pp. 97–100.

# 7

# Can Eagles and Cranes Flock Together? U.S. and Japanese Approaches to Multilateral Security After the Cold War

ANNE M. DIXON

AFTER years of skepticism over the role of multilateral security regimes in East Asia, the United States and Japan embraced multilateralism in the April 1996 Joint Security Declaration (see Appendix 5). Now it is reasonable to ask whether these two states, with their different approaches to security and statecraft, can build a partnership that strengthens Asia's immature multilateral mechanisms or forms new ones. Can eagles and cranes flock together?[1]

The new focus on multilateral security mechanisms stems from shifting international norms and domestic pressures in both countries. "Rebalancing" the U.S.–Japan alliance has become a familiar shibboleth for lightening the U.S. load and giving more voice to Japan. However, it also means less hegemonic authority for the United States and greater responsibility and initiative from Japan. This side of the equation is a bitter pill for both countries to swallow; pursuit of multilateral initiatives and visible cooperation in peace operations may be the sugar coating.[2]

Multilateral mechanisms for dialogue reinforce stability in East Asia and integrate Chinese, American, and Japanese goals, while peacekeeping operations (PKOs) offer an opportunity for Japan to dispatch personnel to crises in a manner consistent with Article 9 of Japan's constitution. Once seen in Washington and Tokyo as Soviet ploys to weaken U.S. naval hegemony in the region or to drive a wedge into the

U.S.–Japan alliance, multilateral initiatives are now viewed by U.S. and Japanese policymakers as necessary complements to an enhanced bilateral security relationship in the post–Cold War era.

Do both countries have the same view of "multilateral security"? The vagueness inherent in familiar European ideas like collective security, in which all of the good guys rally against any bad guy who surfaces, and multilateralism, in which all parties work together to prevent or resolve conflicts that may threaten shared values or security, have broad appeal as palliatives for the stresses and dissonances in the unsettled security environment. But how can these ideas be made concrete in Asia? How can a bilateral relationship strengthen multilateral cooperation without one or the other weakening and losing momentum?[3]

This chapter delineates U.S. and Japanese approaches to multilateral security ranging from dialogue to collective mechanisms and PKOs, and considers the potential for movement of U.S. and Japanese multilateral security policy toward a more operational level of political and military activity. Discussion begins with a brief look at the new regional security environment and considers separately American and Japanese perspectives on multilateralism. Similar discussion of peace operations follows. The chapter closes with a summary of the nature of cooperation possible today and an assessment of obstacles to partnership, and offers concrete recommendations for improving effectiveness and cooperation in the area of peace operations.

## The New Security Environment

Calling the international environment "uncertain" helps paper over important differences and potential sources of tension between the partners. The question that cannot be answered easily, openly, or jointly by the United States and Japan is "who is the threat?" China? Russia? Korea? North Korea? A unified Korea? If Korea reunifies, will U.S. troops be asked to leave? If so, Japan would be very reluctant to be the only nation in the region hosting foreign troops. Without them, how would Japan provide for its security?

The United States and Japan find it easier to discuss these differences over regional uncertainties as little as possible. Submerging differences in both perception and policy seems necessary to assure a basis for new multilateral frameworks, but these issues have a way of irritating the relationship below the surface. The silence allows the United States to continue playing its domineering Cold War role, as it did in its response to the nuclear threat from North Korea and to the Chinese military exercises in 1996—sending a carrier through the Taiwan Strait without consulting Japan. At the same time, it allows Japan to avoid confronting the reality of its own military potential.

Nevertheless, these circumstances do not mean that new Asian multilateral fora will be irrelevant to the alliance or to regional security. They may in fact become a welcome force, releasing U.S. and Japanese partners from their Cold War hangovers and sometimes reactionary fears of a new Co-Prosperity Sphere, if only by encouraging the two countries to talk with one other and with regional neighbors about security issues. In an alliance that accepts and defines a role for multilateral fora, Japan and the United States could first work out agreeable approaches to issues on the bilateral level prior to multilateral dialogues. This may not be pure multilateralism, and some regional partners may not like what they might perceive as exclusivism and bullying by the great powers, but it would help make skeptics in both the United States and Japan more comfortable. If other regional actors believe this will help keep the United States active in Asia, objections may be more muted.

In early 1994, the American Congressional Research Service (CRS) released a report entitled "Regional Security Consultative Organizations in East Asia and Their Implications for the United States." The report identified the following roles for emerging multilateral consultative fora:

- Influence the United States to continue a strong level of involvement in the region;
- Add a collective layer of diplomatic contacts and constraints to the actions of the larger regional powers;
- Reassure countries of the region regarding the intentions and aims of their neighbors;
- Build, in the longer term, an institutional framework for the negotiation of disputes among member states.[4]

Although the goal in Asia is not to build a formal military alliance like NATO, there is certainly a desire to reproduce the political benefits of that alliance. The comparisons are hard to suppress. Perhaps in stating them the regional differences can be brought to the forefront. The old quip about NATO was that it was meant to "keep the Americans in, the Germans down, and the Russians out." The first goal is expressed in Asia now as in Europe then, but the validity of maintaining the military status quo is open to question. The other parts of the old alliance adage are less apt. The Americans and Europeans had no problem identifying the Soviets as the key threat or expressing skepticism about Germany.

Like NATO's approach to Germany, the goal of the Asian multilateral fora is to include countries seen as possible threats. The NATO approach, however, even if it is not openly stated, may not work in Asia, specifically not in China. In postwar Europe, Germany was eager for membership in Europe and NATO and formed close ties with the United States. This is not the case with China, which is a major source of concern in the region. In fact, regional perceptions of China are somewhere between those of Germany and the Soviet Union. "Containing" China will not work and is recognized as a dangerous approach. On the other hand, efforts to persuade the Chinese to participate actively in regional fora have not been successful.

Only time will tell if Asian multilateralism will play a role at all similar to the one it has played in Europe. Security cooperation will not be in the image of Europe; that much is certain. If it is the approach nonetheless chosen, it must be understood that multilateralism in Asia will be more decentralized and far more contentious than it was in Jean Monnet's and Robert Schuman's Europe.[5]

## Multilateralism: Japanese Coming Out Versus American Hunkering Down?

The initial appeal of multilateralism was opposite for the United States and Japan. In the wake of the Cold War, Americans looked forward to the much touted peace dividend. The world's policeman was eyeing retirement—or at least a less demanding beat. The United States immediately took the lead against Saddam Hussein, on the principle of protecting vital national interests. In the more difficult situation in the former Yugoslavia, however, a situation without clear links to national interest in the realist sense, American leaders waited for European solutions to European problems before asserting leadership via NATO.

For Japan on the other hand, with the end of the Cold War, it seemed time to make a formal debut on the international security stage. Calls for Japan to raise its profile began with tensions over economic power and status in the bilateral relationship. After a long period of catch-up, a few outspoken Japanese confidently looked longtime senior partner evenly in the eye. Deployment of a minesweeping group after the end of hostilities was seen as too little, too late. Many Japanese believed that the international community failed to appreciate Japan's contribution of $13 billion to the Gulf War effort. Japan's leaders and intellectuals responded by pushing for a permanent seat on the U.N. Security Council and by passing in a long-debated law providing for Self Defense

Force participation in peacekeeping operations. It was time for Japan to become a normal nation.

Despite the rhetoric, the post–Cold War era has not seen any significant change in the American roles as leader of the free world and senior partner in the U.S.–Japan alliance. Japan, for its part, has continued to follow the United States' lead, though more Japanese now find the U.S. direction less comfortable than in the past. *Gaiatsu*, or outside pressure, has become an ingrained dimension of the policymaking process.[6] However, old patterns of bilateral interaction covered over new pressures for rebalancing and led the leadership in both countries to explore multilateral approaches to security, sometimes in concert, but often leading to difficult experiences and lessons.

## THE UNITED STATES: ENGAGEMENT AND ENLARGEMENT

The Clinton administration initially embraced multilateralism and development of U.N. peace operations, perhaps partly out of a belief that this approach would satisfy both internationalists and less adamant isolationists. After all, multilateral approaches would theoretically remove some of the burden of being the world's policeman, at the same time allowing the United States to remain influential in international affairs.

Clinton's approach was lauded by many foreign observers, including the Japanese. One Japanese international relations scholar believed Clinton was turning America into a normal country. Shinichi Kitaoka wrote,

> In the past the United States constituted not just a single nation with independent national interests but something like a separate world. It was a country that refused to become a regular member of the international community . . . Thus far the United States has never had the experience of cooperating with the other countries on an equal footing.[7]

The day after Clinton's inauguration, then U.S. Ambassador to the United Nations Madeleine Albright voiced administration support for creating a standing U.N. force; increasing the role of the U.N. PKO in regional conflicts; and paying U.S. arrears to the United Nations. Presidential Decision Directive (PDD)-13 advocated an increase of American staff experienced in PKO issues at U.N. headquarters and allowed for the placement of U.S. troops under U.N. command in certain circumstances.

In the second half of 1993, however, policy reversals began. Some Japanese observers attribute the apparent suddenness of these changes to public and congressional reaction to the progress of U.N. efforts in Somalia and Bosnia, specifically the footage of Somalis dragging an American soldier's body.[8] In May 1994, Clinton announced PDD-25, which is almost a direct reversal of PDD-13. It specifies stringent criteria for U.S. military participation in humanitarian and peace operations, which are very close to a restatement of the Powell-Weinberger criteria for U.S. military participation in open conflict.[9] It also reduces U.S. financial support for PKOs and specifies that American troops will remain under national command.

That the United States tends to pursue multilateral options for peace operations on a case-by-case basis is made explicit in the 1995 *National Military Strategy,* under the leeway-giving subtitle, *A Strategy of Flexible and Selective Engagement.*[10] Although Americans are often critical of Japan's consensus-based political decision-making, U.S. officials often abdicate their leadership responsibilities when, in difficult circumstances, they plead "CNN effect" and blame a fickle public for their own lack of conviction.

What the Clinton administration's overall *Strategy of Engagement and Enlargement* offers is, in the words of Andrew Bacevich, a simple checklist, not a strategy.[11] Since the end of the Cold War, the principles of strategists like George Kennan[12] have not fit the world we inhabit. The United States has had no new doctrine since National Security Council (NSC) 68,[13] except perhaps the intervention criteria named above. Strategy has evolved as a by-product of events, whether in Somalia, Rwanda, or Bosnia, or in the American response to the threat of a nuclear North Korea. As Bacevich asserted, however, "a new strategy will not evolve as a by-product of crisis management."

The words used to define American security policy are themselves variously definable, their meaning neither easily inferred nor assiduously explained. As one China analyst has noted, "engagement lacks a clear definition. While the term containment suggests a relatively specific list of policy options, ranging from economic embargoes to military confrontation, the policy choices suggested by engagement are not immediately obvious—beyond simple interaction."[14]

And enlargement? Expanded engagement is a term that in theory seems beneficent, but in reality is rather groping; it is to include the "less popular" countries—the poor ones, or the bullies. Perhaps rightly for the moment, the United States does not see itself as a "normal" country, an equal member of a diffuse international community, but rather as the leader of an elite club. U.S. leaders are betting that others want to join its "free (market/democracy) world club," and that control over membership is a source of influence. In today's Northeast Asia, that may be a bigger gamble than many might suspect, especially with respect to China.

Another aspect of the U.S. Cold War hangover is a strategic focus that remains stubbornly close to the old central front: NATO expansion and the Partnership for Peace. This is in no small part because the same people who managed U.S. foreign policy during the Cold War are still in charge today. Despite nods to trade statistics, many at senior levels still feel closer to Europe, and even to the former Soviet Union, than they do to Asia. Europe is their crucible, and they are often tempted to prescribe European solutions to Asian problems.[15]

The true "Asia hands" still see the United States as the senior partner in the bilateral relationship with Japan. They also see the presence of U.S. troops as the linchpin of the security aspect of the alliance. But does the current American presence support the alliance, or is the alliance used to justify a level of American presence that is neither sustainable domestically in Japan over the medium term,[16] nor strictly necessary for the defense of Japan and of shared Japanese and American interests in the region? What are those shared interests today? If this part of the alliance is off balance, how will it affect new multilateral security initiatives? These issues require serious consideration by the two countries' political leaderships. Furthermore, at least initially, the implications of the discussions for the overall size and structure of the U.S. military should be put aside.

The 1995 *United States Security Strategy for the East Asia–Pacific Region* includes a section on "The Desirability of Exploring New Multilateral Security Initiatives." It quotes President Clinton as saying, "Some in the United States have been reluctant to enter into regional security dialogues in Asia, but I see this as a way to *supplement our alliances and forward military presence, not supplant them*" (emphasis added).[17] The strategy confirms U.S. support for Asia-Pacific Economic Cooperation (APEC), but explicitly identifies the ASEAN Regional Forum (ARF), formed in 1993 and first convened in July 1994, as America's chosen candidate for "Asia's first broadly based consultative body concerned with security issues." The strategy outlines the ARF's roles as follows:

- Conveying governments' intentions and easing tensions;
- Constraining arms races;
- Enhancing preventive diplomacy and developing confidence-building measures;
- Discussing "modest defense transparency measures," which might include limited exchanges of defense data, the publication of

defense white papers, and submission of information to the U.N. arms register;

- Promoting cooperation in disaster relief and peacekeeping.

This basic approach was reaffirmed in the 1998 *East Asian Strategic Report*. Thus the American focus is on traditional security-based multilateralism that arose from European concepts of common security during the superpower confrontation. Its central purpose is the avoidance of war, stressing measures leading toward disarmament. This multilateralism is not based on explicit or treaty-based security alliances; an attack against one is considered an attack against all. The focus differs from that of Japan, a country still debating whether the constitution prohibits it from the rights of collective security articulated in Article 51 of the U.N. Charter. As explained below, Japanese concepts of regional security have been—and have had to be—broader, with a substantial economic component.

While the United States tends to separate economic and security policies more than Japan, whose concept of comprehensive security is discussed briefly below, what Canadian analysts have termed *cooperative security* seems to appeal to both. This concept is similar to common security, but it is broader, recognizing the importance of unofficial interaction and thus allowing for slower and uneven development of multilateral institutions. It is based on reassurance rather than deterrence.

Canadian scholar David Dewitt asserts, however, that key Americans misunderstand this concept. In his view, this is confirmation of "how difficult it is to transcend both academic tradition and political security culture." Dewitt cites the 1992 work, *A New Concept of Cooperative Security*, by William Perry, Ashton Carter, and John Steinbruner for the Brookings Institution, which focuses on coping with military-security problems, such as horizontal proliferation. He concludes that "their employment of the term 'cooperative security' with its focus on military threats does not embrace either the content or the intent of the use of this term."[18]

The issues addressed in the American strategy are clearly of great importance to regional security, but they are too sensitive to be dealt with in the emerging multilateral fora in Asia. The nations of the region are only beginning to publish and share defense white papers. They do not yet have the level of trust or the sense of shared interests and interdependence upon which a sense of common security is built. If U.S. leaders want to play a constructive role in the evolution of multilateralism in East Asia, they must ask themselves what else they can do to contribute to that foundation.

## JAPAN: TO BE OR NOT TO BE?

Broad concepts of security have been articulated by Japanese leaders since the late 1970s. The preventive, economic, and diplomatic dimensions of *comprehensive security* find fairly easy resonance with many Japanese elites. The 1991 *Diplomatic Blue Book* describes a comprehensive national security as a policy that

> secure[s] our national survival or protect[s] our social order from various kinds of external threats which will or may have serious effects on the foundations of our nation's existence, by preventing the arising of such threats, or by properly coping with them in the case of their emergence, through the combination of diplomacy, national defense, economic and other policy measures.[19]

Military security issues, however, have not captured the attention of the Japanese public as a whole; young people in particular seem unconcerned. An October 1995 *Yomiuri* poll showed that less than half of Japanese in their twenties are interested in defense.[20] This is at a time during which Japan's leaders are considering important changes in the role of the Self-Defense Force (SDF): changes that, if confronted fully, would require a revision of Japan's constitution.[21] The *Yomiuri* poll also showed that support for the Security Treaty has waned from a peak of 75.5 percent in 1988 to 61.3 percent in 1995. It is interesting to note that, while support has fallen most dramatically among Liberal Democratic Party (LDP) partisans, support among followers of the Social Democratic Party of Japan (SDPJ) rose significantly in the early 1980s from 49.8 percent in 1981, remaining steady at about 68 percent since the mid-1980s. How does this help contribute to a better understanding of Japanese attitudes toward multilateralism?

The word "multilateralism" entered the Japanese lexicon decades ago, but was punctuated first in 1991 in a speech by Japan's foreign minister and then by President Bill Clinton when he met with the first post-1955 system prime minister, Morihiro Hosokawa. Since then, multilateralism in Japan has evolved in a number of directions:

- It has become a "fashion" and a form of rhetoric to assert Japan's participation in regional and global affairs.
- It is an "excuse" for governing elites, especially the Ministry of Foreign Affairs (MOFA), to push for new roles for the SDF in peace operations.
- Some are concerned that it may serve as a "cover" as Japan seeks a more autonomous security role.[22]

These different perceptions underscore the fact that there is no single vision of "multilateralism" in Japan any more than there is in the United States. The official view, expressed in the Higuchi Commission report and the new 1995 National Defense Program Outline (NDPO) (see Appendix 6a) is that multilateral initiatives serve to complement the bilateral alliance. The document explicitly links Japan's participation in multilateral activities to the alliance.[23] Nonetheless, some Japanese observers warn that at the extreme end of the spectrum there are those who see multilateralism as a step toward supplanting the alliance.[24]

It is important to note that this is not a militaristic response. The new NDPO reaffirms Japan's reliance on the U.S. nuclear deterrent. It also limits Japanese military responses to crises "in the areas surrounding Japan, which will have an important influence on national peace and security [and to] timely and adequate response in accordance with the constitution and relevant laws and regulations."[25] Some "civilian internationalists"—and the pacifist SDPJ—who are firmly opposed to altering the constitution in order to embrace collective security, may see multilateralism pursued via economic interactions and official development assistance (ODA)[26] as a means of distancing Japan from the United States in the region. But it is more likely, given the steady SDPJ support for the security treaty noted above, as well as SDPJ support for limited Japanese participation in PKOs, that they see a division of labor between the security treaty and the bilateral U.S.–Japan alliance, which provide for the defense of Japan proper, and multilateralism meant to increase overall regional security and prosperity and prevent conflict.

In his 1995 work, *Japan: Domestic Change and Foreign Policy,* Mike Mochizuki[27] outlines the debate among elites and intellectuals between concepts of civilian internationalism and great power internationalism, accompanied by the rise of a new Asianism.

Civilian internationalists, such as the first post–1955 system Prime Ministers Morihiro Hosokawa and Masayoshi Takemura, see Japan's international contribution as mainly nonmilitary: Japan would be a "global civilian power." The agenda of the civilian internationalists, who find greater support among the Japanese people as a whole than among the great power internationalists, includes:

- A defensive-only military doctrine and slower increases in defense spending;
- Active support for regional and global arms control;
- Full acknowledgment of Japan's imperialist past and support for human rights and democratization in the region;

- Pursuit of regional economic integration as a means to build regional trust;
- Nonmilitary contributions to international security, including ODA, humanitarian relief, and noncombat roles in PKOs; less focus on economic issues and more support for environmental protection;
- Support for multilateral institutions, such as the United Nations—but without pressing for permanent Security Council membership.

The great power internationalists include former Prime Minister Yasuhiro Nakasone, New Frontier Party visionary Ichiro Ozawa, assertive pragmatist Hisahiko Okazaki, and prominent intellectuals like Seizaburo Sato and Masashi Nishihara. Their goal is for Japan to "assume military responsibilities commensurate with its economic power." Their agenda is a good deal more ambitious, and calls for more cooperation with the United States on military-security issues:

- Expansion of host-nation support both financially and substantively, including support for maintaining U.S. forces in the Pacific beyond Japan;
- Cooperation with the United States in military operations throughout the Asia-Pacific region, and reinterpretation or outright revision of the Security Treaty to provide for a broader Japanese role in regional security and collective self-defense;
- Promotion of defense technological cooperation with the United States, including in the area of theater missile defense (TMD);
- Legislation allowing the SDF to rescue Japanese citizens overseas;
- Active participation in U.N. peacekeeping operations, including combat; eventual participation in peace enforcement; and a permanent U.N. Security Council seat.

Mochizuki also noted three variants of a "New Asianism":

- *Integrationism* calls for better integration between Japan's policy toward Asia and its U.S. policy, mainly by helping the U.S. economic presence in Asia; supporting human rights and democratization; and contributing more for U.S. force presence throughout the region.
- *Asian restoration* sees Japan, already integrated into the industrial West, as arguing for the validity of an "East Asian model of development" based on state cooperation with business. Restorationists, though committed to free markets and democracy, see a need for the West to learn from Asia.

- *Exclusivism,* at its most extreme, sees and is not alarmed by an inevitable parting of the ways between the United States and Japan: the Japan that is not apologetic for its atrocities against its neighbors in World War II. Fortunately, as Mochizuki concludes, exclusivism is not a serious part of the Asianization debate.[28]

How are these visions manifested in official policy? The 1995 revised NDPO (see Appendix 6b) supports Japanese participation in the development of regional security fora, but offers no explicit support for any of them. There is somewhat more attention given to the United Nations, where, with the prominent roles played by Special Representative Yasushi Akashi and the U.N. High Commissioner for Refugees, Japan has played an important nonmilitary role in efforts to resolve current conflicts. Also, public support for permanent Security Council membership rose to slightly above 50 percent following participation in the United Nations Transition Authority in Cambodia, which was seen as a great success.[29]

Beyond articulated policy, Japan has increasingly reached out to other partners, including Australia, the United Kingdom, and the Nordic countries for PKO training, and both bilaterally and multilaterally with eleven European Union countries at the March 1996 Asia Europe Meeting (ASEM). ASEM provoked unease in the United States because the Asian group was limited to the proposed members of the East Asian Economic Caucus (EAEC). Although the focus was mainly on trade and avoidance of either European or Asian bloc-ism, politics and security issues, particularly concern regarding East Asia's overdependence on the United States for its stability, also received much attention.[30] Japan clearly does not want to end its close bilateral relationship with the United States, but it does want opportunities to develop good ties with other nations.

## Regional Multilateral Dialogue: Key Institutions and Initiatives in East Asia

### APEC: ECONOMICS FIRST?

So the question, "whose multilateralism?" cannot be separated from the question of whether Japan should emphasize support for multilateralism in the security realm or continue to develop its international credentials primarily via economic dialogues and interactions. Japan has supported regional economic dialogues; this is well understood and accepted by the Japanese public. The Asia-Pacific Economic Cooperation (APEC)[31] has been the key forum supported by the Japanese.

It is also a forum salvaged from the wreckage of the Cold War. Yoichi Funabashi, former Washington bureau chief of the *Asahi Shimbun*, observes that

> APEC came into being almost simultaneously with the fall of the Berlin Wall. Like the Washington Conference of disarmament after World War I and the Bandung Conference after World War II, this post–Cold War APEC summit reflects a strong urge for and groping toward a new world order. Can the old order, with its emphasis on the Asian pillars, be the foundation for a "new order" of different size and shape?[32]

Funabashi further notes that the old language is being rejected.

> [T]he APEC summit was not an attempt to create a balance of power among major powers nor an eruption of ethnic or ideological passions. Rather it should be seen as the occasion for launching a new philosophy and new relationships that can serve multilaterally and pragmatically—based on the principle of economic interdependence—to achieve peace and prosperity for diverse nations and cultures.[33]

Those words betray American uncertainty about how the new order is to be organized.

Americans, frustrated that APEC appears to be no more than a "talking club,"[34] should remember the long post–World War II transition in Europe; however, the development of multilateralism in Asia should not be expected to mirror postwar Europe. What we know today as the European Union, with all of its political, economic, and security ambitions and fora, began as the small and very limited European Coal and Steel Community (ECSC) in 1950, and it was not until the end of 1960 that the Organization for European Economic Cooperation (OEEC) became today's Organization for Economic Cooperation and Development (OECD).

It will take time for Asian multilateral organizations to take shape, and the security dimension of these organizations is likely to be the slowest and most difficult to develop. It is already clear, however, that APEC is taking on its own life throughout Asia. There are various APEC fora; capitals throughout the region have made extending APEC a priority; and the possibility of an APEC university is being floated.

Eagerness to build institutions with defined roles may lead Americans to overlook the more diffuse stage of cultural development—a necessary precursor to the formation of robust institutions. APEC is developing its own culture, and as its fora and familiarity expand, it is also helping to build trust among its members, something that is fundamental to decreasing regional tensions, though not necessarily yielding immediate concrete results on specific issues.[35] One speaker at the December 1995 conference on which this book is based reminded the group that for a time, the regional attitude toward the U.S.–Japan alliance was "trust but verify." What might that mean for the future of APEC, particularly with regard to security issues?

At the November 1993 APEC summit hosted by President Clinton, the formal agenda was limited to economic issues. However, heads of government met individually to discuss political and security issues. This is a format similar to that of G-7 meetings. Malaysia and China are opposed to such arrangements, however, and other ASEAN members expressed reservations as well.[36] Malaysia's leader, Mohammed Mahathir, has pushed Japan to favor his proposal for a more exclusively Asian organization, the East Asian Economic Caucus, which would exclude not only the United States, but also Australia and New Zealand.

Although Mahathir has put significant pressure on Japan to support the EAEC, Japan's hosting of the APEC summit in Osaka in the fall of 1995 was significant. Furthermore, President Clinton did not attend.[37] His attendance, though not crucial, would have been important for two concrete reasons. First, the meeting was to be the venue for the signing of a declaration reaffirming security ties between the United States and Japan. Second, it would have been a valuable opportunity for the United States to push for faster and stricter trade liberalization in the region.[38] In retrospect, while his absence meant a delay on the security declaration, it was perhaps for the better that Clinton did not have the opportunity to push the trade issue in a multilateral setting.

## THE ASEAN REGIONAL FORUM (ARF): GREAT EXPECTATIONS

The seeds of the security-focused ARF were planted in 1991, when then Foreign Minister Nakayama proposed the development of regional confidence-building measures at the ASEAN Post-Ministerial Conference (PMC). It took two years for ASEAN to embrace the idea,[39] and although both the United States and Japan recognize the organization's limitations, it is the best option for a security-oriented regional organization at present, although both countries' official defense documents do include general references to forming new initiatives focused particularly on Northeast Asia.[40]

Many members of the ARF had previously opposed the idea of an official-level Asia-wide organization modeled on the Organization for Security and Cooperation in Europe (OSCE), to be called the Conference on Security and Cooperation in the Asia Pacific (CSCAP) because it would be too unwieldy given the requirement of unanimous decision-making; because Asia was far more diverse than Europe; and because there was fear that the larger countries would dominate the program, despite the unanimity requirements. Nevertheless, the ARF has taken on many OSCE-like roles; CSCAP, now focusing on unofficial (track II) discussions, supports the ARF through working groups formed to address issues identified in ARF communiqués. ARF agenda items include support for an Asian arms registry, military transparency, and entertainment of other proposals for regional confidence-and-security-building measures (CSBMs).

### TRACK II AND CSCAP

The CSCAP has come to link regional think tanks, research institutes, and nongovernmental organizations (NGOs), all of which study security issues. It is like an umbrella for many track II dialogue groups (e.g., the sea-lanes of communication [SLOC] Steering Committee), and helps to bring together security specialists from academe and both current and former defense officials in unofficial settings where they are able to discuss politically sensitive issues freely.

Track II fora in Asia may for a time be more dynamic and important than the cautious and cumbersome official meetings of APEC and ARF. American scholars and security specialists should actively participate in these fora, but should not habitually seek to set the agenda. Listening to and understanding the debate, while providing experience-based insights into issues of discussion among the other participants, is perhaps more important now than is playing a leadership role.

## U.N. Peacekeeping and Collective Security

Whereas some Japanese officials agree that the U.N. can provide legitimacy, or "cover," for coercive action taken to protect clearly national interests, most Japanese are not comfortable with this view.[41] As Edward Luck has noted, "Article I of the Treaty of Mutual Cooperation and Security Between Japan and the United States of America . . . refers to strengthening the United Nations as one of its primary purposes, while through repeated references it makes clear that its provisions are firmly rooted in the framework of the U.N. Charter."[42]

Masashi Nishihara, however, notes that the United States and Japanese governments take notably different approaches to U.N. peacekeeping activities.

> Both the Japanese and the U.S. governments want to set limits on their involvement in U.N. peace efforts . . . While Japan wants to put legal limits on participation, the United States seeks to place practical limits in terms of cost and benefit. Japan is confined to non-military (civilian) and limited (self-restrained) peacekeeping, whereas the limits imposed by the United States will apply to all peacekeeping. Under these circumstances . . . restrained Japanese peacekeepers can hardly work together. . . . [T]his is exemplified by the situation in Bosnia . . . where Nordic, French, and British troops are deployed on the ground as peacekeepers while the U.S. government urges the United Nations and NATO to take tough punitive air strikes against the Bosnian Serbs. Such action is likely to endanger Nordic peacekeepers. The Japanese troops would not be placed in that kind of situation.[43]

Even more fundamentally than their differences over the U.N. role, the United States and Japan have very different approaches to and capabilities for peace operations. Furthermore, both now have rather strict criteria for their participation, PDD-25 in the United States and the International Peace Cooperation Law in Japan.

## U.S. PEACEKEEPING: THE TOURNIQUET APPROACH

The United States has participated in a range of what it now calls "complex humanitarian emergencies." These often intra-state conflicts were for a time seen as the new mission for the post–Cold War era. This trend began with President Bush's kinder, gentler America and the New World Order. But pursuit of national interests and a very strong strain of unilateralism still persist at both the elite and popular levels. Realists in the United States have long seen the United Nations as an American creature, and have advocated recourse to the Security Council as a means of securing political cover for national interest motivated action.

At the operational level, the U.S. military has little experience in the blue helmet world of traditional peacekeeping. Most military commanders, with the exception of a few like U.S. Marine Corps General Anthony Zinni, Joint Task Force commander in the Somalia withdrawal, *Operation United Shield,* define their role as strictly limited and traditional. In the words of one general, "we clear the area, stop the bleeding, apply a tourniquet, and leave."

In fact, it has been almost as difficult for political authorities in the United States to convince the military to consider "nontraditional" roles in peace operations as it has been in Japan. Americans worry about readiness and training degradation, and diversion of capabilities away from the key "Two Major Regional Contingencies" strategy focused on potential conflict in Korea and the Middle East. Under U.S. law,[44] the military is forbidden to assume policing and law enforcement roles within the United States. These roles are often very important in traditional peacekeeping, but many in the military wonder why American forces should train for and carry out those roles outside the United States.

Public opinion and casualties are also key to the debate. Many analysts have already said that Somalia is the newest memory contributing to "the last war syndrome." When the United States criticizes Japan for its unwillingness to share in the risk of peace operations, the United States itself risks hypocrisy. The United States can say that it is ready to accept losses as a consequence of national-interest-based "real war," but launching silver bullets in techno-war is far safer than being caught in the streets of Mogadishu. The Rangers who lost their lives there were real heroes—as was Atsuhito Nakata, the Japanese U.N. volunteer who was killed in Cambodia.[45] Yet the reaction to his death on the first Japanese foray into U.N. peace operations was nothing like the fevered U.S. response to Scott O'Grady's ordeal in Bosnia.

## JAPANESE PEACEKEEPING: BUILDING ROADS AND TRUST

A poll conducted by the *Asahi Shimbun* on December 9, 1995, showed that 73 percent of Japanese support Japan's SDF participation in peacekeeping operations. However, a good deal of this support is based on the assumption that SDF participation is demanded by the United States and Europe.[46]

The International Peace Cooperation Law was enacted by the Diet in June 1992 after long debate.[47] The law provides for the following missions:

*U.N. Peacekeeping Operations*

1. Monitoring the observance of cessation of armed conflict, withdrawal, or demobilization of armed forces
2. Stationing and patrolling in buffer zones
3. Inspection or identification of the carrying of weapons in or out of the conflict zone
4. Collection, storage, or disposal of abandoned weapons
5. Assistance in designation of cease-fire lines and other boundaries by the parties to armed conflicts
6. Assistance for the exchange of prisoners of war

7. Medical care (including sanitation)
8. Transportation, communication, and construction
9. Supervision or management of fair execution of elections
10. Advice or guidance for and supervision of police administration
11. Advice or guidance in administrative matters not covered by (10)

*Humanitarian Relief Operations*

12. Search or rescue of affected people or assistance with repatriation
13. Distribution of food, clothing, medical supplies, other daily necessities and medical care
14. Installation of facilities or equipment to accommodate affected people
15. Measures for the repair or maintenance of facilities or equipment necessary for the daily lives of affected people
16. Restoration and other measures for facilities and the natural environment damaged in the conflict.[48]

Many of the critical peacekeeping functions (1)–(6) were frozen by the Diet when it passed the bill. Although they were to be reviewed in 1995, the review was delayed. This means that Japanese troops cannot perform such critical peacekeeping functions as disarming the local population or patrolling; they cannot participate in any truly military aspect of peacekeeping. In what are now often called HA/POs (humanitarian assistance/peace operations) or complex humanitarian emergencies, Japan can only assist with the HA portion. This strictly limited mission profile—sending in medical officers or engineers—is one of the issues behind the charge that Japan is not willing to share risks in addition to costs. If and when the freeze is lifted, however, it is conceivable that Japanese troops could be trained by experienced international policing experts to help play a role in police administration, a function that cannot easily be fulfilled by the American military.

Japan's Five Principles for PKO, rather like a Japanese version of the Powell-Weinberger criteria, make clear that Chapter VI peacekeeping is the only form of peace operations to which Japan will be able to contribute—barring a change in the law. The Five Principles are as follows:

1. Agreement on a cease-fire shall have been reached among the parties in the conflict.

2. The parties in the conflict, including the territorial state(s), shall have given their consent to deployment of the peacekeeping force and to Japan's participation in the Force.
3. The peacekeeping force shall strictly maintain impartiality.
4. Should any of the above guideline requirements cease to be satisfied, the government of Japan may withdraw its contingent.
5. Use of weapons shall be limited to the minimum required to protect the lives and persons of the Japanese mission members.

Even if Japan were to lift the freeze on PKO missions, the gulf between the U.S. perspective on operations other than war and the Japanese point of view would still be large. U.S. leaders considered applying the Powell-Weinberger doctrine of overwhelming force in Bosnia, and American national policy identified the Serbs as the aggressors. These clear departures from the principles of impartiality and neutrality would be rejected by Japan. The Japanese vision of PKO is closer to that of Canada or the Scandinavian countries. Realistically, it is hard to imagine that Japan can or should draw mainly from the U.S. experience in peace operations.

Even in the present legal environment, Japanese political officials are nonetheless committed to forming a "habit of participation" in peace operations, at least in part because of their view that participation is required to further Japan's case for a permanent seat on the U.N. Security Council.[49] They have set a goal of continuous SDF participation in peace operations. They are already thinking about where to send troops after the Golan Heights deployment. While the downside of this approach is that it seems to push PKO for PKO's sake, an early decision may be very good for the troops, since they are not allowed to train for PKO until a decision to participate has been reached. This is because PKOs are not named as a key mission in the NDPO. The Japanese sent to Zaire, for example, received only four to six weeks of training.[50]

## Prospects for Bilateral Cooperation in PKOs

This section discusses some PKO issues confronting Japan and the United States and suggests ways in which American experience may assist Japan, ways that Japan may or must adapt, and ways that the United States may or must adapt.

## LOGISTICS NEEDS: AIRLIFT

The SDF has most recently dealt with its evident need for long-distance transport aircraft to send its troops to distant PKOs by using Japanese commercial charter flights for its participation in United Nations Disengagement Observer Force (UNDOF) Syrian Golan Heights.[51] After a failed deal to purchase American C-5s, the Japanese remain interested in a purchase of American military aircraft, possibly C-17s. If American leaders do indeed support an increased international role for Japan in multinational PKOs, they must put aside their concerns regarding Japanese power projection capabilities (Japan already has acquired capable *Aegis* technology for four new destroyers) and supply the aircraft.

William Durch has suggested a possible means of assuaging Americans, the Japanese public, and other regional countries' concerns about the power projection capability of the transport aircraft.

> Were Japan to acquire long-range airlift capability, it would be able to complement U.S. airlift capabilities [and] it could function on an interoperable basis with the United States. Concerns about the appearance of a prohibited military power projection capability might be reduced by permanently detailing these aircraft to a standing International Peace Cooperation Corps headquarters; by pre-designating them for U.N. callup; by making them available secondarily for domestic and regional disaster relief operations; and by relying on American in-flight refueling capacity for long-range deployments.[52]

## FAMILY SUPPORT

Families of Japan's SDF personnel sent overseas need support and advice. Unlike American families, who know they must face—and know something about how to face—the separation, anxiety, and difficulty of long and distant deployments, most Japanese families of SDF officers have no reason to expect this kind of family stress. The United States could offer the SDF access to its studies on family support issues. Promoting supportive relationships through family partnering programs between SDF families and American families stationed in Japan may be an additional gesture of goodwill.

## RULES OF ENGAGEMENT

The Office of the Secretary of Defense has opened a dialogue on rules of engagement (ROE) at Japan's request. Japanese and American officers have participated together in conferences that discuss ROE. However, no mere discussion will solve the problems faced by Japanese troops lost in the jungle of conflict with no ROE to guide how they react as a group to difficult and life-threatening situations. Avoiding the ROE issue may seem initially to be the easiest path for Diet members and Tokyo bureaucrats who do not want to confront constitutional or PKO law.[53] However, issues regarding use of weapons by units rather than individuals acting in self-defense, confusion, and death—made public in both Japanese and international media—could bring disaster to attempts to increase Japan's participation in PKOs. The United States can provide history, options, advice, and training. No number of command post exercises, however, will solve the problems for troops sent overseas without approved and understood ROE. Conferences and gaming could be done in Japan, perhaps at the National Institute for Defense Studies or the U.N. University, and include Diet members and other decision-makers who may not be familiar with ROE issues, but who have a role in making the decision to send Japanese troops on overseas deployments.

## LANGUAGE BARRIERS

The U.S. military plans to expand the number of foreign area officers (FAOs) in its ranks, people well trained in foreign languages and cultures. Until now, soldiers have "ended up" as FAOs; it is a pox on a military career. The prestige of the position and the potential for advancement must be raised if the military is serious about bringing its best into the FAO ranks. In some instances, "language barriers" can be a convenient excuse: faced with unpleasant situations or unpalatable compromises, either party can "not understand." The United States needs to increase understanding in the relationships among soldiers both at home and in the field so that this becomes less likely.

## INTELLIGENCE/INFORMATION SHARING

There is a great need in the SDF for well-trained regional analysts. However, since the role of the SDF is essentially limited to the protection of Japan, this cadre of officers has not been developed. Cooperative International Military Education and Training (IMET) programs could help to address this need over the short term, but the problem will not go away until the SDF explicitly avows a role for its members beyond Japanese boundaries. On the operational level, U.S.–Japan cooperation in intelligence-sharing works well on a service-to-service level, but the intelligence-sharing from the Defense Intelligence Agency to U.S. Forces Japan (USFJ) and then to the Japanese intelligence organizations needs improvement. This should be an agenda item for future staff talks at the level of the Department of Defense. On the multilateral level, the possibility of creating a regional "information clearing house" has been discussed by Japan and Australia; the Unites States should lend both political and technological support and assistance to any initiatives that result.

## UNITED NATIONS PEACEKEEPING OPERATIONS

Japanese leaders have focused their PKO activities on the United Nations for a variety of reasons, some of them discussed above. Now all officials involved in making decisions to delegate Japanese units to peace operations, and Japan's SDF itself, must learn more about the long history of U.N. peacekeeping. They must also incorporate lessons learned from their own deployments. An easy way to begin would be to send liaison officers and staff to local U.N. headquarters to learn about the area of responsibility, U.N. structures and their relationships with other entities and within the U.N. chain of command, and the requirements, division of labor, and rules of engagement for the proposed or actual operation.

Japan's need to learn, if actively pursued, might also serve as an important catalyst for reforms in training for U.N. peacekeeping. Japan and the United States should work together to promote their implementation. Edward Luck and Masashi Nishihara have proposed the following:

- U.N. coordination of the development and application of training standards and procedures for military peacekeepers and civilian personnel;
- Establishment of national mobile training teams to "train the trainers" in smaller-troop contributing states;
- Use of command-post exercises for likely future staff officers of U.N. operations, with eventual establishment of a U.N. command and staff college;
- Development of a policy for priority recruiting of peacekeepers from among states and units that have completed U.N.-standard training;
- Japanese sponsorship (with American support) of a joint-peacekeeping training center as either a staff or field training center for

both civilian and military personnel from regional countries. The center could "facilitate joint training of U.S. and Japanese peacekeeping scenarios as part of the two countries' program of joint defense exercises, and it could be co-located with a reserve stockpile of equipment maintained by Japan in cooperation with the United Nations for peacekeeping contingencies in Asia." [54]

These are ambitious goals for Japan. The response to the Hanshin earthquake revealed the grave difficulties that the SDF faces with crisis action planning (CAP). The American military stationed in Japan has offered significant support in improving Japanese CAP, but progress is slow.

The new NDPO offers a much better basis for Japanese participation in pure disaster relief operations in the region. There is still concern that sending Japanese troops to regional PKOs may trigger memories of Imperial Japan—though, somewhat surprisingly, some Southeast Asian nations have been supportive of a regional PKO role for Japan. Given America's honest broker role in much of the region, the cooperation of U.S. forces with SDF troops in any future PKOs is essential to building trust. But USFJ does not at present see a place for PKO/HA exercises even in the current joint exercise program. The key annual exercise, Keen Edge, is dedicated to the defense of Japan, and cannot include scenarios beyond Japan.[55] Thus, U.S.–Japanese operational cooperation in real PKOs may not be realized for some time.

Furthermore, Japanese sponsorship of necessary joint (cross-service) training for PKO deployments would not be realistic at present, even if it assumed U.S. participation. Most joint military activities are still taboo for Japan because of the power projection capability that jointness seems to imply. Japan's SDF is in fact exploring increased jointness, if only to interoperate with the United States, but the United States has been very cautious about encouraging jointness because of the lack of clear high-level political support for it.[56] Currently, USFJ support for jointness is limited to sharing American experience at the operational and tactical levels.

Perhaps, given the limits imposed by the current PKO law freeze, the best means of pursuing the above options is to focus training first on humanitarian operations and disaster relief for the near to medium term. This would allow Japan to build regional goodwill toward its forces. At the same time, SDF officers could continue to be trained by experienced Nordic or Canadian forces in traditional peacekeeping activities. American forces could also benefit from such training, and the United States could bring new applications of its superior information technology to the table.

## CIVILIAN CONTROL

It is not surprising that the SDF, difficult to justify under the Peace Constitution, is squarely under the thumb of the civilian authorities. The prime minister's office (PMO) and the Ministry of Foreign Affairs control participation in peace operations, and the Diet can influence how troops are deployed and when.

Normally, one does not consider the problems of civilian control. The United States has worked hard to teach other countries about the importance of civilian control and its role in fostering legitimacy and trust in the military as an institution that serves society. Japan has special problems with society's acceptance of the SDF due to obfuscation about its status as a true military and its status in society, but it is possible Japan has too much civilian control. This is evidenced by an incident in Cambodia. When the Japanese engineers there were asked to build a much-needed well, they were required to first obtain permission directly from the prime minister's office. By the time they had gone up the chain of authority, it was too late. Others had built the well.

Part of the difficulty lies in huge gaps in the chain of command. In U.S. operations, the field commander of a Joint Task Force (JTF) is a field-grade officer who either makes decisions independently or takes the issue to a regional commander in chief (CINC), who usually has the necessary decision-making power. If not, the CINC's clout in Washington means that prompt attention will be given to the question. By contrast, the SDF officer in charge is a lieutenant colonel with almost no decision-making power, and who must communicate directly with the PMO—not even via a higher-ranking officer in the service, the Japan Defense Agency (JDA), or the Joint Staff Office (JSO).

One way to immediately improve the situation would be to put higher-ranking officers in charge in the field, and to accord the field commander more, and clearer, decision-making authority. The most effective means of resolving the chain of command issue would be bureaucratic reorganization, giving more status to the JDA and JSO and involving them at high levels in decisions about the deployment and in resolving problems that arise during the deployment. This would, however, make it difficult for the Japanese to suspend concerns about the constitutionality of the SDF.

The desire for safe and effective participation in overseas deployments, with their inherent risks to Japanese personnel and subsequent public opinion backlash, may play a role in forcing the Japanese government to engage in an open dialogue with the Japanese people about the SDF, its role, and the constitution. American observers, no matter how frustrated they may be with the status quo, must realize that this dialogue can only take place when both the public and the leadership are ready. The United States can offer insight from its own experience in developing JTFs and international combined JTFs and about defense reorganizations. However, simply offering the American model as a template to be copied is not appropriate, as the two countries try to rebalance the bilateral relationship.

## Conclusion

Multilateralism in Asia has acquired a life of its own. This does not negate the alliance between Japan and the United States, but it does signal a change in the relationship and its role in regional security. Still, security-related multilateralism in Asia will be slow to develop. The best role for the U.S.–Japan alliance is to accept this evolution and to provide reassurance to Japan and to the rest of Asia as it occurs. The United States should promote a positive multilateralism that is not motivated mainly either by the fears of countries in the region concerning U.S. departure or by frustration with U.S. intransigence over either economic issues or changes in Japanese support for U.S. bases in Japan. American goals should be to promote an integrationist vision of Asianization, and at the same time to remain open to listening to and learning from our Asian partners.

For now, multilateral approaches will probably not lead to the resolution of real conflicts or territorial disputes, such as those in the South China Sea. While American leaders and many of their experienced Japanese interlocutors may prefer the great power internationalist vision side of the debate among Japanese intellectuals and some officials, they must recognize that the Japanese people, nor many Asians, are ready for an assertive Japan. Many aspects of civilian internationalism and great power internationalism, however, are not mutually exclusive. Some of the best ways of building the necessary confidence for a more activist Japan are included in the civilian internationalist agenda.

Neither the United States nor Japan has a clear vision of what it hopes to accomplish through peace operations. Participating in them for the sake of playing an international role or reaffirming the importance of military forces is dangerous. Both countries must resolve many issues about the role of their forces in promoting peace and stability throughout the world. They must think about these issues both separately and together.

They may find complementary roles, with the United States having the major role in stopping conflict initially, and Japan focusing on the more humanitarian and nation-building aspects of building a new peace. Both must face the risks that are part of any phase of an intervention, as well as the responsibilities inherent in taking one's own ideals abroad. Both are taking part in a very complex human experiment, and neither can predict the results.

## Notes

1. This is a natural impossibility: eagles are not flocking birds; the eagle is an apt symbol for the American individualist. Flocks of white cranes, like parks filled with cherry blossoms, reflect the Japanese appreciation for the beauty and power of a homogeneous group, rather than a distinctive individual.
2. Peace operations, spanning the spectrum from peacemaking via diplomacy to traditional blue helmet U.N. peacekeeping à la "Chapter 6½", to Chapter 7 peace enforcement, and even to the relatively unmined potential for regional action in Chapter 8, have been ordained as a key means of implementing, or operationalizing multilateralism. Despite great differences in capability, philosophy, and goals, the United States and Japan have focused many of their efforts to build a more multilaterally oriented post–Cold War alliance on creating a vision for cooperation in peace operations.
3. Japan's long acceptance of American paternalism in the security relationship is coming to an end. "The old self-doubt has been replaced by self-confidence, sometimes overblown. In many respects, Japanese reckon they know better than MacArthur's heirs—and plenty of Americans are willing to agree with them." "America and Japan: Friends in Need," *Economist*, April 13–19, 1996, p. 21.
4. CRS Report for Congress 94-79-F, Larry Niksch, January 14, 1994.
5. Jean Monnet, accorded the moniker of "the first statesman of interdependence" by biographer François Duchêne, was the greatest advocate for European unity following World War II. The 1950 Schuman Plan to create a common Franco-German steel market was named for the contemporary French Foreign Minister, Robert Schuman.
6. *Gaiatsu* became something of a convenience for Japanese politicians who wanted to go along with the United States on various issues, but faced domestic opposition. The Japanese could blame the strong and aggressive Americans for leaving them no option.
7. Shinichi Kitaoka, "Putting Old Diplomatic Principles into New Bottles," *Japan Echo* 21 (Spring 1994): 64–71.
8. See, for example, the report from Asian Forum Japan's October 1994 conference, "Challenges and Prospects for the Multilateral System In Asia," *A Call for a Multilateral Strategy for Japan*, p. 9.

9. The "six points" elaborated by former Secretary of Defense Caspar Weinberger and General Colin Powell to define the proper set of circumstances to commit military forces are (1) vital interests are at stake; (2) sufficient forces are committed to ensure the operation's success ("overwhelming force"); (3) political and military objectives are clearly defined; (4) the relationship between forces and objectives is continually reassessed; (5) the operation has the support of the American people and the elected members of Congress; (6) the decision to use U.S. forces is a last resort, following diplomatic, political, and economic efforts. The Clinton administration's criteria for participation in multilateral peace operations are (1) involvement supports U.S. interests, and the international community is interested in addressing the problem; (2) peace and security are threatened; (3) the mission is understood; (4) means to conduct an operation are available; (5) the consequences of inaction have been weighed and are unacceptable; (6) objectives are clear and the end state realistic; (7) both the public and the Congress support the defined end state.

10. See *National Military Strategy of the United States of America: A Strategy of Flexible and Selective Engagement,* Chairman of the Joint Chiefs of Staff, 1995, p. 9.

11. Andrew Bacevich heads the Foreign Policy Studies Institute at the Paul Nitze School of Advanced International Studies. The remarks cited above were made at the NDU/SAIS/IDA conference that serves as the basis for this book.

12. "Long Telegram," written in 1946 while he was chargé d'affaires in Moscow, concludes that the USSR's view of a world split into capitalist and socialist societies, could not live on "permanent peaceful coexistence," and that the Soviets had a "neurotic view of world affairs." Kennan urgently conveyed that Soviet expansion had to be stopped; and is thus known as the "father of containment." However, in *A+A Century's Ending: Reflections 1982–1995,* Kennan concludes that Cold War military competition harmed us as well as the Soviets.

13. National Security Memorandum No. 68 (NSC-68) outlined "United States Objectives and Programs for National Security." It was written under the supervision of Paul Nitze, Director of the Policy & Planning Staff, following the expansion of the first Soviet atomic bomb and the "loss" of China. NSC-68 articulates the bipolar world view of the Cold War.

14. Christopher B. Johnstone, " 'Managing' China: American and Japanese Policies and Prospects for Cooperation," *JEI Report* 13A, (5 April 1996): 4. As Johnstone notes, Judith Kornberg points out that "comprehensive engagement is not a framework that can guide America in its China policy development and implementation; rather, comprehensive engagement is a negotiating tactic." Robert Manning concludes that "engagement is just a gift-wrapped word for diplomacy."

15. One colleague suggested that any Japanese need for further nuclear reassurance from the United States in the more fragmented and fluid post–Cold War environment could be addressed by placing Pershing IIs outside of Tokyo—a solution that in fact proved unworkable in Germany in 1983!

16. Only 7 percent of Japanese support maintaining the bases at their current size. *Economist*, April 13–19, 1996, p. 21. See also "Okinawa Speaks," *Economist*, September 14–20, 1996, pp. 34–39. A *Wall Street Journal* (U.S.) and *Nihon Keizai Shimbun* (Japan) poll in March 1995 found that while 76 percent of Americans believed that the U.S. would come to Japan's defense were it attacked, only 49 percent of Japanese believed so. This is down from 84 percent in the United States and 58 percent for Japan recorded in a November 1991 poll done by CBS, the *New York Times*, and the Tokyo Broadcasting System. See Everett Carll Ladd and Karlyn H. Bowman, *Public Opinion in America and Japan* (Washington, D.C.: AEI Press, 1996), p. 30.

17. *United States Strategy for the East Asia-Pacific Region*, Department of Defense Office of International Security Affairs, February 1995, p. 13.

18. David B. Dewitt, "Common, Comprehensive, and Cooperative Security in Asia-Pacific" (Toronto: CANCAPS, March 1994). Paper no. 3, p. 14, note 41.

19. *Diplomatic Bluebook, 1991: Japan's Diplomatic Activities* (Japan: Ministry of Foreign Affairs, December 1991), p. 30. Cited in Ibid., p. 4.

20. "Vacuum in Defense Attitude: People Indifferent to National Security Top 40 Percent; Back to the 'Leaving-It-to-Someone-Else' Pattern," *This Is Yomiuri*, October 1995. 53.6 percent of twenty-somethings polled described themselves as "not interested" in security issues.

21. Article 9 of the constitution renounces the use of force as a legitimate means of settling international disputes.

22. Interviews with Yoichi Funabashi, Washington bureau chief of the *Asahi Shimbun*, and Kinichi Yoshihara, Asian Forum Japan.

23. From the subsection on Japan–U.S. Security Arrangements: "[T]his close cooperative bilateral relationship [with the U.S.], based on the Japan–U.S. security arrangements, facilitates Japanese efforts for the peace and stability of the international community including promotion of regional, multilateral security dialogues and cooperation as well as various United Nations activities."

24. The view that the bilateral is no longer necessary in the wake of the Cold War has been expressed by some Japanese thinkers, including former president of Hitotsubashi University Shigeto Tsuru and former Tokyo University professor Yoshikazu Sakamoto.

25. Prior to the release of the new NDPO, Mike Mochizuki observed, "In taking the lead in drafting a new policy outline, the JDA [Japan Defense Agency] has adopted the following approach: Consult widely, develop a strong con-

sensus behind the country's defense policies, and minimize political controversy. Accordingly, the agency will refrain from pushing initiatives that may go far beyond the majority public opinion. This means that the agency will support maintaining a strictly defensive military posture and will only gingerly promote the idea of deepening military cooperation with the United States for regional security beyond defense of the home islands." See Mike M. Mochizuki, *Japan: Domestic Change and Foreign Policy* (Santa Monica, CA: RAND National Defense Research Institute, 1995) p. 71.

26. Japan's policy is to use ODA a tool for conflict prevention. Its four ODA principles link aid to recipients' trends in military spending, democratization, market economics, and environmental protection. However, Japan's difficulty in suspending a portion of aid to China in response to initial missile tests, and the failure to maintain suspension in the face of repeated Chinese belligerence, raises doubts about Japan's commitment to those principles.
27. The following discussion draws heavily on Mochizuki, 1995, pp. 47–55.
28. Mochizuki notes, "The ascendancy of exclusivism will occur only if relations between Japan and the U.S. worsen because of an intensification of bilateral economic conflicts coupled with a weakening of America's security commitment to Japan."
29. Interview with Yoichi Funabashi.
30. See Christopher Johnstone, "Asia-Europe Summit Emphasizes Cooperation," *JEI Report* No. 9B, March 8, 1996, pp. 8–11.
31. APEC was established in 1989. It supported the General Agreement on Tariffs and Trade (GATT), and now the World Trade Organization (WTO). It also seeks to foster economic cooperation in the region. Its membership is Australia, Brunei, Canada, China, Hong Kong, Indonesia, Japan, Korea, Malaysia, New Zealand, the Philippines, Singapore, Taiwan (as Chinese Taipei), Thailand, and the United States.
32. Interview with Yoichi Funabashi.
33. Ibid.
34. Japanese officials also see both the ASEAN Regional Forum and APEC as "immature institutions." But they have lent them support, seeing value in expanding dialogue. Interview with Japanese Embassy official, December 1995. Perhaps they share the philosophy of Jean Monnet: "Nothing is possible without men; nothing is lasting without institutions." Cited in Alfred Grosser, *The Western Alliance: European Relations Since 1945* (New York: Vintage Books, 1982), p. 102.
35. One such issue concerns the disputed Senkaku Islands. Tensions increased over this matter in September 1996. For more information, see Steven Mufson, "Chinese Warnings Heighten Tension over Island Dispute with Japan," *Washington Post*, September 25, 1996.
36. CRS Report for Congress 94-79-F, Larry Niksch, January 14, 1994, pp. 9–10.

37. Nor did Clinton attend the 1998 APEC Summit in Kuala Lumpur, due to tension with Iraq over U.N. weapons inspections. Furthermore, the U.S. and Malaysia clashed following Vice President Gore's open support for Anwar Ibrahim and the "brave people" trying to topple Mahathir.

38. See "Japan Conquers APEC," *Economist*, November 11, 1995, pp. 33–34; Sebastian Moffett, "The Devil's in the Details," pp. 14–15, and Nigel Holloway, "Missed Opportunities," p. 16, both in *Far Eastern Economic Review*, November 30, 1995.

39. Its formal birth was at the July 1993 meeting of the ASEAN-PMC. The ARF met for the first time in July 1994.

40. The ARF has a very broad membership: the six ASEAN countries (Thailand, Malaysia, Singapore, Indonesia, Brunei, and the Philippines), the United States, Japan, Australia, New Zealand, the EU, South Korea, Russia, China, Vietnam, Laos, and Papua New Guinea.

41. Interviews with Japanese officials, December 1995.

42. Edward C. Luck, "Layers of Security: Regional Arrangements, the United Nations, and the Japan–U.S. Security Treaty: American Perspective," in Selig S. Harrison and Masashi Nishihara, eds., *UN Peacekeeping: Japanese and American Perspectives* (Washington, D.C.: Carnegie Endowment for International Peace, 1995), p. 117.

43. Masashi Nishihara, "Japan-US. Cooperation in UN Peace Efforts: Japanese Perspective," in Harrison and Nishihara, 1995, p. 170.

44. To ensure civilian control, the *posse comitatis* law contravenes military action directed at U.S. citizens.

45. See his father's (Takehito Nakata) touching essay, "Coming to Terms with My Son's Death," *Japan Echo* 20(Autumn 1993): 19–22.

46. Interview with a JSDF official, December 1995.

47. For an excellent exposition of the debate and the progress of the bill, see Naoki Saito, *The Passing of the PKO Cooperation Law: Japan's Struggle to Define Its International Contribution*, IIGP Policy Paper 102E (Tokyo: International Institute for Global Peace, November 1992).

48. *Defense of Japan*, 1993, p. 130.

49. See Takahiro Shinyo, "The Conditions of Permanent Membership in the U.N. Security Council," *Japan Echo* 21(Summer 1994): 57–61, for a view that this is not the case. The author observes that "[o]ne factor making the Japanese hesitant about permanent membership on the council is concern over what this might mean in terms of a military contribution to the U.N. But . . . there is no direct link between the two."

50. Interview with an official at the Japanese Embassy, December 1995.

51. Yet this option is not always readily available; when the U.S. government requested commercial planes to help transport American troops and their

equipment to the Gulf War theater, the Japanese government was forced to refuse because Japan Airlines and All Nippon Airlines unions saw the risks as too great. Japan instead procured American commercial planes to fulfill the request. As Masashi Nishihara notes, "Japan needs emergency laws that empower the Prime Minister to procure airlift and sealift capabilities from the private sector." See Harrison and Nishihara, 1995, p. 168. This is only a partial solution if American and Japanese leadership are serious about expansion of PKO cooperation.

52. William Durch, "Japan–U.S. Cooperation in UN Peace Efforts," in Harrison and Nishihara, 1995, p. 159.

53. The problems with establishing ROE for Japanese units began during debates in the Diet before the PKO law was passed. The government, in making its case for the constitutionality of sending SDF personnel abroad, claimed that sending them to participate in PKO did not constitute an "overseas dispatch of troops" *(kaigai hahei)*, but merely an "overseas dispatch [of personnel]" *(kaigai haken)*. It also determined that SDF units could not exercise a group right to self-defense; only individuals could do so—the individual right to self-defense being universal. See Yoshihiko Seki, "Concluding the Debate on War-renouncing Article 9," *Japan Echo* 20 (Summer 1993): 21–22.

54. Luck, 1995, p. 156; See also Masashi Nishihara, "Trilateral Country Roles: Challenges and Opportunities," in John Roper et al., *Keeping the Peace in the Post–Cold War Era: Strengthening Multilateral Peacekeeping* (New York, Paris, and Tokyo: The Trilateral Commission, 1993); and Barry M. Blechman and Matthew Vaccaro, *Training for Peacekeeping: The United Nations Role* (Washington, D.C.: The Henry L. Stimson Center, May 1994).

55. Written interview with United States Forces Japan, December 1995.

56. However, Admiral Archie Clemins has raised the need to plan for jointness to ensure basic interoperability and to make sense of future cooperation, both operational and in technology sharing; our jointness pushes theirs. Interview with Admiral Clemins, December 1994.

# 8

# The Alliance Implications of Theater Missile Defense

PATRICK M. CRONIN, PAUL S. GIARRA, AND MICHAEL J. GREEN

IN A WORLD in which law-abiding nations like the United States and Japan could be subjected to blackmail by nuclear or biologically tipped missiles controlled by Kim Jong-il or Saddam Hussein, the strategic arguments for bilateral cooperation on Theater Missile Defense (TMD) are compelling. However, the challenges of TMD for management of the U.S.–Japan security alliance are immense. Since tacit bilateral missile defense cooperation began in the late 1980s as an alliance management initiative bent on cementing tangible military-to-military cooperation, TMD has become a manifold political, strategic, doctrinal, and technical challenge for the alliance. The strategic arguments for bilateral cooperation on TMD are still strong, but Tokyo and Washington will have to sort out myriad technical and political issues in the process of developing and eventually deploying missile defense systems.

The approach to TMD cooperation with Japan, given bipartisan support in the U.S. Congress, had seemed fairly straightforward. To the surprise of many, however, the TMD question in the U.S.–Japan alliance has grown increasingly complex in the last few years. If brought to fruition in any rational way, TMD will drive a broad array of operational initiatives, force changes to bilateral doctrine and command and control, and motivate the integration of Japan's Self-Defense Forces (SDF). In short, TMD has the same implications for bilateral integration at the operational and support level as does the Defense Guidelines, with even more tangible definition and consequences for the bilateral alliance and the way that the United States and Japan must plan, procure, consult, and operate in the future.

This chapter reviews the arguments for and against TMD in the United States and Japan, the technical and operational challenges that will emerge with any joint R&D or deployment, and the steps that Tokyo and Washington can take to ensure that the alliance relationship, U.S. national capabilities and force protection, and Japan's own security will be stronger as a result of bilateral cooperation on TMD.

## Background

TMD encompasses a range of lower- and upper-tier systems intended to intercept and destroy short- and medium-range ballistic missiles with ranges up to 3,500 km. Lower-tier U.S. systems now under development include the Aegis-based Navy Block IV A ("Navy Area Defense") fleet defense system and the upgraded Army Patriot ("PAC-3") with a hit-to-kill capability. These systems, effective against missiles with ranges up to 1,500 km, are close to deployment, and are clearly permissible according to the 1972 Anti-Ballistic Missile (ABM) Treaty.

U.S. upper-tier TMD systems now being developed include the Army land-based, deployable Theater High Altitude Air Defense (THAAD) system, and the Navy Theater Wide (NTW) system. These systems would provide hit-to-kill capability against longer-range, higher-speed ballistic missiles. While the implications for the ABM Treaty are still debated, under current plans these systems will be detuned to stay beneath ABM Treaty thresholds. The upper-tier systems will not be deployed for some time, and they face numerous technical and budgetary obstacles. Deployment of Japanese systems would likely not come before the end of the next decade.

After years of tacit discussion limited to industrial studies during the Strategic Defense Initiative Office Western Pacific (SDIO WESTPAC) Architecture Study (1989–93), the United States and Japan initiated a formal political dialogue on Theater Ballistic Missile Defense in the early 1990s. Its goal was to demonstrate tangible cooperation based on mutual defense requirements generated by proliferation of ballistic missile technology. Alliance managers recognized that successful cooperation on a new defense requirement would be good for an alliance battered by economic and political disagreements and an uneasy sense of drift and divergence. Moreover, Iraq's use of short-range Scud ballistic missiles during the 1991 Persian Gulf War, coupled with North Korea's test of the No Dong missile into the Japan Sea in 1993, presented clear evidence of the threat to the U.S.–Japan alliance from theater ballistic missiles.

Japan's excruciatingly distant official technical participation in the Strategic Defense Initiative (SDI) was marginal to the overall U.S. program, but by 1993 trade tensions between Washington and Tokyo made it imperative in the minds of many Americans that Japan should play a more central role in funding, research, and procurement of U.S. TMD systems. There were to be no more "free rides" on defense technology for Japan, and the initial U.S. approach on TMD focused almost entirely on the issue of technology reciprocity. When Secretary of Defense Les Aspin visited Tokyo in October 1993 and first asked for formal Japanese participation in TMD, the Japan Defense Agency (JDA) and Japanese industry reported to the press that Tokyo had been given only three options: joint development (involving the transfer of some Japanese technology to the U.S. side), buying TMD off-the-shelf, or engaging in gradual technology exchanges.[1] Production agreements without Japanese technology cooperation would no longer be permitted.

This deliberate U.S. approach was seen as a threat to Japan's own technological and industrial base, with many in Tokyo interpreting that the U.S. side was more interested in obtaining Japanese technology and cash than in helping Japan defend itself against ballistic missile threats. It soon became clear to officials in the Departments of State and Defense that the U.S. side had overplayed its hand, and they had done so without any clear definition of what the United States really wanted from Japan, or of what Tokyo might have to offer.

Accordingly, in 1994, the U.S. and Japanese governments recast TMD as an alliance management issue with the establishment of the bilateral U.S.–Japan Theater Missile Defense Working Group. Initially led on the U.S. side by the Office of Asian and Pacific Affairs in the Secretary of Defense's policy organization in the Pentagon, the TMD Working Group focused on the political hurdles holding Japan back from an objective examination of its own requirements for missile defense and potential for bilateral collaboration. The earlier acrimony of the technology dialogue faded, if only because the U.S. side never could define its technology requirements or desired Japanese technologies, and as the new economics-based competitive policies toward Japan foundered or were overtaken by events.

Based on data provided through a bilateral TMD study initiated by the Working Group, as well as reflecting Japanese industry and the Japanese Maritime Self-Defense Forces (JMSDF) preferences (as well as Air SDF indifference), the JDA concluded internally by 1997 that the most logical area for bilateral technological cooperation would be in the Navy Theater Wide (NTW) program, which appeared to be the system capable of defending Japan most effectively (albeit with a number of difficult strategic and operational consequences). The JMSDF already had the platforms (Aegis ships), and the NTW development program was still immature enough that some level of programmatic participation from Japanese industry might be possible. This followed significant pressure from the U.S. Navy, which was intent on broadening support for its own underfunded programs, and which paralleled the JMSDF and the Japanese shipbuilding industry's interest in building more Japanese Aegis destroyers. The longer timeline for NTW development also gave Japanese industry time to hone its skills on co-production of lower-tier PAC-3 and indigenous development of the Chu-SAM replacement for the Hawk air defense missile. Building pressure for a particular choice in Japan was the result of acquisition-based preferences, not strategic or policy choices.

A formal decision on participation in the NTW program had been expected by the summer of 1997, but it was postponed indefinitely at that time due to the lack of consensus in Japan and because of pressure from Beijing. The difficult part for the Japanese government remained the building of budgetary and political support from a Liberal Democratic Party (LDP) skeptical about the technical feasibility and cost of TMD, and especially concerned about vocal Chinese opposition—this despite the clear implications for Japanese security of China's demonstration of the ballistic missile capabilities of the People's Liberation Army (PLA) against Taiwan in March 1996.

In the summer of 1998 the Japanese press speculated that the decision would have to be postponed again. That political calculation changed abruptly, however, when North Korea test-fired its new three-stage Taepo Dong missile directly over Japanese territory on August 31, 1998. Bilateral TMD cooperation returned to its incremental, but forward momentum.[2] Nevertheless, the debate continues in both the United States and Japan.

## The Debate in the United States

For the United States, Japanese participation in TMD offers the potential to enhance bilateral security cooperation, in addition to providing technology, funding, and customers for a complex and expensive program.

Nevertheless, there are deep-seated and unresolved disagreements among U.S. experts and government officials regarding the efficacy of upper-tier TMD cooperation with Japan. Functional and regional experts focus in particular on TMD's implications for China policy, and its impact on arms control and overall U.S. nuclear strategy. These debates reflect the broader arguments about TMD now under way in academic and policy circles. One way to judge these debates is to consider that the United States inevitably will deploy TMD systems as they become available to defend U.S. forces deployed overseas, including in Japan and wherever fixed installations have been established. The American debate is surveyed below.

## THE EFFICACY OF TMD COOPERATION WITH JAPAN

American critics challenge the severity of the ballistic missile threat, the utility of missile defenses to U.S. strategy in East Asia, and the advantages to Japan's own national security.

### *The threat*

It is often pointed out that bilateral TMD cooperation with Japan is premised on the long-term North Korean missile threat, while the Department of Defense argues in other forums that the Pyongyang regime will probably not last through the rest of the decade. Alternate post–North Korea threat scenarios based on unstable Russian or Chinese military commanders are similarly dismissed by some regional experts as unrealistic. In response, the advocates of missile defense argue that Northeast Asian politics are fluid and uncertain enough to allow any number of troubling political scenarios, and they point out that threat assessment based on intentions and capabilities must take account of the steady proliferation and modernization of ballistic missiles and weapons of mass destruction (WMD) warheads in the region (to include residual Russian arsenals and emerging North Korean capabilities). Arms control advocates counter that this aspect of the threat could be controlled with proper implementation of the Missile Technology Control Regime (MTCR), but here the two communities are divided by fundamentally different assumptions about international relations.

### *The utility of missile defense to U.S. strategy in East Asia*

Critics of TMD challenge the general assumption that TMD for Japan as part of an active counterproliferation strategy is crucial to U.S. strategy in East Asia. U.S. TMD advocates, on the other hand, posit the following arguments:

- TMD shores up the U.S. extended nuclear deterrent against newly emerging rogue states, limited ballistic missile threats, and chemical and biological threats—which, for moral, political, and strategic reasons, cannot be deterred by nuclear retaliation alone.
- TMD protects coalitions against intimidation. In a Korean or Taiwanese scenario the threat of limited ballistic missile strikes against

Japan could deny the United States its base of operations in the region. Active defenses fortify allied solidarity in the face of such a threat.

- TMD demonstrates an American commitment to defend Japan and a Japanese commitment to shield U.S. forces based in Japan.
- TMD will be deployed to defend forward-deployed American forces around the globe, regardless of the political decision taken bilaterally with Japan. It follows that it simply is not tenable for the United States to protect its forces in Japan and leave the Japanese population exposed. Similarly, U.S.-only deployment of missile defense would seriously undermine interoperability and defense cooperation with Japan's Self-Defense Forces.
- Both for moral and strategic reasons, Japan will not want to rely on the extended U.S. nuclear deterrent alone in the face of limited ballistic missile threats. Without TMD, Japan becomes at least marginally more predisposed in the eyes of its neighbors to its own nuclear deterrent[3]
- Furthermore, TMD is a necessary precursor to National Missile Defense, and will be ineffective without an effective homeland defense to prevent strategic blackmail by a regional opponent with an intercontinental ballistic missile capability.

*The implications of TMD for Japanese security.*

U.S. critics argue that TMD will overwhelm Japan's limited national security capabilities. They maintain that the SDFs are not ready to handle the complexity and jointness of missile defenses, and that the government of Japan is not ready to handle the strategic responsibilities involved in a more explicit role in the extended U.S. nuclear deterrent. Finally, they point out that the cost will prove prohibitive.

Advocates of TMD in both the United States and Japan argue that for precisely these reasons it is essential that Japan not be left behind as the United States proceeds with missile defense development and deployment, and that the alternative would be to gut the alliance.

## THE CHINA DIMENSION

The most vociferous opposition to TMD cooperation with Japan comes from those concerned about its impact on Sino–U.S. relations. Some China experts and arms control advocates argue that a U.S.–Japan decision to develop TMD would cause the People's Republic of China (PRC) to incorporate into its long-range multiple-independently-targeted-vehicle (MIRV) warheads capability, and submunitions into short- and medium-range ballistic missiles, thereby escalating vertically from a strategy of minimum deterrence to a more threatening one of limited deterrence. Moreover, they point out that TMD would set both Japan and the United States on a collision course with Beijing that would undermine their broader strategic objectives for integrating China into the regional and global community of nations. Beijing has reinforced these concerns with its active and vocal opposition to TMD. Some opponents of TMD advocate an approach to Beijing that would instead be based on arms control and confidence-building measures, because this would strengthen China's burgeoning arms control community and constrain the hawks in the PLA.[4] Ultimately, there is a fundamental difference between a China that aspires to work within the boundaries of the international community and a pariah regime operating outside such constraints. As China builds a role in the maintenance of global arms control regimes, the United States and Japan will have a stronger basis for confidence-building with Beijing related to TMD.

While acknowledging the importance of not handing China excuses for expanding the PLA's strategic rocket and submarine-launched ballistic missile (SLBM) forces, TMD advocates question the causality between the development of missile defenses and Chinese decisions to modernize its strategic military forces. TMD advocates point out that Chinese officials invoke the logic of the ABM treaty while the PLA quietly develops its own missile defense.

Moreover, China's arguments that Japanese TMD would undermine Chinese deterrence suggest that China targets Japan, contradicting Beijing's own "no first use" policy, thereby only increasing Japanese fear of Chinese missiles.

Finally, Chinese Cold War era doctrinal arguments ignore the fact that missile defenses raise the barrier for proliferators and decrease the likelihood that nuclear weapons would have to be used in response to limited strikes.

## THE ARMS CONTROL VERSUS DEFENSE DEBATE

Ultimately, the controversy building around TMD cooperation with Japan is larger than that of American regional strategy, the bilateral security relationship, or Sino–U.S. relations, pitting basic American arms control objectives against a fundamental requirement to protect U.S. forces and allies against an emerging threat. Arms control advocates focus on the risk that upper-tier missile defense deployments might undermine existing arms control agreements, setting back future negotiations to reduce the number of nuclear weapons. TMD supporters focus on the threat, believing that security is ultimately guaranteed by deterrence and not arms reduction.

## The Debate in Japan

For Japan, TMD has several basic advantages. First, TMD could enhance Japan's defensive capabilities against a significant new threat to the home islands. Second, TMD would strengthen U.S.–Japan alliance cooperation. In addition, the prospect of integrating the technological sophistication of TMD, and the potential to relax arms export control rules through cooperation with U.S. counterparts, has won many enthusiasts in Japanese industry. TMD also will be a force-builder for the Self-Defense Forces, especially the JMSDF.

Japan is now much more likely to introduce certain soon-to-be-available lower-tier systems and to participate in R&D on the NTW program, but eventual procurement and deployment decisions for upper-tier systems, and their effective operation, will hinge on a broad range of complex and expansive issues.

### *The missile threat from North Korea and China*

There is growing public recognition in Japan of the ballistic missile threat since the March 1996 missile demonstrations by the PRC during the Taiwan Strait crisis and the August 1998 North Korean Taepo Dong test.

### *The cost*

The cost problem has been compounded by a recent Ministry of Finance decision to limit defense increases for the foreseeable future, and by the current Japanese recession and banking crisis. Projected TMD costs compare with other major air defense programs such as the F-15J and the FS-X/F-2. (For comparison, projected F-2 program costs, including R&D and procurement of 130 aircraft, are estimated at $15 billion.) However, this does not simplify the funding problem for JDA and the SDFs, which have yet to determine where the funding might come from, or which major defense programs will be cut to make way for TMD.

### *The technical success of upper-tier programs in the United States*

The Japanese government is still waiting to see if U.S. upper-tier, hit-to-kill prototypes will work, as U.S. tests on THAAD continue to fail (although so far not because of basic TMD hit-to-kill technology, proved in earlier National Missile Defense and recent navy tests, but rather due to failures of individual components). In fact, most experts agree that the United States eventually will be able to field effective systems that "hit a bullet with a bullet."

*Implications for strategic relations with China*

Japan is increasingly willing to hedge in its long-term view of Chinese intentions and stability, but remains focused on improving relations with Beijing. Fear of confrontation with China over defense-related issues such as TMD can have a major impact on internal Japanese decision-making.

*The potential for and implications of significant change in bilateral technology cooperation*

Collaboration with the United States might require relaxation of the Three Principles on Arms Export (see Appendix 7) to allow component export or third country transfer—an option supported by industry and their supporters in the LDP, but strongly opposed by the political left in Japan.

*The ABM Treaty*

The Japanese government is watching closely U.S.–Russian negotiations on whether upper-tier systems will be prohibited by the ABM Treaty. The Japanese government will resist participation in an arrangement that threatens arms control regimes. In January 1999 the United States announced its intention to opt out of the treaty if the TMD issue cannot be resolved.

*The industrial impact*

Japanese industry is cautiously optimistic about the impact of TMD cooperation on the defense industrial base, but remains concerned that the vast U.S. technical lead might still relegate Japan to the position of licensed production or even off-the-shelf arrangements with U.S. industry.

Resolving these issues and getting tangible bilateral TMD cooperation under way will take at least a decade. During that period, in addition to fielding the interceptor missile systems themselves, Japan's air defense system infrastructure will have to be rebuilt from the ground up. This is the almost universally neglected long-lead-time component of effective missile defense of the Japanese archipelago. Rebuilding Japan's air defenses will have to proceed from a clear understanding of the necessity for effective bilateral integration in sensors, systems, doctrine, and Command, Control, Communications, Computers, Intelligence, Surveillance Reconnaissance ($C^4$ISR). This will lead inexorably to the requirement for systemic bilateral coordination and rationalization of design, development, procurement, fielding, doctrine, and operations.

Moreover, the manifestation of TMD by Japan and by the United States in and around Japan will necessitate significant changes to both the mechanics of bilateral cooperation and Japanese self-defense. Given the physical realities of very short warning times—and the absolute necessity of effective, seamless, unimpeded command and control of disparate sensors and weapons, commanded by both nations, and controlled by a variety of military organizations—the alliance will have to institute profound and complex structural changes.

## Back to the Alliance Management Problem

If mismanaged, the TMD issue will do significant damage to the alliance. A failure of American perseverance on bilateral cooperation after pressing Japan to participate in joint programs would undermine political credibility. Perceptions of the U.S. commitment to the alliance depend on Washington's not retreating in the face of pressure from Beijing. Also at stake is Japan's confidence in the extended U.S. deterrent, the terms of which are bound to change if Japan assumes an active role in what amounts to strategic defense. Moreover, pushing TMD on a technological/acquisition track without resolving enormous strategic and doctrinal debates on the U.S. side would not only undermine the rationality of an important and complex capability; it would also confirm suspicions in Japan that the United States seeks Japanese money and technology without regard for the strategic requirements of defending Japan.

However, the incremental Japanese approach to TMD, although problematic for DoD's acquisition strategy (the window for Japanese participation will steadily close with time and North Korea's Taepo Dong series may not be adequately defended against by lower-tier capabilities alone), is probably a blessing for policy officials and alliance managers. The timeline for decisions on upper tier allow the United States and Japan to hold in abeyance fundamental decisions about the future of North Korea and strategic relations with China.

## IMPLICATIONS FOR ALLIANCE CHANGE: PREDICTIVE DECLARATIONS AND POLICY PRESCRIPTIONS

There is nothing like a startling external event, unimagined by the most ardent of alliance supporters, to push forward the maturation of the bilateral U.S.–Japan security alliance. Like the 1994 North Korean nuclear crisis, previous North Korean No-Dong missile launches into the Sea of Japan, the 1995 Okinawa rape crisis, and the 1996 Taiwan Strait crisis, the August 1998 North Korean missile launch—this time *over* Japan and into the Pacific—has galvanized the attention of Japanese citizens and security experts alike.

Before this significant juncture TMD had grown on its own momentum to the point where it promised a broad range of tangible bilateral cooperation, based on new mutual defense requirements emerging from the proliferation of ballistic missile technology. The 1998 released Rumsfeld Report on National Missile Defense will also affect the broader national debate in the United States, and has the potential for moving TMD along as a regional and bilateral issue.

There are now so many moving parts to TMD that management of its progress would be very difficult under the best of political and bureaucratic circumstances. Distinctions having blurred over the last decade, serious consideration of TMD now includes a broad range of complex and expansive issues surveyed above: the missile threat from North Korea, implications for strategic relations with China, the potential for significant change in bilateral technology cooperation, consequences for the politics of National Missile Defense, the Anti-Ballistic Missile Treaty, formulation of effective bilateral command and control structures, the potential for truly integrated combined missile defense operations, and bilateral military connectivity that would go far beyond anything so far contemplated in the bilateral security relationship.

It might help to clarify the arguments over TMD, sketch out necessary steps, and animate policy prescriptions with a few predictive declarations on the subject.

- TMD will succeed technically, despite a highly publicized but flawed test program—and insufficient quality control by the contractor—for THAAD (as opposed to flawed technology).
- The United States will deploy TMD in sufficient numbers and in necessary locations to provide deterrent and war-fighting protection for U.S. forces deployed overseas, including Japan.
- For present purposes, it is understood that the United States will not assume the entire mission of missile defense of Japanese territory.
- Given the significant concentrations of American troops and facilities in Japan, deployed U.S. TMD systems will enhance Japanese air and missile defense in the future.

- Since Japan already operates the precursor systems that form the basis for an effective TMD capability (the Aegis weapons system and the Patriot missile system), Japan will not be able to resist the logic of fielding advanced Japanese systems of American origin that modernize and extrapolate those capabilities already in service with the Self-Defense Forces.
- American operational plans will dictate Japanese requirements, and serve as a logical starting point for Japanese operational and procurement planning. For instance, the United States will plan to defend its forces in Japan centered on bases and facilities in and on Okinawa, Sasebo, Iwakuni, the bases on the Kanto Plain, and Misawa. American TMD capabilities will be either permanently located in Japan to defend U.S. forces on short notice, or deployed there in a crisis.
- These notional U.S. plans, based on what we know now and can reasonably anticipate about future capabilities and requirements, are a necessary—and readily available—present template that will give substance and texture to Japan's own TMD planning. If such American plans have not yet been derived, they must be prepared very soon to inform long-lead planning in both countries. They need not be perfect, merely sufficient to outline national and bilateral requirements.
- Tokyo has a number of options. Japan could do nothing at all (unthinkable in any alliance context), fill in the gaps left by American deployments (the niche plan), or field a system that overlaps and defends all of Japan, including U.S. bases (the overlap plan).
- Fielding TMD in Japan will necessitate significant changes to the mechanics of bilateral cooperation and Japanese self-defense. Given the physical realities of very short warning times, it will be absolutely necessary to achieve effective, seamless, and unimpeded command and control of disparate sensors and weapons, commanded by both nations, and controlled by a variety of interconnected military organizations that are doctrinally interconnected.
- For the first time, Japan's individual Self-Defense Forces will become motivated to cooperate operationally with each other, and required to do so with U.S. forces in unprecedented intimacy.
- Japan and the United States will have to learn to integrate command and control functions, either implicitly or explicitly.
- Japan's air defense system will have to be rebuilt from the ground up. Modernization of the Base Air Defense Ground Environment (BADGE) system according to TMD specifications is the neglected

long-lead-time component of effective missile defense of the Japanese archipelago, and in the long run will prove to be significantly more important than symbolic technology cooperation.

- Rebuilding Japan's air defenses will have to proceed from a clear understanding of the necessity for effective bilateral integration, leading inexorably to the requirement for systemic bilateral coordination and rationalization of design, development, procurement, fielding, doctrine, and operations.
- Systems and components will be overwhelmingly American in origin, and the United States will have to step up to political and technical leadership for design and integration. Japan will have to come to grips with this fundamental reality.
- Given the time and capabilities required, direct Japanese costs for TMD will be affordable, ending up roughly comparable to the expense involved in fielding other recent major air defense systems such as the F-15J or the F-2.
- Japan for the first time will have a significant hand to play in regional and global arms control and proliferation initiatives.
- Not inconsequentially, Japan will have to craft a careful rationalization of how its role in missile defense does not detract from the sensitive notion of the American nuclear umbrella, heretofore an exclusive alliance contribution of the United States.
- It is not entirely unreasonable that fielding of American and Japanese TMD capabilities might lead eventually to an Asian Intermediate Nuclear Force (INF) reduction agreement. This would remove the fundamental problem of intermediate-range Chinese missiles from Asia, as did the original INF agreement for Soviet missiles in Europe, thereby finessing the issue of TBM defenses. The alliance will have to conduct itself in the interim in such a way that there are no insurmountable surprises should that result come to pass.

In short, the process will take well more than a decade to play itself out, but TMD will succeed technically and be affordable (that is, no more expensive than other major air defense systems procured by Japan). Most important, the United States will deploy TMD to protect its forces. As a result Japan will have to do so as well, and should use basic American intentions as a bilateral planning template. In the long run, what began as an alliance management initiative may instead become an alliance-defining initiative, on the leading edge of the revolution in military affairs as part of a system that inherently mandates unprecedented connectivity, compatibility, and seamless command and control.

## Next Steps

Alliance managers in Tokyo and Washington will have to make a virtue out of necessity by channeling Japanese TMD development into the least confrontational but most flexible avenue available, while addressing the larger strategic issues in a way that does not damage security cooperation.

### IN THE UNITED STATES

The Office of the Secretary of Defense (OSD), after concerted interagency deliberations, will have to bring together the disparate tracks that are now shaping the TMD debate, building a consensus on the larger strategic issues, along the following lines:

- Engage the services and theater and functional U.S. military commanders in chief (CINCs) on the operational requirements for Japanese missile defense in an alliance context. This will require a study of the utility of a range of missile defense options for Japan in terms of U.S. strategic objectives.
- Engage the acquisition/Ballistic Missile Defense Organization (BMDO) community by pursuing agreement on realistic modalities and timing for possible future Japanese programmatic/technological participation in TMD, including, but not limited to, NTW cooperation as agreed upon in 1998.
- Engage China in an agenda for possible arms control and confidence-building measures that would test Chinese intentions and reduce unnecessary rhetorical confrontation over TMD. This might include, for instance, the possibility of incorporating China into regional missile defense regimes.
- Build U.S. interagency consensus on the role of missile defenses and counterproliferation in extended deterrence doctrine.

### TOGETHER WITH JAPAN

- Hold in abeyance decisions on joint fielding of upper-tier systems, but move forward with joint research on systems such as NTW (and other systems and subsystems such as C4ISR).

- Provide Japan with a predictable American operational template of sufficient detail that Tokyo can proceed with and play off of what the United States will deploy to Japan and how those American TMD forces will operate.
- Reach bilateral agreement to introduce PAC-3 (which is within the ABM Treaty specifications and would not undermine arms control).
- Work to enhance interoperability with Japan's air defense infrastructure. Japan's current air defense system (the BADGE system) is not capable of defending against modern and future ballistic missile threats in terms of sensors, command and control, and connectivity with U.S. forces. This is the time to initiate an effective bilateral approach on Japan's infrastructure development in anticipation of near term ballistic missile threats and possible longer term introduction of upper-tier systems.
- Initiate bilateral studies on counterproliferation and the broader strategic context of missile defenses (to expand Japanese expertise).

## Conclusion

If recent history is our guide, then diplomacy and deterrence are essential yet insufficient instruments for preventing pariah regimes from acquiring intermediate- and long-range ballistic missiles tipped with chemical, biological, or even nuclear weapons. After all, Iraq's Saddam Hussein has been able to hold at bay the tightest international arms control regime devised in history. The United Nations Special Commission (UNSCOM) designed to enforce and monitor Iraq's compliance with U.N. resolutions regarding missiles and weapons of mass destruction has been gradually weakened. It appears increasingly possible that Saddam Hussein may someday announce that he has nuclear-tipped missiles aimed at regional capitals.

Similarly, the October 1994 Agreed Framework, while useful in defusing a crisis that would have led to conflict and stemming North Korea's known nuclear program, never actually guaranteed the elimination of a North Korean nuclear threat. Moreover, it did nothing to deal with the North's burgeoning missile program and perhaps a covert biological and chemical weapons effort. Deterrence, while preventing deliberate conflict, also was useless in responding to North Korea's August 1998 Taepo Dong missile launch over Japan. Thus the question becomes, "Do law-abiding states like the United States and Japan have a right to defend themselves against potential blackmail, or worse, from Saddam Hussein or Kim Jong-il?"

Clearly, there are several obstacles to fielding defensive systems, not the least of which are political. Obviously, such systems also have to be cost effective and technically reliable—and thus far they are neither. However, information technologies give the defense the advantage over the offense, and a concerted effort by the two highest-technology states in the region can lead to breakthroughs in the development of more effective and cheaper ways of fielding a defensive system against ballistic missiles.

More than technology, however, the key missing ingredient remains the political decision to collaborate on a realistic basis dictated by the realities of the physics, ballistics, and flight times involved, and centered on specific requirements—that already can be clearly articulated—which define the systems, doctrines, and command architectures necessary for successful missile defense.

## Notes

1. For details see Michael Green, *Arming Japan: Defense Production, Alliance Politics, and the Post-War Search for Autonomy*, (New York: Columbia University Press, 1995), p. 137.
2. Senior LDP and opposition politicians called publicly for participation in the TMD project in the days after the Taepo Dong test, which dominated the Japanese newspapers during the week of August 31, 1998, albeit from some quarters with an emphasis on independent Japanese capabilities to the exclusion of alliance cooperation.
3. See, for example, Stephen A. Cambone, "The United States and Theatre Missile Defence in Northeast Asia," *Survival* 39, No. 3 (Summer 1997): 66–84; and Michael J. Green, "Theater Missile Defense and Strategic Relations with China," in Ralph A. Cossa, ed., *Restructuring the U.S.–Japan Alliance: Toward a More Equal Partnership* (Washington, D.C.: Center for Strategic and International Studies, 1998), pp. 111–18.
4. A well-researched case for this position can be found in Alastair Iain Johnstone, "China's New 'Old Thinking,'" pp. 5–42, and Banning Garrett and Bonnie Glaser, "Chinese Perspectives on Nuclear Arms Control," pp. 43–78, both in *International Security* 20, no. 3 (Winter 1995–96); and Johnstone, "Prospects for Chinese Nuclear Force Modernization: Limited Deterrence vs. Multilateral Arms Control," *China Quarterly* (Spring 1996): 548.

# III

# The Politics of the Alliance

# 9

# Alliance Politics and Japan's Postwar Culture of Antimilitarism

THOMAS U. BERGER

THE HISTORY of the U.S.–Japanese alliance has been characterized by repetitive cycles of rising U.S. expectations followed by disappointment, acrimony, and renewed pressures for increased Japanese burden-sharing. Time and again, American and Japanese leaders have produced bold initiatives proclaiming a new era of cooperation on regional security issues. With depressing regularity these initiatives have produced only relatively small changes in Japan's actual defense policy. While there is little doubt that there has been significant progress in U.S.–Japanese military cooperation over the past two decades, the improvements focus almost exclusively on the defense of Japan's territory.

With the Security Declaration of April 1996, once again a new proposal for an improved U.S.–Japanese partnership on regional security was floated.[1] However, direct Japanese military support in the event of a regional security crisis, on the Korean Peninsula or in the Taiwan Strait, for example, remains as uncertain today as it was in the 1950s and 1960s. In light of the earlier history of the alliance, the natural question now is whether the two countries are on the threshold of a genuinely new era of cooperation on regional security matters, or whether there is likely to be another round of frustratingly small changes in Japanese policy, followed by renewed U.S.–Japanese diplomatic tension.

The answer depends in large measure on whether the factors that induced Japan to cling stubbornly to a minimal defense posture in the past are still active today. Analysts have tended to account for Japan's highly parochial approach to defense and national security during the Cold War in one of two ways. One prominent school of thought, associated with realist theory in the field of international relations, attributes Japanese passivity in security affairs to its position in the international system. As a weak, isolated nation dependent on the United States for its security, Japan was unable to provide for its own security during much of the Cold War. Even after its economy had recovered sufficiently to allow Japan to take on a broader security role, the free ride on security provided by the United States robbed Japan of any incentive to do so. Why should Japan expend blood and treasure to maintain regional security when the United States had already proven itself willing to do so?[2]

Other analysts, mostly area experts more intimately familiar with the politics of the region, have stressed domestic political factors. They argue that pacifist sentiments in broad segments of the Japanese public, buttressed by the state's distinctive institutional structure, most notably Article 9 of the Japanese constitution under which Japan relinquishes its right to use force to settle international disputes, are the chief factors accounting for Japan's reluctance to assume a greater military role.[3]

Despite their differences, both perspectives lead one to anticipate a softening of Japanese intransigence on military security. Internationally, Japan is no longer the weak, isolated nation it was in the 1950s when the general contours of its approach to national security first emerged. Today Japan has the world's second-largest economy; it has acquired a technology base that rivals and in some cases even surpasses that of the United States; and it plays a leading political and economic role in the rapidly growing Asian-Pacific region.[4]

Moreover, American commitment to Asian security has been put into question by the collapse of its communist Soviet rival, while at the same time new security threats have emerged in the shape of a more assertive China and a possibly nuclear armed North Korea. In short, the international context in which Japan finds itself has undergone a fundamental transformation, making a new approach to defense all but inevitable.

On the domestic level as well there have been shifts suggesting that the forces of pacifism and foreign policy inactivity have been decisively weakened. The 1955 system of unbroken Conservative Party hegemony has come to an end and the main left-wing party, the Japanese Social Democratic Party, apparently has abandoned its traditional pacifist views.[5] Public opinion, too, appears to have shifted, and survey data indicate public support for, or at least acceptance of, the participation of Japanese troops in peacekeeping operations in places as far away as Mozambique and Somalia, breaking the once inviolable taboo forbidding the overseas dispatch of military forces.[6] In light of these many changes, both internal and external, it seems reasonable to expect that Japan will soon emerge from its half-century of military semi-isolationism.

This chapter argues that such a shift is unlikely to occur. While both geostrategic factors and Japanese pacifism have undoubtedly played an important role in discouraging Japan from assuming a larger security role, they tell only part of the story. The chief factor inhibiting the emergence of a more active Japanese approach to defense and national security has been neither the benign security environment created by its strategic relationship with the United States, nor the institutional support for pacifism provided by its constitution, although both of these are important factors. Rather, the decisive element behind Japanese security behavior has been the emergence in Japan of a peculiar culture of antimilitarism. This culture is based on lingering doubts in the Japanese general public as well as in considerable segments of the nation's elite regarding the strength of Japanese democracy and its ability to control the armed forces. In a very real way, the Japanese defense debate has been more a debate regarding the strength of Japanese democracy than a discourse on how to best meet external military threats.[7] Japan's pronounced antimilitarism is reinforced by a highly decentralized, fragmented policymaking environment. Policy elites, such as those in the defense establishment who operate in such an environment without the backing of a powerful network of interest groups or a national consensus favoring new policy directions, are able to effect only marginal changes in the existing policy line.

At this fundamental level, the roots of Japanese foreign policy passivity have remained unchanged since 1991. Public doubts about the strength of Japanese democracy and its ability to contain the military remain strong, while the current upheavals in Nagatacho have made Japanese policymaking more fractured and directionless than ever. As a result, the prospects for a fundamental shift in defense policy are poorer than is commonly appreciated. To be sure, Japan is responding to its altered circumstances, but these changes are slow and proceed only in an incremental fashion. Ultimately only a major new external shock or a much more far reaching transformation of the domestic political system than anything seen thus far will be sufficient to bring about a major change in the direction of Japanese defense and national security policy.

The next section outlines the origin and function of the domestic political determinants of the Japanese approach to defense and national security. Special attention is paid to the extent to which this constellation of factors has changed since the end of the Cold War in 1991. Finally, consideration is given to the probable direction of change in Japan, as well as to some of the strategic implications of the foregoing analysis.

## The Origins of Japanese Antimilitarism

It is commonly assumed that the lack of Japanese war guilt indicates the Japanese have not learned any lessons from their devastating experiences of the 1930s and 1940s.[8] This view is mistaken. It is not that the Japanese did not draw any lessons from their recent past, but that the lessons drawn are not the ones the outside world feels are appropriate. Rather than feeling guilt or shame over the horrendous atrocities Japanese forces committed throughout Asia during the war and before, public opinion in Japan is strong that the Japanese people had little say in the events that led up to the war. Like almost all significant political changes in modern Japan up to that point, the imposition of the military dictatorship is seen to have been another revolution from above, engineered by a cabal of high officials, powerful industrialists, and shadowy string-pullers operating behind the scenes.[9]

Instead of guilt as defined by the West, after 1945 the Japanese people came to feel what could be called a sense of dual victimization. On the one hand, they felt victimized by the United States, a country they believed had waged war against them with a ruthlessness and racially motivated disregard for human life that culminated in the dropping of the atomic bombs on Hiroshima and Nagasaki.[10] On the other hand, they felt victimized by their own government, and especially by the military leadership, which had dragged Japan into a hopeless war that could not be won, but which the military men refused to give up regardless of the horrific suffering that had been inflicted upon the nation.[11]

As a result, the chief lesson learned by the Japanese people concerned the dangers of an overly strong state. Internally this led to the maintenance of a decentralized police force and fear of avoidance of an overconcentration of power in the hands of a single government authority, especially of the kind of police and administrative powers that formerly had been held by the old Japanese Internal Ministry (*naimusho*). Externally, this led to the advancement of an approach to defense and military security that relied largely on the alliance with the

United States and sharply constrained the size and missions of the new Japanese military establishment.

There was nothing automatic about the lessons drawn. In the immediate postwar period a variety of different domestic political actors with sharply diverging policy agendas and ideological world views contended with one another in the Japanese political arena.[12] Each of these groups had a different interpretation of Japanese history and of the lessons they felt should be drawn from the past. On the left there was a large and well-organized peace movement, spearheaded by the newly emergent labor movement and the left-wing Socialist and Communist Parties, and led by many of Japan's leading intellectuals, including Masao Maruyama and Ikutaro Shimizu. The lesson they drew from the past was that any involvement in military ventures could lead to hypernationalism and war, with potentially horrific consequences in the nuclear age. To avoid this fate, they vowed to make Japan into a "peace nation," a neutral power that sided with neither camp in the Cold War. Instead, Japan was to become a model that would inspire the world through its principled renunciation of war as a tool of foreign policy and its adoption of a foreign policy of unarmed neutrality. The left was bolstered in its campaign for neutrality by widespread war weariness combined with the pacifism of a defeated and occupied nation.[13]

On the right there was an alliance of conservative forces favoring a reversal of the more liberal aspects of the occupation era reforms, including the constitution imposed by the United States. Those on the right envisioned the reemergence of Japan as a powerful regional military power, aligned with the United States in the battle to contain communism, but retaining a substantial margin of independence from its powerful Western patron. From this perspective, Japan had done nothing morally wrong by going to war; rather, Japan's prewar and wartime calculation that it could carve out an autarkic sphere of its own in opposition to the United States and the Soviet Union had been mistaken. Japan would be better off if it were to ally itself with one power, preferably the United States, and in this way recover its great power status. The right enjoyed support from a large segment of Japan's old political and bureaucratic elites and also received backing from the heavy-industry sector, which was interested in the potential for defense production.[14] They further enjoyed the advantage of being in government as part of the conservative coalition that came to power during the American occupation.

The ruling coalition, however, was deeply divided within itself. A significant portion of the Japanese political and economic elite favored a more moderate policy of a lightly armed Japan than of a Japan aligned with the West, while eschewing a major military buildup in favor of an emphasis on economic growth and development. This approach to foreign policy was associated with Shigeru Yoshida, the centrist prime minister of the early 1950s. He promoted his own vision of Japan as a merchant nation (*shonin kokka*) aligned with the United States in order to counter the left's image of Japan as a nonaligned, pacifist nation. This approach came to be known as the Yoshida Doctrine.

Like the right, the centrists were vehemently anticommunist. They were able to rally support from more moderate elements in the bureaucracy and the political parties, and they were backed by certain economic elites, especially in the financial and light-industrial sectors. During the crucial period from 1950 to 1955, the centrists were able to shape the broad contours of Japanese foreign policy under the leadership of Prime Minister Yoshida. Conservatives like Hitoshi Ashida who pushed a strong, anticommunist, pro-defense message, were defeated decisively by Yoshida's Liberal Party in national elections.[15] Yoshida and his allies prevented the reentry of conservative officers into the nascent Japanese military establishment and established a system of tight bureaucratic controls over the new armed forces.[16] A whole series of legal safeguards, or brakes (*hadome*), were designed to contain the armed forces, including a ban on the overseas deployment of the Self-Defense Forces (SDF); a ban on the export of weapons; and a Diet resolution declaring Japan's entry into collective security arrangements unconstitutional.[17]

Yoshida, with the help of moderate Japanese business leaders and the Ministry of Finance, managed to prevent the formation of a significant industrial bloc which could have engaged in defense production and which might have lobbied for expansion of the armed forces.[18]

In 1955, centrists and the right formed a single bloc to contain the rising power of the left, creating what came to be known as the 1955 system (*gojyunen taisei*) under the banner of the Liberal Democratic Party (LDP). This coalition dominated Japanese politics until 1993. To do so they had to paper over their very significant differences on defense and other issues.[19] This center–right alliance was in many ways a precarious one, especially on foreign policy issues. Whenever conservative leaders attempted to push their foreign policy and defense agenda, the alliance quickly came apart, as it did in spectacular fashion during the 1960 controversy over the revision of the Mutual Security Treaty (MST) with the United States.[20]

In the late 1950s, the conservative wing of the LDP achieved a dominant position in the party when Nobosuke Kishi became prime minister in 1958. Kishi had been a prominent member of the wartime regime, and as munitions minister under General Hideaki Tojo he had been one of the signatories of the declaration of war on the United States. During the postwar period, after being briefly imprisoned as a possible war criminal by the Americans, Kishi returned to politics and became a leading proponent of large-scale rearmament and constitutional revision. As a result, proposals to revise the MST with the United States sparked widespread fears that the Kishi government was using the alliance as a tool to effect far-reaching transformation of Japan's foreign and domestic policies.

Of particular concern was the insertion into the treaty of a clause (Article 6) committing Japan to a broader security role. Critics worried that this clause would commit Japan to sending forces to support American military operations in regional conflicts like Korea and Vietnam. The fear was that Japanese forces would become bogged down in fighting a land war on the Asian mainland and domestic political dissent would grow, giving the conservatives the excuse they needed for cracking down on the left-wing opposition. Foreign military crises would thus become, as in the 1930s, the catalyst for the collapse of democratic government and a return to authoritarian government and militarism.[21]

Based on these fears, hundreds of thousands of protesters took to the streets, while inside the Diet building, opposition parliamentarians and their staffs made every effort to block the proposed revisions, at times resorting to physical violence in order to disrupt parliamentary proceedings. As the violence escalated and the Kishi government contemplated calling out the SDF to suppress the protesters, centrists in the ruling party, the bureaucracy, the media, and the business community began to fear for the stability of Japanese democracy. Only a few months later in neighboring South Korea, the democratic Chang Myon government, unable to cope with student protesters, was brought down by a military coup d'etat.[22] While condemning the violent methods of the protesters, Japanese centrists turned on their own government and called for the removal of Prime Minister Kishi. Although the treaty was eventually revised, the conservative Kishi government was toppled and the more moderate Hayato Ikeda, a protégé of Yoshida, took over as prime minister.[23]

The 1960 treaty debate proved a seminal event in the formation of the domestic political context of Japanese defense policy. The LDP, fearful that further internal divisions could split the party and allow an anti-alliance Socialist coalition to come to power, chose to follow the centrists and support the more moderate foreign policy course associated with Yoshida. A tacit moratorium on defense and national security issues was agreed upon while the country focused on the tasks of economic growth and development. When the defense issue reemerged, future generations of Japanese leaders had learned to proceed with caution. Certain issues, most notably constitutional revision, were taken off the political agenda, and the pattern of centrist defection whenever the right wing seemed to test the boundaries of permissible debate was set.[24]

## Japanese Antimilitarism During the Cold War

For the next three decades, Japan followed the strategy set out by the Yoshida Doctrine. Although the evolving international environment necessitated numerous changes, the core orientation toward defense and foreign policy established in the 1950s remained unchanged. This did not mean, however, that defense and national security became devoid of controversy. On the contrary, the prevailing approach to defense was challenged constantly, by both the left and the right, and defense policymaking on the whole was plagued by a string of scandals and political controversies that periodically rocked the Japanese political world. However, until 1990 the net result of these challenges was more a reaffirmation and strengthening of the Yoshida Doctrine, rather than rejection thereof.

The continued power of the antimilitary animus in the Japanese defense debate and the way in which it hampered U.S.–Japanese defense cooperation can be seen in the 1965 controversy over the "Three Arrows Plan," a secret set of contingency plans leaked to the Japanese opposition concerning how the SDF might respond to a military emergency on the Korean Peninsula. Even though these plans were purely hypothetical in nature and in no way formally committed Japan to assist the United States in the event of a military conflict, their very existence was considered inflammatory in Japan, where it recalled the emergencies used by militarists to launch the invasion of China in the 1930s. When word of these plans was leaked, public opinion and concern over civilian control in the ranks of the party compelled the conservative Eisaku Sato government to place a virtual ban on such research for over thirteen years.[25] Other legal safeguards were similarly reinforced, most notably a strengthening of the ban on the export of weapons and the introduction of the "Three Non-Nuclear Principles" (see Appendix 9) whereby Japan resolved not to acquire, to allow the stationing of, or to permit the transit through its territory of nuclear weapons.[26]

In the early 1970s, the perceived decline of a U.S. commitment to Asian security in the wake of the Vietnam War posed a serious challenge to the Yoshida line and led many Japanese leaders to urge the adoption of a more independent military posture within the context of the U.S.–Japanese alliance. Senior Japanese officials, including Prime Minister Eisaku Sato and the then director general of the Self-Defense Agency Yasuhiro Nakasone seriously considered a major expansion of Japan's military forces, including the possible acquisition of nuclear weapons.[27] In the end, however, the movement favoring the establishment of an autonomous defense posture (*jishuboei*) came to naught when Japanese leadership concluded that the domestic and international political costs of pursuing such an option would be too costly. Instead, they sought to strengthen the security relationship with the United States rather than to embark on a major arms buildup and a concomitant reorientation of Japan's security policy.[28]

In a similar fashion, factionalism, bureaucratic in-fighting, and persistent suspicions regarding the military hampered Japanese defense policymaking after the reintensification of the Cold War at the end of the 1970s. New Soviet troop deployments in the Far East also placed the subject of military security on Japan's political agenda once again. Controversy flared again in 1979 when a senior officer warned that in an emergency situation, Japan's highly restrictive rules of engagement could compel the SDF to take extralegal action and respond to a Soviet attack without waiting for civilian approval.[29] Furthermore, in 1986 when Prime Minister Nakasone linked raising defense spending above 1 percent of GNP to a revival of Japanese national pride and defense consciousness, LDP moderates and rival conservatives like Fukuda Takenori sided with the leftist opposition to delay defense spending.[30]

Despite recurrent controversy, however, Japan's defense and security policy continued to evolve. The two most important changes were the upgrading of the U.S.–Japanese military relationship in the late 1970s and early 1980s and the redefinition of national security during the 1980s to include a broad range of areas beyond military defense, as described by Sheila Smith in this volume. Both of these developments, however, did not add up to much more than an elaboration of the Yoshida line. In a very real sense they should be viewed as a cautious modification of that doctrine to meet Japan's changed position in the international system.

Following the decision to reject *jishuboei,* the Japanese government began to seek ways to strengthen the U.S.–Japanese alliance. In 1975, for the first time in the postwar era, the Japanese Diet approved a mission statement and procurement plan for the Self-Defense Forces. It was known as the National Defense Policy Outline (NDPO, or *taiko*). The *taiko,* unlike earlier Japanese defense plans, made explicit for the first time the reliance of the Japanese SDF on U.S. assistance for dealing with a large-scale military threat. Formulation of Guidelines for U.S.–Japanese Defense Cooperation in 1978 subsequently set the stage for joint U.S.–Japanese training and collaboration in hypothetical defense planning.[31] While widely criticized by the left at the time, these initiatives represented not a remilitarization of Japanese foreign policy, but rather a reaffirmation of the Yoshida line's commitment to a minimal defense establishment and the continued reliance on the United States.[32] Not only did the successful implementation of these policies obviate the need for a defense buildup, many Japanese policymakers also saw the intensified security relationship with the United States as another way to monitor and contain the Japanese armed forces.[33]

Despite a renewed emphasis on security ties to the United States, Japan faced the problem of matching its security role to its new economic status. The solution that maintained the Yoshida line was put forth by the government of Masayoshi Ohira in 1980; it was the concept of "comprehensive security." No longer would Japan seek to maintain external security through military means alone; instead it would pursue its goals through a wide range of other, nonmilitary policies deemed crucial to national security. These other policy options included stockpiling energy supplies, maintaining a certain degree of self-sufficiency in food production, promoting regional institutions such as the Pacific Economic Cooperation Council (PECC); and furthering regional development through the generous provision of Overseas Development Assistance (ODA) funds.[34]

Comprehensive security can be seen in part as having been merely a means of logrolling increases in defense spending with other issues in order to win bureaucratic and Diet approval. At a more fundamental level, however, these policies were designed to stave off U.S. pressure on Japan to assume a larger military role. In addition, they helped open the way for the wave of Japanese foreign direct investment (FDI) that swept through East and Southeast Asia during the 1980s and 1990s.[35] The promotion of economic development, one of the two pillars on which the Yoshida Doctrine rested, was no longer seen as a purely domestic Japanese matter. With comprehensive security, the Japanese government endeavored to extend the doctrine to cover the entire East Asia region. At the same time, both implicitly and explicitly, the Japanese were offering a new division of labor to the United States. America would retain primary responsibility for military security, while Japan would concentrate on providing the economic underpinnings of regional, and perhaps even global stability.

It is far from accidental that Japan chose to pursue this particular set of policies. Other options were considered and rejected by the Japanese leadership at various points during the Cold War. They were rejected primarily because they were believed to be unsustainable for domestic political reasons. Policies that were in place by the late 1950s, however, became the templates for future policies designed to meet the exigencies of a changed international environment. The peace and prosperity that Japan enjoyed during the Cold War increased considerably the domestic political legitimacy of this approach. Public opinion data reveal steadily growing support for the institutional structures of the Japanese approach to defense, including the SDF, the alliance with the United States, and the postwar constitution.[36] At the same time, both left- and right-wing criticisms of government policies became more muted. In the early 1970s, the left could mobilize thousands of demonstrators to protest government policies, but by the late 1970s the turnout at such protests was greatly diminished.[37]

These policies were intended by Yoshida to be purely provisional. Once Japan had recovered from its wartime defeat, Yoshida and other conservative Japanese leaders fully expected Japan to reassume the role of a great power. Their aim was not to turn Japan permanently into a civilian power, but rather to undo what they believed had been the fundamental mistake of the militarists: pitting Japan, a nation dependent on commerce and overseas markets for its survival, against the primary maritime power of the age, the United States.[38] The Yoshida Doctrine, however, proved to be the one policy behind which it was possible to form a minimal political consensus. It was in this way that Japan's minimalist approach to security survived long after the domestic and international political conditions that had created it ceased to exist.

## Antimilitarism in the Post–Cold War Period

To what extent have things changed in the post–Cold War period? As outlined above, the three chief features behind Japanese defense passivity were fear of the impact of a more active military policy on democracy, factional and bureaucratic paralysis, and a weak pro-defense constituency coupled with the absence of a strong consensus favoring reform. Closer analysis of the current Japanese defense debate reveals that these factors have changed less than is commonly supposed.

Despite the fact that fewer and fewer Japanese have had any direct experience with the militarist regime and that the SDF have played a relatively quiescent role in Japanese politics, deeply ingrained fears of the armed forces as a potential threat to democracy persist. Nowhere were these fears more evident than during the Gulf War, when Japan came under intense pressure from the United States to go beyond checkbook diplomacy and send at least logistical forces in support of the war effort against Iraq. Not only did the Kaifu government stubbornly refuse to dispatch forces—against the advice of many of the government's top defense and foreign policy experts—but for the first few months of the war, Toshiki Kaifu forbade cabinet members to speak directly with uniformed personnel for fear they would be contaminated by military thinking.[39]

In 1993, the end of the LDP's 38 years of dominance in Japanese politics, marked by the formation of the government of Morihiro Hosokawa, seemed to breathe new life into Japanese democracy. The unspoken fear of the Cold War era that the conservatives had to be held in check in order to preserve Japan's fragile democracy seemed to have been undermined with the LDP's fall from power. At the same time, the Socialist Party's abandonment of its anti-alliance, pacifist defense policies signaled the demise of the old left–right cleavage that had for so long paralyzed Japanese defense policymaking. Ichiro Ozawa, the leader of the largest of the new opposition parties, the New Frontier Party, seemed in the eyes of many observers to herald the arrival of a new era in Japanese politics by boldly calling on Japan to become a "normal nation" and to assume a larger international security role through participation in both peacemaking and peacekeeping operations.[40]

Ozawa's call for a new international activism, however, was viewed with suspicion by many of the other members of the Hosokawa coalition, especially the Socialists and left-of-center former LDP politicians, and was seen as further evidence of his authoritarian character.[41] Concerns about Ozawa's long-term ambitions and his growing influence within the coalition government led eventually to the dissolution of the Hosokawa cabinet. Ozawa revived traditional fears about the antidemocratic tendencies of advocates of a more active security policy. Other members of the new generation of conservative leaders, including former Prime Minister Kaifu, leaned toward a more moderate version of the left's old concept of Japan as a peaceful nation, emphasizing its duty to promote international disarmament and eschewing a more active military role.[42]

In short, political realignment and the apparent disappearance of the old ideological cleavage between the right and the left have not laid the defense debate to rest. Instead, the cleavages that have long existed inside the LDP between centrists and rightists have spread to become one of the dominant cleavages running throughout the Japanese political system.[43]

The prolonged crisis and increased factionalism that has gripped Japanese politics since 1989 has further reinforced the system's tendency toward fragmented decision-making. Each ministry continues to jealously guard its bureaucratic prerogatives, while lack of direction at the political center leads to a mode of policymaking in which new policies are made in ad hoc fashion. Under these conditions, the Japanese defense establishment holds a particularly weak set of cards. The Japan Defense Agency (JDA) remains a second-rank power in the bureaucratic hierarchy, and Japanese defense spending, like other segments of the budget, has come under increased budget-cutting pressures in recent years.[44] The domestic constituency for increased defense spending and military effort remains relatively weak,[45] and although public opinion has proven supportive of a continuation of the present array of policies, opposition remains strong to Japan's assumption of a broader military security role.[46]

## Conclusion

As the 21st century arrives, the question arises whether in light of its history Japan is likely to remain forever on the sidelines in military security affairs. Are efforts like the Nye Initiative, which seeks to encourage Japan to assume a larger regional security role, condemned to failure? Or perhaps, while the foregoing analysis suggests that, mutatis mutandis, a fundamental change in Japan's outlook on security is not on the horizon, there are also grounds for cautious optimism that some progress can be made, much along the lines of the limited, but significant improvements in U.S.–Japanese security cooperation achieved in the late 1970s and early 1980s.

Both public and elite opinion in Japan remain supportive of the SDF and of a continuation of the MST system. The uproar in 1995 over the rape of an Okinawan schoolgirl by U.S. servicemen highlighted the continued sensitivities centering around the presence of American forces on Japanese territory. At the same time, the Hashimoto government's successful effort to contain the controversy and find a new modus vivendi under which American troops can continue to be stationed in Japan underlined a continued appreciation on the Japanese side of the importance of maintaining the security relationship.[47]

Japan's foreign policy elite are keenly aware of the emergence of potential new security threats in the region, such as the acquisition of nuclear weapons by a North Korean regime that only recently threatened to turn southern Japan into a "sea of fire," as well as the emergence of an increasingly assertive People's Republic of China.[48] Hence, the perceived need for continued American commitment to Japanese and regional security is as great as ever. Certainly, Japan can contain these threats more easily on its own today than it ever could the Soviet military threat during the Cold War. Furthermore, Asian fears of Japanese intentions, while still quite strong, have diminished, especially during the last twenty years. Yet the domestic political obstacles to pursuing a more independent stance on military issues remain as strong as ever.[49]

In the future, the kinds of initiatives that are likely to have the greatest chance for success in inducing Japan to expand its security role are ones that do not run counter to the grain of Japan's antimilitaristic culture. In this context, proposals that seek to expand Japan's military forces purely within the framework of the old U.S.–Japan alliance suffer from two major drawbacks. First, they automatically revive domestic political fears of U.S. political dominance. Second, such initiatives historically have been seen as a potential channel for a right-wing revival. Instead, it may be more fruitful to anchor an expanded Japanese security role within the context of a new regionally based security order. The precise contours of such a multilateral institution depend a great deal on the further evolution of international relations in East Asia, and care must be taken to construct institutions that will not become the focus of a new left-wing neutralism, as the Conference on Security and Cooperation in Europe did at certain times in Europe during the 1970s and early 1980s.[50] For such a new security order to emerge, however, the United States will have to take the lead.

## Notes

1. Regarding some of the details of the proposed research, see *Asahi Shimbun*, September 15, 1996, p. 1. See Appendix 5.
2. See, for example, Christopher Layne, "The Unipolar Illusion: Why New Great Powers Will rise," *International Security* 17 (Spring 1993): 41–45; and Kenneth Waltz, "The Emerging Structure of International Politics," *International Security* 18 (Fall 1993). A number of Japan experts make similar arguments; see Chalmers Johnson, "Rethinking Asia," *National Interest* 32 (Summer 1993). Perhaps the most widely known of this view is George Friedman and Meredith Lebard, *The Coming War with Japan* (New York: St. Martin's Press, 1992). For a more moderate version of this position, see Susan Pharr, "Japan's Defensive Foreign Policy and the Politics of Burden Sharing," in Gerald L. Curtis, *Japan's Foreign Policy after the Cold War* (Armonk, NY: M.E. Sharpe, 1993).
3. Tetsuya Kataoka, *Waiting for Pearl Harbor: Japan Debates Defense* (Stanford, CA: Hoover Institution Press, 1980); and Peter J. Katzenstein and Nobuo

Okawara, *Japan's National Security: Structures, Norms and Policy Responses in a Changing World* (Ithaca, NY: Cornell University Press, 1993). Appendix 5.

4. On Japan's new regional role, see Walter Hatch and Kozo Yamamura, *Asia in Japan's Embrace: Building a Regional Production Alliance* (New York: Cambridge University Press, 1996); Edward J. Lincoln, *Japan's New Global Role* (Washington, D.C.: Brookings Institution, 1993), especially chap. 5; Peter J. Katzenstein and Martin Rouse, "Japan as a Regional Power in East Asia," in Jeffrey Frankel and Miles Kahler, *Regionalism and Rivalry: Japan and the United States in Pacific Asia* (Chicago: University of Chicago Press, 1993).
5. *Yomiuri Shimbun*, July 9, 1996, pp. 1, 2.
6. *Yomiuri Shimbun*, July 3, 1993, p. 2.
7. For a more detailed articulation of this argument, see Thomas U. Berger, *Cultures of Anti-Militarism: National Security in Germany and Japan* (Baltimore, MD: Johns Hopkins University Press, 1998).
8. For a fascinating analysis of Japanese thinking about the war and contrasted with Germany, see Ian Buruma, *The Wages of Guilt* (New York: Farrar, Straus and Giroux, 1994).
9. On the character of the prewar Japanese political system and the events that led to the collapse of Taisho democracy and World War II, see Gordon Berger, *Parties Out of Power in Japan, 1931–1941* (Princeton, NJ: Princeton University Press, 1977); Richard J. Smethurst, *A Social Basis for Prewar Japanese Militarism* (Berkeley, CA: University of California Press, 1974); Murayama Masao, *Thought and Behavior in Modern Japanese Politics* (New York: Oxford University Press, 1963); Akira Iriye, *The Origins of the Second World War in Asia and the Pacific* (London and New York: Longman, 1987).
10. The impact of the atomic bombing on Japan's national psyche is hard to underestimate, and the event proved seminal in providing the emotional focus for the subsequent development of the Japanese peace movement. For a scholarly discussion, see John Dower, "The Bombed: Hiroshimas and Nagasakis in Japanese Memory," and Seiitsu Tachibana, "The Quest for a Peace Culture: The A-Bomb Survivors' Long Struggle and the New Movement for Redressing Foreign Victims of Japan's War," both in Michael J. Hogan, ed., *Hiroshima in History and Memory* (New York: Cambridge University Press, 1996). For an overview of the impact of these events on Japanese culture in general, see John Whittier Treat, *Writing Ground Zero: Japanese Literature and the Atomic Bomb* (Chicago: University of Chicago Press, 1995). On the general brutality of the Pacific war as waged by both sides, see John Dower, *War Without Mercy* (New York: Pantheon, 1986).
11. On the Japanese debate over war guilt in general, see *Sekai* (February 1994), special issue on war guilt, especially Shinichi Arai, "Senso Sekinin to wa Nani Ka"; and Tanaka Akira, "Nihon wa Senso Sekinin ni do taishite kita

ka." Recently this debate has received additional impetus as a result of the domestic and international political uproar regarding new revelations about the Japanese government's involvement in organizing sexual slavery for the Japanese forces during World War II. As a result, the Japanese government has begun to grudgingly acknowledge its moral obligation to compensate the victims of Japanese wartime actions. See *Asahi Shimbun*, June 15, 1995, p. 1. See also George Hicks, *Comfort Women* (New York: Norton, 1994).

12. For other descriptive typologies of the different ideological groupings in Japan, see Michael Mochizuki, "Japan's Search for Strategy," *International Security* 8 (Winter 1983–1984); Tetsuya Umemoto, *Arms and Alliance in Japanese Public Opinion*, (Ph.D. diss., Princeton University, 1985); Kobun Ito, *Japan's Defense: Its Present and Future* (National Institute for Defense Studies, 1985); Kiyofuku Chuma, *Saigumbi no Seijigaku* (Tokyo: Chishikisha, 1985).

13. An early and influential expression of this point of view can be seen in the influential article, by Tatsuo Morito "Heiwa Kokka no Kensetsu Kenso Kaiso" (January 1946). See also the impassioned plea of Tokyo University president Shigeru Namboro, *Heiwa no Sengen* (Tokyo: Tokyo Daigaku Shuppanbu, 1951).

14. In the early 1950s there was tremendous interest concerning Japanese business and bureaucracy concerning the possibility of using defense production to revive the then still moribund postwar economy. See Hideo Takeo, "Nihon ni okeru 'Gunsankan fukugotai keisei no Zasetsu," in Hideo Otake, ed., *Nihon Seiji no Soten* (Tokyo: Sanichi Shobo, 1984).

15. Hideo Otake, *Saigumbi to Nashinaruzumu* (Tokyo: Chukoshinsho 1988), chap. 3.

16. On the battle to keep conservative officers out of the new military, see John Welfield, *An Empire in Eclipse: Japan in the Postwar American Alliance System* (London: Athlone Press, 1988), pp. 71–78. On type of controls that are placed on the military, see Akira Nishioka, *Gendai no Shiberiian Kontroru* (Tokyo: Chishkisha, 1988); and Katsuya Hirose, *Kanryo to Gunjin: Bunmintosei no Genkai* (Tokyo: Iwanami Shoten, 1989).

17. By which was meant regional security arrangements such as NATO. For an overview of these restrictions and the legal battles fought over them see Osamu Nishi, *The Constitution and the National Defense Law System in Japan* (Tokyo: Seibundo, 1987). See also Tsuneharu Higuchi, "'Shudanteki B eiken' to 'Kokurengun e no Sanka' o meguro Seifukaishaku no Henyo," in *Shinbei Ronshu* 19 (September 1991).

18. See Hideo Otake, "Nihon ni okeru 'Gunsankan fukugotai' keisei no Zasetsu."

19. On the complex maneuvers of the time, see Hideo Otake, 1988, pp. 178–81.

20. See Appendix 2.

21. For a summary of the (often well-grounded) criticisms being made by the left, see Martin E. Weinstein, *Japan's Postwar Defense Policy* (New York: Columbia University Press, 1971), chap. 5.

22. On the collapse of Korean democracy around this time period, see Sungjoo Han, *The Failure of Democracy in South Korea* (Berkeley: University of California Press, 1975). All across Asia during this time period democratic governments that had emerged in the wake of the decolonization process were collapsing. Minxin Pei, "The Fall and Rise of Democracy in East Asia," paper delivered at the Conference on "Democracy in East Asia," Washington, D.C., March 14–15, 1996. Although democracy in Japan had deeper, indigenous roots, Japan's prewar democracy had been strongly flawed. Moreover, as the example of the collapse of democracy in Weimar Germany only fourteen years after World War I had demonstrated, the presence of a large middle class and a certain level of material prosperity provided was no guarantee that the democratization could not be reversed.

23. For what is still the most comprehensive English language account of the events and politics surrounding the 1960 Security Treaty struggle, see George Packard, *Protest in Tokyo: The Security Treaty Crisis of 1960* (Westport, CT: Greenwood Press, 1966). Perhaps the best scholarly Japanese work on the subject, outstanding for its coverage of the debate within the LDP and the Foreign Ministry, is Yoshihisa Hara, *Sengonihon to Kokusaiseiji: Ampokaitei no Seijirikigaku* (Tokyo: Chuokoronsha, 1988).

24. Yonosuke Nagai, "Moratoriumuron," *Chuokoron* (Spring 1980).

25. For good overviews of the Three Arrows controversy, see Takeo Ishikuro, "Mitsuya Kenky to Shibirian Kontororu rongi," in *Rippo to Chosa* (June 1980) and Hans Georg Mammitzch, *Die Entwicklung der Selbstvertidigungs-Streitkräfte und Aspekte der zivil-militärischen Beziehungen in Japan* (Ph.D. diss., Rheinische Friedrich-Wilhelms-Universität, Bonn, 1985), pp. 156–74.

26. It is generally believed that certain exceptions to this last point—the non-transit of nuclear weapons—were negotiated in a secret memorandum of understanding in order to permit nuclear-armed U.S. ships to dock at U.S. bases in Japan.

27. It was recently confirmed by influential Japanese political scientist Royama Michio that in the late 1960s Prime Minister Sato Eisaku secretly established a large study group including military officers to look into the issue of nuclear weapons acquisition. *Asahi Shimbun*, November 13, 1994.

28. The definitive study of the politics of this period remains Hideo Otake, *Nihon no Boei to Kokunaiseiji* (Tokyo: Sanichi Shob, 1984), esp. chap. 1.

29. *Asahi Shimbun*, January 20, July 20, and July 27, 1978; Otake, *Nihon no Boei to Kokunai Seiji*, pp. 186–87.

30. See Akio Kaminishi, *GNP 1% Waku* (Tokyo: Kadokawa Bunko, 1986); and Shintaro Akasaka, "1% Waku de Tsumazuita Nakasone Shush," *Bungeishunju* (January 1986). An excellent English overview of the 1% issue in the context of the debate over U.S.–Japanese burden sharing is Joseph Keddell, *The Politics of Defense in Japan* (Armonk, NY: M.E. Sharpe, 1993), esp. pp. 126–56.

31. See Kiyofuku Chuma, *Saigumbi no Seijigaku* (Tokyo: Chishikisha, 1985), pp. 45–94; and Takeo Hideo, *Nihon no Seiji to Kokunai Boei,* chaps. 9, 10.

32. For an example of the kinds of fears that these policies sparked on the left, see Kazuo Yasuhara, "Kishimihajimeta Sengo Boei no Wakugumi," *Ekonomisuto,* July 10, 1984, pp. 12–13.

33. Katsuya Hirose, *Gunjin to Kanryo: Bunmin To se no Genkai* (Tokyo: Wanami Shoten, 1989), pp. 187–88.

34. See the report of the Comprehensive Security Research Group, *Sogoanzenhosho kenkyuu gruppu hokokusho,* delivered to the prime minister, July 2, 1980.

35. Walter Hatch and Kozo Yamamura, *Asia in Japan's Embrace;* Robert M. Orr, *The Emergence of Japan's Foreign Aid Power* (New York: Columbia University Press, 1990).

36. For a review of long-term public opinion trends during this time period, see Shinkichi Eto and Yoshinobu Yamamoto, *Sogoanzenhosho to Mirai no Sentaku* (Tokyo: Kodansha, 1991), pp. 213–24.

37. See Akio Kaminishi, *GNP 1% Waku.* Introduction.

38. Regarding Yoshida's long-term expectation that eventually Japan would rearm, see Kiichi Miyazawa, *Tokyo-Washington no Mitsudan* (Tokyo: Jitsugyo no Nihonsha, 1956), p. 160. For more background on Yoshida's thinking, see John W. Dower, *Empire and Aftermath: Yoshida Shigeru and the Japanese Experience, 1878–1954* (Cambridge, MA: Harvard University Press, 1979).

39. The most comprehensive summary to date of Japan's reaction to the Gulf is Asahi Shimbun, "Wangankiki" Shuzaihan, *Wangan Senso to Nihon* (Tokyo, Asahi Shimbunsha, 1991). See also Courtney Purrington and K. A. "Tokyo's Policy Responses During the Gulf Crisis," *Asian Survey* 21 (April 1991). The author also benefited from conversations with mid-level officials from the JSDA and Ministry of Foreign Affairs regarding the decision to insulate the cabinet from "military thinking."

40. Ichiro Ozawa, *Blueprint for a New Japan: The Rethinking of a Nation* (New York: Kodansha International, 1994).

41. See Mike Mochizuki, *Japan: Domestic Change and Foreign Policy,* pp. 9–12.

42. For a review of the different parties' positions on defense, see *Asahi Shimbun,* October 12, 1996, 1, 2. On the persistence of deep differences between the LDP and the Socialists (now Social Democratic Party), see, for instance, *Asahi Shimbun,* October 27, 1996, p. 1.

43. Mike Mochizuki argues that the new cleavage is between "great power internationalists" and "civilian internationalists." See Mike Mochizuki, *Japan: Domestic Change and Foreign Policy*, pp. 47–50. I, on the other hand, would contend that the two groups have long existed in the Japanese political system, and should be traced back at least to the debates inside the LDP around the time of Prime Minister Masayoshi Ohira in 1980.

44. Masao Fujii, "Maniawase no 'Nobiritsu' Shogen," *Ekonomisuto* (February 1, 1993): 104.

45. On the role of the Japanese defense industry in the Japanese economy, see Michael Green, *Arming Japan: Alliance Politics, Defense Production and the Postwar Search for Autonomy* (New York: Columbia University Press, 1995); and Richard J. Samuels, *Rich Nation, Strong Army: National Security and the Technological Transformation of Japan* (Ithaca, NY: Cornell University Press, 1994).

46. *Yomiuri Shimbun*, July 3, 1993, 2; and April 30, 1993. 1. A five-country study showing that whereas on the average 53–68 percent of Americans and Europeans support an increase in U.N. PKO missions, in Japan a mere 40 percent do. *Yomiuri Shimbun*, April 30, 1993, 1. For an overview on recent developments in public and elite opinion, see Mike M. Mochizuki, *Japan: Domestic Change and Foreign Policy* (Santa Monica, CA: RAND, 1995), esp. chap. 4.

47. For an overview of Japanese government thinking on the Okinawa crisis, see *Asahi Shimbun*, December 9, 1996, p. 6.

48. Christopher Hughes, "The North Korean Crisis and Japanese Security," and Michael Green and Ben Self, "Japan's Changing China Policy: From Commercial Liberalism to reluctant Realism," both in *Survival* 38 (Summer 1996).

49. Whereas the Soviet Union had thousands of warheads and hundreds of launchers that could be aimed at Japan, the PRC has only approximately seventy deliverable warheads. See *The Military Balance: 1995–1996* (New York: Oxford University Press, 1995). The author is indebted to Professor Lyman Miller of the Johns Hopkins School for Advanced International Studies for bringing this data to his attention and sharing his commentary on the subject. On Japan's nuclear potential, see Selig Harrison, ed., *Japan's Nuclear Future: The Plutonium Debate and East Asian Security* (Washington, D.C.: The Carnegie Endowment for International Peace, 1996), Part I, esp. pp. 18–21.

50. For an elaboration of this argument, see Thomas Berger, "Unsheathing the Sword; Germany, Japan and the Perils of Multilateralism," in *World Affairs Quarterly* 158, no. 4 (Spring 1996): 188–91.

# 10

# The Alliance and Post–Cold War Political Realignment in Japan

W. LEE HOWELL

THIS CHAPTER is a parsimonious look at the influence of the U.S.–Japan alliance over a shifting body politic in Japan. On October 20, 1996, a historic election for the lower house of the Diet was held under a new electoral system. At the time of this election, Japan was governed by a remarkably resilient, and unprecedented, coalition of conservatives and socialists. Many still anticipated, therefore, that at least one of the two major conservative parties would emerge with a clear majority in the October poll. No single party, however, achieved an absolute majority in the lower house of representatives, but the largest member of the ruling coalition government, the Liberal Democratic Party (LDP), won 239 of the Diet's 500 seats. Their plurality—coupled with the tacit support of seventeen members from its junior partners in the former coalition government—was enough for the sitting prime minister, Ryutaro Hashimoto, to form a second, and exclusively LDP, cabinet. Despite suffering heavy losses in the election, Hashimoto's left-wing coalition partners from the recent past, the seventeen members from the Social Democratic Party of Japan (SDP) and Sakigake, agreed to form a "loose union" with the LDP: the two parties would not officially join the new government but would nonetheless commit their bloc of votes in support of LDP rule.

Two years later, in a sudden reversal of fortune, Hashimoto was forced to resign as the head of the LDP as a result of his party's poor performance in a bellwether upper house election on July 12, 1998. In the July election, 61 contested seats were under LDP control and retention of these seats was assumed to be highly likely if not a given. Half of the 252 upper house seats of the Diet are up for election every three years for a fixed six-year term.

Although in the midst of a major economic recession, the LDP leadership publicly maintained that its definition of success would be for the party to win at least sixty-four seats—a majority of the contested races. Upper house elections historically have been plagued by low voter turnout, but the July election had an unanticipated 59 percent of the voters going to the polls. By contrast, only 44 percent went to vote in 1995. The LDP suffered a dramatic loss of seventeen seats forcing Hashimoto to resign as prime minister just days prior to scheduled state visits to France and the United States. Keizo Obuchi, the leader of the LDP faction to which Hashimoto belonged, was elected LDP president and prime minister in August.

This chapter focuses primarily on the October 1996 lower house election. The lower house is the principal lawmaking body with authority to elect the prime minister; it is the election that matters most in Japanese politics. Moreover, the October election was the first under new electoral reforms. The U.S.–Japan alliance was also the salient issue for Japan's major political parties throughout the 1996 election campaign. In contrast, the upper house election of July 1998 was about the mismanagement of Japan's economy. Although dramatic in outcome, it did not force the LDP out of power but instead shook the LDP from their complacency about the domestic economy.

The July elections did, however, force the LDP to consider revamping its incremental, and often ad hoc, policymaking process in the wake of strong opposition to its fiscal stimulus and tax cut remedies. The LDP, without an upper house majority, found its legislative and budgetary proposals challenged by vocal and energized opposition parties. Under the constitution, any bill passed by the lower house can be delayed in the upper house for sixty days. The lower house, after the sixty-day period, can then vote to pass the bill into law by a two thirds majority. Such a scenario, however, runs counter to Japan's political culture where a premium is placed on forming a consensus in advance of voting on new legislation. The LDP, therefore, was forced to tread cautiously in this new environment. In this political setting, the onus is placed firmly on opposition parties to capitalize on voter discontent by developing consistent party platforms and more compelling political themes in preparation for the next lower house election.

Although the LDP's support for a U.S. military presence in Japan remains strong, the inherently unstable political arrangement brought on by Hashimoto's departure poses more questions than answers for the future of the U.S.–Japan security relationship. For example, what does Japan's economic malaise mean for the future of the alliance? How will Japanese domestic political factors affect the bilateral relationship, and what issues are likely to be the most explosive? These are some of the issues explored in this chapter.

## The October 1996 Election

The Japanese public voted, after an intense twelve-day political campaign, in an unprecedented election on October 20, 1996. Under a new electoral system, voters elected 500 representatives to the lower house of the Diet. The political stakes in the October election were high; multimember districts were eliminated and replaced by 300 new single-seat districts. The electoral changes were mandated by major political reform bills (*Seijikaikaku Kanrenhoan*) passed on January 29, 1994, during the tenure of Prime Minister Morihiro Hosokawa, in the wake of intense criticism of several major corruption scandals.[1]

Under the new single-seat system, the top vote-getter became the sole representative for each district. The remaining 200 seats of the Diet were apportioned based on a party's election performance in fourteen regional districts; in practice, the parties submitted a list of candidates to fill regional seats administered proportionally. A record 1,500 candidates campaigned for 500 lower house seats. Under the new system Japanese voters dispense two votes—one for their district's single seat and one for their preferred party on the proportional slate.

The expectation of political analysts was that the new electoral system would work against pork barrel politics and encourage a straight debate on policy issues. That debate did not emerge on security issues during the campaigns in 1996, but the fluidity of factional alliances and coalitions that resulted from the new electoral rules has opened up the potential for future political debate and realignment based on security issues. Hints of that fluidity came in the political debate that took place in Tokyo—though not in the election districts—about U.S. bases on Okinawa, and the constitutionality of emerging Japanese defense policies.

## Okinawa and Domestic Politics

Japanese and American defense officials were concerned that U.S.–Japan security relations would become a major political, and poten-

**Table 10–1 The Election Results and Political Realignment**

| Parties | Numbers of Seats: District | | Proportional | | Total |
|---|---|---|---|---|---|
| Liberal Democratic Party (*Jimin-to*) | 169 | + | 70 | = | 239 |
| New Frontier Party (*Shinshin-to*) | 96 | + | 60 | = | 156 |
| Democratic Party of Japan (*Minshu-to*) | 17 | + | 35 | = | 52 |
| Japan Communist Party (*Kyosan-to*) | 2 | + | 24 | = | 26 |
| Social Democratic Party (*Shamin-to*) | 4 | + | 11 | = | 15 |
| Harbinger Party (*Sakigake*) | 2 | | | = | 2 |
| Independents | 9 | | | = | 9 |
| Others | 1 | | | = | 1 |
| Total | 300 | + | 200 | = | 500 |

| *Top Four Parties* | *Percentages of District and Proportional Votes* |
|---|---|
| Liberal Democratic Party | 38.6% District, 32.8% Proportional |
| New Frontier Party | 28.0% District, 28.2% Proportional |
| Democratic Party of Japan | 10.6% District, 16.2% Proportional |
| Japan Communist Party | 12.5% District, 13.2% Proportional |

*1998 Political Realignment in the Lower House*

| *Party* | *Seats* |
|---|---|
| Liberal Democratic Party | 263 |
| Democratic Party of Japan | 92 |
| *Heiwa Kaikaku* | 47 |
| Liberal Party | 40 |
| Japan Communist Party | 26 |
| Social Democratic Party | 15 |
| Independent Club | 5 |
| *Sakigake* | 2 |
| Independents | 10 |
| Total | 500 |

tially divisive, issue with Japanese voters in the 1996 lower house elections. The U.S. military presence in Japan had come under intense public scrutiny in the wake of a brutal rape of an Okinawan schoolgirl by American servicemen in September 1995. Moreover, only a month before the election, Okinawans in a nonbinding referendum voted overwhelmingly (by a ten-to-one margin) for the reduction of U.S. forces stationed on the island (74.9 percent of all U.S. military installations in Japan are concentrated in Okinawa, Japan's southernmost prefecture). Okinawa plays a critical role in the U.S.–Japan security alliance. In 1996, American bases occupied some 10 percent of the total area of the multi-island prefecture and about 18 percent of the land on the main island of Okinawa.

The potential for political crisis was acute in the weeks before the election because the erosion of public support for American military bases spread beyond the residents of Okinawa prefecture. Concerning basing U.S. troops in Japan, an October 1995 *Louis Harris/Asahi Shimbun* poll found that 76 percent of Japanese polled wanted the United States to reduce its forces gradually, and 14 percent wanted the bases withdrawn immediately.[2] The poll reflected the public's outrage over the Okinawa incident; however, a recent extensive study of Japanese and American public opinion data has concluded that "Japanese doubts about U.S. troop presence are [in fact] long-standing."[3]

Okinawa was a key issue affecting Japanese domestic politics in 1996. The prefectural governor of Okinawa, Masahide Ota, has long advocated a reduction of U.S. forces on the island. Frustrated with the central government's policies toward the prefecture, Ota refused to authorize the renewal of expired leases for properties located in U.S. military installations. His refusal generated great media coverage and eventually forced the prime minister to respond by exercising his authority to sign the leases, which in turn led to a legal challenge in Japan's supreme court, the *Saiko Saibansho*. The high court upheld the central government's authority to renew the leases in the national interest. The widespread devastation and civilian casualties suffered by Okinawans during the World War II laid a historic foundation for their distrust of, and reluctance to cooperate with, central government authorities in Tokyo. Therefore, a much anticipated September 1996 meeting between socialist governor Ota and conservative Prime Minister Ryutaro Hashimoto was interpreted as a necessary first step before the LDP could call a national election.

In their meeting, Hashimoto expanded on the closing of U.S. military bases (including the Marine Corps air station in Futenma) as well as the consolidation and elimination of military training activities on Okinawa. He also pledged to follow through on a variety of public works and deregulatory initiatives aimed at improving economic conditions in the prefecture. The media and political pundits alike gave a good review of the September meeting, and Hashimoto became more comfortable with the idea of calling an election soon thereafter, but the question remains as to why the controversy over Okinawa and the ensuing debate over the future of the U.S.–Japan security alliance failed to resonate with voters in the October election. The answer involves consideration of four factors.

1. The ideological collapse of Japan's largest liberal opposition party—the Social Democratic Party (formerly the Japan Socialist Party)—resulted in the disaffection of traditional left-wing, pacifist, and antimilitarist voters.
2. A much heralded, but hastily formed alternative liberal party, the Democratic Party of Japan, failed to articulate clearly its defense policies and therefore did not generate political momentum on the issue.
3. Political concern over the transition to a new electoral system coupled with uncertainty surrounding the demise of the "1955 system" of single-party dominance in Japanese politics chilled serious debate on defense issues among leading conservatives.
4. Voter turnout was only 59.9 percent—a twenty-year low for a lower house election. About 66 percent of Japanese voters are over forty years old. The majority grew up during a period of high growth and achieved relative prosperity under the current security framework; they are a moderate/conservative constituency unlikely to challenge the status quo.

## Collective Self-Defense and the Constitution

Another issue that might have colored the lower house elections was the constitutionality and proper scope of Japan's emerging defense policies. Although policymakers have begun to restructure the U.S.–Japan security alliance in light of emerging post–Cold War challenges, public support of their efforts lags far behind in both the United States and Japan. An October 1995 Gallup/*Yomiuri Shimbun* survey found that 30 percent of Americans—but only 19 percent of Japanese—said it was definitely in their respective national interests to keep the U.S.–Japan Security Treaty the same.[4]

Assuming the two publics remain unfamiliar with alternatives to the existing framework, one conclusion that can be drawn from the poll is that the United States may have oversold the utility of the security alliance during the Cold War while Japan undersold it to its public in recent years. By contrast, tension over Chinese missile testing across the Taiwan Strait, heightened anxiety over a potential crisis in North Korea, and the revival of territorial disputes in Northeast Asia made it very apparent to policymakers on both sides of the Pacific that the future of the Security Treaty rests with avoiding what one scholar warns as "divergent responses in crisis affecting mutual security."[5] The erosion of public support for the alliance, of course, increases the likelihood of such a risk. Although defense officials continue to work diligently on revamping existing Guidelines and clarifying roles and missions to avoid such a hazard, many observers felt that public debate over whether or not Japan should exercise the right of collective self-defense would do much to buttress their efforts and to educate the Japanese public on security issues in general.

Japan's government has interpreted its constitution as allowing the right of "self-defense" (against direct attack). However, the government has never had the political support necessary to assert the right of collective defense (assisting a close ally under attack). With the 1996–97 review of the Defense Guidelines, the U.S. and Japanese governments agreed to work within the existing framework of the alliance and the Japanese constitution to avoid a political conflagration over the constitutional issue. They believed that nearly all aspects of enhanced defense cooperation could be managed within a more flexible interpretation of "individual self-defense." Nevertheless, political conservatives in Japan remain eager to test the constitutional issue, while doves remain cautious.

In November 1994, an appeal was made—outside of the political arena—to engage the Japanese public in a debate over their country's constitution. The *Yomiuri Shimbun,* Japan's largest circulating daily newspaper, proposed the revision of the constitution of Japan and published the findings of its private Constitution Study Council chaired by Dr. Masamichi Inoki.[6] The study acknowledged that Japan's postwar recovery, political stability, and economic prosperity owed much to the current constitution enacted in 1946. *Yomiuri Shimbun*'s rationale for proposing a revision was clear and simple: "the Cold War regime has collapsed and national politics have been transformed."[7] On the issue of defense, the report characterized the interpretation of the current constitutional language on the Self-Defense Forces (SDF) as having "been very much confused and [having] resulted in debate after sterile debate—a situation not to be disregarded."[8]

Most Americans who have witnessed prolonged political debate over a balanced budget amendment to the U.S. constitution through most of this decade have come to appreciate the complexity of constitutional change and understand the necessity for maintaining strong political momentum for its success. Constitutional revision, in most democracies, comes as a result of the state having to face the consequences of, or recognizing the potential for, social, political, or economic upheaval that would result from maintaining the status quo. In contrast, confusion over bilateral defense obligations, a growing nonfinancial role in international peace and humanitarian efforts, and concern over inefficiencies in decision-making at the cabinet level forced the issue of constitutional revision in Japan. The issue of collective self-defense and the U.S.–Japan alliance was not directly addressed in the Yomiori proposal. Collective self-defense was examined, only tangentially, by the study. One of its primary goals, in terms of foreign policy impact, was "to make it clear that there will be eventualities in which it will be appropriate to provide a part of our SDF to support peacekeeping and humanitarian efforts of international organizations and that we are determined to play our part when such occasions arise."[9]

The foreign policy dimension to any constitutional debate in Japan remains quite large. Although the American hand in drafting the constitution was great in 1946, the proposals put forth by *Yomiuri Shimbun* did not result from *gaiatsu* (foreign pressure). The proposals reflect a new political reality that is very much based on recent past experience, as opposed to the reactions and counterproposals from liberal newspapers such as the *Asahi Shimbun.* The recent past experience of the Persian Gulf War symbolized for many the constitution's restrictions on foreign policy and the country's lack of political leadership.

In his book *Japanese Politics: Decay or Reform?*, Frank McNeil describes the Persian Gulf War as Prime Minister Toshiki Kaifu's "great headache."[10] Kaifu, leader of the smallest faction in the LDP, was called up to head a government rocked by the "Recruit" scandal of 1989. He then won a general election victory, only to have to face the Gulf War and a protracted domestic political debate over Japan's role during the crisis. McNeil's explanation for Kaifu's fall from power in 1991 is a helpful reminder that domestic political interests more often than not override foreign policy concerns in Japan.

> Rivals tried to push him out because of 'lack of leadership.' . . . It was not foreign policy but Kaifu's desire to reform the Lower House electoral system along lines recommended by a select commission that brought him down. When he sought to dissolve the Diet to stand for election on that issue, the party leadership refused. Unable to exercise his constitutional prerogative of dissolving the Diet, Kaifu resigned.[11]

In 1997, as the Defense Guidelines were under review, the growing consensus among Japanese defense experts was that a constitutional amendment is unnecessary to reverse the existing ban on collective self-defense. Their argument was based on the fact that the current prohibition (i.e., the Yoshida Doctrine) is essentially a product of the bureaucracy. The Yoshida Doctrine, it was argued, is based on a constitutional interpretation by the cabinet's Legal Affairs Bureau (*Naikaku*

*Hoseikyoku*) and has no legal standing. This new rationale, however, reflects only a tactical shift on the part of those bureaucrats and academics endorsing collective self-defense. The ultimate resolution rests either in the supreme court or in the political arena. The difficulty is that no one knows which way the political wind will blow when faced with such a choice.

In August 1996, *Bungei Shunju,* a popular and influential monthly magazine, published the results of its extensive survey of 215 Diet members about Japan's right of collective self-defense as well as its constitutionality (the deregulation of the economy was the other major question polled).[12] 190 Diet members were asked to choose one of four policy positions related to the exercise of collective self-defense.

Position One: Collective self-defense is constitutional and the government should revise its interpretation and proceed with joint U.S.–Japan operations necessary for the security of the country. (Favored by 10 percent of those polled).

Position Two: Collective self-defense presents a conflict with the constitution but the current interpretation is too restrictive in security matters and therefore a public debate to amend the constitution should be proposed. (Favored by 22 percent of those polled).

Position Three: *Collective self-defense is unconstitutional,* but matters related to U.S.–Japan military cooperation should be reviewed as to their constitutionality on a case-by-case basis. (Favored by 41 percent of those polled).

Position Four: *Collective-self defense is unconstitutional.* This view is critical of any military cooperation in general and instead supports peaceful means of international cooperation as an alternative to using military force. (Favored by 17 percent of those polled).

(10% of those polled did not respond to any of the aforementioned choices.)

Position three garnered the most support (seventy-seven members) from among those participating in the poll, in part because it is the perfect "hedge" answer. While it does not challenge the conventional wisdom about collective self-defense, it does allow for flexibility in the event of a crisis. U.S. experts in the past understood the utility of such a hedging strategy as "a reflection of uncertainty about U.S. intentions and Japanese domestic political developments."[13] The appeal of position three is that it permits political leaders to pursue what is now referred to as an "incremental shift" toward collective self-defense.[14]

The success of an incremental approach relies on the fact that positions two and three differ only slightly, and the two points of view can be reconciled with little or no political fallout. Position two proposes a well-defined way to remedy much of the ambiguity surrounding Japan's response to a regional crisis, while position three simple acknowledges the complexity of the problem. The key point here is that moderates and conservatives that advocate position three are likely to pursue the means prescribed by position two to resolve this issue should it come to fore. (An example of this would be some exigent regional crisis.) Public debate in favor of amending Japan's constitution (position two) would of course be welcomed by proponents of position one as well. Given the aforementioned policy options and political climate, the start of an incremental shift toward collective self-defense is a distinct possibility.

Will the bases issue and the constitutional problem shape political realignment in the next election? Absent a major regional security crisis, a second, or even third, election campaign under the new system is necessary before pundits and politicians can make an accurate assessment of the influence of defense policy on Japanese voters. In the long term, the combined effect of the demise of the 1955 system and the creation of new electoral districts will make national security policy a key determinant in predicting the success of various parties in electoral districts currently accommodating military installations or encouraging investment in defense-related industries.

## The New Electoral System

An unintended effect of new electoral changes will be that two traditional functions of parliamentary representatives—to serve as the local delegate representing the interest of a constituency and to act as a trustee in the interests of the nation as a whole—are likely to be treated as mutually exclusive within the divided ranks of the Diet under this new system. Simply put, 300 Diet members, now responsible solely for the welfare of their respective districts, are expected to be more responsive to the specific needs of their constituencies. The remaining 200 members, many of whom lost district races but all of whom were elected via the proportional list method, need only maintain close faction ties and avoid intraparty disputes to ensure their reelection. How such fundamental political shifts are likely to affect Japan's security posture is best illustrated by a succinct examination of the political economy of defense policy.

In a paper speculating on Japan's security policy orientations in the year 2010, Princeton University's Kent Calder anticipates that under the single-district system:

> [p]oliticians will have to make much broader political appeals than in the past. Rather than cultivating a small target constituency of 10 to 20 percent of the electorate (the minimum required to be elected under the old multiple-member constituency system), they will be seeking a plurality of 40 to 50 percent of the total vote. Distributive politics—such as promises of roads, bridges, or subsidies to specialized constituencies—will likely become less important. Symbolic appeals—to consumer interests or nationalism, for example—conversely become more so.[15]

An earlier book by Calder focusing on the multimember system, *Crisis and Compensation*, argued that during the 1970s and 1980s Japanese defense budgets were low, "first and foremost because counterpressures from agriculture, public works, and other grassroots-oriented sectors of the Japanese political economy have been strong, due to the ratchet effects of the crisis and compensation dynamic.[16] He identified "the electoral system and the grassroots-*koenkai* structure" as generating civilian counterpressures to defense spending. With multimember districts, conservative politicians were forced to compete against one another, and, in Calder's words,

> [t]o prevail in such competition, since World War II the successful among them have developed so-called *koenkai*, or support organizations. These bodies often have many small businessmen, especially public works contractors, among their members. They continually demand pork-barrel benefits as quid pro quo for continued cooperation, thus forcing Dietmen to press the Ministry of Finance for national budgets oriented heavily toward such distributive allocations.[17]

In the wake of the October 1996 elections, the above statement appears an apt description of the future of Japanese politics in the near term. A decline in distributive politics appears unlikely despite an end to multimember districts, in large part because of Japan's continued economic recession. Although Japan's national debt is now an enormous 440 trillion yen (equal to over 90 percent of the country's annual GDP), Keynesian solutions are not easily abandoned. In the last four years alone, the country's bureaucrats and politicians have spent some 60 trillion yen for economic stimulus with little noticeable result, but this remains the most familiar, and favored, method of business for politicians. Economic hardship, and the requisite political pain, are nevertheless unavoidable when considering the fact that the Japanese government's latest public estimate was that the banking sector carried 76.7 trillion yen in bad or questionable loans ($580 billion).[18] The announcement was received as good news in Japan. Although more than double the amount of previous official estimates, it was well below the figures bandied about in Tokyo's financial circles. In October of 1998, the Diet passed a 25 trillion yen bank recapitalization bill. A month later, the Obuchi government announced yet another stimulus package worth 24 trillion yen.

Any expected increase in symbolic appeals in political campaigns is likely to emanate from the politicians elected on the representational ballot as they begin to operate independently from constituent pressure, as opposed to the members who are preoccupied with issues directly related to their district. Although multimember districts are a thing of the past and intra-party competition has decreased, the grassroots *koenkai* structure remains imbedded in Japanese politics and has proved to be essential for political success. Moreover, local *koenkai* grow stronger in influence as they concentrate much of their organizational and financial support on a single candidate. This new pressure has already surfaced. In November 1996 the LDP secretary general, Koichi Kato, created a political uproar by telling the Japanese media that the ruling party planned on rewarding its supporters and punishing its enemies with budgetary favors for districts that elected LDP candidates. Kato explained that with the electoral change "we [candidates for political office] go through life-or-death fights, [and] it is unavoidable [that we would] distinguish between the districts that helped us and those that did not."[19]

Kato's attitude toward distributive politics (shared by many in the opposition) also influences Japan's defense policy, as well as the bilateral security relationship. Members of the Diet with either U.S. or Japanese military bases and/or defense-related industries located in their districts may advocate initiatives at odds with central government policy if such policies affect, or interfere with, local commercial, environmental, and land-use (zoning) concerns. In the alternative, these very same members may be supportive of an increase in defense-related government spending or military activities if their district stands to gain economically. In the past, membership in a particular intra-party faction (*habatsu*) established a member's political pedigree. Intra-party power-sharing ensured that each faction would have some measure of representation in any new cabinet. Within each faction, a seniority system determined whether a member would assume a junior ministerial or senior cabinet appointment. The system also determined which issue-oriented or special interest *zoku* (political caucus) a member supported, although a *zoku* would often cross faction lines. For example, membership in former prime minister Noboru Takeshita's faction also meant support of Japanese policies that were pro-mainland

China as opposed to pro-Taiwan. Political lineage permitted outside observers to neatly categorize politicians and their pet issues. With the breakup of the 1955 system, political pedigrees have been tainted by a Diet filled with party defectors and members belonging to more than one faction. Understanding the political mood of those districts with either a high concentration of defense industries or military (United States and Japanese) facilities will be critical in forecasting Japan's defense posture. This may become more difficult if the role of local civic groups, such as the *kichi taisaku iinkai,* which serve as important intermediaries over base issues in their municipalities, were to diminish under the new electoral system. Although political power is concentrated under one representative, the corridor to influence soon becomes crowded with local organizations that were always heard by at least one Diet member in the old multiparty system. Constituent groups will now have to compete among themselves to gain the attention of their sole representative.

Demographics will also play an important role in determining the longer-term impact of the new electoral system. Despite electoral reforms, sharp imbalances remain. From the perspective of one analyst, "Japan's electoral system continues to be heavily rigged in the LDP's favor. Even though the country is highly urbanized, the traditionally pro-LDP rural vote packs a mighty punch. Because of gerrymandering, the rule of thumb for the lower house is that one rural vote is equivalent to two city votes."[20] The influence that gerrymandering will have on the future of American bases in Japan (outside of Okinawa) is yet unclear, but many major installations are located in relatively urban locales. The LDP's poor showing in urban centers in the 1998 upper house election is the first sign of an emerging polarization in Japanese politics.[21] As one Japanese analyst observes, "[the LDP] will keep control of the rural areas, but opposition influence will grow in the cities, attracting new, independent constituencies concerned about the political economy."[22] The pace and profile for this polarization will be influenced greatly by Japan's increasing aging population—currently, more Japanese are over the age of sixty-five than are under the age of sixteen. This change will profoundly alter the country's political landscape as 25 percent of Japanese will be over the age of sixty-five by the year 2030.

In terms of American interests, the October 1996 election results did not challenge the current alliance structure in the short run. There was no correlation between the location of a base and the margin of victory for the LDP candidate. On Okinawa, two of the three electoral districts were won by NFP members, but the third district of Okinawa went to Kosuke Uehara of the SDP. It is too soon to predict the policy leanings of these new members on future issues related to national security. The importance, however, of these and other key districts, in terms of their symbolic appeal and impact on the defense budget process, should not be underestimated. If the behavior of their American counterparts are an indicator, then it is not premature to assume that Japanese representatives (with vested interest in defense issues) will advocate policies supported by their constituencies.

Okinawa's November 1998 gubernatorial election best illustrates the possible broad appeal in working local economic concerns into future political debates over base issues. The national press had framed the Okinawa election exclusively as a referendum between immediate base closings and gradual force restructuring. In reality, the ideological posturing over defense policy has fatigued voters. The problem's importance did not necessarily diminish, but residents of one of Japan's poorest regions did not want their other main concern—the state of the local economy—to go unheeded. By pledging to improve the prefecture's political dialogue with the central government (and thereby improving the likelihood of securing much needed federal assistance), Keiichi Inamine defeated incumbent Governor Masahide Ota by a 5 percent margin in an election with a voter turnout of 77 percent. Inamine, a conservative candidate backed by the LDP, shared views similar to Ota's with regard to base closures; he had pledged to limit the use of Futenma airfield by U.S. Marine Corps helicopter forces to 15 years. His campaign, however, focused on improving the local economy and ignored base issues.

## The Future: New Actors and Ideas

The creation of a new liberal party, the Democratic Party of Japan (*Minshu-to*), by former moderate LDP members (including former Prime Minister Morihiro Hosokawa) and socialists a few months before the October elections raised the expectations of voters and the media concerned about a return to the 1955 system. There was also apprehension over the prospect that the two major conservative parties (LDP and NFP) would cooperate to form a powerful right-of-center coalition majority (*hoho-rengo*) after the October election.

Lacking both the organizational reach and financial pull of its more conservative opponents, the Democratic Party's electoral success relied heavily in the October 1996 election on the charisma of its leaders. These included Yukio Hatoyama, who has a distinguished political pedigree that includes a former prime minister (grandfather), a former foreign minister (father), and a fellow lower house member (brother, Kunio); and Naoto Kan, another former member of Sakigake, who exposed the bureaucratic cover-up of tainted blood supplies during his tenure as minister for health and welfare in the Murayama cabinet. Hatoyama and Kan were the principal figures in increasing the party's national exposure. As the third largest party at that time, the Democratic Party faced some difficulty in distinguishing its policy proposals from the two major parties.

On the economic front, all parties in the 1996 elections, including incumbents, campaigned promising greater progress on *kisei kanwa* (the reduction of government regulations) and *gyosei kaikaku* (administrative reform of the bureaucracy). It was on national security policy where the Democratic Party made some attempt to distinguish itself from the rest of the pack. In early October, Yukio Hatoyama told foreign reporters that his party considered the Security Treaty outdated, and that a new security treaty was needed that "does not necessitate the full-time existence of U.S. military bases in Japan."[23] Although his comments stirred the foreign media, critics in Japan attacked his ideas as being vague and not well thought out (which was not the case for his party's economic message). Indeed, his preelection comments lacked both a strategic vision and an alternative framework and therefore did not resonate with voters. His party's position in the Diet remains about the same as before the election. That said, the Democratic Party is now refining its message on national security. Its revamped policies are finding some favor in both media and academic circles.

In his November 1996 article in the *Bungei Shunju*, Hatoyama articulated a vision of "A Security Treaty Without Stationing Troops During Peacetime."[24] In his essay, Hatoyama acknowledged the importance of the role of the U.S.–Japan security relationship, but addressed in greater detail the necessity of promoting multilateral regional forums. He also reaffirmed his opposition to an expanded interpretation of the right to collective self-defense. Two proposals captured the most attention from observers in both countries.

- A comprehensive review of the U.S.–Japan Security Treaty with the aim to remove U.S. forces on Okinawa and on mainland Japan by the year 2010 while concurrently concluding a U.S.–Japan free-trade agreement
- Dividing Japan's Self-Defense Forces into three new units by the year 2010: a defense-oriented unit that comprises a navy and an air force; an international peacekeeping unit comprising army troops; and a disaster rescue unit

The political future of Hatoyama's proposals is yet unclear given some reactions from within his own party. A month after the article's publication, the Democratic Party's Security Affairs subcommittee chairman, Seiji Maehara, wrote in an editorial that the two proposals "will be the basis of debate in the Democratic Party, but at the moment they are nothing but [Hatoyama's] personal views."[25] An intra-party division, however, did not happen because the issue lost its political appeal. The Democratic Party backed off the issue because it recognized that its future interests were with supporting the labor agenda during a period when anxiety is still high over Japan's management of its slow-growth economy. Moreover, the few remaining old-guard socialists retreated to their past hard-line stance on base issues. The Democratic Party saw their neglect of the labor vote, which is moderate on security issues, as an important opportunity to shore up the party's support with workers.

After the NFP's poor showing in 1996 lower house elections, former prime minister Tsutomu Hata left in December to form the Sun Party (*Taiyo-to*) in large part because of disappointment in Ichiro Ozawa's leadership. A new voting bloc, calling itself "*Minyuren,*" consisting of the four opposition parties, was formed in January 1998. The new group collectively held ninety-eight seats in the lower house and forty-four seats in the upper house. In March 1998, this bloc merged into a newly expanded Democratic Party. The Democratic Party, in the wake of the July 1998 upper house election, is the dominant opposition party. It is now the party best poised to capitalize on the shifting political mood for the next lower house election, but its tent is even larger, and its voices on security even more diverse than before.

Meanwhile, in the LDP a new generation of political leaders took control of the factions and Prime Minister Obuchi formed a coalition with Ozawa's remaining followers in the Liberal Party. This next generation of conservative leadership has yet to set its course on security policy.

The concept of maintaining the Security Treaty without U.S. forces in Japan is gaining strong support from many in academic and media circles who had opposed the security relationship up until the early 1990s. Japan's influential liberal newspaper, *Asahi Shimbun,* in a editorial, put its support behind the idea of a bilateral security relationship that does not involve the basing of U.S. forces in Japan.[26] Although political opposition and public demonstrations no longer challenge the U.S.–Japan security relationship, a more corrosive hollowing-out of the alliance may occur if this new line of thinking begins to appeal to voters and politicians alike.

A few months prior to the July 1998 upper house election, Morihiro Hosokawa announced his retirement from the Diet. Long perceived as the "Hamlet" of Japanese politics, Hosokawa has seen his reformist appeal steadily diminish over time; however, analysts have understood his importance in reconciling the policy differences, particularly on defense issues, between young center-left leaders such as Kan and older conservatives such as Hata. It was startling to some, therefore, to find him in favor of the alliance yet advocating the removal of U.S. forces from Japan by 2000 in an article published in *Foreign Affairs*.[27] He was careful to acknowledge the strong public support behind maintaining the alliance, but urged Americans to recognize that this same majority supports a reduction of U.S. military bases in Japan. Hosokawa maintained that diminishing regional security threats and Japan's growing financial debt burdens would force a reassessment of the current American military presence sooner and not later. Written just prior to his retirement and with the intention of distinguishing the Democratic Party's defense platform from that of the ruling conservatives, Hosokawa's article is telling about the future direction of his former party. Democratic Party president Naoto Kan, unlike Hosokawa and Hatoyama, has yet to fully expound on his views about Japan's security policy. Nevertheless, his personal appeal with voters remains very high. On economic issues, Kan continues to promote his own version of "third way" politics, popularized by Britain's prime minister Tony Blair. Critical attention should now be focused on Kan's "third way" as it relates to Japan's future defense strategy.

Naoto Kan is both his party's principal asset and largest liability. His personal charisma and popular appeal have lifted the Democratic Party, but he has yet to articulate what "third way" politics mean for Japan. Kan's party still defies any label and the party is increasingly left vulnerable to shifts in his personal popularity. When rumors of an extramarital affair with a television news anchor were reported in weekly gossip magazines, Kan's poor handling of the allegations led to a significant drop in his popularity as well as a noticeable one for the Democratic Party. The real scare for the party was the negative reactions coming from an increasingly influential constituency—women. Kan did recover from the scandal to win a second term as Democratic Party president in January 1999. Nevertheless, it is clear to many party leaders that there are indeed limits to riding on Kan's coattails.

## Conclusion

As for the outlook for Japan's political system, there are significant changes that lie beyond the scope of this chapter but which nonetheless necessitate further study. First, Japanese voters' distrust of both national politicians and central government bureaucrats, particularly with regard to national economic policy, remains intense. With the bursting of a speculative real estate "bubble" in the early 1990s (with land values dropping over 60 percent), Japan's stock market has over time lost almost half its value from its 1989 Nikkei Index high of 38,915. The firm entrenchment of single-member parliamentary districts (with its promise of a more responsive political culture) should over the long term ameliorate voter frustration, but public and media attention will remain focused on the business cycle and consumer confidence in the near term.

Second, as observed on Okinawa, the role of local and prefectural government will also increase as voters search for alternatives to solve a variety of pressing issues. And many of these issues, although domestic in nature, will undoubtedly impact Japan's future ability to carry out its defense obligations. And lastly, the difficulties posed by financial deregulation of the economy, budget deficits, demographic change, and banking reform will force Japan's leaders to make delicate political decisions; the impact of their decisions will undoubtedly be felt in the national security arena. The process is well on its way.

After the October 1996 election, the Ministry of Finance proposed to Hashimoto that he sponsor a larger financial reform package modeled after Margaret Thatcher's major overhaul of the British securities industry in 1986—the London "Big Bang." Making up for lost time, the Tokyo Big Bang aimed to not only reform the securities business but also liberalize other aspects of the financial system. Moreover, the much publicized bankruptcies of some major agricultural lenders and regional banks had undermined the election base of the LDP.

Since 1997, political debate about the security alliance has taken a backseat to criticism of the elite Ministry of Finance and outrage over sensational cases of fraud and mismanagement in the banking sector. The stunning financial collapse of a number of East Asia economies has also shifted focus away from defense issues. Policymakers in the United States have made it abundantly clear that Japan's weak economic performance during Asia's deflationary spiral threatens the rest of the world with recession. The moribund Japanese financial system, backbone of the second largest economy and top lender to the world, has now become the greatest drag on Asia's recovery.

In the midst of a recession, the LDP government has backed off its initial plan to balance the budget by 2005 and instead has been forced to propose a variety of tax-cutting measures and new spending to stimulate the economy. The aggregate effect has been a change in the mood within Japan's body politic and general public about the economic merits of maintaining the U.S.–Japan security alliance at current spending levels.

The limitations imposed by fiscal and budgetary constraints on defense obligations is well understood in the United States, but will this be the case for Japan? This chapter examined the dynamics of Japan's political change and described the new electoral system. One conclusion is that the consolidation of political power in single-member electoral districts will result in a greater awareness in political circles of local concerns about defense and base-related issues. This awareness is all the more welcome in that it comes during a moment of political realism when Japan's major parties are in agreement over the constitutionality of the Self-Defense Forces and the U.S.–Japan Security Treaty. Yet this newfound reality remains shielded from fiscal and demographic challenges. Although political issues such as "collective self-defense" are no longer shielded from public debate, we should heed with some caution Former Prime Minister Ryutaro Hashimoto's dictum on Japan's effort at budget and government reform—"there are no sanctuaries." It could easily be applied to future budgetary support for the security alliance.

## Notes

1. "Diet Passes Political Reform Bills," *Daily Yomiuri*, January 30, 1994.
2. Everett Carll Ladd and Karlyn H. Bowman, *Public Opinion in America and Japan: How We See Each Other and Ourselves* (Washington, D.C.: AEI Press, 1996), p. 36.
3. Ibid.
4. Ibid., p. 35.
5. Jonathan D. Pollack and Hyun-Dong Kim, eds., *East Asia's Potential for Instability & Crisis: Implications for the United States and Korea* (Santa Monica: RAND, 1995), Section V., "The Future of Japan–U.S. Security Relations: The Challenge of Adversity to Alliance Durability," by Courtney Purrington, p. 225.
6. "A Proposal for the Revision of the Text of the Constitution of Japan" (English translation), *Yomiuri Shimbun*, November 3, 1994.
7. Ibid., p. 1.
8. Ibid., p. 2.
9. Ibid., p. 7.
10. *See* Frank McNeil, *Japanese Politics: Decay or Reform?* (Washington, D.C.: Carnegie Endowment for International Peace, 1993), p. 39.
11. Ibid.
12. "Japan: Dietmen on Defense Rights, Deregulation," FBIS-EAS-96-151 (English translation), August 5, 1996, p. 19.
13. Patrick M. Cronin and Michael J. Green, *Redefining the U.S.–Japan Alliance: Tokyo's National Defense Program*, McNair Paper 31 (Washington, D.C.: NDU Press, November 1994), p. 10.

14. Ibid., p. 2.
15. Kent Calder, "Japan 2010: Prospective Profiles," Center for Naval Analyses (February 1996).
16. Kent Calder, *Crisis and Compensation: Public Policy and Political Stability in Japan* (Princeton, NJ: Princeton University Press, 1988), p. 420.
17. Ibid.
18. Sheryl WuDunn, "Japanese Government Downplays Fear over Bad Bank Loans," *New York Times*, January 13, 1998.
19. "Kato Talks of 'Retribution Budget.' Shinshinto Demands Retraction," *Daily Japan Digest*, December 2, 1996, p. 2.
20. John N. Neuffer, "Poised to Prevail," *Behind the Screen: Roundup of Japanese Politics* (July 3, 1998), no. 55 (electronic mail newsletter).
21. The LDP did not win a single seat in Tokyo, Kanagawa, Saitama, Aichi, Osaka, Hyogo, and Kyoto.
22. Akihisa Nagashima, "The End of Kabuki Politics? Reforming Japan's Political Economy," *Japan Digest Forum*, July 15, 1998.
23. Mary Jordan, "Tokyo Party Is Cool to U.S. Bases," *Washington Post*, October 4, 1996.
24. "Political Platform of DPJ's Hatoyama Noted," FBIS-EAS-96-203, November 1, 1996 (English translation).
25. Seiji Maehara, "Japan's Security Policy: A Time for Realism," *Japan Digest Forum*, December 11, 1996.
26. "Shusho no shigoto wa kore kara da: Nichibei anpo o kangaeru," *Asahi Shimbun* (Editorial), December 3, 1996.
27. Morihiro Hosokawa, "Are U.S. Troops in Japan Needed: Reforming the Alliance," *Foreign Affairs* (July–August 1998).

# IV

# Economics, Technology, and Security

# 11

# Economics and Security: A Conceptual Framework

MIKE M. MOCHIZUKI

JAPAN knows well the effect of security factors on economics. After its devastating defeat in World War II, it benefited enormously by relying on the United States for its security needs. Instead of having to spend huge amounts on the military, Japan concentrated on economic reconstruction and development. Peace among the advanced industrial countries enabled Japan to prosper through trade and the absorption of foreign technologies. The security linkage with the United States made Japan's external economic expansion more palatable to its East Asian neighbors. Japan even saw the positive effect that war can temporarily have on an economy. U.S. military procurements during the Korean War gave the Japanese economy a big boost in the early 1950s. The Japanese experience is by no means unique. Peace and security provide an international and domestic environment conducive to long-term investment, trade, and economic growth. Wartime production can even stimulate demand.

While most analysts would agree about the impact of security on economics, the effect of economics on security is more controversial. In addressing the question of how economics might affect security in the Asia-Pacific region, this chapter is divided into three parts. The first section summarizes the different theoretical traditions that have grappled with the security implications of economic developments. Next, the essay applies some of the arguments that emerge from this theoretical literature to contemporary developments in the Asia-Pacific region. The final section discusses the policy implications of the preceding analysis for the United States and Japan.

## Different Theoretical Traditions in Economics and Security

Three separate theories offer very different propositions on how economic factors can affect traditional security concerns such as the prospects for war or peace. The liberal tradition tends to see the relationship primarily in positive terms. One argument in this tradition focuses on the relative material costs and benefits of international economic exchange and peace on the one hand and of autarkic economic policies and war on the other. Unlike interstate security rivalries, economic competition in the context of international trade and investment is a positive-sum, rather than zero-sum, game. No matter how fierce international economic competition may be at the international level, countries that trade with each other can all benefit economically in absolute terms—at least at the aggregate national level. As the amount of international trade increases, the absolute benefits from trade will also increase. Consequently, as transnational economic interdependence deepens through greater international trade, the mutual economic benefits of peaceful commercial relations will grow relative to the possible benefits of military competition and aggression.[1] The recent transformation of economic activity driven by the information-technology revolution as well as the inordinately high costs of modern warfare have reinforced this calculus. This calculation at the aggregate national level will be buttressed by ruling social coalitions within the trading states themselves that will want to maintain international peace for the sake of their own economic interests. Based on this logic, greater international trade and economic interdependence will over time mitigate traditional geopolitical rivalries among states and therefore promote international peace. Conversely, a reduction of international trade and interdependence and the emergence of exclusive trading blocs will tend to exacerbate geopolitical competition and make interstate war more likely.

A second argument in the liberal tradition about the positive effect of economics on security relates to the political implications of economic development. Although states can develop economically under either democratic or authoritarian regimes, once a country reaches a certain threshold of economic advancement, sociological factors are likely to steer it toward democratic political processes. In the course of industrialization, a middle class will emerge that will be a strong proponent of political liberalization and will eventually serve as the social foundation for stable democratic politics. Insofar as liberal theorists argue that democracies are more likely to have peaceful relations among themselves, the spread of democratic states in the international system will make peace more likely.[2] One recent caveat to this liberal thesis about the linkage between democracy and peace is that democratizing states may have fragile political systems that can deteriorate into militarist regimes.[3] Once countries develop stable democratic systems, however, the evidence that democracies do not fight each other is quite strong.

Theorists in the realist tradition are skeptical of the positive effects of economics on security. While making claims about the absolute economic gains from international trade, liberal economic theory does not say much about how these gains might be distributed across states. It is quite possible that some countries might benefit more than others from international commercial relations. History has shown how some countries that lag behind economically can catch up to and even surpass the more advanced states by absorbing technologies of the leading economies and by marshaling national resources behind industrial development. To the realist, relative gains from international commerce matter more than absolute gains because states in the context of international anarchy are likely to use their economic capabilities to enhance their military power.[4] Therefore, differences in relative economic gains could eventually transform the military power balance in favor of one country or coalition of countries relative to another. A rapid shift in the power balance could make the international system ripe for war because the leading state or coalition of states may fear the rise of a new power or because the states that maintained the old balance of power will not respond quickly enough to cope with the new power equation. The only way to preserve the peace in the context of these power shifts is to enhance military capabilities and mobilize alliances to deter military expansion by challengers. For realists, economic interdependence is therefore subordinate to these traditional security concerns.

In addition to the relative gains argument, some realists posit that economic interdependence can aggravate, rather than mitigate, geopolitical rivalries.[5] Under a condition of anarchy, states will be anxious about economic dependencies with other states. They will fear that during a security crisis, access to critical raw materials and markets might be severed with dramatic negative consequences for their economic well-being. To reduce this vulnerability, states may choose to gain political control over these resources or markets by territorial expansion or other means. According to the realist argument, this logic makes security competition and war more likely as economic interdependence increases. In a refinement of this realist claim, one scholar has written recently that the liberal argument about economic interdependence promoting peace may be valid when there is an expectation that trade will increase in the future. If the expectations about future trade are pessimistic, however, then the realist logic about wanting to reduce economic vulnerabilities will kick in and steer states toward aggression.[6]

The third theoretical tradition that links economics and security encompasses those who view international political economy through the lens of mercantilism and imperialism.[7] One line of argument in this tradition is an extension of the realist claim that states seek to reduce their external economic dependencies by expanding political control beyond their borders. By extending their political realm, imperialist states secure the various inputs necessary to sustain their economies. In the industrial world, this dynamic can increase the probability of war among the most advanced economic states as they compete fiercely for foreign resources and markets. Although imperialist theories might interpret the two world wars in terms of this interimperialist rivalry, such military conflicts are by no means inevitable. It is also possible that the ruling classes of the leading capitalist states might cooperate to avoid war in order to preserve their common economic interests. Such a calculation would converge with the liberal notion regarding the greater economic benefits of peace over war in the context of liberal commercial relations among states.

A second line of argument found in mercantilist and imperialist writings concerns the problem of hierarchy in international political economy. One aspect of this problem would be the domination of less economically developed countries by the more technologically advanced states. Rather than being a mutually beneficial relationship, there is a danger that the latter will exploit the former. This pattern of exploitation can also manifest itself domestically. The ruling class of an exploited country may in turn exploit the weaker social classes in that country as part of an overall international system of economic domination and subservience. Such a system is potentially destabilizing because it sows the seeds of rebellion and revolution. As elite control in the exploited country weakens, anticolonial wars could emerge that threaten peace at the systemic level.

Finally, even within countries that are either economically developed or enjoying economic growth through international commerce, social problems may emerge that can have negative security consequences. Although at the aggregate level states will benefit mutually from international trade, these benefits may not be distributed equitably within the states themselves. Moreover, trade will hurt some societal sectors due to competition from more efficient and advanced foreign producers. An absence of public policy measures to make more equitable the domestic distribution of the benefits and costs of international trade could produce an internal political backlash against free trade and for protectionism. Even worse, social forces could mobilize nationalistic sentiments against foreign trade partners, and the ruling economic classes might prefer to fan the flames of this nationalism rather than to compensate the social groups being hurt by trade. Such a dynamic could sour interstate relations and even promote security competition.

To summarize, liberal theories tend to see the security implications of economics in primarily positive terms. Although the realists recognize potential security problems emerging from economic dynamics, they usually seek solutions to these problems by traditional security means such as deterrence and power balancing. Generally, theories of imperialism and mercantilism stress the negative security implications of international economic interactions. How then do these theoretical perspectives fare in the context of contemporary developments in the Asia-Pacific region?

## Assessment of the Asia-Pacific Region

At first glance, the Asia-Pacific region seems to be quite consistent with liberal views about the positive effect of economic development and interdependence on security. Except for a few exceptions, most of the states in the region are concentrating on strengthening their economies through trade rather than through enhancing their power via military expansion. Many of the countries are actively seeking foreign capital and investments as a way to enhance their indigenous industrial and technological capabilities. For the moment, there is very little economic incentive to engage in security competition or territorial expansion. In fact, to the extent that there are regional territorial disputes, states have tended to put such conflicts aside for the sake of commercial interaction. After China and Vietnam embarked on economic reform and liberalization, commercial relations have dissolved the old ideological divide between capitalist and communist states in the region. Even Myanmar (Burma) with its repressive regime is trying to integrate itself in the regional economic system. With the loss of its economic patrons China and Russia, North Korea now seems interested in moving away from its *juche* ideology of self-reliance to attract foreign capital and investments. Despite the dispute about sovereignty, economic links between mainland China and Taiwan have grown dramatically during the last two decades.

In the words of one Japanese analyst, "deepening interdependence has greatly increased the opportunity cost of conducting war for most of the countries in the region, and military options have become a much less attractive tool to resolve disputes."[8] Even a rising power like China has a keen interest in a stable and peaceful international environment so that it can concentrate on economic growth and technological development. As part of this national strategy, China wants to sustain its access to foreign capital, markets, and technology. Its leaders would like to avoid conflicts with the more advanced states like the United States and Japan that are critical to this access. China therefore is a conservative, not a revisionist power.[9] By the same token, the attractiveness of a growing China market should increase the incentive of Japanese and American leaders to cultivate stable and cordial relations with China.

The East Asian economic turmoil that began with the Thai baht crisis in July 1997 does call into question the liberal optimism that economic interdependence will promote great power cooperation rather than conflict in the region. In an era of rapid and largely unfettered international flows of capital, interdependence can quickly transmit bad economic tidings as well as good across states. Although China has thus far avoided the economic contagion because its financial system has been less integrated with the rest of the world, the regional crisis has dragged the Japanese economy down from stagnation into a deep recession and worsened even more the terrible conditions in Russia. As American leaders began to worry about the possible negative consequences for the United States, relations between Tokyo and Washington soured because of differences on how to respond to the crisis as well as U.S. frustration with Japan's inability to revitalize its economy. But eventually, the worsening of the crisis did motivate the U.S. and Japanese governments to temper their disagreements and cooperate bilaterally as well as multilaterally to prevent a further downward spiral. Much will depend upon how quickly the regional economies can be turned around. A prolonged crisis could steer countries to adopt nationalistic economic responses (even beyond controls on capital flows) that could rekindle geopolitical tensions. An American economic downturn in the context of a burgeoning U.S. trade deficit with Japan could strain the bilateral political-security relationship as well.

There has also been some progress on the other liberal argument about the connection between democracy and international peace. Until recently, Japan had been the only democratic state in the East Asian region; and this democracy was established in the context of foreign occupation after war. During the last decade, more countries in the region have moved toward democratization. The People-Power Revolution of 1986 restored democratic processes after many years of Ferdinand Marcos's corrupt and dictatorial rule in the Philippines. Six years later, Fidel Ramos succeeded Corazon Aquino as president after a relatively fair election. The same year, the Republic of Korea elected Kim Young Sam president in a popular vote. A year later Singapore did the same. After the failure of the 1991 military coup, Thailand instituted competitive electoral politics. In 1996, Taiwan held its first contested presidential election. As these countries develop economically, a growing middle class is likely to give these nascent democracies a more solid social base. The liberals argue that as stable democracies become more widespread in the region, the possibility of military conflicts could decline.

In the foreseeable future, one should not be too sanguine that the democratization trend will reinforce regional peace. As Edward D. Mansfield and Jack Snyder have argued, states in the transitional phase of democratization could become militarily aggressive and fight wars with democratic states.[10] In such transitional democracies, popular control over foreign policy is likely to be partial, and the possibility of autocratic deterioration is high, especially in the face of international security and economic pressures. Many of the East Asian democracies are indeed fragile. Although Singapore is an urban middle-class society, its protection of civil liberties remains dubious. Labor unrest and corruption could undermine South Korean confidence in democratic political processes. Despite the deserved praise for Taiwan's presidential election in March 1996, democratic politics could aggravate, rather than ameliorate, the conflict with mainland China because the Taiwanese majority is likely to become more vocal about its desire for political independence. For democracy and peace to take hold in East Asia, the big states in the region like China, Indonesia, and Vietnam will also have to liberalize their politics. Ultimately, economic progress could produce democratic politics in even these states. Since the process of political liberalization has hardly begun in these states, the transitional phase is likely to be long and difficult.

How do realist theories fare in the context of the Asia-Pacific region? Although initial restraints on military spending may free resources for economic take-off, once states move up the economic ladder, they gain the capacity to invest in military capabilities without jeopardizing further growth. Virtually every successful economy in the region is now engaged in modernizing its military forces through foreign arms purchases, and in some instances, indigenous production. At this point, these military modernization efforts primarily involve a quest for greater defense self-reliance and have yet to become a full-blown interactive arms race. Nevertheless, there is cause for concern. Recent arms acquisitions by states in the region have increased offensive capabilities, which have in turn heightened mutual suspicion and raised the danger of miscalculation and inadvertent escalation.[11] In the wake of China's large-scale military exercises in the Taiwan Strait, neighboring countries are eager to accelerate their military modernization programs.[12] How are these trends affecting the regional balance of power, which is the real concern of realists?

The collapse of the Soviet Union has certainly weakened Russia's ability to project military power in the region. Therefore, even with cuts in U.S. defense spending after the end of the Cold War, the United States remains the predominant maritime power in the Asia-Pacific theater. If one adds the air and naval capabilities of Japan, then the U.S.–Japan alliance is unchallenged. Even while maintaining tight political constraints on its military policies, Japan has modernized its defense forces into one of the most advanced in the world. Even as Japan has gained relative to the United States in economic power, the military gap between the United States and Japan has not narrowed. Even if Japan has the economic and technological potential to be a military challenger of the United States in the region, such a course would be counterproductive for Japan as long as its alliance with the United States is secure. In fact, Japan's dependence on the United States for security makes Japan's economic expansion into the region more palatable for its East Asian neighbors.

Although much has been made of China's military modernization and its recent purchases of Russian weapon systems, it will take much more than a decade or two before China can challenge the United States and Japan militarily in the coastal waters and air space of the East Asian continent. Even across the Taiwan Strait, the military balance generally favors Taiwan over China. Compared to its potential adversaries like the United States, Japan, and Taiwan, China's military is large in size but technologically backward.[13] By integrating itself into the world economy and strengthening its technological base, China might be able to narrow this military technology gap somewhat. Beijing is trying to compensate for its military deficit by strengthening its ballistic missile arsenal. Ballistic missiles will give China the ability to intimidate its neighbors from undermining its core interests, such as restraining Taiwan from declaring independence. Such weapons will be of limited use for territorial aggression. Moreover, even as China modernizes its military, the United States and Japan are unlikely to stand still technologically. If China did become threatening to these two powers, they would have the economic and technological ability to blunt the Chinese challenge. As long as the U.S.–Japan alliance is solid and the United States maintains its key air and naval assets in the region and its ability to project military power rapidly from the American continent during a crisis, the rise of China should not be threatening to states on China's periphery. The defense modernization programs of the Southeast Asian states should be more than adequate to balance against China. The United States and Japan should not fear that the coastal states of the East Asian continent will bandwagon with China as its economy expands. From a strict realist perspective, the current balance of power, which is favorable to both the United States and Japan, is likely to continue. Put differently, the relative economic gains by China and other East Asian industrializing states will not upset the regional power balance. Despite its economic difficulties, Japan will remain the preeminent industrial and technological power in East Asia for the forseeable future.

What about the other realist concern that economic interdependence might motivate security conflict because states will want to minimize their vulnerabilities? As Kent Calder of Princeton University has pointed out, industrial development will make the East Asian economies hungrier for secure energy supplies.[14] This quest for energy security could exacerbate regional geopolitical rivalries and even provoke conflict in the following ways. First, it could drive states in the region to proceed with nuclear energy programs that might increase the risk of proliferating nuclear weapons technology and materials. Second, the hunger for energy may make territorial disputes in the region more difficult to manage and resolve because of interstate competition to control possible petroleum and mineral deposits in the seabeds near disputed islands (e.g., the Spratlys, the Senkaku or Diaoyu Islands, and Takeshima or Tokdo). Finally, insofar as the Middle East is likely to be the largest source of oil imports for East Asia, the security of the sea-lanes from the Middle East as well as stability in that part of the world will be of paramount importance. Realists argue that these vulnerabilities will steer states to beef up their military capabilities and ultimately engage in zero-sum territorial competition.

At this point in time, such an assessment appears too alarmist. Despite recent problems over contested islands, the states in the region have tried to put the sovereignty issue aside and work toward joint economic and scientific development of the seabeds. Multilateral security dialogues such as the Association of Southeast Asian Nations (ASEAN) Regional Forum have defused tensions over the Spratly Islands for the moment. Concerning the danger of nuclear proliferation, Japan is becoming increasingly interested in developing a regional nuclear energy regime to enhance safety and transparency and to minimize the danger of nuclear weapons proliferation. The common problem of Middle East oil supplies can steer the states in the region toward cooperation to secure the vital sea-lanes rather than toward self-defeating military competition. Moreover, the issue of energy resources may not be as acute as some say due to the increase in petroleum output resulting from advances in drilling technology and the tapping of new oil fields in the North Sea and central Asia. Moreover, the regional economic contraction in the wake of the 1997 currency crisis has significantly reduced energy consumption. Finally, dependence on foreign trade seems unlikely to trigger territorial aggression. Future expectations about trade growth are generally optimistic. Despite periodic concerns that the United States might restrict access to its markets for East Asian products, America's support for the World Trade Organization (WTO) and the Asia-Pacific Economic Cooperation (APEC) process has reassured most East Asian states that Washington will not defect from free trade principles. Moreover, the expansion of intra-regional trade will provide a hedge against potential American moves toward protectionism.

Finally, what about applicability of the negative linkage between economics and security that theories of imperialism and mercantilism posit? In the post–World War II period, anticolonial struggles posed perhaps the greatest security challenges in East Asia, and some of these struggles became entangled in the Cold War rivalry with devastating consequences. After the end of the Vietnam War, however, the region moved steadily out of the shadows of Western imperialism to embrace the dream of economic prosperity. In contrast to the problematic dependent development patterns experienced by many of the Latin American states, the successful East Asian economies have maintained a remarkable degree of domestic social equality while utilizing foreign economic assistance and direct investments to pursue an export growth strategy. This strategy has paid off handsomely as the newly industrializing economies of East Asia have gained relative to the advanced industrial states rather than being economically dominated and exploited by them as some imperialist or world system theories might predict.[15] For the most part, East Asian countries have escaped in recent years the vicious cycle of underdevelopment and political turmoil that has plagued much of the so-called Third World.

Despite the positive features of East Asian development, however, it would be misguided to be overly optimistic about the prospects of current trends continuing without setbacks toward the liberal vision of prosperity and a democratic peace. Theories critical of capitalist development offer appropriate warnings for the region's future. Rapid economic growth is not only producing severe social problems associated with migration, population growth, and rapid urbanization, but also jeopardizing the egalitarianism that gave political legitimacy to developmentalism under authoritarian rule. As popular expectations of a better livelihood become more widespread, redistributing the fruits of development to sustain at least a semblance of economic equity will be essential for domestic political stability. Yet it is far from clear whether the political regimes now in place will adequately handle this task without deteriorating into corruption. Failure to handle such issues could reignite the civil conflicts that convulsed much of East Asia during the first seventy-five years of the twentieth century. This internal strife could easily spill over into the international arena.

In addition to the problem of domestic political economy, another issue might stand in the way of cultivating a Pacific community based on economic interdependence. East Asia may have liberated itself from the pernicious pattern of economic domination and exploitation of the weak countries by the strong, but the problem of economic hierarchy and mercantilism remains. Although Japan does not have the ability or the will to create a regional economic bloc that it can control, it has successfully expanded its production networks throughout East Asia. By replicating their *keiretsu* networks in the region, Japanese corporations have developed markets for their machinery as well as technologically advanced intermediate goods and components.[16] Instead of being hit by an East Asian economic boomerang, Japan has racked up significant trade surpluses with virtually all non–oil exporting East Asian countries. In 1995, its trade surplus with East Asia totaled $71 billion. It would, however, be misleading to argue that Japan is using East Asia primarily as an export platform. Japanese subsidiaries in East Asia sell more goods in local regional and Japanese markets than in the North American market, and Japan's imports from East Asia have indeed increased.

Whereas Japanese subsidiaries in East Asia serve three markets—the local regional, the Japanese, and the North American—U.S. subsidiaries there tend to direct their products back to the United States and to some extent the local regional market, but have difficulty penetrating the Japanese market. Since Japanese corporate networks can in effect modulate sales to their home markets, Japan is better able to temper the dislocating effects of imports from East Asia than the United States. Moreover, Japan's trade surplus with many of the East Asian countries pressures these economies to export aggressively abroad in order to improve their balance of payments.

The United States, with the most open market, is the easiest target for this export drive. Put differently, the difficulty in penetrating the Japanese market deflects East Asian exports to the United States. As a result, America's trade pattern in the Asia-Pacific region is the reverse of

Japan's. The United States has large trade deficits with both Japan and the rest of East Asia, while Japan has large trade surpluses with both the United States and the rest of East Asia.

Even with the leap-frogging by some East Asian competitors in some sectors (e.g., South Korean semiconductor manufacturers), East Asian development still follows a stratified pattern that approximates the famous flying geese model. With the region's reliance on Japanese aid, investments, and production technology, Japan's position as the lead goose appears relatively secure. As the East Asian newly industrialized economies (NIEs) have moved up, Japan has turned its attention to new Asian economic frontiers like China, Vietnam, and even Burma, while deepening its stake in the ASEAN Four. It remains to be seen to what extent Chinese entrepreneurial networks and Korean *chaebol* can challenge the Japanese in East Asia's dynamic regional economy. Overseas Chinese might rival, or even surpass, Japanese conglomerates in some third markets, but Japanese firms will still dominate at home. Asia may not be in Japan's embrace, but Japan is well-positioned to reap the benefits of East Asian growth, once it resumes, while moderating the negative social consequences of expanding imports from the region.

This pattern of regional economic interdependence has two negative security implications. First, unless the East Asian development pattern moves away from its current hierarchical ordering, regional suspicion toward Japan will persist, especially since the Japanese are having such difficulties coming to terms with their country's militarist past. Rather than developing a regional community based on liberal economic principles and equality, East Asian states may seek counterweights to balance against Japan. The logic of geoeconomic balancing and competition could then obstruct transnational economic integration along more organic lines. Under such conditions, the role of the United States as the outside power balancer will continue to be critical to regional security. But this leads to the second negative implication. A continuing asymmetry in regional trade patterns between Japan and the United States will make more challenging the task of sustaining the U.S.–Japan security relationship. Unless Japan absorbs more imports from both the United States and the rest of East Asia, Americans hurt by the influx of Japanese and other East Asian imports will question why the United States must maintain its security commitments to the region. Instead of seeing these commitments as promoting American commercial access into the region, they may charge that the U.S. military presence in East Asia merely preserves a security order conducive to Japan's economic dominance in the region. Some may even argue that the United States should use its regional security commitments as leverage to pry open

Japanese and other East Asian markets for American goods and services.[17] Even though such arguments may not determine actual U.S. policy, the political climate of U.S.–Japanese and even U.S.–East Asian relations in general could deteriorate enough to damage irreparably the basic security framework forged during the Cold War era.

## Policy Implications for the United States and Japan

The dynamics of regional economic development and interdependence do not confirm the arguments of one theoretical tradition to the exclusion of others. Each of the three theoretical arguments discussed in this chapter offers important insights for policy. The current trends in East Asia favor in general terms the optimistic outlook found in liberal perspectives. Therefore, both Washington and Tokyo have security and economic interests in helping to revive regional economic growth. It is certainly better for the United States and Japan that the countries of East Asia concentrate on economic development rather than military aggrandizement. There is, however, still enough truth in the less optimistic theories of realism, imperialism, and mercantilism that it would be imprudent to rely solely on economic interdependence strategies for regional security. Despite economic globalization, security issues must still be dealt with on their own terms.

The United States and Japan should therefore maintain their security alliance even after the end of the Cold War in order to reassure the region as China increases its power through economic modernization. Without U.S. security engagement in the region, the power balance will eventually shift in China's favor given its mammoth size. Because of regional suspicions about Japan, it is hard to imagine that a maritime alliance led by Japan would form to balance China. History combined with geopolitical suspicions and bilateral economic frictions will make it difficult to forge a stable cooperative relationship between Japan and China in the foreseeable future. The realists are also right to argue that the desire for energy security might inject a zero-sum competitive element to regional economic relations. To prevent an escalation of military rivalry, the United States and Japan should therefore support multilateral processes that can help defuse territorial disputes and reduce the risk of nuclear proliferation. American and Japanese insistence on navigational freedom will also help the cause of maintaining the flow of oil from the Middle East.

Just as economic interdependence does not render irrelevant the traditional tools for maintaining security, it would be wrong for Tokyo and

Washington to neglect the way economic factors can mitigate or aggravate the security environment. Current trade imbalances, both bilateral and regional, between Japan and the United States can have a corrosive effect on American domestic support for the bilateral security relationship. U.S. economic and security interests with respect to Japan do intersect politically. At a time when the United States no longer faces an acute direct military threat from East Asia and when Americans are being asked to make hard choices for the purpose of domestic renewal, the political sustainability of U.S. security commitments to Japan will increasingly require that Japan not be seen to undermine U.S. economic interests. To the extent that Japan produces more and more of the important inputs for U.S. defense systems, the United States has a security interest in maintaining stable supplies of such inputs and accessing Japanese dual-use technologies.

An aggressive U.S. trade policy toward Japan will inevitably strain political relations with Japan and may make Japanese leaders somewhat more reluctant to work with the United States on security-related issues. Given the absence of an attractive strategic alternative, Tokyo will not dilute or dismantle the security alliance because of Washington's pressures on trade. Japan will move away from its side of the bilateral strategic bargain not because of U.S. economic policies, but because of developments in the security arena, such as changes in the strategic environment, misgivings about U.S. defense policy, or irritations about the American military presence in Japan. Within reason, the United States should not hesitate to pursue its economic interests vis-à-vis Japan for fear of damaging the security relationship.

Does the pursuit of U.S. security interests undermine its economic interests? Not necessarily. Defining security interests in expansive terms, there is the danger that the United States will be saddled with much larger military expenditures as a percentage of GNP than other major powers.[18] The problem is not that big defense budgets might crowd out business investments. Attractive businesses should be able to raise adequate funds in capital markets. But overblown military spending may make it difficult to sustain and develop the public programs necessary to ease the social adjustments to economic globalization. A choice in favor of the former would be unjust and would tear America's social fabric. It might even weaken U.S. political will for international engagement. The remedy is to restructure the military establishment and foreign deployments in order to enhance efficiency while continuing to perform the critical roles and missions. Japan can help this process by assuming more of the burden and responsibility for regional security.

If security and economics are inextricably linked, then should the United States explicitly leverage its defense commitments to Japan in order to extract Japanese concessions on economic issues? While theoretically enticing, this author has serious doubts that Washington can execute such a strategy with the subtlety necessary to obtain the desired result. Moreover, given the current political climate, the Japanese are just as likely to accept the hollowing out of the security alliance as they are to submit to American economic pressures. Of course, although an explicit policy of linking security to trade may be unwise, U.S. leaders should always remind their Japanese counterparts that continuing American public support for the alliance depends greatly on whether bilateral economic relations are seen as fair and reciprocal. But in terms of actual policy, the best course is to pursue vigorously both economic and security interests simultaneously on their own terms.

Looking beyond the bilateral relationship, the United States and Japan should work more closely together to coordinate economic incentives and disincentives on behalf of regional security interests. Greater U.S.–Japan collaboration on economic issues concerning China, its accession to the WTO, for example, would reduce Beijing's ability to play Washington and Tokyo off of each other. Such coordination would also clarify to Beijing the acceptable terms of China's incorporation into the regional and global economic system. The smoother and quicker China's integration into international economic regimes, the more likely that a political elite will emerge in China that will be more cooperative on the security front. Economic policy instruments could also be put to good use regarding the Korean question. The United States and Japan in coordination with South Korea could extend economic benefits to North Korea, such as economic aid and investments, in exchange for Pyongyang's cooperation on security issues like confidence-building measures, the pulling back of military forces from the demilitarized zone, progress on North–South talks, and restraints on ballistic missiles and other military systems. All of this suggests the need to develop a comprehensive security strategy for the Asia Pacific region that integrates the military, diplomatic, and economic dimensions.

## Notes

1. Richard Rosecrance, *The Rise of the Trading State: Commerce and Conquest in the Modern World* (New York: Basic Books, 1986).
2. Michael W. Doyle, "Liberalism and World Politics," *American Political Science Review* 80 (1986): 1151–69.

3. Edward D. Mansfield and Jack Snyder, "Democratization and the Danger of War," *International Security* 20 (Summer 1995): 5–37.
4. John J. Mearsheimer, "Back to the Future: Instability in Europe after the Cold War," *International Security* 15 (Summer 1990): 5–56.
5. Kenneth Waltz, *Theory of International Politics* (New York: Random House, 1979), p. 106.
6. Dale C. Copeland, "Economic Interdependence and War: A Theory of Trade Expectations," *International Security* 20 (Spring 1996): 5–41.
7. For a survey of imperialist theories, see Anthony Brewer, *Marxist Theories of Imperialism: A Critical Survey* (London: Routledge & Kegan Paul, 1980).
8. Matake Kamiya, "Hopeful Uncertainty: Asia-Pacific Security in Transition," *Asia-Pacific Review*, no. 3 (Spring–Summer 1996): 114.
9. Robert S. Ross, "China II: Beijing as a Conservative Power," *Foreign Affairs* 76 (March–April 1997): 33–44.
10. Mansfield and Snyder, 1995.
11. Desmond Ball, "Arms and Affluence: Military Acquisitions in the Asia-Pacific Region," *International Security* 18 (Winter 1993–94): 78–112.
12. Tetsuya Shimauchi, "Tensions in the Taiwan Strait and the Security of the Asia-Pacific Region," *Institute for International Policy Studies Policy Paper* 166E (February 1997), pp. 14–16.
13. Ronald Montaperto and Karl Eikenberry, "Paper Tiger: A Skeptical Appraisal of China's Military Might," *Harvard International Review* 18 (Spring 1996):28–31; Paul H. B. Godwin, "From Continent to Periphery: PLA Doctrine, Strategy and Capabilities," *The China Quarterly* 146 (June 1996): 464–87.
14. Kent E. Calder, *Pacific Defense: Arms, Energy, and America's Future in Asia* (New York: William Morrow, 1996), pp. 43–82.
15. See, for example, Immanuel Wallerstein, *The Capitalist World-Economy* (Cambridge: Cambridge University Press, 1979).
16. Walter Hatch and Kozo Yamamura, *Asia in Japan's Embrace: Building a Regional Production Alliance* (Cambridge: Cambridge University Press, 1996).
17. An example of this argument is Chalmers Johnson and E.B. Keehn, "The Pentagon's Ossified Strategy," *Foreign Affairs* 74 (July–August 1995): 112.
18. Lawrence J. Korb, "Our Overstuffed Armed Forces," *Foreign Affairs* 74 (November–December 1995): 22–34.

# 12

# Whither Trade and Security? A Historical Perspective

**LAURA STONE**

*SPRING 1994: Washington is planning for the possibility of a shooting war on the Korean Peninsula. North Korea has flaunted the authority of the International Atomic Energy Agency, refusing to permit inspections of its nuclear facilities, suggesting the possibility that it has reprocessed enough plutonium for a nuclear weapon. The Clinton administration has identified nonproliferation as a top post–Cold War foreign policy objective. The United States must take action against such an arrogant proliferator. At the very least, sanctions against North Korea seem inevitable. At most, it is possible that sanctions will drive the isolated North Korean regime into a "use-or-lose" situation. Faced with dwindling material resources that jeopardize its war-fighting capability, Pyongyang could launch a desperate attack on South Korea or Japan, hoping to capture enough land to sue for peace, or to at least go down fighting.*

*It is universally accepted in both Washington and Asia that Japanese cooperation will be vital to the success of the sanctions. North Korean permanent residents of Japan remit substantial funds to their homeland, and Japan has risen to become the North's third-largest trading partner. The degree of Japanese cooperation is a critical variable determining the overall loss of American lives if the long-standing Cold War on the peninsula suddenly turns hot. Much of America's air, naval, and rapid-reaction support for its troops in South Korea are based in Japan. According to the Security Treaty, Tokyo's approval is necessary to send the Japan-based troops into combat. If that approval is not forthcoming, an American decision to proceed without it—in the event of a surprise attack, for example—would likely sound the death knell for the alliance as it now exists.*

*In another corner of Washington, the trade warriors are simultaneously planning the next salvo in a seemingly endless low-intensity trade war with Japan. The president has also defined "economic security" as one of the top foreign policy priorities of the administration. Not only are Japanese trading practices seen as a threat to U.S. jobs, but previous trade agreements are considered suspect and unenforceable. In order to force Tokyo to commit to a more stringent enforcement regime, Washington is preparing to threaten sanctions on imports of Japanese-made cars and auto parts. Someone close to the trade negotiations was asked whether the timing for sanctions might be modified if the situation on the Korean Peninsula further deteriorated. His answer was telling: "Why should we? There is no connection between trade and security."*

## Ah, What a Tangled Web . . .

Some evidence supports the argument that for the U.S.–Japan relationship trade and security ties are not connected. Few would argue that the U.S–Japan trade relationship has deteriorated over the last thirty years. Beginning in the 1960s, government-to-government economic and trade ties became increasingly strained. The parent-child economic relationship fostered by both sides in the immediate postwar period was challenged, first in textiles, later in steel and automobiles, and through the production cycle to semiconductors and cell phones. Over time, Americans' frustration with their inability to stem relative Japanese economic advances manifested itself in more hostile rhetoric and tougher trade negotiations. Often, these trade battles were waged as much on the front pages of Japan's and America's major dailies as across the negotiating table.

In contrast, the defense relationship has gradually strengthened and expanded. In fits and starts, Japan has assumed greater responsibility for the alliance, both financially and in terms of roles and missions. The completely one-sided defense relationship of the immediate postwar period has been transformed into a maturing alliance that, while far from equal, is evolving toward a more equitable allocation of responsibilities.

Is it realistic to view the U.S.–Japan defense relationship as an isolated, or isolatable, aspect of the overall relationship? Can discussions of strategic planning, common threats, and new roles and missions take place without concern for trade balances, auto parts, and technology transfers? The answer is not satisfying: "occasionally yes, usually no." It is possible to insulate certain important practical decisions and planning from the vagaries of the economic relationship. However, throughout the postwar period, trade and economics have become intertwined with the defense relationship. This is not a new development. What has evolved is the impression by many on the U.S. side that achieving its defense objectives has an unacceptable cost in terms of trade.

Security relations can affect trade.[1] Relative spending rates for defense as a proportion of a country's GNP can affect growth rates. Depending on how the funds are spent, defense spending can have a positive or negative effect on the development of certain industries. On a broader scale, defense affects global trade patterns. Much like purely trade oriented customs unions, defense relationships have trade-distorting properties—a state is much more likely to trade with its allies than its enemies, even if the enemies offer better terms of trade. Defense concerns can also encourage a less contentious approach to trade policy, in order to prevent offending tentative allies and to promote goodwill.

However, economic interactions can also spill over into the defense relationship. Trade can promote goodwill and feelings of mutual trust and understanding, or it can damage those feelings when trade is seen as unfair or confrontational. Because of its tendency to segregate production, trading patterns over time breed dependence on other states for certain products, which can include the parts and technology necessary for war-fighting. This can be stabilizing, since it ties states firmly together, but it can also be disconcerting for defense planners accustomed to freedom of action. Finally, defense procurement often is trade, and is thus subjected to all of the pressures of promoting trade objectives, as well as the goals of the defense relationship. This chapter briefly examines the historical approach to managing the effects of trade on the alliance.

Alliance managers in both Tokyo and Washington are well aware of the pressures that trade and economics exert on the alliance. If trade appears to have a modest effect on the alliance as a whole, it is only because these foreign policy experts seek to insulate the defense relationship from the more detrimental effects of trade whenever possible.

## In the Beginning There Was Trade. And It Was Good.

The early postwar years established positive trade spillovers for the alliance. Washington saw an open door policy toward Japan as a low-cost method of reinforcing the defense relationship. Tokyo adopted the same stance and came to view economic growth and trade ties as the most important components of its security. Most important, this period demonstrated that trade can create goodwill and confidence vital to the strength of an alliance. Both states viewed expanded bilateral defense relations as having positive spin-offs for their respective producers and consumers in terms of defense sales for the United States and technology transfers through joint defense production for Japan.

In Washington, the concept of free trade as a tool for defense germinated in the late 1940s. As Soviet–American relations deteriorated and the strength of the Chinese communists grew, the United States began casting about for an firm strategic ally in the Pacific. Japan was a logical choice, but the occupation was not preparing Japan for its role of anticommunist bulwark. MacArthur's democratizing reforms were having a destabilizing effect on the Japanese populace, and newly legalized trade unions and leftist parties found fertile ground among the demoralized, hungry Japanese. The occupation authorities, as supreme rulers of Japan, could easily restrict the left-leaning political action. Indeed, they revised legislation to allow purges of communist sympathizers from jobs in government, education, industry, and unions. Such a dictatorial approach, however, would not yield the strong independent ally that Washington sought. It was determined that Japanese leftism had to be attacked at its source: the poverty and loss of confidence that pervaded Japan. George Kennan argued that once the Japanese prospered under capitalism, only then could they be depended on to help defend the Western system against the spread of communism. Thus, encouraging Japanese economic recovery became a strategic priority. Worries that Japan's relative economic growth could jeopardize American power or prosperity would have seemed ludicrous at that time. The Japanese economy was insignificant compared to America's. If there were any concerns about relative growth, they were centered on keeping the Soviet Union and China from reaping the benefits of trade with Japan.

Economic recovery for Japan was not easily engineered. After clamping down on monetary policy to get inflation under control, the occupation authorities eased the money supply and loosened strict antimonopoly rules. Still, these internal reforms were not enough. Washington realized that trade would be necessary to ensure Japan's economic recovery. Before and during the war, manufacturing had been the engine of Japanese growth. However, the manufacturing sector required natural resources and markets in order to function. Japanese consumers, even if they could have furnished the demand to jump-start the manufacturing industry, could not provide dollars to buy oil, coal, or raw materials. Exports were essential. U.S. markets were thrown open, but it was assumed in Washington that low-quality Japanese consumer products would never sell in the United States. Originally, there was some hope that Japan could reestablish its colonial trading patterns with

Manchuria, exporting finished goods in return for Chinese resources. But the loss of China to communism dashed these hopes. Trade was seen as a force that tied countries together, and having Japan beholden to communist China was out of the question. To replace China, Washington developed a dollar recycling scheme. Washington provided dollar-denominated aid to Southeast Asian countries, which in turn were encouraged to purchase Japanese products. This gave Japan the dollars to buy raw materials, often from Southeast Asia. The plan was augmented by the Korean War, when the U.S. military provided a massive dollar generating market for Japanese industrial products.

Washington's belief that the expansion of Japanese trade was vital to American security affected its entire Asia policy in the 1950s.[2] Japanese manufactured products were beginning to penetrate the U.S. market, but Japan was still very dependent on trade with Southeast Asia. Washington national security planners feared that, even if Southeast Asia moved into the communist camp, Japan would have to continue trading with them. Japan would be forced to accommodate anti-Western regimes, particularly China. This was unacceptable to Washington. Concerns about Japan's need for continued access to the markets of Western-leaning Asian nations merged with the nascent domino theory, resulting in the infamous NSC-68. Some have argued that U.S. involvement in Vietnam had its roots, at least partially, in Washington's desire to ensure Southeast Asian markets for Japan, in order to guarantee Japan's place in the Western security system.[3] Security goals lead to trade goals. Trade goals lead to security goals.

Washington's policy of encouraging Japanese economic growth without asking for contributions to the defense of Japan would have been impossible if Congress had seen much cost associated with this approach. However, costs were low: Japanese imports were gradually increasing, but they did not threaten American jobs. During the 1950s and 1960s most Japanese export production absorbed labor-intensive production cycles that had grown unprofitable in America. Because the U.S. economy was functioning at close to full employment, workers could find alternative, higher-paying jobs in other manufacturing industries. In fact, for the American defense industries, the alliance was a net gain, in the form of military sales and licensed production. Licensed production was particularly valuable to U.S. defense contractors, allowing them to continue to earn revenue on older systems while turning domestic production over to newer products with higher profit margins. The commitment to defend Japan almost certainly benefited the larger U.S. economy as well. By formalizing Japan's pro-American orientation, the alliance created a bias toward

U.S. products and investment. Insofar as the U.S.–Japan defense relationship contributed peace and stability in Japan and Asia, American businesses profited.

Even in the 1950s, some American interests took issue with the open door approach to Japan. Textile manufacturers in particular had competed with Japanese imports before the war, and sought to defend their American market share against reviving Japanese industry. However, this industry was an unusual case, based in the less economically vital South. The textile problem was settled by a series of agreements starting in 1957 under which Japan voluntarily agreed to restrict imports, under threat of having de jure import quotas placed against it. Throughout this period, there were few Americans who saw Japanese imports as a threat to American jobs or economic interests.

On the Japanese side, this view of trade as a route to security gained converts as Japan recovered after the war. In return for quickly regaining its sovereignty, Japan had signed on to the U.S.-led Western alliance. As part of this agreement, Tokyo regained some of its basic defense rights, previously denied during the years of the occupation. However, the use of these rights was restricted by both popular and elite opinion in Japan. Many Japanese, disillusioned by the failure of Japan's militaristic ambitions during the war, had lost faith in the security establishment and even in the concept of security. In 1953, polls showed that as many Japanese favored a neutral Japan, friendly with both the Eastern and Western blocs, as wanted a commitment to the West.[4] Acknowledging these widely held views, while still providing for Japan's defense, Prime Minister Shigeru Yoshida's cabinet developed an approach later known as the "Yoshida Doctrine." Japan would rely on the United States for physical security while focusing on economic recovery. This approach coincided nicely with Washington's hopes for Japan. Japan was allowed to expand and protect its economy, thus contributing to the bilateral security relationship.

More than seeing trade as a route to security, Tokyo also came to see the bilateral security relationship as a motor for economic growth and progress. Taking a lesson from its role during the Korean War, Japan pursued defense production in order to jump-start various heavy industries. All Japan's defense procurement decisions took place under the watchful eye of the Ministry of International Trade and Industry. The licensed production of the F-86 helped revive the decimated Japanese aerospace industry, and on a smaller scale, production of small arms and other equipment infused capital and technology into Japanese industry. For elites in Tokyo, the defense relationship proved extremely compatible with Japan's economic and trade goals.

## With Friends Like These . . .

The comfortable trade and defense comity began to have problems in the 1960s. As trade relations became more conflictual, the mood infected the alliance. Initially, the impact on the alliance was psychological, a crisis of confidence. However, because the alliance was, at base, psychological—a belief that the United States would risk American lives to come to Japan's aid—diminished goodwill had a serious effect on the defense relationship's integrity. Some Americans questioned why the United States would do so much to defend an ungrateful ally. This questioning had an echo effect in Tokyo, leading Japanese opinion leaders to wonder whether the United States remained committed to the defense of Japan. As Japan's Study Committee on National Security Problems concluded in a 1970 report, " 'cooperation in the case of an emergency' will not work when political relations are strained." Insofar as trade negotiations strained political relations, they damaged the defense partnership. Ironically, it ultimately strengthened the alliance by forcing Japan and the United States gradually to transform the alliance into a more equal partnership.

### THE FIRST TRADE BATTLE

As Japan recovered from the destruction of war and began to grow rapidly in the 1960s, Americans began to question Japanese trade practices. During this decade, the United States and Japan had extremely different economic experiences. Japan achieved then-astonishing double-digit growth. The United States, for a variety of reasons, was gradually moving into a trade deficit with the rest of the world, while Japan was going into surplus. Furthermore, dollars were increasingly flowing out of the United States, putting great pressure on the currency, while the yen was still pegged at an exchange rate favorable to exports. On the bilateral trade front, Japanese products were beginning to make firm inroads into the American market while protectionist trade and investment policies still kept U.S. products and business out of Japan. By the end of the 1960s, Japanese imports were competing with American-made products, and beating them. This phenomenon was particularly disruptive in the South, where textile manufacturers were shutting doors and laying off workers.

American frustrations with the bilateral trading system were not appeased in the 1960s. Japan was pressured to restrict some specific exports. But with the Cold War raging, and the United States expanding its battle against communism in Asia, Washington's foreign policy and defense establishments still felt that encouraging Japanese export–led economic growth and stability was more important than addressing sectoral trade concerns.[5] Because security arguments were used to suppress trade demands vis-à-vis Japan, it was inevitable that those pressing a trade agenda would blame the alliance for many of America's economic problems. Threatened American business interests, their U.S. workers, and their congressional representatives began questioning the utility of defending Japan. This criticism was reinforced by the lopsided nature of the defense relationship. Tokyo throughout this period spent only 1 percent of its GNP on defense, and relied heavily on American security guarantees. Charges that Japan was getting a free ride on defense from U.S. workers and taxpayers became common.[6] American "Japan experts," particularly in the State Department, resisted this criticism: they had negotiated the 1960 Treaty Revision that had brought down the Japanese government and felt that asking Japan to assume a greater defense burden could sign the death warrant for the alliance. However, these experts' voices were increasingly drowned out as dissatisfaction with the unbalanced trade and defense relationships rose.

Criticism of the alliance reached Tokyo and raised concerns among Japan's foreign affairs elite. Tokyo's willingness to give up its ability to defend itself had been based, at least in part, on faith that the United States was a reliable ally. Any doubts about American ability or willingness to risk American lives for Japan's defense represented a serious weakening of Japan's security. Americans' rising disillusionment with the war in Vietnam was already raising questions about how long the U.S. electorate would remain willing to defend Asia, as well as concerns about the U.S. military's war-fighting capability. American complaints also reinforced Japanese worries, born of Japan's recent economic successes, that the United States was a declining power and would not be able to afford adequate force projection into Asia in the future.

American criticism of the relationship and Japanese anxieties about the U.S. commitment were intensified by the first U.S.–Japan trade war. The constant back-and-forth, the growing antagonism on both sides, and the final result with a "loser" and a "winner" was not conducive to improved relations.

By 1968, American unhappiness with the Japanese import and capital controls was widespread. Nixon took advantage of these complaints for electoral advantage: to gain support in the politically important Southern states, he pledged to restrict Japanese imports of wool and synthetic fibers. Initially playing by the script that had worked for previous sectoral trade disputes, Prime Minister Sato agreed to voluntary export restraints (VERs) for the sake of preserving the alliance and smoothing the Okinawa reversion. He was forced to back down in the face of domestic criticism, especially from the Ministry of International Trade and Industry (MITI). Japan's economic bureaucracy, flush with the success of the previous eight years, had picked this time to take a stand against American trade demands. A low-intensity textile dispute had been going on for years, so MITI textile officials were prepared with free trade arguments against Nixon's demands for new export restraints. A period of deadlock ensued, with U.S. trade negotiators proposing solutions, Tokyo rejecting them, and the U.S. Congress threatening import quotas. Tempers rose on both sides. Nixon felt that Sato was negotiating in bad faith and could not be trusted. In the middle of the textile negotiations, and just after his normalization with China without prior notification of Tokyo, Nixon presented Tokyo with the "dollar shock," a 10 percent surcharge on all imports entering the United States. While the surcharge was applicable to all foreign goods entering the United States, it had a particularly strong impact on export-dependent Japan. Nixon took this unilateral approach in part out of frustration resulting from months of fruitless negotiations with Japan. Immediately thereafter, Congress threatened to apply the Trading with the Enemy Act to Japan in order to force Tokyo to concede on textiles. Japan's new prime minister, Tanaka, saw no way to salvage the overall relationship without yielding. Japan had lost. The United States had won.[7]

In the confusion of Nixon's first term, it is impossible to determine exactly what damage this trade battle did to the alliance. Given the general disregard with which Nixon and Kissinger held relations with Tokyo, the Japanese had a host of reasons to question the U.S. commitment to Japan's defense. In fact, normalization with China, the Nixon Doctrine—which threw back responsibility for allies' defense—and the drawdown in Vietnam did as much to compromise the U.S.–Japan defense relationship as the textile talks and dollar devaluation issues together. However, a few results can be identified. First, the trade battle introduced a feeling of rivalry and antagonism into the alliance. The goodwill established in earlier years was shattered, with U.S. popularity in Japan plummeting to the lowest level since the war. Second, the experience decreased Japanese confidence in the alliance. Some defense experts were already questioning America's willingness to defend Japan. This is evident in Japan's 1970 Fourth Defense Plan, which called for increased autonomous defense spending, as well as plans for independent defense of Japan. The rationale for the defense relationship was dimming as the China and Russia threats were at least partially mollified. Commentators on both sides of the Pacific wondered aloud if it made sense for one adversary to be so utterly dependent on the other for its defense. The new primacy of trade in the U.S–Japan relationship discredited the traditional defenders of overall relations. These "Japan experts" and "America experts" were routinely shoved aside, especially in the Nixon White House, leaving the alliance increasingly vulnerable to pressure.

## SAVING THE ALLIANCE

The mid-1970s saw the United States and Japan both beginning to slowly back away from the alliance. The United States sought to operationalize the Nixon Doctrine, calling for Japan to assume greater independent defense capabilities. Washington also continued to press a trade agenda, leading to the 1973 soybean embargo and the 1974 steel import restrictions, as well as a litany of other complaints. This period of trade unrest was followed by Carter's election pledge to remove troops from Korea. Tokyo politicians, pundits, and planners began considering how to secure Japan's defense when the United States "inevitably" withdrew from Japan as well. Japan normalized relations with China, and was pursuing talks with the Soviet Union. However, when the underpinnings of the alliance appeared to be weakening, it was saved. It was rescued by the very "experts" that had been increasingly marginalized as trade issues rose to the top of the bilateral heap.

Japan experts at the Defense and State Departments in Washington admitted that Japan needed to change its trade policies in order to keep the alliance strong, but argued that pressure on Japan would irreparably damage defense relations. In Japan, the experts were mostly in the Ministry of Foreign Affairs (MOFA), with the defense establishment increasingly divided between pushing a more independent course, and continuing to place faith in the alliance. In both Japan and the United States, these pro-alliance experts had numerous allies in academia, and a few in their respective legislatures and media corps. By the late 1970s, they arrived at a new approach to alliance management. Rather than trying to stifle trade attacks, they would simply seek to insulate the alliance and deflect criticism. If the alliance was challenged as being too unequal, they would work to equalize it. While many disagreed with the premise that Americans were bearing too great a burden, given the benefits the alliance and bases afforded the United States, they recognized that the unequal defense relationship made the alliance an easy target. To divert attention, Japan would have to begin assuming more of the costs of its own defense, both financially and in terms of expanded roles and missions. This would involve procurement from the United States, which would yield the additional benefit of decreasing the trade deficit—an old trick that Japan had used since the 1960s to deflect pressure on trade from Washington. The threat of trade souring the alliance forced both Tokyo and Washington to strengthen the alliance, increase security cooperation, and stimulate joint defense production and interoperability.

The first step toward greater Japanese responsibility was the 1976 National Defense Program Outline (NDPO) (see Appendix 6a). In the NDPO, Japan committed to defending itself against a limited invasion and to calling for U.S. assistance only if unable to repel the invasion on its own. There were barriers to the assumption of this new burden on both sides. In the United States, there were still anxieties that Japan could not be trusted with its own defense. In Japan, the opposition to an independent military capability was even greater. The idea of the right to military defense still did not go very deeply into the Japanese popular mind. The reluctance of most Japanese politicians reflected this military allergy.

To assuage these concerns, the United States and Japan crafted a document to provide political cover for future defense cooperation. It became known as the 1978 Defense Guidelines (see Sheila Smith's chapter in this volume for details). This nonbinding study called for limited expansion of Japan's defense responsibilities to include the defense of the islands of Japan, but placed this expanded capability firmly in the framework of a continued U.S.–Japan alliance. The significance of this document went beyond its intended purpose of allowing for more of the defense burden to be shifted to Japan. In drafting the Guidelines, the Japanese and American defense elite proved they could work together to reinforce the alliance even while trade disputes continued. By carefully returning this aspect of the relationship to the level of experts, the alliance was safely insulated from the citizens who cared more about trade than the sanctity of defense.

Even as trade relations continued to deteriorate in the late 1970s, the defense relationship became stronger. In 1977, the Carter administration, concerned about the sluggish U.S. economy and rising trade deficit with Japan, tried using the alliance to get trade concessions. After several months of harsh negotiations, a reluctant Japan committed to reducing its current account surplus, cutting tariffs, and increasing its growth rate to 7 percent. Tempers on both sides ran high during the negotiations. Washington also went after Tokyo for excessive exports of television sets. The 1978 Congress heard more about how Japan's free-riding was jeopardizing the U.S. economy. However, that same year,

Japan made its first tentative commitment to work toward defending its sea-lanes of communication to 1000 miles. It was argued within the United States that an American withdrawal from the region was feared in Japan, and that only a small percent of Japanese believed the United States would come to Japan's defense if it were attacked. Prime Minister Ohira, however, rejected the proposition that the single most fundamental change in the international situation in the 1970s was the end of American military and economic superiority. He subsequently rejected calls for an autonomous or at least an increased independent defense capability for Japan. Ohira choose to rely on the U.S.–Japan defense relationship and, after initial hesitation, followed Washington on sanctions against the Soviet Union for the invasion of Afghanistan.

Since that time, trade negotiations have continued to raise interest in both countries. When faced with the inevitable emotional backlash from contentious sectoral trade negotiations, however, the alliance managers have simply circled the wagons and set about the task of modifying the defense relationship to present an even smaller target by reducing the apparent defense burden on the United States. Thus, while trade relations have worsened, defense cooperation has expanded.

The famous Ron-Yasu dialogue—connoting the good working relationship between President Reagan and Prime Minister Nakasone—was a particularly good example of the division between defense and trade. During this period, Prime Minister Nakasone agreed to President Reagan's requests for increased host nation support toward the stationing of U.S. troops on Japanese soil, agreed to Strategic Defense Initiative (SDI) commitments, broke the 1 percent GNP barrier for defense spending, increased joint maneuvers, and began to operationalize its pledge to defend sea-lanes. This cooperation was strengthened by the renewed intensity of the Cold War, which provided the necessary rationale that the alliance had been missing in the 1970s. In fact, by 1984 Paul Wolfowitz felt comfortable saying in congressional testimony that, while trade problems still existed, "the general consensus of administration officials and long-term observers of U.S.–Japan relations is that our defense relationship with Japan has never been better."[8] This improvement came despite the fact that while the Reagan administration was speaking positively of the alliance, it was still pursuing a separate trade agenda at the behest of industry and Congress. The Reagan administration initiated auto negotiations, resulting in more VERs. They were followed by the market-oriented, sector-specific talks in 1985 to deal with specific trade issues. These talks did not always proceed smoothly. In 1986, Japan was forced to agree to more VERs, and Washington enacted a 100 percent tariff on imports of Japanese semiconductors. By

1987, still obsessed with charges of free-riding by Japan, both the House and the Senate voted that Japan should spend at least 3 percent of its GNP on defense. The damage from these trade salvoes was contained: the administration's "traders" at the Department of Commerce and the Office of the United States Trade Representative were balanced with the traditionalist experts at State and the Pentagon, yielding a "separate but equal" policy on trade and defense.

## HISTORY REPEATS

History repeats itself. The diminished Cold War threat of the late 1980s again opened the door to trade disputes. Surging Japanese imports and investment accompanying the strong U.S. dollar resulted in demands that Japanese trade practices be seriously addressed. These renewed demands for action on trade, combined with the diminished security threat brought by glasnost in the U.S.S.R., weakened arguments used for suppressing contentious trade policies. Congress took the lead in providing the executive branch's trade warriors with the bureaucratic weapons they needed. The Super 301 trade provision in 1987 was the most powerful trade weapon ever developed. It allowed the United States Trade Representative to identify countries that restricted U.S. commerce, and it was aimed almost exclusively at Japan.

A straight line can be drawn between this period of renewed trade rhetoric and the policies adopted four years later by President Clinton. However, the final breakup of the Soviet Union expanded the freedom of action of the Clinton White House's economic team. The Japan experts were, for a time, partially discredited on matters relating to trade. And just as in the early 1970s, the years of trade conflict began to wear on the defense relationship. Once again, commentators questioned U.S. reliability, and parts of the Japanese defense establishment began casting about for alternative methods of guaranteeing Japan's physical security.[9] This resulted in the 1993 Hiraiwa Report to the Japanese government. While still recognizing the importance of the bilateral alliance, it also suggested that Japan should pursue autonomous defense and multilateral arrangements. The backlash against this report among the U.S. defense and foreign policy elite led to the Nye Initiative, which reaffirmed the importance of the alliance. It also led to a move to restructure the 1978 Defense Guidelines in order to strengthen the operational side of the alliance. Once again, the defense relationship is to be managed by those who know the alliance. And once again, their main task is to equalize the defense relationship so that it is less vulnerable to the vagaries of trade.

## My Kingdom for a Flat-Panel Display

The alliance managers were able to insulate the defense relationship from the negative effects of others' efforts to deal with unequal growth. But they could not insulate the alliance from the actual effects of that growth. War-fighting in the postwar period become increasingly dependent on high technology. However, at the same time much of the world's production was segregated by country. Although most developed countries produced most of the inputs that went into high-tech weaponry, a few important inputs were produced only in one country. Furthermore, for products that could be produced anywhere, often the most advanced technology, which was necessary for precision weapons, was available from just one supplier. Unequal growth, particularly in certain high-technology sectors, had made the United States dependent on Japan for some of its defense capabilities.

As Japanese industry grew and prospered, it began to drive American producers out of some businesses or to buy the U.S. production facilities. American's free trade policy—its lack of protection for and subsidization of companies—made this possible. Even in industries where American producers continued to operate, Japanese technology surpassed American in some militarily applicable fields. A 1980 report to Congress stated that the United States had become "Japan's plantation, haulers of wood and growers of crops, in exchange for high-technology value-added products."[10] This was an exaggeration, but it led to another report examining the relative technological superiority of Japan versus the United States in various militarily relevant technologies. It was discovered that in no fewer than seven fields, the United States was dependent on Japan.

This dependence was particularly problematic due to Japan's "three principles" governing arms exports. The principles stated that Japan could not export to communist states, states under U.N. sanction, or states likely to engage in war. This was interpreted to include all militarily related exports, including exports of technology, to all countries, including the United States—a country likely to engage in war. In 1982, the United States convinced Japan to ease the three principles so that technology exports to American defense companies were not prohibited. However, Japanese companies were not required to export the technology to the United States, leaving the U.S. military's dependence on Japan intact.

Furthermore, the United States was not simply dependent on Japan for technology. It also relied on Japanese-made products for some dual-use parts required to make current weapons operate. These included special batteries, semiconductors, and displays.

This sort of dependence on another state for American war-fighting capability was extremely disconcerting for the U.S. defense establishment. For the first time, American military independence was jeopardized. While it may be possible to argue that dependence on Japan, as a close ally, should not have been a problem, this was contradicted by several facts.[11] First, Japan did not share America's approach to use of force. The idea of Japan holding U.S. forces hostage to Tokyo for want of spare parts frightened U.S. military planners. Second, the U.S. military was not necessarily accorded top priority for scarce supplies. This problem became particularly apparent during the Gulf War, when Japanese suppliers balked at rushing semiconductors to U.S. defense contractors over their other, nonmilitary clients. Third, Japanese manufacturers were not always willing to sell their most advanced technology to the United States. This was due in part to suspicions that the Pentagon, given its close relationship with American defense suppliers, could not safeguard the technology. It was also partially due to the "defense allergy" of large Japanese firms.[12] Finally, American planners would not have been comfortable with dependence on anyone. Dependence on another state for defense capabilities automatically decreased American security. One state's dependence is another's power, thus Japan was not troubled by the American dilemma. Looking at the big picture, American dependence may have actually increased U.S. security by increasing Japanese confidence that the United States had to remain committed to the alliance. In the short term it limited American capabilities and freedom of action.

In attempting to address this problem, the Pentagon began looking at managed trade solutions. America's free trade policies were taking some vital production and research out of the United States. In order to eliminate this dependence on Japan, U.S. industry would have to be subsidized and trade would need to be controlled.

This movement had advocates in the 1980s. Congress took a particular interest, proposing legislation that would restrict defense procurement to U.S. firms or protect U.S. defense contractors from foreign competition. The Defense Production Act Amendments of 1990, for example, would have repatriated defense industries so that almost all essential defense production took place onshore.[13] Encouraging domestic production, however, became a tentative government policy only after the Gulf War, when the problem of acquiring semiconductors from Japanese firms clearly demonstrated U.S. military dependence on Japanese industry. A program to rectify this situation for at least one test product was initiated. Frustrated by their inability to obtain advanced flat-panel display technology from Sharp, a Japanese company, the Department of Defense decided to create an American supplier. Seed money and a guaranteed market would be provided. In this endeavor, the Pentagon found allies among those advocating managed trade to counter unfair Japanese trade practices. It, however, encountered opposition from the administration's free trade advocates at the Council of Economic Advisers and the National Economic Council. The program was received with little corporate enthusiasm, and was allowed to languish. The effort did demonstrate the concern with which Washington regarded American dependence on Japan. The American guardians of the alliance had once again sought to insulate it from the negative effects of trade, although in this case with little success.

## Alliance Wise, Trade Foolish

There is one area that is impossible to isolate from trade: defense procurement. Procurement is big trade. Trade agendas can have a very immediate effect on procurement decisions. The purchase of one $50 million fighter can compensate for a large number of $300 VCRs. Likewise, the domestic manufacture of top-flight weapons systems can keep a lot of workers in jobs, promote domestic industry, and encourage the development technology and experience that is applicable in nonmilitary production. Defense production and defense trade thus attract constituencies that are not normally concerned with daily alliance management. These interests bring with them the concerns that dominate the trade side of the relationship. These trade interests often run counter to purely security-related objectives, such as autonomy or joint operability.[14]

Both Japan and the United States have long been aware of the power of defense trade to help or hurt their respective economies. As noted earlier, through the 1950s and 1960s the United States was happy to supply equipment and licensed production to Japan, while segments of the Japanese defense and industrial establishments were willing to produce under license. Both sides realized the utility of defense trade in strengthening the alliance. Most prime ministers, when meeting with their American counterparts, brought promises to purchase more American weapons in order to deflect trade criticism. Co-production accelerated in the late 1970s as part of this effort. The licensing system kept both sides happy because it seemed to benefit both the United States and Japan equally.

This production relationship faltered as the United States became increasingly concerned about technology losses to Japan. The problem was a perception that Japan was reaping disproportionate technological benefits from joint production. In the late 1970s, the Pentagon and its contractors developed a list of technologies that they were interested in getting from Japan. They attempted to negotiate a technology sharing program in 1980, but met with resistance from Tokyo. As a result, the U.S. Department of Defense decided to "black box" (refuse to transfer) most of the base technology for Japan's licensed production of the F-15. Ironically, it was Japan's production of this black-boxed plane that brought Congress into the game. The General Accounting Office (GAO) in a 1982 report noted that F-15s were being built under license in the same hanger as commercial jets.[15] It concluded that American technology was unfairly used to help a Japanese industry that would compete with American companies. According to GAO, Japan accrued unequal gains from the arrangement by acquiring new production technology, providing experience to workers and producers, and subsidizing the development of the necessary infrastructure. Once Congress was interested in co-production deals, they remained attentive.

This legislative interest in Japan's aerospace defense production resulted in one of the U.S.–Japan defense relationship's most contentious postwar chapters: the negotiation of the FSX development agreement. The story of how Japan acquired a replacement for its aging F-1 fleet has been handled in detail elsewhere, but a summary is useful here.[16] The State Department and the Pentagon had originally negotiated an agreement to co-produce a fighter. U.S. negotiators were aware that the U.S. defense aviation industry would be interested in the project, and worked to ensure that some benefits from the deal might flow back to the United States in terms of workshare or technology. To insulate the negotiations from rising trade tensions, they intentionally excluded Commerce and United States Trade Representative (USTR) officials. Ultimately this approach caused more problems than it solved. Despite the negotiators' best efforts, Commerce and USTR still found the agreement too lopsided in terms of economic benefits. They insisted on renegotiating, this time with their participation. On the Japanese side, MITI took up the challenge and agreed to renegotiation. With familiar trade adversaries sitting at the table, the renegotiation of the development agreement took on many of the characteristics of trade discussions. The contentious and disturbing intrusion of trade players and trade rhetoric into defense negotiations was a negative experience for both American and Japanese defense elites, and did little to further defense goals in the short term. It also provided the ammunition for those in Japan who advocated autonomous production. At a time when Japan and the United States were trying to increase cooperation and interoperability, such autonomy ran counter to the goals of the defense relationship.

The "technology for technology" initiative by the Pentagon in the early years of the Clinton administration was an attempt to smooth defense co-production by ensuring that the U.S. economy received the same benefits from defense trade that Japan's did. Like the flat-panel display effort, it floundered for lack of business interest; the framers of the initiative had overestimated U.S. corporate interest in Japanese technology, as well as the level of control Japan's defense elite had over Japanese defense technology. The entire undertaking proved again the need to equalize the economic benefits accruing to the United States and Japan from the alliance, as well as the difficulty of insulating the alliance from such concerns.

## It Is All Relative—A Conclusion

The postwar period begun with positive trade spillovers for the alliance by the end of the Cold War turned into mostly negative spillovers. The Japanese economy's relative growth led Washington to promote trade negotiations, which negatively affected confidence in the alliance. Its relative growth resulted in Japanese suppliers having more and more control over American war-fighting capabilities. Its relative growth also made Washington increasingly conscious of the unequal benefits accruing to Japan in defense co-production, leading to efforts to modify those arrangements.

The source of these problems appears to be American concern about unequal growth yielding unequal costs and benefits. Growth throughout most of the postwar period has, indeed, been lopsided. Between 1956 and 1975, Japan's GNP went from 4 percent of the world total to 9 percent, while the United States dropped from 31 percent to 24 percent.[17] This disparate relative growth continued through the 1980s and early 1990s.

Debate over whether a state should be concerned about relative gains has raged for decades.[18] This normative judgment does not much matter for the purpose of alliance maintenance. The fact is that Americans are concerned about such gains. American fear of Japanese relative gains is borne out by a variety of polls of Americans showing that most would prefer slower but equal growth for the United States and Japan over higher but unequal growth that favors Japan.[19] Other polls indicated that, at the height of the Japanese "bubble" economy, more Americans saw Japan as a threat to American security than the Soviet Union.[20] This hostility does not bode well for the future of the alliance.

The insulationist approach to managing the alliance can mitigate these adversarial feelings, borne of relative gains and suckled on trade disputes. It must be noted, however, that this policy of insulation carries with it serious problems for the long-term future of the alliance. First, because the alliance has operated without needing much support from the populace, understanding of the necessity of the alliance to the security of both American and Japanese interests has not been well articulated to the masses. As a result, the alliance has remained suspect in the eyes of both the American and Japanese general populations. The 1995 rape of an Okinawa schoolgirl by American servicemen underscores this problem. The initial dramatic popular outcry in Japan against the alliance had its roots in unstable domestic politics, general popular dissatisfaction with Tokyo, and bureaucratic bumbling, but it also demonstrated that understanding of the rationale for the defense relationship has not penetrated Japan's political culture. Ironically, by taking the alliance out of its protective insulation and into the general debate in Japan, the underlying long-term strength of the relationship may have been enhanced.

Second, alliance management cannot counteract the fact that trade continues to have a real effect on the alliance. Attempts to protect U.S. security from these dependencies have not succeeded, and never will without drastic trade distorting efforts. Finally, quiet alliance management cannot protect the defense relationship from trade disputes over defense trade. Since procurement is intrinsically part of both the defense and trade relationships, it is destined to be buffeted by both.

There is light at the end of this tunnel. The source of America's troubles with Japan may also carry with it the roots of resolution. If concerns about relative growth are straining the defense relationship, then the current decline in Japan's growth rate should remove many of these tensions. In fact, if Chinese growth rates continue to outstrip Japan's for any length of time, American interest in Japan is likely to diminish. Current efforts to further equalize the defense burden within the alliance should also reduce pressure on the defense relationship from trade concerns. Defense can never be separated completely from trade. But with Japan no longer viewed as an economic threat, nor as a free-rider on the backs of American citizens and soldiers, the positive effects of trade on the alliance could again come to the fore.

## Notes

1. See, for example, Kar-yiu Wong, "National Defense and Foreign Trade: The Sweet and Sour Relationship Between the United States and Japan";

and Robert Dekle, "The Relationship Between Defense Spending and Economic Performance in Japan," both in John Makin and Donald Hellmann, eds., *Sharing World Leadership?: A New Era for America and Japan* (Washington, D.C.: American Enterprise Institute for Public Policy Research, 1989).

2. Michael Schaller, "Security the Great Crescent: Occupied Japan and the Origins of Containment in Southeast Asia," *Journal of American History* (September 1982): 394.

3. Andrew Rotter, *The Path to Vietnam: Origins of the American Commitment to Southeast Asia* (Ithaca, NY: Cornell University Press, 1987).

4. Douglas Mendel, *The Japanese People and Foreign Policy: A Study of Public Opinion in Post-Treaty Japan* (Berkeley and Los Angeles: University of California Press, 1961), p. 43.

5. Roger Buckley, *U.S.–Japan Alliance Diplomacy 1945–1990* (Cambridge: Cambridge University Press, 1992), p. 126.

6. Gerald Curtis, "American Policy Toward Japan in the Seventies: The Need for Disengagement," in Gerald Curtis, ed., *Japanese-American Relations in the 1970s* (Washington, D.C.: Columbia Books, 1970).

7. I. M. Destler, Haruhiro Rukui, and Hideo Sato, *The Textile Wrangle: Conflict in Japanese-American Relations, 1969–1971* (Ithaca, NY: Cornell University Press, 1979).

8. Paul Wolfowitz, "Taking Stock of U.S.–Japan Relations" (Washington, D.C.: U.S. Department of State, Bureau of Public Affairs, July 1984).

9. See, for example, Tatou Takahama, "What Future Does the Japan–U.S. Security System Have?" *Journal of Japanese Trade and Industry* 3(1995):35–37; and Yoshihisa Kumori, "The Impact of Auto Talks on the U.S. Security Pact," *Shukan Bunshun* (June 8, 1995): 50–51.

10. Ellen Frost, *For Richer, For Poorer: The New U.S.–Japan Relationship* (New York: Council on Foreign Relations, 1987).

11. James Meiskel, "Domestic Industry and National Security," *Strategic Review* (Fall 1991): 23–32.

12. With defense manufacturing still tainted in Japan, many high-tech companies chose to stay out of the business rather than tarnish their reputations.

13. Meiskel, 1991, p. 24.

14. Gregg Rubinstein, "Arms and Technology Cooperation in U.S.–Japan Security Relations," unpublished paper, December 12, 1995.

15. U.S. General Accounting Office, *U.S. Military Coproduction Programs Assisting Japan in Developing Civilian Aircraft Industry.* Report to the Chairman, Subcommittee on Trade, U.S. House Committee on Ways and Means (Washington, D.C.: GPO, March 18, 1982).

16. Michael J. Green, *Arming Japan: Defense Production, Alliance Politics, and the Postwar Search for Autonomy* (New York: Columbia University Press, 1995).
17. *International Economic Report to the President, 1977* (Washington, D.C.: GPO, 1977).
18. For the debate of the economic effects of relative gains, see Samuel Huntington, "America's Changing Strategic Interests," *Survival*(January–February 1991); Paul Krugman, *Strategic Trade Policy and the New International Economics* (Cambridge, MA: MIT Press, 1986), and Fred Hirsch, *The Social Limits of Growth* (Cambridge, MA: Harvard University Press, 1976). For a discussion of the larger effects of relative gains, see Samuel Huntington, "Why International Primacy Matters," *International Security* (Spring 1993); Robert Jervis, "International Primacy: Is the Game Worth the Candle?" *International Security* (Spring 1993); and Robert Gilpin, *U.S. Power and the Multinational Corporation* (New York: Basic Books, 1975).
19. Urban Lehner and Alan Murray, "Will the U.S. Find the Resolve to Meet the Japanese Challenge?" *Wall Street Journal,* July 2, 1990.
20. Michael Oreskes, "Americans Express Worry on Japan, As Feelings in Tokyo Seem to Soften," *New York Times,* July 10, 1990.

# 13

# U.S.–Japan Armaments Cooperation

GREGG A. RUBINSTEIN

AN ESSENTIAL factor in U.S.–Japan security relations, armaments cooperation has nevertheless seldom received the attention given to other defense issues by policymakers and analysts.[1] This chapter reviews the development of armaments cooperation from the Cold War pattern of security assistance through the convergence of defense and economic interests in post–Cold War security relations. It also covers the evolution of defense technology collaboration and its role in armaments cooperation.

## Security Assistance: 1954–1985

Following the first U.S.–Japan Mutual Cooperation and Security Treaty of 1952, the Mutual Defense Assistance Agreement (MDAA) of 1954 provided the framework for U.S. assistance in the arming and training of Japan's newly formed Self-Defense Forces (SDF).[2] Through MDAA-based programs, Washington assisted the development of both operational and industrial bases for Japanese defense efforts. Defense industrial programs with Japan developed through several phases.

*The 1950s:* provision of surplus U.S. defense equipment under Military Assistance Programs (MAP); maintenance and repair of U.S. systems in Japan.

*The 1960s:* MAP ends; sales of major U.S. defense systems; increasing co-production of U.S. equipment by Japan; Japanese development of basic defense hardware.

*The 1970s:* extensive U.S. sales and co-production; increasing indigenous research and development (R&D) and production in Japan.

*The 1980s:* co-production of first-line U.S. defense systems; growing number of Japanese development programs; technology transfer becomes a significant issue. By the 1980s, Japan's inventory of purchased and co-produced U.S. defense equipment exceeded that of any other U.S. ally.

**Table 13-1 Japan's Procurement of U.S. Defense System**

| System | Japanese Procurement | | | |
|---|---|---|---|---|
| | MOU[a] agreed | from when | how | upgrade in |
| F-15 | 1978 | 80s | FMS[b]—>license | 88, 94 |
| F-4 | 1969 | 70s | license | 82, 89,93 |
| E-2C | — | 80s | FMS, DCS[c] | |
| AWACS | — | 90s | FMS | |
| C-130 | — | 80s | FMS | |
| P-3C | 1978 | 70s | FMS → license | 88, 93 |
| AH-1S | 1982 | 80s | FMS → license | 91, 93 |
| CH-47 | — | 80s | commercial license | 93 |
| SH-60 | 1989 | 80s | license | 93 |
| MH-53 | — | 80s | DCS | |
| PATRIOT | 1985 | 80s | license | 92 |
| 1-HAWK | 1977 | 80s | license | 82, 86, 91 |
| HARPOON | — | 70s | FMS | 82 |
| Sidewinder -9B, 9E, 9P, 9L | 1982 | 50s | FMS → license | 73, 75, 80 |
| Sparrow -7E, 7F, 7M | 1969 | 70s | license | 80, 89 |
| Sea Sparrow -7E (improved), 7F, 7M (VLS) | 1969 | 70s | license | 77, 82, 90, 93 |
| Standard Missile: SM-1, SM-2 (VLS) | — | 70s | FMS | |
| Stinger | — | 80s | FMS | |
| TOW | — | 80s | FMS | 89, 91 |
| VLS | — | 90s | FMS → DCS | |
| AEGIS | — | 90s | FMS | |
| ASROC | — | 60s | license | |
| Mk-46 | 1982 | 80s | license | |
| PHALANX | — | 80s | FMS | |
| MLRS | 1992 | 90s | FMS → license | |

[a] Memorandum of Understanding.
[b] Foreign Military Spaces.
[c] Direct Commercial Sales.

For many years Japan occupied a unique place in U.S. government thinking on defense industry programs. Japan was neither a NATO ally with whom the United States had extensive partnership relations in armaments procurement, nor a recipient of direct military aid. Defense programs with Japan fell somewhere between NATO and the third world—sales and co-production[3] of some of the most advanced U.S. defense systems continued to be implemented in a security assistance framework.[4]

These arrangements have served well-established interests in both countries. U.S. officials justified the release of front-line defense systems for licensed production as a means of strengthening security relations with Japan, especially in improved Japanese defense capabilities and interoperability with U.S. forces. Interest in technology transfer focused on the release of advanced U.S. technologies in licensed production programs. There was little perceived need for attention to transfers of technology from Japan. (See "Defense Technology Cooperation" section below.)

Critics of defense programs with Japan have charged that in their preoccupation with alliance objectives, U.S. officials neglected the equally important implications of licensed production programs for Japan's economic competitiveness. The first project in which these concerns became evident was in co-production of the F-15 fighter. Arguments against co-production emphasized that direct sale of this aircraft would have provided greater economic benefit to the United States and prevented Japanese use of F-15 technology and manufacturing experience in the development of its own aerospace industry.[5]

U.S. officials involved with Japanese defense programs have emphasized an awareness of income and market share concerns, as well as a conviction that Japanese industry benefits were incremental and acceptable trade-offs for continued Japanese reliance on U.S. defense systems. It was generally accepted that if the "full loaf" (off-the-shelf purchase of a U.S. system) option was not a realistic expectation, then a "half loaf" of licensed production was preferable to an indigenous Japanese system or a third country purchase.[6]

This debate among U.S. proponents and critics of defense industrial programs with Japan remains unresolved.[7] A tendency on both sides to speak past each other's concerns reflects years of deliberate intent to separate defense and economic issues in U.S.–Japan relations. While understandable as a response to misguided linkages of security relations to U.S.–Japan trade problems, this position encouraged an insensitivity among many U.S. officials to the interaction of defense and economic interests in armaments programs. This attitude reinforced a marginal view of defense industrial activities (technical issues of little policy significance) and a lack of attention to developments in co-production and technology transfer activities that no longer fit within a security assistance framework.

While Japanese government and industry officials predictably endorsed the idea that cooperation in security matters should not be affected by trade disputes, it has always been clear in Japan that defense industry programs are both defense and economic activities. The development of modern defense capabilities has been an important concern in Japan's procurement planning, but defense programs have also been a significant channel for the introduction of advanced technologies and the strengthening of Japan's industrial base.[8] Japanese officials have never been secretive about this agenda, nor has Japan been exceptional in emphasizing the economic and technology benefits of its defense programs. However, Japanese demands for licensed production and technology transfers in defense programs became increasingly controversial as they grated against growing trade problems with the United States—a point not well understood then in either Washington or Tokyo.

## Transition: 1985–1989

By the mid-1980s Japan's emergence as a leading economic power and competitor to the United States had called into question the traditional security assistance rationale for defense industrial cooperation. Major defense programs with Japan raised concerns in the United States over potential compromises of sensitive technologies and commercial exploitation by Japan. Defense industrial activities with Japan became a lightning rod for U.S. trade officials concerned by the economic implications of military sales and licensed production programs, but largely uninvolved in their development and negotiation.[9]

Dissatisfaction with defense industrial cooperation programs in the United States was matched by pressure in Japan for indigenous development as well as production of defense systems. Steady growth in defense budgets, increasing Japanese industrial capabilities, and the surge of national confidence that marked Japan's "bubble economy" years all supported visions of autonomy in defense acquisitions and more advantageous dealings with the United States among many Japan Defense Agency (JDA) and the Ministry of International Trade and Industry (MITI) bureaucrats as well as industry and political supporters in the Diet.[10]

Traditional security assistance attitudes toward U.S.–Japan defense programs could not answer effectively either economic criticism in the United States or posturing for autonomy in Japan. By the late 1980s, a collision of these interests became inevitable; all that was required was a flash point.

Even among the few observers who warned that Japan's Fighter Support Experimental (FSX) program could become a serious problem, none were prepared for the intensity and bitterness of the ensuing controversy. In the early to mid-1980s, JDA initially wanted to replace its F-1 support fighter with an indigenous aircraft based on both domestic and foreign systems—a pattern familiar to U.S. officials working on Japan programs. While willing to support the FSX program, DoD insisted that cooperation take place under a government agreement with provisions for protection of information and technology flowback.[11]

Faced with what they believed to be unrealistic JDA options for acquiring FSX, DoD first raised the idea of co-development in late 1985. At that time there was no firm position on the question of new development versus use of an existing airframe for FSX. However, frustration with perceived Japanese inflexibility combined with awakening political interest in the FSX program had by early 1987 hardened Washington views on use of an existing U.S. airframe for FSX. By late 1987, after a cabinet-level confrontation over "U.S.-based" versus "indigenous" options for FSX, Tokyo had agreed to co-development based on the U.S. F-16 fighter. This led to the FSX Development Memorandum of Understanding (MOU) the following year.

Ironically, agreement on a joint FSX program triggered an even greater controversy. Posturing over FSX had little to do with the substance of the program; FSX had become a symbol for inflated Japanese expectations of aerospace leadership, just as it was a target for frustration over trade problems and fears for the U.S. industrial base in Washington. Misfortune also played a role; the coincidence of the FSX MOU with the confusion of the Reagan-Bush transition provided an opportunity that was quickly exploited by political critics of the program.[12]

Political problems aside, U.S.–Japanese interaction on the FSX project also revealed serious differences in perceptions reflective of Cold War patron–client attitudes and the security assistance approach to U.S.–Japan programs.

*Japanese interests:* JDA announced three options for FSX selection—use of upgraded F-4s in Japan, adoption of an existing foreign aircraft, and development of a new aircraft. The preference, however, was clearly domestic development. FSX was expected to strengthen Japan's industrial base and Japanese officials assumed that U.S. support for the program would be available as needed—as it generally had been.

*U.S. interests:* While Japanese interests in FSX remained relatively constant, however misguided in their reading of the United States, American expectations shifted; first from concern with technology transfer to insistence that FSX be based on a U.S. airframe, and eventually back to a renewed emphasis on technological cooperation. In all cases, U.S. positions were reactive; negotiations on FSX development were carried out by officials who neither fully appreciated the wider economic and technology concerns raised by FSX, nor were prepared for the political consequences.

*Co-development:* Although the United States and Japan agreed to development of FSX based on the U.S. F-16 fighter, the two sides had basically different ideas of what co-development meant. For the United States, FSX was one more security assistance program, an extension of co-production.[13] In Japan, co-development meant a maximum of indigenous development with U.S. support, but minimal U.S. oversight. These approaches were never reconciled and continued to complicate the FSX development program.

Whatever one's view of the FSX controversy and subsequent development, there is little question that its effect spread well beyond the bounds of defense industrial programs. While economic concerns cannot be held hostage to security interests, or vice versa, FSX proved that defense and economic issues between the United States and Japan cannot be maintained on separate tracks. More than any other single event, FSX brought defense industry and technology issues from the periphery to the mainstream of U.S.–Japan security relations.

## Armaments Cooperation: 1990–Present

The FSX controversy coincided with the beginning of post–Cold War adjustments to defense programs as well as economic recession in Japan. These developments changed the focus of defense industrial activities between Japan and the United States from security assistance to armaments cooperation. Armaments cooperation policy recognizes a connection of defense and economic interests in sales, licensed production, and joint R&D activities.[14]

Washington's objectives in armaments cooperation programs with Japan have overlapped with those of earlier years concerning allied defense capabilities and interoperability between U.S. and Japanese forces. However, armaments cooperation policy also recognizes Japan as not only a customer, but as both an economic competitor and potential partner in systems and technology development. This reality has been evident in emphasis on workshare for U.S. industry in sales and licensed production projects, as well as in efforts to achieve greater balance in transfers of defense-related technologies between the two countries.[15]

While Japan's post–Cold War defense budgets have not been reduced as sharply as those of the United States, JDA also has had to contend with a decline in procurement funding.

Together with the general economic recession in Japan, this declining trend in defense spending has deflated much of the enthusiasm for autonomous defense acquisition that fueled the FSX controversy. The conclusions of JDA-sponsored studies on indigenous defense production and R&D capabilities echo those reached in other countries: it is necessary to protect essential capabilities, but complete autonomy is not feasible.[16] Despite the negative legacy of FSX, Japanese government and industry sources acknowledge that industrial cooperation

**Table 13-2 Japan's Initial Defense Budget**

| year | total budget (billion yen) | % of GNP |
|---|---|---|
| 1977 | 1690.6 | 0.88 |
| 1978 | 1901.0 | 0.9 |
| 1979 | 2094.5 | 0.9 |
| 1980 | 2230.2 | 0.9 |
| 1981 | 2400.0 | 0.91 |
| 1982 | 2586.1 | 0.93 |
| 1983 | 2754.2 | 0.98 |
| 1984 | 2934.6 | 0.99 |
| 1985 | 3137.1 | 0.997 |
| 1986 | 3343.5 | 0.993 |
| 1987 | 3517.4 | 1.004 |
| 1988 | 3700.3 | 1.013 |
| 1989 | 3919.8 | 1.006 |
| 1990 | 4159.3 | 0.997 |
| 1991 | 4386.0 | 0.954 |
| 1992 | 4551.8 | 0.941 |
| 1993 | 4640.6 | 0.937 |
| 1994 | 4683.5 | 0.948 |
| 1995 | 4723.6 | 0.949 |
| 1996 | 4845.5 | 0.968 |
| 1997 | 4941.4 | 0.946 |

*Note:* The FY 1997 budget is not including the cost for Special Action Committee on Okinawa (SACO) related projects accounts, which accounts for 6.1 billion yen.
*Source: Bouei Hand Book,* 1997 (Tokyo: Asagumo Shinbunsha, 1998).

with the United States continues to serve important defense and economic interests.[17]

Although unlikely to match the steady stream of defense sales and co-production programs that marked the 1970s and 1980s, the negotiation and management of major procurement projects such as AWACS early warning aircraft, AEGIS air defense ships, and possible procurement of Theater Missile Defense (TMD) systems will continue to be important issues in U.S.–Japan security relations. However, the most significant development in the transition from security assistance to armaments cooperation has been an increasing emphasis on technology transfer—an issue that in recent years has taken on a life of its own in defense programs with Japan.

## Defense Technology Cooperation

While potential U.S. interest in defense technology cooperation with Japan was noted in the MDAA,[18] it remained dormant in the context of security assistance programs. By the end of the 1970s Japan's growing technological capabilities had attracted the attention of the U.S. defense community—a development that coincided with the collapse of détente with the Soviet Union and Washington's interest in a more active security relationship with Japan. While the United States and Japan developed "Guidelines for Defense Cooperation" to cover operational matters, officials from DoD's Defense Research and Engineering Directorate proposed consultations with JDA acquisition and R&D interests. These discussions led to the establishment in 1980 of the U.S.–Japan Systems and Technology Forum (S&TF).[19]

Despite agreement to strengthen consultations on defense procurement and technology development, it quickly became apparent that Japanese restrictions on arms exports made the implementation of cooperative development programs all but impossible. First adopted in 1967 in response to criticism of Japanese logistic support for U.S. forces engaged in Vietnam, Japan's "Three Principles" policy banned arms exports to members of the Soviet bloc, countries under U.N. sanctions, and nations in or near a state of hostility. "Guidelines" to the Three Principles announced by the Japanese government in 1976 virtually banned arms exports, including defense production equipment and technologies. These measures were reinforced by a Diet Resolution adopted in 1981.[20]

Washington officials were soon urging their Japanese counterparts to allow the transfer of defense-related technologies to the United States despite Three Principles restrictions. At this point defense technology became part of the "burden-sharing" agenda that dominated U.S.–Japan security relations during the 1980s. While initially reluctant to risk controversy over any attempt to revise Three Principles–related positions, the Japanese government finally announced in 1983 that transfers of military technologies to the United States would be exempted from its ban on arms exports.[21]

This statement was confirmed later the same year by an Exchange of Notes between the two governments. These Notes provided a U.S.–Japanese government channel—the Joint Military Technology Commission (JMTC)—for military technology transfers and confirmed that commercial technologies with defense application (often known as "dual-use technologies") were freely available to the United States.[22] U.S. interest in access to Japanese technologies was also reflected in the incorporation of explicit technology flowback provisions into co-production MOUs with Japan.[23]

Subsequent release of reports on industrial and technology cooperation with Japan by both the Defense Science Board (an industrial advisory group to DoD) and DoD-sponsored Technology Assessment Teams further encouraged expectations (as well as fear) of possible U.S.–Japan activities.[24] In fact, events neither justified forecasts of technology harvests from Japan nor threatened expansions of Japanese industrial capabilities. Collaboration on defense technology issues remained minimal and largely symbolic through the 1980s. Policy statements notwithstanding, there was little support in Washington for serious pursuit of defense R&D projects with Japan. Japanese officials meanwhile saw no reason to change their view of defense technology issues as problems to be contained rather than opportunities to be pursued, and Japanese industry continued to follow the lead of its government.[25]

By the early 1990s post–Cold War reductions in defense resources had encouraged more Defense Department interest in international collaboration for systems and technology development. In the case of Japan this development first became evident in efforts to reinvigorate the S&TF through work on several joint R&D projects.[26] However, the first real expression of post–Cold War concern over armaments cooperation with Japan emerged with the " Technology-for-Technology" (TfT) concept introduced early in the Clinton administration.[27] TfT set itself apart from earlier Department of Defense approaches primarily in its emphasis on "equal" returns of Japanese dual-use technologies for access to the technologies of advanced U.S. defense systems.

While U.S. interest in dual-use technologies was a well-established issue, its expression through TfT soon raised insurmountable problems.

TfT tended to distort evaluations of defense programs by stressing technology acquisition as an end in itself rather than as one of several factors (industrial work share, interoperability, etc.) that contribute to armaments cooperation. More seriously, TfT-related proposals blurred the distinction between technologies controlled by the Japanese government and dual-use items clearly developed and owned by Japanese industry. The use of DoD–JDA channels to access commercial technologies proved impracticable.

These substantive problems were aggravated by a premature linkage of TfT ideas with discussions of Japanese participation in TMD programs.[28] A widespread belief in both countries that the TfT concept embodied a "managed trade" economic agenda that slighted defense interests was encouraged by the lack of a clearly articulated policy on security relations with Japan during the early Clinton years.

Progress in revitalizing U.S.–Japan security relations (as seen in the recently revised Guidelines for Defense Cooperation—see Appendix 3) has allowed defense officials to more credibly integrate technology cooperation with other defense acquisition interests. Promotion of the TfT concept has been supplanted by DoD policy that emphasizes Japan as not only a customer of U.S. products, but a partner in the development of future equipment and technology.[29]

As demonstrated in current S&TF programs, Japanese officials have also shown a willingness to broaden cooperation in basic research to the joint development of advanced defense systems.[30] Common recognition of budgetary and technology limitations, mutual interest in defense acquisition reform, and increasing reliance on commercial sourcing for hardware and technologies have given the United States and Japan a shared stake in armaments cooperation that was not apparent in the 1980s.

The trend toward "partnerships" in the development of defense equipment and technology has also been strengthened by a significant change in perceptions of U.S.–Japan engagement. Popular 1980s images of an adversarial Japan in the United States and an America in terminal decline in Japan have receded with more recent economic and political developments in both countries. As noted in other chapters in this volume, post–Cold War realities have tended to revalidate rather than undermine the relevance of close U.S.–Japan security relations.

The most telling demonstration of changing conditions for armaments cooperation can be seen in the 1996 MOU for production of the F-2 (former FSX). Agreement on a program that had only a few years earlier triggered a political uproar, and become a serious incident in

U.S.–Japan relations, attracted only limited attention in Japan while passing almost unnoticed in the United States.[31] Still, FSX/F-2 will affect perceptions of U.S.–Japan cooperation in defense programs for years to come. Avoiding another FSX experience has become a by-word in considering future collaboration.

It now appears that TMD systems could provide the first major challenge for the concept of defense partnerships with Japan.[32] Pentagon interest in Japan not only acquiring TMD systems but also assisting the United States in their development is consistent with U.S. approaches to other allies on R&D collaboration. While Japan's internal deliberations on the acquisition of a TMD capability remain unresolved, cooperation with the United States in missile defense R&D may evolve in the future. Interaction on TMD will follow an incremental path—procurement of basic systems through sales and licensing programs in parallel with joint efforts on more advanced capabilities.

Continued evolution toward partnerships in defense equipment and technology development is already occurring in less conspicuous areas. For example, recent agreement to jointly develop an improved ejection seat for fighter aircraft marks the first DoD–JDA project to focus not on basic research, but on full development of a product.[33] Current emphasis on a defense requirements dialogue in the S&TF reflects the reality that partnership activities must be based on an understanding of common interests in future equipment and technology needs.

Further development of armaments cooperation cut will depend not only on closer contact between government agencies, but also on more effective interaction with industry. Discussion of an industry advisory group that would provide a counterpart to the S&TF dates back almost to the beginning of the S&TF itself, but bureaucratic resistance to the idea of private sector involvement in "government activities" blocked attempts at implementation.[34]

However, the concept of defense partnerships—which depends in part on substantial industry involvement and initiative in cooperative programs—has encouraged a more positive view of a U.S.–Japan industry dialogue on defense programs. With Defense Department and JDA support, the National Defense Industry Association and the Defense Production Committee of Keidanren recently established an Industry Forum for Security Cooperation (IFSEC). IFSEC recommendations on problems that obstruct armaments cooperation should both encourage closer industry dialogue and provide an agenda for future government–industry exchanges.[35]

## Conclusion

The development of armaments cooperation activities between the United States and Japan reflects the evolution of their security relationship and has become an important factor in driving that evolution. Despite charges of unbalanced benefits, defense equipment and technology programs with Japan over the past forty years have continued to meet basic U.S. needs—modernized Japanese defense capabilities, interoperability, and significant benefits for U.S. industry—while also satisfying Japanese security, political, and economic interests.

For the foreseeable future, interaction on defense industrial programs will continue to reflect a trade-off among sales of U.S. defense systems, licensed production in Japan, and R&D collaboration. However, the balance in this trade-off has changed. There will be fewer new defense programs in Japan, and U.S. interest in sales and licensing opportunities that do emerge will be challenged by pressure for indigenous programs and alternatives from third countries.[36] Interoperability concerns will continue to be important for U.S. policymakers, but the content of future U.S.–Japan defense programs will be driven at least as much by considerations of industrial work share and technology transfer opportunities.

While pressure in Japan for autonomy in defense R&D and production has receded in the face of limited technology and budgetary resources, Japan has hardly given up its indigenous options. Officials in JDA and MITI will continue to protect both national security and industry interests in what they see to be essential defense development and manufacturing capabilities. Despite budgetary limitations, Japan can be expected to play the indigenous card where possible—an alternative that will be encouraged by U.S. reluctance to release defense systems for production in Japan.[37]

The skill with which competing U.S. and Japanese interests in armaments cooperation are negotiated and managed will do much to determine which of two paths future U.S.–Japan defense programs follow.

1. Rigid U.S. and Japanese positions on licensing and technology release result in occasional U.S. sales, third country procurements, and indigenous Japanese programs. Industrial collaboration gradually erodes as U.S. participation in Japanese defense programs recedes and Japan is increasingly distanced from its primary source of advanced defense equipment and technology.
2. More flexible postures toward technology transfers and joint programs supports collaboration that meets specific defense and eco-

nomic interests on both sides and *provides a positive linkage of defense and economic interests in a vigorous U.S.–Japan security relationship.*

Only a few years ago the first alternative appeared more likely as suspicion over FSX combined with bureaucratic inertia to limit defense industrial activities. However, recent progress in U.S.–Japan programs supports the second, more positive prospect—there are no longer insurmountable obstacles to further evolution toward partnerships in equipment and technology programs. Whether this trend continues depends on a mutual understanding of several critical factors.

- Armaments cooperation has become a key determinant in post–Cold War U.S.–Japan security relations. As shown by the FSX experience, defense and economic concerns in U.S.–Japan relations converge on armaments programs. The economic impact of such activities will continue to engage a degree of public attention and political interests usually untouched by other issues in the security relationship.
- The security assistance framework for managing defense programs with Japan reflected realities of the Cold War period. This framework has since become outdated, but was far from thoughtless in conception or practice. Trade-offs among defense capabilities, interoperability, and industrial benefits that determined the content and terms of defense programs at that time remain (together with technology access) valid measures today.
- If the security assistance approach did not give full weight to economic and technology concerns, it is also true that economic-focused criticisms of U.S.–Japan armaments programs have failed to appreciate valid defense interests. Contrary to the impression left by polarized debates over FSX, security and economic interests are not zero-sum issues in Japanese defense programs—any more than they are in the United States or elsewhere.
- Post–Cold War armaments programs in both countries underline the importance of access to a broad range of technologies. However, the development and transfer of defense-related technologies cannot be a stand-alone issue in U.S.–Japan relations. "Technology cooperation" must be managed within a coherent framework of armaments cooperation.
- The past practice of separating sales and licensed production from technology development in U.S.–Japan programs is no longer realistic. Equipment sales and R&D activities are not mutually exclusive, but increasingly interdependent.

- Similarly, alliance concerns will no longer suffice to impose U.S.-based procurements on Japan, as was the case with FSX (and Japan's more recent acquisition of AWACS). "No more FSXs" can best be understood as insistence—from both sides—on programs that balance operational needs with mutual industrial–technology benefits.

## Notes

1. The meaning of "armaments cooperation" in this chapter corresponds to the accepted usage of this term in DoD: a broad range of defense programs including arms sales, licensed production, joint R&D, and cooperative development efforts like the FSX.
2. Quoted in *Defense of Japan 1996* (Japan Defense Agency), p. 317.
3. Though often used interchangeably, co-production and licensed production are different terms. Licensed production means foreign manufacture under commercial agreement with government approval through an export license. Co-production refers to activities under umbrella agreements—such as a Memorandum of Understanding (MOU)—that can include government or commercial sales, manufacturing licenses, and local procurements.
4. This situation largely reflects institutional bias. Officials responsible for sales and co-production programs in DoD's Defense Security Assistance Agency (DSAA, now the Defense Security Corporation Agency [DSCA]) are widely separated—in both organization and attitude—from those managing joint development programs in DoD Acquisitions.
5. A good example of such criticism can be found in Government Accounting Office, *U.S. Military Coproduction Programs Assist Japan in Developing Its Civil Aircraft Industry* (Washington, D.C.: GAO Report ID-82-23, 13-205192; March 18, 1982).
6. Interview with former DSAA deputy director Glenn Rudd (September 12, 1994).
7. Continuing ambivalence on the need for cooperation with Japan vs. discomfort with Japanese capabilities and intentions can be seen in Defense Science Board *Defense Industry Cooperation with Pacific Rim Nations* (Washington, D.C.: U.S. Department of Defense, 1989), pp. 41–59; and National Research Council, Committee on Japan, *Maximizing U.S. Interests in Science and Technology Relations with Japan* (Washington, D.C.: National Academy Press, 1995).
8. Accounts of defense programs and the development of Japan's industrial/technology base can be found in Michael W. Chinworth, *Inside Japan's Defense* (Washington, D.C.: Brassey's, 1992); Richard J. Samuels, *Rich Nation/Strong Army: National Security and the Technological Transformation of*

*Japan* (Ithaca, NY: Cornell University Press, 1994); and Michael J. Green, *Arming Japan* (New York: Columbia University Press, 1995).

9. See revised introduction in Clyde V. Prestowitz, Jr., *Trading Places* (New York: Basic Books, 1989), pp. 1–13.
10. Chinworth, 1992, pp. 124–39; Green, 1995, pp. 72–85. Though Japanese posturing was aimed at leveraging access to U.S. systems, hubris clearly played a role as well.
11. Discussion of early FSX development is based on direct experience while at the Mutual Defense Assistance Office of the U.S. Embassy, Tokyo. JDA/industry plans for FSX acquisition were very similar to those used for upgrading Japan's co-produced F-4 fighters and procuring the SH-60 naval helicopter. While JDA insisted that SH-60 avionics were to be indigenously developed, the evident input of U.S. industry caused DoD to insist that the program be managed under a government agreement. The SH-60 example was readily applied to FSX. See also Green, 1995, pp. 86–97.
12. Extensive discussions of FSX can be found in Chinworth, 1992, pp. 132–61; Samuels, 1994, pp. 231–44; Green, 1995, pp. 86–124. For the most detailed account of FSX development and U.S.–Japanese interactions available at present, see Mark Lorell, *Troubled Partnership* (Santa Monica, CA: RAND, 1995). Polemical accounts of FSX in Prestowitz, 1989, pp. 1–58; and Jeff Shear, *The Keys to the Kingdom* (New York: Doubleday, 1994) underscore both the fears and the political agendas that fueled the FSX controversy.
13. For example, DSAA officials argued that FSX could not be a co-development program since no U.S. government funds supported the project—a point correct on the letter of regulation, but misleading in any other sense.
14. The rationale for this approach toward Japan was first presented in *Defense Industrial Cooperation with Pacific Rim Nations*, e.g., vii-xi. It has since been evident in the Technology-for-Technology Initiative and current DoD emphasis on industrial partnerships with Japan.
15. Workshare became the driving factor in negotiation of a MOU for co-production of the Multiple Launch Rocket System (MLRS) in 1991, while assessment of opportunities for Japanese technology transfers have become a standard issue in U.S. approaches to all defense MOUs with Japan.
16. JDA Equipment Bureau (*Boeisobikyoku*), "Report of the Advisory Group on Defense Equipment Procurement" (*Boei Sobihin Chotatsu Kondankai Hokoku Sho*) (December 1993) and "Report of the Advisory Group on Defense Industry and Technology" (*Boei Sangyo Gijutsu Kondankai Hokoku Sho*) (March 1994).
17. While time and budget overruns in FSX development are routinely blamed on the United States, the program proved a sobering experience for government and industry officials in Japan who had repeatedly underestimated the difficulty and cost of such an undertaking.

18. The MDAA includes provisions for the cooperative development of equipment and technology, an idea also reflected in a DoD–JDA agreement on R&D cooperation concluded in 1962. However, Japan's subsequent adoption of arms export restrictions discouraged follow-up actions and the issue was all but forgotten.

19. While the S&TF has gradually evolved into a substantial organization supporting numerous projects, its establishment and development occurred largely apart from bilateral interactions in other areas of the security relationship.

20. See Appendix 9. As with the Constitution and Mutual Security Treaty, Japanese positions on defense-related exports are as much a matter subjective bureaucratic interpretation as actual law and regulation. Practice on applying Three Principles policy has become more flexible in recent years but still poses significant problems for collaboration on defense programs.

21. *Defense of Japan 1996*, p. 320.

22. For texts of the Military Technology Transfer Notes and Detailed Arrangements, see U.S. Department of Defense, Office of the Under Secretary for Research and Engineering, *Japanese Military Technology: Procedures for Transfers to the United States*, (February 1986).

23. There has been some confusion on use of the term "flowback." This refers specifically to the transfer of Japanese improvements to U.S.–derived technologies obtained through licenses in defense programs. Flowback provisions in MOUs were first made explicit in the revised F-15 MOU signed in January 1985. On the other hand, the Military Technology Transfer Notes apply to Japanese-developed (that is, non-derived) technologies. Differences over what constitute derived and non-derived technologies continue to be a point of contention in U.S.–Japan programs.

24. Defense Science Board, *Report of the Defense Science Board Task Force on Industry-to-Industry International Armaments Cooperation—Phase II—Japan* (Washington, D.C.: GPO, 1984); and Department of Defense, *Electro-Optics Millimeter/Microwave Technology in Japan* (Washington, D.C.: GPO, 1985).

25. The initial JMTC case concerning the Japanese "Keiko" surface to air missile was never implemented, while subsequent cases concerning shipbuilding technology were arguably not military technology at all. Negotiation of an agreement on SDI cooperation in 1987 proved to be an isolated and largely unfruitful exercise. JDA's narrow view of S&TF activities was matched by counterparts in MITI who, unhappy with the 1983 Notes and stung by the Toshiba technology transfer incident of 1987, adopted a very restrictive approach toward dual-use technology transfers.

26. JDA proposed several areas for cooperative R&D projects in 1988; DoD followed up with additional proposals in 1990. The first of several current projects, joint research on ducted rocket engines, was launched in 1992.

Although small in scale, these activities have established useful precedents for evolution toward more ambitious joint development programs.

27. This concept underwent several changes in title (originally and somewhat erroneously known as "the Perry Initiative") and presentation before becoming known as TfT. However, the basic idea of reciprocity in technology transfers remained unchanged and, magnified by sensationalized reporting through media and industry channels, continues to cast a shadow over armaments cooperation activities.

28. Green, 1995, pp. 136–42. Linkage of TfT and TMD interests was strongly implied during September 1993 discussions between then under secretary of defense John Deutch and senior Japanese officials. The negative publicity that arose from these talks compromised TMD proposals made by Secretary of Defense Aspin in Tokyo the following month and all but undermined the credibility of TfT.

29. This concept is best expressed in a Department of Defense briefing paper "U.S.–Japan Defense Equipment and Technology Cooperation" released by the Office of the Under Secretary for Acquisition and Technology, May 1996.

30 Statements by Japanese officials at recent S&TF meetings have for the first time openly acknowledged an interest in moving beyond research on basic technologies toward systems development projects. JDA and MITI officials have also voiced support for Japanese industry interest in a more flexible application of the Three Principles policy to facilitate cooperative programs with the United States (see the Japan Federation of Economic Organizations *(Keidanren)* paper, "A Call for a Defense Program for a New World Order," May 1995).

31. The F-2 production MOU was signed in July 1996 and completed congressional review in October. Negotiation of this agreement covered more than a year of often contentious posturing but remained largely free of public scrutiny, even by previously outspoken FSX critics.

32. Japan Economic Institute, *JEI Report* No. 39B (October 16, 1998): 8.

33. The "Crew Escape System" MOU was signed in March 1998. U.S. interest in possible third country transfers if improved ejection seat equipment raised Three Principles–related concerns (i.e., third party use of military equipment based partly on Japanese technology) that will be handled through case-by-case consideration of future transfers.

34. As confirmed by minutes of S&TF-related discussions and briefing memos, DoD officials expressed interest in an industry adjunct to the S&TF as early as 1981. Fearing unwelcome public exposure of S&TF activities, JDA continued to resist such ideas through the early 1990s.

35. See National Defense Industrial Association–Japan Federation of Economic Organizations, "Joint Report: U.S.–Japan Industry Forum for Security Cooperation," October 1997.

36. The option of defense procurements from third countries has often been raised both through campaigns by third-country parties and by Japanese officials seeking to gain leverage in dealings with the United States. In fact, Japan has usually turned to third-country acquisitions only when a particular requirement cannot be met by either a U.S. or indigenous source. The continued domination of U.S. defense systems in Japan—even as countries like South Korea have gone out of their way to seek non-U.S. alternatives for defense needs—is testimony to Japan's view of its security environment and relationship with the United States. Nonetheless, as other countries become more sophisticated in their approaches to the Japanese defense market (and more flexible in their positions on technology transfers) the attractiveness of third-country procurements to Japan is bound to grow.
37. An excellent example of what can happen is evident in current JDA consideration of a future radar-guided air-to-air missile for its fighter aircraft, a choice between the U.S. AMRAAM and an indigenously developed counterpart known as AAM-4. Although performance, cost, and interoperability considerations would appear to argue for the selection of AMRAAM (with some provision for licensed production to meet industrial base needs in Japan), a combination of fierce domestic lobbying for AAM-4 and apparent DoD concern over AMRAAM technology has resulted in JDA approval for AAM-4 production.

# 14

# The Technology Factor in U.S.–Japan Security Relations

MICHAEL CHINWORTH

## Introduction

JAPAN'S defense budgets throughout the postwar period have remained relatively small but have risen in relative and absolute terms. The rate of spending increases generally has dropped from year to year, however, culminating in a budget crunch for the Japan Defense Agency (JDA) in recent years. The result of these trends is a defense budget that has been able to support (with the help of budgetary and contracting mechanisms) a sizable defense industrial structure, but which is increasingly hard pressed to initiate major new procurement programs while maintaining existing equipment. From a political standpoint, this industrial base is both criticized and praised. It is criticized for its lack of depth and emphasis on absorption of U.S. technology, but praised for the extent to which modern equipment has been deployed relative to deployments of other American allies.

Defense research, development, and production in Japan have been viewed by observers in the United States with changing perspectives over time. Throughout the postwar period there have been questions concerning Japan's challenge to American competitiveness, and about the intent of government and industry in Japan in pursuing such production. With the emergence of Japan as a global competitor in numerous commercial industries, there have been increasing calls for greater defense technology reciprocity with the United States to bring about technology transfers from Japan to the United States that would be comparable in economic value and significance to those that have taken place under cooperative defense programs. Recognizing the desire to constrain growth in indigenous defense production in Japan by preserving the existing policy framework, policymakers in this country are examining alternatives for bringing about that end.

This chapter reviews briefly technology transfers and the economic and competitive aspects of the security relationship. It also offers a set of alternatives for taking the security relationship to a new level that would be characterized by more mature and reciprocal arrangements in defense production and technology transfers.

## Technological and Competitive Aspects of Defense Programs with Japan

Military-related production in Japan during the Korean conflict (1950–53) provided a significant boost to the Japanese economy. That assistance did not go unnoticed by Japanese industrialists, who urged resumption of defense production in part to stimulate the domestic economy. To a certain degree, some U.S. government officials were sympathetic to this view, although they were cautious to keep it under wraps, motivated more by lingering concerns about Japan's political intentions than by competitive reasons. Long before there was ever discussion of "dual-use" technology, the U.S. military helped revive the domestic Japanese electronics industry through radio licensing and production. Spin-offs from the radio industry helped stimulate development of the commercial television industry many years later.[1] To the extent that economics and competitiveness entered the picture, U.S. officials generally viewed these trends as positive given their concern for the development of Japan's economy in order to avoid its becoming a long-term burden on the United States. Of equal concern was the possibility that prolonged economic difficulties would contribute to the popularity of indigenous communist political movements.

As aid programs were replaced permanently by local production, the economic implications of defense production became more pronounced and attracted greater attention in the United States. Cognizance of the industrial implications of licensing policies was indicated in a statement by Lockheed engineers who at the time were responsible for launching F-104 production in Japan. As one executive noted long before the FSX debate, "We were paid to put them in business, and we gave them everything we had."[2]

Through the 1980s, Japan benefited more than any other U.S. ally did from licensed production (Figure 14–1). The peak of licensing activity was reached in the late 1980s with the Patriot surface-to-air missile co-

**Figure 14–1**

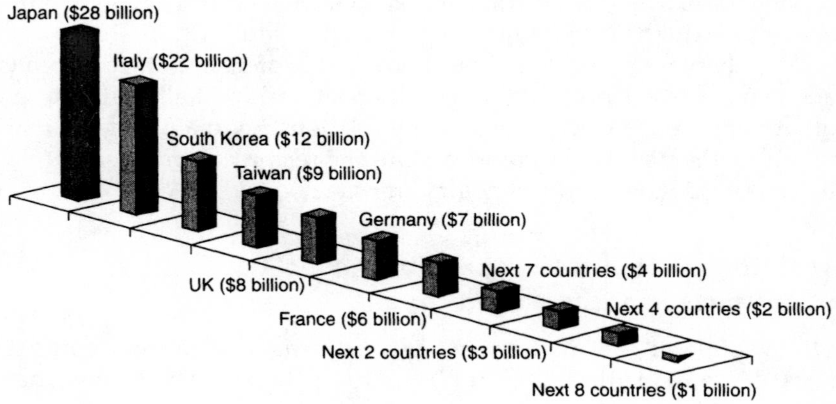


production program, which resulted in the licensing and transfer of virtually every element of hardware and early generations of software in the system. This program continues with various upgrade packages, although production of the Patriot missiles and launchers has stopped. No program attracted more political fire, however, than the subsequent FSX/F-2 co-development program, which utilized the U.S. F-16 fighter aircraft as the basis of a heavily modified Japanese variant that included numerous indigenous technologies developed by government and industry in Japan. The FSX at one point looked like it might become the first major cooperative program in postwar history to be overturned by a vote of Congress.[3]

As noted earlier, various Japanese industry and government officials have sought continuation of defense production for economic reasons. U.S. concerns over bilateral defense programs for their economic ramifications have not gone unnoticed in Japan, but those concerns often are interpreted as evidence of U.S. hostility toward Japan; envy of its technological prowess; or a desire to maintain Japanese dependency on U.S. military systems in general.[4] More balanced perspectives on the relationship of economics and security in bilateral security ties exist, but even these agree with the observation that a relative decline of the U.S. economy, coupled with a rise in Japanese economic strength, have heightened U.S. concerns over the security relationship in general and defense programs in particular.[5]

In both the United States and Japan there have been periods in which government and industry officials noted the economic and competitive implications of defense and security policies. One of the questions often asked by security policy analysts is why government officials did not notice these implications earlier. As indicated, however, by the comments of Lockheed engineers in the F-104 case, U.S. industry and government were well aware of these consequences, although admittedly in varying degrees.

U.S. government and industry officials were not unconcerned about these implications. Given the state of Japan's economy, however, there was little reason to believe that the progression of policies and programs over the decades would emerge as a purely competitive issue. The U.S.–Japan trade balance favored the United States until the 1960s; by the 1970s, the trade balance favored Japan. Yen appreciation, which was both a symbolic and tangible manifestation of Japan's global economic clout, did not come until a decade after that. While the viewpoint may have been shortsighted, few American officials ever believed that Japan would pose a serious competitive challenge to the United States. Even as Japanese products came to dominate markets once held primarily by U.S. brands, few defense or civilian officials truly believed that Japan would be able to crack the most advanced and technologically demanding sectors such as missile and aircraft research, development, and production. Skills such as systems integration, it was believed, were still beyond the capabilities of Japanese government and industry and remained an American stronghold.

Growing belief in the United States of widely dispersed dual-use technological capabilities within the Japanese economy, as well as such developments as its move toward systems integration with the FSX project, challenged the view of Japan as a benign partner and caused a reassessment of Japan's intentions and capabilities. This perception, coupled with more visible and advanced defense programs, increased political attention toward economic considerations of defense relationships. The peak of interest came with the General Accounting Office's report on the F-15.[6]

Consequently, concerns over the competitive implications of bilateral defense programs remain. Expressed crudely, the United States remains uncertain over whether Japan is an economic ally or challenger when it comes to its aims and capabilities in defense programs. The FSX debate represented the high-water mark of political attention to the economic aspects of the security relationship. The articulation, however vague, of a "technology-for-technology" policy *(TfT)* by the Department of Defense was motivated in part by these sentiments.[7] Criticisms, however, continue. A 1995 report by the Defense Task Force of the National Research Council (NRC) represents the most penetrating criticism of the technology relationship, on the basis that defense has been used essentially as an excuse by Japan to draw technology from the United States for the purpose of its own economic development. The NRC report flatly declares that under these circumstances the technology relationship with Japan cannot continue, and that major realignment is necessary.[8]

In contrast to these views is the opinion that technological spin-offs from defense production in advanced nations should not be surprising. Japan's history is replete with examples of incremental improvements made to imported and domestically developed technologies for the past three centuries.[9] Furthermore, since Japan has benefited from more defense technology transfer and licensing programs than any other country in the world, it is almost surprising that the list of spin-offs from defense production is not longer. According to some analyses, European nations have been far more successful at developing domestic aircraft industries and enhancing electronics production and other major industries with less generous transfers than those experienced throughout the postwar period by Japan.[10] Concerns on this matter have subsided somewhat in recent years, for several reasons.

*Few new, large-scale defense programs have begun between the United States and Japan since the FSX/F-2.* Production of the U.S. AWACS system based on a Boeing 737 airframe has begun, but despite the cost, volume is limited and few critical technology issues are involved in the case. The F-2 production Memorandum of Understanding (MOU), at this writing, is seen as beneficial to U.S. industry because it will generate far greater sales than would have been possible had the original F-16 been sold "off the shelf" to Japanese producers.

*U.S. competitiveness is perceived as having rebounded.* While actual relative performance may be debated, there is a perception in the United States that the competitiveness of important industrial sectors such as the automotive and semiconductor industries has improved dramatically compared with world-class producers, including Japanese companies. This may have led industry and government officials in the United States to become somewhat less concerned about the Japanese economic challenge, compared with earlier periods.[11]

*The Japanese bubble economy has burst.* Coupled with the rise of U.S. competitiveness has been a decline in Japanese competitiveness. In the 1990s Japan's economy was characterized by slow or stagnant economic growth, complicated by a precipitous decline in real estate prices; an uncertain stock market (having dropped by more than 50 percent in value following the burst of the bubble); an unsound financial system; and erratic trading of the yen in international markets. These conditions have led many in Japan and the United States to discount the possibility that Japan will seriously challenge the United States economically in the immediate future.

*"New Japans" have emerged in Asia.* Rather than minimizing concern over Japan, political leaders in the United States may have placed greater emphasis on the competitive challenges posed by such nations as the People's Republic of China, thus demoting the relative importance of Japan in the U.S. economy. In addition, European economic integration may have attracted increased attention due to the implications raised by the dimensions of a unified market.[12]

*The U.S. government now addresses the competitive implications of defense programs with Japan.* One of the most notable bureaucratic shifts within the U.S. government resulting from the FSX fallout has been the inclusion of the Department of Commerce in reviews of MOUs negotiated by the two governments. To date, the Commerce Department has not exercised its new authority to reject an MOU on this basis. Supporters of the process argue that the very inclusion of Commerce assures negotiation of MOUs that are more favorable to U.S. economic interests.

*The Department of Defense (DoD) accepts the unity of economics and security policies.* The TfT notion vaguely articulated early in the Clinton administration managed to establish the fact that business as usual would not continue within DoD. Acquisition reform within DoD encourages this thinking as well, to the extent that it encourages policymakers in the defense arena to follow the examples established within commercial sectors regarding international teaming and technical assistance.

Other possibilities are on the horizon that could reverse this situation. While still in its formative stages, TMD would represent a major joint development and production effort if the two countries reach an agreement on jointly deploying a system in Japan. In the near term, upgrades of existing systems could always raise economic considerations. In addition, DoD seeks expanded cooperative relations in the area of research and development, as indicated in the September 1996 meeting of the Systems and Technology Forum (S&TF). Previous research and development programs have been the source of minor controversies, suggesting that future programs also could come under political scrutiny. Political dissatisfaction with the broader economic relationship, of course, can also influence security programs at any time. This is perhaps the most uncertain and unpredictable element in the equation. Economic factors will be connected with bilateral defense for the foreseeable future.

In examining the coupling of defense and economic elements in the bilateral relationship, it is important to keep the defense elements in perspective relative to total economic activity between the two countries. While bilateral defense programs generally involve advanced technologies and high-profile systems, their total economic value nevertheless represents only a fraction of total economic activity between the United States and Japan. The entire FSX/F-2 program, from research to development and production, is likely to span over fifteen years with a total program cost of $12 to $16 billion, a figure dependent on exchange rates and other factors.[13] The trade in automobiles and automotive parts between the United States and Japan in a single year amounts to more than $44.2 billion, and total merchandise trade between the two countries currently exceeds $169 billion annually.[14] Thus, while not a trivial element of the economic relationship with Japan, its importance should not be exaggerated compared to the totality of economic ties between the two countries. American competitiveness vis-à-vis Japan extends far beyond the military relationship.

## The Next Phase

As long as there is a security relationship, however, economic considerations will be involved. Thinking about this matter should include how the United States can best preserve its interests while assuring mutually beneficial ties.

Economic factors enter into the security relationship largely due to the existence of cooperative technology development and defense equipment production programs. The challenge for current and future policymakers is how to structure these programs and create new alternatives in a manner that will preserve U.S. economic interests and expand opportunities for the U.S. economy and businesses as well. It should be noted also that there are numerous defenders of the status quo, since programs with Japan have been highly profitable for U.S. industry and have resulted in satisfying Defense Department's aim of seeing Japan deploy more advanced and capable systems for its defense. In addition, new approaches must conform to the present Japanese security framework, unless policymakers are willing to enter into discussions with Japan concerning such controversial subjects as expanded arms exports. Moreover, the budgetary climate in both countries is unlikely to change for the foreseeable future, so DoD must identify means of achieving these aims within the bounds of its current and projected budgets.

There are several options for bringing greater economic benefits to the United States while preserving the qualities of bilateral defense programs that both countries have found beneficial throughout the postwar period.[15] Many of these options would require only marginal changes in policies and budgets; most already have well-established precedents. What they do require is creative thinking and implementation on the part of government and industry in both countries, qualities central to the effective management of a security relationship during a period of transition.

The first set of options is based on present practices. Options reflect a continuation of existing programs, including *co-production, basic research and development,* and *limited development.*

The second set includes three approaches that would require no changes in, or expansion of, existing policies, but rather would involve attitudinal changes that must be addressed if the options are to be expanded broadly enough to bring new economic benefits to the United States. They include *contract research and development, feasibility studies,* and *joint development (non-munition).*

Finally, other options are available if policymakers in both countries can accept new interpretations of old policies. They include *expanded component purchases/transfers* and *joint development/production (defense systems).*

Each alternative has several advantages and potential drawbacks (see Table 14–1). All offer the potential for technology access/flowback or industry-to-industry partnering, which is often a precursor to more extensive cooperation. These merits and challenges are worth examining briefly.

## CO-PRODUCTION

It is important to note that of all the forms of defense programs that have been utilized between the United States and Japan throughout the postwar period, only one—security assistance—is no longer in effect. All other programmatic approaches remain in effect and can serve as the starting point for future relations as well. Of these, co-production remains an avenue popular to both government and industry in Japan and the United States. It is well understood, having been utilized for decades and for various systems. It is relatively straightforward for the companies involved, and the mechanisms used to implement the programs are familiar.

**Table 14-1 Future Options for Cooperative U.S.-Japan Defense Technology Programs**

| Option | Precedents ITY/Author | Advantages | Issues |
|---|---|---|---|
| Co-production | Well established; several programs ongoing (F-15; others) | Well understood; familiar mechanisms; future systems may be appropriate candidates for co-production | "Reverse co-production" from Japan would require re-examination of arms policies; unclear how JMTC procedures would be involved; no administrative authority on JDA side |
| Basic research and development | MDAA; 1983 Technology Transfer Notes; 1985 Detailed Arrangements; S&TF-JWG projects | Low profile; competitive implications minimized | Current experience indicates slow implementation time |
| Limited development | FSX provides some precedent | Direct flowback potential; attractive option for common upgrades | Heavy baggage from FSX/F-2 experience; implementing technology transfers from Japan raise derived/non-derived, intellectual property, other issues |
| Contract research and development | TRP; Nunn amendment programs | Flexibility | Political sensitivity: U.S. reticence to fund Japanese companies; Japanese corporate nervousness about participating in arms development programs |
| Feasibility studies | WESTPAC study for SDI | Low cost; no commitment; builds industry teams | WESTPAC less than optimal precedent in terms of results |
| Joint development (non-munition) | Weapons R&D, development programs | Non-lethal but still serving defense needs | Commercial interests/considerations likely to be very strong |
| Expanded component purchases/transfers | Japanese content in U.S. systems; special products/services (Kyocera packaging) | Technology access in form of products; presumed cost savings; reflects commercial practices | Direct clash with arms export policies in Japan; no obvious technology flowback benefits for U.S. |
| Joint development, production (defense systems) | FSX; JWG projects | Direct technology flowbacks through "hands-on" activities | Extensive administrative issues; Japanese arms export policies come into play |

Critics of co-production programs, of course, remain concerned with the potentially marginal, slow technology flowbacks to the United States that, if beneficial at all, will aid only a limited number of U.S. defense contractors. Changes instituted in co-production programs have enabled modest technology flowback to the United States.[16] However, these changes have not been sufficient to provide the United States with technology transfers from Japan comparable to those that have taken place in the opposite direction through past and current programs.

There is another alternative in the realm of co-production that should be explored. That is U.S. production of a Japanese system under arrangements comparable to those carried out between the two countries for the production of U.S. systems in Japan. Through "reverse co-production," interested U.S. firms could produce promising Japanese systems such as its air-to-air or anti-ship missiles (which were themselves developed as import substitutes for U.S. systems), complete with technology transfers and licensing rights. This approach could also be applied to upgrades for common systems.

There are several problems with this approach. Japan's arms export policies clearly would need reexamination. Whether a blanket exception or a case-by-case evaluation of proposed programs, some policy precedent would be necessary for the United States to produce a Japanese system.[17] The procedures of the Joint Military Technology Commission (JMTC), established to facilitate implementation of the 1983 technology transfer notes between the United States and Japan, have been criticized as impediments to technology transfers to the United States. It would likely be a factor in this scenario, which would in turn raise the question of whether the JMTC has outlived its usefulness.

An additional drawback might be that U.S. interest in producing a Japanese system would in fact encourage more extensive and independent research, development, and production of domestic systems. It is also unclear whether Japanese firms would willingly license production or co-production of their systems by U.S. firms. Finally, reflective of Japan's arms export policies, no office exists within JDA to implement or oversee such a concept. Internal discussions required for determining an appropriate office for such a program would be time-consuming.

Nevertheless, advantages to reverse co-production do exist. Technology transfers gained through the local production of a Japanese system could be significant, and the initiative for such a program would not necessarily depend on U.S. industry interest. American co-production of Japanese systems would offer Japanese firms benefits such as additional income through license fees, added production and revenues through initial sales of knock-down units, and follow-on potential.

## BASIC RESEARCH AND DEVELOPMENT

Joint basic research and development programs already implemented have resulted in some technological benefits to the United States. To assure continued benefits, future programs and projects should retain a focus on 6.1–6.2 categories.[18] Basic R&D programs will help support existing mechanisms such as the Joint Working Groups (JWG) established under the S&TF framework.

Basic research activities through JWGs have allowed DoD and JDA research organizations to interact in a relatively noncontroversial forum that is fully covered by U.S.–Japan agreements on technology cooperation (see Appendix 8). Results to date have not been dramatic, but experience suggests that they have been valuable learning experiences that will facilitate further cooperative efforts.

There are, however, drawbacks. For example, the time required from an initial proposal to conclusion of a MOU and the implementation of a project is as long as five years, ultimately raising questions about projects' timeliness and relevance because technological progress does not come to a convenient halt while governments attempt to establish and implement time-consuming bureaucratic procedures.

These programs are likely to be most appropriate when issues such as marginal productivity and budgetary constraints come into play. Specific incentives for companies, however, remain unclear given their basic orientation, lack of specifics prior to program launch, and time-consuming implementation. Technology transfer, however, takes place largely through tangible activities, and this would remain one means of encouraging and implementing such activities in a manner that would enable U.S. technical specialists to secure tangible gains from Japanese capabilities.[19]

## LIMITED DEVELOPMENT

The popularity of bilateral co-development programs has not benefited from the FSX/F-2 experience, which is viewed as a highly politicized and costly example of pursuing too much, too soon, and under false assumptions. However, it is likely that U.S. participation through technology inputs will be factors in future Japanese defense programs, both in new development programs and upgrades to current systems. Limited co-development programs offer the potential for mutual benefits similar to those of co-production, with greater emphasis on use of Japanese technology. They would allow significant cooperation in projects where neither straight adoption of existing U.S. systems nor bilaterally funded joint R&D activities are feasible. Limited co-development is also an approach to upgrades of current systems in common use.

The disadvantages of co-production, including pressure for off-the-shelf purchase of U.S. systems and criticisms of technology transfers to Japan, have an even greater impact on limited co-development programs. More concrete problems focus on the difficulties of implementing technology transfers from Japan. Such programs also raise problems of implementing technology transfers, all of which must be resolved in order for the projects envisioned in the following scenarios to ever develop.[20]

## CONTRACT RESEARCH AND DEVELOPMENT (R&D)

Contract R&D offers immense flexibility and the potential for access to specific technologies or capabilities that would have value beyond the defense sector. DoD could exercise this avenue through government-to-government, company-to-company, or government-to-industry avenues. Programs could actively solicit specific companies for specific needs, or passively utilize mechanisms like the Broad Agency Announcements (BAAs) or more targeted requests for proposals (RFPs).[21]

Numerous precedents exist for this method of gaining defense, commercial, and dual-use technology inputs from other countries, including Japan. In this case there is the example of the U.S. government assigning research contracts to Japanese firms for the development of Josephson junctions for the Strategic Defense Initiative (SDI).[22] Nunn Amendment programs, the short-lived Technology Reinvestment Project (TRP) of the Advanced Research Projects Agency (ARPA; now renamed the Defense Advanced Research Projects Agency—DARPA), and sample purchases of Japanese artificial diamonds through the University of North Carolina all underscore the fact that this already is a well-established practice that, if applied more aggressively and broadly, could reap considerable benefits for the U.S. economy and individual firms.[23] Research subsidies and direct purchases through the Defense Production Act's Title III program are other alternatives under this concept.

These options are not without some political risk. Congress would likely challenge the general notion of paying foreign firms, especially Japanese ones, for developing advanced technologies for the Defense Department. Concerns about heightened American vulnerability could be mitigated by teaming arrangements, as well as by the low cost of this approach. Its flexibility, its distinct possibilities for targeted flowback, and the potential for relatively detached administration by government all make this a highly attractive alternative for utilizing U.S–Japan competitiveness for enhancing the bilateral relationship.[24]

## FEASIBILITY STUDIES

Feasibility studies alone will not address technology transfer or economic competitiveness issues. Nevertheless, they can be used to indicate Defense Department interest in specific areas and can help develop bilateral industrial teams affecting technology transfers to this country, thus strengthening U.S. competitiveness. Joint or unilateral funding are both options, allowing the Defense Department more opportunity to entice Japa-nese companies into direct participation in U.S. programs with the aim of transferring Japanese capabilities to this country. Feasibility studies are aimed strictly at concept definition and limited basic research. They can lead to projects because they are conducive to industry team-building, are representative of government commitment to specific courses of action, and are very low profile—thus more likely to attract Japanese firms fearful of the implications of their participation in Japan's arms policies. Projects could be developed within the existing policy framework in both the United States and Japan. While not necessarily the most widely praised final product, the Western Pacific (WESTPAC) study in support of SDI provides sufficient precedent for this approach.[25]

## JOINT DEVELOPMENT OF NON-MUNITION ITEMS

Using the well-established ties of the security relationship, the United States may be able to identify opportunities for joint development of non-munition items that would benefit commercial enterprises and competitiveness in the United States. Environmental protection and restoration technologies, for example, have been identified as areas in which both Japanese and U.S. firms have considerable commercial interest and identifiable Defense Department needs.[26] The nonmilitary, nonlethal focus of this strategy, plus its obvious commercial and social benefits, could help contribute positive policy precedents without encountering problems associated with the Three Principles, by helping firms remain engaged in "defense business," even if not directly related to defense systems (see Appendix 7). The JWG approach could easily be utilized for such projects, as in the case of ceramic engine technologies, further strengthening the value of this particular mechanism for the United States. Almost by definition, technologies pursued under this approach would be dual-use without the need to be concerned about JMTC procedures. Finally, it offers potential for building allies within the government of Japan for DoD and JDA cooperative programs.[27]

## EXPANDED COMPONENT PURCHASES/TRANSFERS

Commercial firms routinely decide whether to develop a component internally or purchase it externally, often from a competitor, at a competitive price and without the investment required to develop it internally. As a result of its procurement reform efforts, DoD increasingly will be faced with similar decisions, and Japan is a country to be considered in this context. The rationale of this decision is the same as that for the commercial firm: technology transfer occurs in many forms, including the purchase of a specific product. If access to technology is an important policy priority for the United States, it must address the possibilities of technology access in the form of component purchases.

Component purchases from Japan already are an established precedent, despite arms export restrictions. Many Japanese commercial products such as vehicles, communications systems, and electronic components have been applied to military use, while U.S. weapons systems have significant Japanese content.[28] Most items with significant sales quantities are either unique or are commodity items, but the precedent has been set.

These practices can be expanded in the current environment. Japanese firms are looking for export sales, and U.S. interests are likely to be restricted to materials and components rather than systems or major subsystems. Thus, arms export issues are distant factors, although critics of the notion would argue that expanded precedents would open the floodgates to widespread Japanese military exports. Some components clearly could be military rather than commercial, although most sales that take place are commercial. To minimize the political ramifications of this step in the United States, purchases could be coupled with informal encouragement from the Defense Department to produce locally or to license the underlying technology to a U.S. partner.

The potential drawbacks of such practices cannot be belittled. The leverage of the U.S. government in these instances is dubious. There are significant disincentives for Japanese firms to sell to the United States or other countries for military purposes, given the country's arms export policies. Still, unresolved dependency issues raised by U.S. reliance on foreign suppliers would not be minimized by expanding the practice of purchasing directly from Japanese suppliers. Finally, expanded component purchases pose challenges to the aforementioned Three Principles.

Despite the drawbacks, however, for a relationship in which competitive concerns are ever present and where justification for the fundamental security relationship itself needs reevaluation, the two countries may have reached a point in which direct component sales are not only desirable, but essential to assure mutual benefits in the relationship.

### JOINT DEVELOPMENT/PRODUCTION OF DEFENSE SYSTEMS

A final option would be a move by both countries toward full and joint development and production of military systems. Critics of technology transfers to Japan have been concerned with the one-way flow of technology from the United States to Japan, noting further the lack of maturity in the relationship characterized by Japan's reluctance to provide technology in return. Both concerns are addressed by the concept of true joint development and production of advanced weapons systems.

Full co-development would advance the bilateral defense industrial technology relationship well beyond the FSX experience and the basic research of current JWGs under the S&TF. It would involve consideration of joint requirement definitions, joint funding, common logistics and contingency planning, and unified production. In short, it would represent a move toward an equitable security relationship between the United States and Japan, complete with reciprocal technology transfers and the economic benefits resulting from defense production.

In the short term, this notion could apply to upgrades such as those anticipated for F-15 aircraft deployed in both countries. Longer-term options would require establishment of mechanisms to assure common requirements definition and agreement on common interests well before entering into discussions of common systems. An extensive time requirement for the definition of common requirements is a complicated process with potential for bureaucratic resistance since it assumes identity of interests between the United States and Japan. It would not be surprising if moving from requirements definitions, even if they could be agreed upon, to implementation of a program would require as much as ten to fifteen years, given the dimensions of the policy implications involved.

## Obstacles to Implementation

One of the desirable features of all the proposals above is that they can utilize relatively passive mechanisms to facilitate technology transfers. Many of the specific decisions and incentives in each proposal are left in the hands of industry, assuring that they will be made on the basis of economic interest rather than on the basis of politics. In those instances in which technology cooperation makes business sense, companies will presumably make the effort to complete arrangements resulting in technology transfer to the United States. Some degree of oversight from DoD and the Department of Commerce would, however, be desirable to reinforce this situation. Relegating as many of these issues to the private sector as possible and out of negotiating circles—including flowback, intellectual property rights, derived/nonderived technologies, and third country transfers—is in the interests of the United States if it truly seeks expeditious and reciprocal benefits in cooperative programs.

Many of these plans have potential for controversy. They imply a degree of dependency with which the United States has yet to come to terms. The involvement of Japanese firms in the United States defense technology/industrial base is a particularly controversial issue for both countries. It is possible that mergers or acquisitions would be desirable, necessitated, or encouraged by the changes outlined above, which is another move fraught with political risk. In many cases, the United States would find itself in the position of buyer rather than seller, a mode to which the country is unaccustomed after decades of sales and licenses to Japan. Finally, it is difficult to escape the fact that stimulating flowback to the United States involves some element of sacrifice by the United States in one or another of the areas above.

Despite the seemingly infinite number of policy implications and mechanisms that would come under reexamination with these proposals, it is worth noting that two factors stand out above all others for these and other alternatives under consideration with the goal of equalizing economic benefits in the security relationship. On the Japanese side, almost every change in current practices ultimately raises concerns about Japan's arms export policies. At the very least, a more flexible interpretation of Japan's arms export principles is needed to realize any of the specific programmatic approaches outlined here.

In the case of the United States, attitudes more than legal or policy restrictions impede the prospects for success in many of the proposals outlined above. Policy constraints, particularly "Buy America" provisions, cannot be underestimated, but the more fundamental problems involve long-standing concerns over foreign dependency, the development of potential Japanese competitors, and role reversal involving Japan as seller and the United States as buyer. It is difficult to imagine any of these proposals in which technology transfers are stimulated without requiring a measure of compromise over these issues. The author's subjective assessment of these attitudes and obstacles is portrayed in Figure 14–2.

**Figure 14–2**

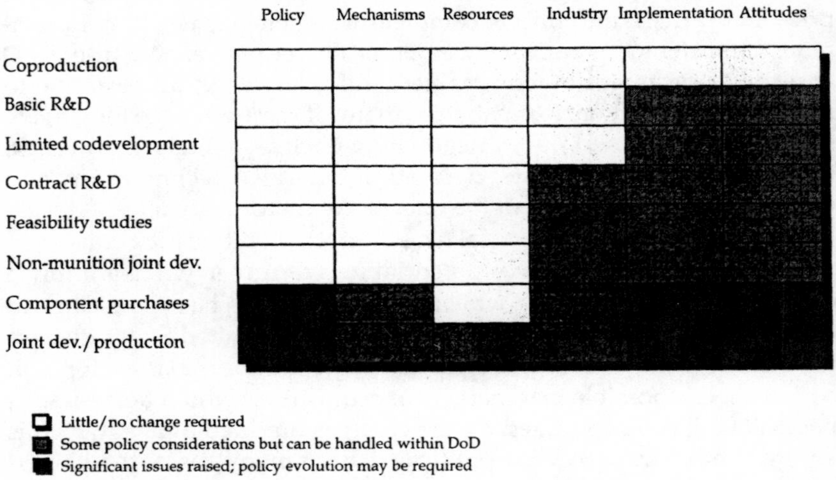

Policy Mechanisms Resources Industry Implementation Attitudes

Coproduction

Basic R&D

Limited codevelopment

Contract R&D

Feasibility studies

Non-munition joint dev.

Component purchases

Joint dev./production

Little/no change required

Some policy considerations but can be handled within DoD

Significant issues raised; policy evolution may be required

Source: Michael W. Chinworth and Gregg A. Rubinstein, "U.S.-Japan Technology Cooperation: Policies and Future Scenarios," October 1, 1995, Final Presentation to OUSD(A&T)/IP, p. VI-7.

Shedding a part of the Cold War era policy structure would not damage the cause of instilling confidence by industry and implementing more extensive, reciprocal technology relations. A candidate in this regard is the Joint Military Technology Commission (JMTC). The JMTC's function is to determine whether technologies under consideration for transfer from Japan to the United States are military, commercial, or dual-use, and thereby decide the appropriate channel of the Japanese government and related mechanism through which the transfer should be implemented in the process.

JMTC has been criticized as a bottleneck in the cause of promoting technology transfers from Japan to the United States. Its defenders argue that its intent and processes are not well understood and have not been exercised aggressively. Regardless of which viewpoint more accurately represents reality, it has no place in the present environment, and is unlikely to serve a constructive role in the future. U.S. companies are skeptical about the process, and interest rests primarily in technologies having multiple applications. When the U.S. government sought a means of encouraging technology transfers from Japan by establishing a track record of precedents, JMTC was viewed as a suitable means for achieving those goals. Today it is an anachronism that should take its place with other aspects of defense programs that have been set aside in the face of changing international conditions and the desire for a more mature relationship.

## Conclusion

There is no doubt that Japan has benefited economically and technologically from its security relationship with the United States. One can argue that the time for new approaches to the relationship has come, and that the United States must be able to point to comparable economic and technological benefits in order to sustain political support for the bilateral Security Treaty with Japan. However, the United States is not simply entitled to such benefits by virtue of past actions. It is in the interest of both countries to assure that both parties benefit mutually from the Security Treaty. Increased economic and technological benefits for the United States are one aspect of those interests.[29]

While it may be difficult for Washington policymakers to accept the notion, the United States must be ready and willing to provide incentives or other measures to the Japanese government and industry in order to achieve its goals of mutually acceptable technological and economic benefits under the auspices of the Security Treaty. The United States must identify what it is willing to sacrifice in order to receive these benefits.

This may be the most difficult part for the United States to accept as the bilateral relationship moves into a new phase. Japanese industry and government paid for the technology transfers under programs that have been the source of concern in the United States. If the competitive aspects of the relationship are to be channeled for productive purposes, the United States must also be ready to make a similar sacrifice, knowing that global sensitivity to international competitiveness is likely to raise the price for such access. The United States is not entitled to Japanese technology by virtue of having sold its own technology in previous decades. But the costs of such access can be minimized through some of the low-profile program options mentioned above, and their aggressive pursuit will help counter the concerns that the relationship is one-sided in economic terms and therefore no longer worth preserving.

The Japanese government and industry must also examine what they are willing to sacrifice in moving toward a new phase in the security relationship in order to assure preservation of the benefits of the treaty. In this case, "sacrifice" suggests moving from the posture of helplessness with regard to technology transfer and cooperation with the United States, currently embraced by both industry and government, to a more pragmatic and businesslike posture that is appropriate for a mature relationship between allies.

As new alternatives are considered, it would be wise for policymakers to reexamine many of the assumptions that have governed perceptions underlying the security relationship. TfT, for example, assumed American and Japanese agreement on the mutual benefits of technology transfers. However, elements in both countries believe that such benefits are outweighed by consequent net technology and competitiveness gains by the other country. The assumption that Japan possesses abundant commercial technology with direct application to U.S. military equipment needs must also be examined closely. While it may be true, attempts to support such an assumption systematically have fallen short. DoD has identified technologies of general interest, but it has not been able to match these with specific DoD program applications.

In examining new alternatives, it is assumed that the United States maintains considerable leverage due to the existence of the bilateral Security Treaty. Leverage is indeed critical, but such leverage is constrained in most proposals outlined above. Insistence on technology transfers alone will not be sufficient to produce results, as experience to date has demonstrated. Defining incentives, on the other hand, is difficult given the divergent interests of the two countries. Identifying self-enforcing mechanisms that do not require extensive attention by U.S. government officials is equally difficult. One of the greatest challenges in this regard is to implement practices and procedures that are assured of industry support in both countries and that will produce automatic results. It is doubtful, however, that increased technology transfers from Japan to the United States will take place without extensive, active participation by government and industry in the United States. Simply establishing mechanisms or policy principles and then expecting technology to flow naturally is unrealistic given the history of the relationship in the postwar period.

Technology transfer takes place through "hands-on" activities, including research, development, and, most important, production. Given the history of the bilateral relationship, it can be assumed that high-profile programs are less likely to succeed than low-profile initiatives; the latter tend to be less visible and therefore less politically sensitive. Japanese companies in particular are likely to shy away from highly publicized initiatives involving military technology transfers. A lower profile also minimizes the likelihood that Japanese corporate participation will require new policy declarations or positions. Thus, the challenge facing policymakers will be to institute new mechanisms and practices quietly over time, but in a fashion that assures equitable political, security, technological, and economic benefits.

## Notes

1. Masanori Moritani, *Gijutsu Kaihatsu no Showashi* (Asahi Shimbunsha, 1986), pp. 9–55; Society of Japanese Aerospace Companies, *Aerospace Industry in Japan, 1987–88* (Tokyo, 1989), pp. 3–13; Daniel L. Spencer, "Military Transfer: International Techno-Economic Transfers Via Military By-Products and Initiatives Based on Cases from Japan and Other Pacific Countries," Defense Technical Information Center, Defense Logistics Agency, AD6606537, March 1967, 32–34, 52–56.
2. G.R. Hall and R.E. Johnson, "Transfers of United States Aerospace Technology to Japan," in Raymond Vernon, ed., *The Technological Factor in International Trade* (New York: National Bureau of Economic Research, 1970), p. 317.
3. Michael W. Chinworth, *Inside Japan's Defense: Technology, Economics & Strategy* (New York: Brassey's, 1992), p. 153. A thorough case study of the FSX can be found in Mark Lorell, *Troubled Partnership: A History of U.S.–Japan Collaboration of the FS-X Fighter* (Santa Monica, CA: RAND, 1995).
4. Examples of the more vitriolic analyses sharing these perceptions include Yasushi Kibino, *Nichibei Haitekku Massatsu: SDI to Nihon no Mirai (U.S.–Japan High-Tech Frictions: SDI and Japan's Future)* (Tokyo: Gijutsu to Ningen Shuppansha, 1987); Shinji Otsuki and Masaru Honda, *Nichibei FSX Senso* (*U.S.–Japan FSX War*) (Tokyo: Ronsosha, 1991); and Ryuichi Teshima, *Nippon FSX o Ute (Shoot Down the Japanese FSX)* (Tokyo: Shinchosha, 1991).
5. See, for example, Yuzo Murayama, *Amerika no Keizai Anzen Hosho Senryaku (America's Economic Security Strategy)* (Tokyo: PHP Kenkyusho, 1996).
6. The F-15 was the most advanced aircraft the U.S. had to offer at the time; Japan remains the only country in the world to which the aircraft was licensed. See U.S. General Accounting Office, "U.S. Military Coproduction Programs Assist Japan in Developing its Civil Aircraft Industry," GAO/ID-82-23, March 18, 1982. The GAO report represented the first official government assertion in public that Japan was utilizing U.S. defense technology for promoting its commercial aircraft industry. The advanced technology embodied in the F-15, along with early Japanese interest in licensing arrangements (official interest in licensed production was made clear before the aircraft entered into production in the United States), raised the profile of this program relative to earlier, less controversial programs such as the F-4. For details of the F-15 production program with Japan, see Michael W. Chinworth, *Inside Japan's Defense: Technology, Economics, and Strategy* (New York: Brassey's, 1992). See esp. chap. 4, "Past and Prologue: The F-15." pp. 96–131.
7. Kenneth Flamm laid down the notion of "TfT"—"technology for technology"—when he was assistant secretary of defense for international affairs

in the Department of Defense. The basic notion was that the United States would expect greater technology transfers from Japan as part of a continued defense technology relationship with Japan. The policy did not necessarily imply a strict quid pro quo for each defense technology transfer from the United States to Japan, but it indicated U.S. government expectations that Japanese government and industry would "bring something to the table" in future cooperative programs that, over time, would bring greater balance in mutually beneficial technology transfers between the two countries. This posture was underscored by Secretary of Defense William Cohen shortly after taking office. See Memorandum from the secretary, "DoD International Armaments Cooperation Policy," March 22, 1997.

8. National Research Council, *Maximizing U.S. Interests in Science and Technology Relations with Japan: Report of the Defense Task Force* (Washington, D.C.: National Academy Press, 1995), pp. 1–7.

9. For an insightful overview of technological development in Japan from a historical perspective, see Tessa Morris-Suzuki, *The Technological Transformation of Japan: From the Seventeenth to the Twenty-First Century* (Cambridge: Cambridge University Press, 1994).

10. For details, see U.S. Congress, Office of Technology Assessment, *Arming Our Allies: Cooperation and Competition in Defense Technology*, OTA-ISC-449 (Washington, D.C.: GPO, May 1990); and U.S. Congress, Office of Technology Assessment, *Global Arms Trade: Commerce in Advanced Military Technology and Weapons*, OTA-ISC-460 (Washington, D.C.: GPO, June 1991).

11. Measures of U.S–Japan trade vary depending on the specific method of calculation. Using figures of the Japan Economic Institute, one of the more reliable and consistent sources of data in this area, shows a continued increase in the bilateral trade balance in Japan's favor over the 1990–94 period, although with somewhat slower rates of increase. The United States, on the other hand, experienced an increase in global exports as well as to Japan, due heavily to dollar depreciation and sharp yen appreciation.

12. The collective GDP of EU members at the beginning of 1995 was $6.7 trillion, with a per capita GDP of $18,000. *Encyclopedia Britannica 1997* (Chicago: Encyclopedia Britannica), pp. 754–55. See also the EU home page at http://www.echo.lu/.

13. This is admittedly a "back of the envelope" estimate, but a fair one given the program costs to date and future costs based on past histories of defense aircraft production programs in Japan. Research and development funding for the FSX program totaled approximately $3.5 billion, based on an average annual exchange rate of U.S. $1.00 = Y130.9 billion, approximately Y11.9 billion—almost $100 million—per aircraft at the same exchange rate. See Japan Defense Agency, *Defense of Japan 1996* (Tokyo: Japan Times), p. 295. The purchase of forty-seven F-2s has been authorized under the five-year procurement program from Japan FY1996–2000 (*Defense of Japan 1996*, p. 292), and supporters are calling for as many as 200 aircraft to be

produced for the life of the program, although a lower number is more realistic. Exchange rates, learning curve efficiency gains, and other factors will affect dollar calculations, but assuming a total production run of 80 to 120 aircraft at current production rates, the program would require $12 to $16 billion over a period of fifteen years from initial research through production of the last aircraft. This would not include enhancements, service life extension programs, or other costs that may come once the aircraft are deployed. See also U.S. GAO, "U.S.–Japan Fighter Aircraft: Agreement on F-2 Production," Letter Report GAO/NSIAD-97-761, February 2, 1997.

14. Japan Economic Institute, "Statistical Profile: International Transactions of Japan and the United States in 1995," *JEI Report* 34A, September 1996, pp. 6, 7, 9–14.

15. The options discussed here were drawn from Michael W. Chinworth and Gregg A. Rubinstein, "U.S.–Japan Technology Cooperation: Policies and Future Scenarios," January 15, 1996, Final Presentation to OSD(A&T)/IP. A Japanese language summary of the presentation was published by the Keidanren Defense Production Committee in Keizai Dantai Rengokai, *Boei Seisan Iinkai Tokuho* no. 254, November 11, 1996, pp. 59–133.

16. Technology flowback clauses are standard in all recent Memoranda of Understanding (MOUs), and JMTC procedures have been used for Japanese developed items adopted in co-produced U.S. systems (computers in Japanese P-3Cs). In addition, interactions between U.S. and Japanese companies offer numerous opportunities for informal and unofficial exchanges that constitute effective technology transfer (in the course of past and current programs, Japanese firms have offered literally thousands of suggested improvements, often involving production technologies and processes, for U.S. programs).

17. The upgrade alternative might be able to sidestep this issue, however.

18. The Defense Department characterizes its research and development programs in five basic stages, with each corresponding to the line item designation in budgets. The categories are as follows: 6.1: Basic research (research into basic principles); 6.2: Exploratory development (conduct of research and development to demonstrate a proof of concept); 6.3: Advanced development (development to the point of prototype production); 6.4: Engineering development (improvement of prototypes and limited production of items for field use); and 6.5: Program management (full scale production and deployment of an item/system).

19. In postwar practice, Japanese companies have been expected to provide half the cost of domestic research and development programs that have been recovered partially through production contracts, in contrast to practices in the United States that will provide full reimbursement of research and development costs, regardless of whether a system moves into full-scale

production. Thus, Japanese companies have little interest in entering into basic research if they do not have reasonable assurance that the program ultimately will move into production. See Chinworth, 1992. See esp. chap. 2, "Research, Development, Production, and Procurement," pp. 30–66.

20. Co-production programs have been criticized as being inefficient in cost terms compared with direct purchases with the United States. The same criticisms have been applied to the FSX-F-2 program, a co-development effort with generous licensing from the United States. The cost of the F-2 is at least twice that of the current model of the F-16, the aircraft upon which the Japanese plane is based. Criticisms of technology transfers to Japan on the basis of their commercial/competitiveness implications were noted earlier in the form of the National Research Council report assessing U.S.–Japan technology relations. These considerations are compounded further when considering the precedents and policies that might be required in order to promote defense related technology transfers to the United States. Japanese companies are likely to be no less concerned about cost recovery and competitiveness when considering technology transfers to potential competitors in the United States. Japanese firms are likely to insist on similar derived/nonderived rights as those in place for the FSX/F-2 (that is, absolute right to free party and the opportunity to license anything in the program developed by the other side). Third country transfers remain a sticking point in bilateral programs; to minimize opportunities for inadvertent transfers of U.S. technology to hostile countries as well as to minimize potential damage to U.S. competitiveness, the United States government has not allowed transfer of any defense technology from the United States to Japan to third parties by Japanese firms or the government, except in certain cases with prior approval. Japanese firms no doubt would seek similar restrictions for the same reasons in limited development programs, complicating the task of increasing transfers to the United States from Japan.

21. Broad Agency Announcements (BAAs) allow a government organization to solicit research, development and/or production concepts or ideas from the private sector with no commitment to pursue individual contracts with any organization submitting such ideas. Unlike formal competitions, BAAs ask contractors to submit white papers outlining the broad notion for addressing a particular problem. The agency sponsoring the BAA can then select those ideas that appear to have technical merit and then request more comprehensive and detailed proposals from the contractors. The initial step in the BAA process allows companies and government agencies to exchange ideas with far less cost involved than would be possible through a full-fledged procurement competition. Requests for Proposals (RFPs) are formal procurement solicitations requiring detailed information on cost—including all hardware, software, and personnel costs, management approach and project implementation. Winners are legally bound to cost figures, where any costs

indicated in a BAA submission are considered to be good faith, "order of magnitude" estimates. From a submitting company's standpoint, RFPs require far more time for preparation, therefore representing higher costs and risk, than do the relatively low-cost, low-effort submissions for the initial phase of the BAA process.

22. The Strategic Defense Initiative (SDI)—known commonly by its less flattering moniker "Star Wars"—was a research program during the Reagan administration that consolidated several preexisting research initiatives under a single umbrella organization to further the cause of land- and space-based defenses against long-range missiles of other countries, primarily the former Soviet Union. Japanese firms were viewed as having a possible lead in the area of Josephson junctions—high-speed semiconductor switching technology—due to materials development and manufacturing strengths.

23. "Nunn amendment" programs are research programs utilizing funding earmarked for international cooperative efforts. The program is named after former senator Sam Nunn, one-time chairman of the Senate Armed Service Committee. The Technology Reinvestment Program under the first Clinton administration sponsored targeted development of dual-use technologies for application to both commercial and defined military needs.

24. The government could be relatively detached from the program because, unlike other situations, in this case, issues such as intellectual properties, third country sales and others, which are normally the realm of government negotiation in co-production programs, would be relegated to individual companies instead.

25. WESTPAC was a joint feasibility study conducted by Japanese industry in cooperation with U.S. industry for the Japan Defense Agency that addressed possible SDI deployment configurations for the Western Pacific region, including Japan. The final report of the effort has never been released formally.

26. See, for example, "Cooperation in Environmental and Demilitarization Fields," U.S.–Japan Technology Forum, May 3 and 4, 1993. Technical Report No. 15, U.S.–Japan Center for Technology Management, Vanderbilt University.

27. This could be expanded to include the respective environmental protection agencies of the two countries, the Japanese Ministry of Transportation, the Maritime Safety Administration, the Ministry of Posts and Telecommunications, and others.

28. Martin Libicki, Jack Nunn, and Bill Taylor, *U.S. Industrial Base Dependence/Vulnerability; Phase 2—Analysis* (Washington, D.C.: National Defense University, November 1987); Erland H. Heginbotham et al., "Dependence of U.S. Defense systems on Foreign Technologies," Institute for Defense Analyses, December 1990; U.S. Department of Commerce, Office of Indus-

trial Resource Administration, "National Security Assessment of the Domestic and Foreign Subcontractor Base: A Study of Three U.S. Navy Weapon Systems," Washington, D.C., March 1992.

29. Two surveys conducted by the MIT Japan Program, Massachusetts Institute of Technology, illustrate the promise and potential pitfalls of bilateral cooperation. See Michael Green, "The Japanese Defense Industry's Views of U.S.–Japan Defense Technology Collaboration," MITJP 94-01, January 1994; and Matthew Rubiner, "U.S. Industry and Government Views on Defense Technology Cooperation with Japan: Findings of the MIT Japan Program Survey," MITJP 94-03, March 1994.

# Conclusion: From Reaffirmation to Redefinition—An Agenda for the Future

PATRICK M. CRONIN AND MICHAEL J. GREEN

THE 1995 revision of Japan's National Defense Program Outline (NDPO), the April 1996 Joint Security Declaration, and the September 1997 revision of the Guidelines for Defense Cooperation have all begun to reestablish credibility for an alliance that many in the Asia-Pacific region once thought would not survive the transition to the post–Cold War era. The alliance—once in danger of becoming a source of uncertainty in Asia's strategic future—is back on a trajectory that will enhance regional stability. The question now is whether or not this asset will be squandered by political leadership in Tokyo and in Washington, distracted by the Asian and global economic crises and domestic problems and paying only sporadic attention to international security affairs.

Critics will still argue that the real problem with the alliance is persistent asymmetries in the division of military roles and missions between the two states. Even with the revision of the Guidelines, they will point out, Japan's role is limited to rear area functions and Tokyo is under no obligation to come to the defense of the United States when Japan's own security is not directly affected. However, the critics miss some salient points. First, few alliances are forged by states with identical capabilities and interests. Second, the military role described for Japan in the Guidelines is nontrivial and surpasses the requirements the U.S. military has for Japanese support in responding to contingencies. Third, pushing for bilateral symmetry in combat responsibilities in places such as the Korean Peninsula would severely undermine regional stability. In fact, the South Korean side, while supporting the Guidelines review, has clearly and unequivocally rejected a Japanese combat role on the peninsula. Fourth—and most important—asymmetries in the bilateral division of military roles and missions are less relevant than the overall balance in the broader sharing of responsibility for regional stability.

This latter point—the definition of the U.S.–Japan alliance in broader comprehensive terms—will be the greatest challenge to maintaining the long-term credibility of the bilateral relationship. Division of labor and compartmentalization of responsibilities are no longer sufficient for the circumstances we face at the end of the twentieth century. In short, U.S.–Japan relations are far beyond the original Cold War calculus of "bases for defense" and the complete separation of economics from security issues.

As the Asian economic crisis deepened in 1998, the U.S. Congress and the media were asking, "where is Japan?" The inability of the Japanese government to mount a decisive and convincing response to its own banking crisis and economic slowdown doomed the rest of the region and cast a pall over the U.S.–Japan strategic partnership that had emerged with the Joint Security Declaration of 1996. The bilateral trade deficit was always an irritant to the alliance, but never a threat in the way that macroeconomic factors have become since the Asian currency crisis. Japanese politicians know what they must do to recover economic growth, but the resolution of the country's banking crisis will be a protracted and difficult process, during which drastic action on the economy will be political *seppuku.* In the meantime, the confidence of U.S. policymakers in Japan as a partner will be strained and Japanese resentment and nationalism in response to U.S. pressure could increase. Japan will eventually recover its economic growth and will remain the most important U.S. ally in the region well into the future, but the management of the alliance over the next decade will require a steady hand.

Based on this broader long-term view of bilateral relations and drawing on the analysis and recommendations in this volume, we suggest an agenda for the future of the U.S.–Japan alliance that focuses on four themes: incremental enhancement of military cooperation, engagement of China, development of a global security partnership, and preparation for a long-term commitment to forward U.S. presence in Asia.

## Enhancing Military Cooperation

A broader U.S.–Japan security partnership has always been predicated on a reliable bilateral military relationship. The 1997 Guidelines set the correct tone for such a relationship, but the spirit and letter of the Guidelines will have to be fully implemented through a series of Japanese legislative changes in the years ahead. The Guidelines outline areas of cooperation under the *existing* framework of the alliance relationship. Any changes in this framework in the current strategic environment should be incremental, because the alliance contributes to regional stability by reducing uncertainty, not by introducing sudden change. If the strategic environment does change drastically, however, then more significant structural change in the alliance may also be appropriate. (The point is that we cannot structure the alliance for the extreme worst-case scenario without undermining stability in the near term and making that worst-case scenario even more likely.)

A Japanese debate on security policy is unfolding, and is long overdue. As a matter of policy, however, the Japanese side must first divisive, debate, and implement the Guidelines-related legislation that will allow U.S. defense officials to sit down with their Japanese counterparts and plan for regional contingencies. Defense planners face myriad potential crises in the region and cannot afford to wait for a protracted debate about the Japanese constitution before getting to work. The larger debate can and should occur in time, but practical near-term steps must be taken. This means amending the Self-Defense Forces (SDF) law to clarify rules of engagement. It also will require changes in laws covering the Ministries of Transport, Home Affairs, and Posts & Telecommunications so that these important ministries have a legal framework for providing rear area support (civilian airports, telecommunication frequencies, etc.) to the U.S. and Japanese forces in the event of a contingency. It may also require the Japanese side to strengthen the emergency powers of the Prime Minister's Office—a controversial subject given Japan's history but an essential task in Tokyo's unfolding efforts at administrative reform. In exchange, the U.S. side will have to intensify consultation with Tokyo on the objectives and options for responding to crises in the region. If the supporting Japanese role outlined in the Guidelines is credible (based on enabling legislation, planning, and training), then U.S. defense officials should also examine turning over certain rear area functions in regional contingency planning to Tokyo. For example, by the next Quadrennial Defense Review, the Pentagon may be able to save considerable budgetary resources now dedicated to medical personnel, military police, and logistical personnel who would be deployed to Japan to support a Korean contingency—if Japan can cover those responsibilities as advertised in the Guidelines.

Building this level of trust in the U.S. defense establishment will always prove challenging. This challenge is far more difficult because the United States and Japan lack a joint and combined command structure. The 1997 Guidelines compensate for that deficiency by establishing new coordination mechanisms more appropriate to the U.S.–Japan relationship and Asia in general than the trans-Atlantic model. Looking into the next century, "virtual" joint and combined commands could also be established with joint operations centers for humanitarian relief and peacekeeping operations. Such centers could have a permanent bilateral staff that would coordinate with U.N. authorities and nongovernmental organizations (NGOs) in planning for and responding to noncombat operations. From such a precedent, the U.S. and Japanese militaries could then move on to consideration of a NATO-style joint command for the full range of operations. However, as Sheila Smith points out, there is still a strong Japanese resistance to joint command (and even in the prewar period Japan's only experience with combined command was during the ad hoc response to the Boxer Rebellion). Tokyo will have to modernize its own command and control system, including enhanced authority for the Prime Minister's Office in times of crisis, before the Japanese people will trust the SDF in a more joint and combined arrangement with the United States. If the future security environment is more benign than at present, however, the consideration of a joint command could be less germane.

From a U.S. and regional perspective, the credibility of the U.S.–Japan alliance is also measured by the level of Japanese support for U.S. forward presence. Traditionally, this dimension of military cooperation has had more political saliency (particularly in the U.S. Congress) than the level of cooperation in roles and missions. Japan's host nation support has been the most generous of any U.S. ally, though that "generosity" has also been in Japan's national self-interest. With the end of the Cold War and the September 1995 Okinawa rape incident, however, pressure has increased on U.S. forces in Japan to consolidate bases. When the Diet had to vote on whether or not to overrule the Okinawa government and extend the leases on U.S. bases in March 1997, 80 percent of the politicians voted in support of extension. However, this same level of support may not appear after 1999 when the Diet has to vote on whether or not to sustain the current level of financial support for U.S. forces through an extension of the Special Measures Agreement. The United States and Japan reaffirmed in April 1996 and in subsequent bilateral communiqués that a U.S. force level of approximately 100,000 is appropriate in Asia's current strategic environment. Unless there are measurable reductions of the threat and new levels of regional stability in the years ahead, this same logic will apply. However, there is still room for considerable consolidation of existing U.S. military bases in Japan and for greater joint use of facilities with the SDF (as described in Paul Giarra's chapter). Moreover, even without a more favorable security environment, advances in military means may allow for fewer numbers of troops while not reducing U.S. military capabilities. These steps should be taken to reinforce political support for a continuation of the current level of U.S. forces in Japan in a time of decreasing Japanese budgetary resources. Greater joint use of bases—including SDF command of some bases—will also strengthen the trend toward a closer bilateral command and control relationship. All of this depends, of course, on the implementation of the Defense Guidelines described above.

As Gregg Rubinstein and Mike Chinworth demonstrate in their chapters, it is also critical that the United States and Japan take steps to strengthen bilateral armaments and technology cooperation. The first task is to eliminate the bureaucratic stovepiping of the defense technology relationship. The Systems and Technology Forum (S&TF) has always existed in a separate realm from the policy-oriented Security Consultative Committee (SCC). However, armaments and technology cooperation should be considered integral to bilateral policy deliberations, and a formal coordination process between the SCC and the S&TF is long overdue. The perpetuation of this bifurcated bureaucratic organization will impede real progress toward closer consultation and coordination in the alliance. Better coordination between the two has been urged for some time now by the Defense Science Board and the National Research Council. Closer integration of the technology and policy components of the U.S.–Japan alliance will increase the prospects for a bilateral requirements dialogue that will reduce redundancy of systems and anticipate areas for technology cooperation on new weapons before it is too late (i.e., before production has begun). A more integrated approach will also facilitate adjustments to Japan's Three Arms Export Control Principles so that bilateral joint development can proceed to the production stage. Keidanren (the Federation of Economic Organizations) has argued for a relaxation of the arms export rules, but exceptions should only be made on a bilateral case-by-case basis. This will be particularly important as the United States and Japan enter joint development or co-production of Theater Missile Defense (TMD) systems. Increasingly, Japan's strength will be at the subsystems and components level, while the United States will dominate at the systems level. Logic dictates that Japanese industry should therefore concentrate on contributing dual-use technology to U.S. weapons at the subsystems and components level, rather than pushing for indigenous Japanese aircraft and missile systems for the SDF. Old habits die hard, however, and Japanese industry may find abandonment of *kokusanka* (indigenization) as difficult as U.S. industry finds designing-in Japa-nese subcontractors.

Over the longer term, technology will also shape U.S.–Japan military cooperation at the operational level. The revolution in military affairs, even if only half of the experts' predictions are accurate, will increasingly result in an enormous U.S. lead in information-based warfare in the next century. Only the United States will have the capabilities to integrate weapons systems and information at the level of "systems-of-systems." This will challenge interoperability with even high-tech allies like Japan. The United States may have more options for shaping presence in Japan (at the margins) as U.S. forces explore simulated "virtual" training or establish longer-range strategic airlift. In addition, the United States military may have increased capacity for unilateral intervention in crises (with smart weapons fired offshore, for example), which might dilute the incentive for consultation and joint action with Japan. Overall, the pressure will be on Japan to prove itself a credible ally and to maintain interoperability with U.S. forces as it adapts to new high-tech systems and doctrines.

The need for greater integration of technology and security policy-making in the alliance begs a larger point about the overall bureaucratic framework of the U.S.–Japan security relationship. The greatest obstacle to coordination between the S&TF and the SCC is that the S&TF is dominated by the Ministry of International Trade and Industry (MITI) and the Pentagon's Office of Acquisition and Technology, while the SCC is controlled by the traditional managers of the alliance in the Ministry of Foreign Affairs (MOFA), Japan Defense Agency (JDA), and the Departments of State and Defense. These old turf wars are a problem. The alliance has outgrown the day when a handful of like-minded defense and foreign affairs officials in the two countries could control the full range of bilateral security cooperation. The Guidelines will bring in new civilian agencies on the Japanese side. Technology and armaments cooperation (not to mention nonproliferation and other technical issues) will increasingly bring in MITI and the Commerce Department. The political controversy over basing issues in Japan is bringing more and more Japanese politicians into the process. And one can never anticipate when and how the U.S. Congress will intervene in the security relationship. The alliance still requires a small elite group of officials to manage crises and set the overall direction of policy, but as the security cooperation expands and becomes more comprehensive, other bureaucratic and political actors will have to be let inside the gate.

## Coping with China

Beijing's criticism of the 1996 U.S.–Japan Security Declaration and the 1997 Defense Guidelines demonstrated that U.S.–Japan defense ties do not and cannot exist in a vacuum. The Chinese leadership concluded that the revitalization of the U.S.–Japan alliance was aimed at containing China. This impression was reinforced by the fact that President Clinton and Prime Minister Hashimoto announced the reaffirmation of the security relationship only one month after the People's Liberation Army conducted ballistic missile tests in and around the Taiwan Strait. In fact, the Clinton summit had been planned with Prime Minister Murayama for the previous fall, but was canceled due to the domestic budget crisis in Washington at the time. Nevertheless, there is no denying that because it took place after the March 1996 Taiwan Strait incident, the U.S.–Japan Security Declaration attracted far more attention and political support in both the Congress and the Diet than would have been the case otherwise.

Some critics have charged that U.S. and Japanese officials have seen the collision with China over the cross-strait issue coming as a result of emphasizing "areas surrounding Japan" in the new Guidelines. Beyond the unintended timing mentioned above, however, these critics either misunderstand the new Guidelines or give excessive credence to politically motivated Chinese concerns about developments in Taipei. That is, the Guidelines neither call for a SDF role in a "Taiwan scenario" nor encourage Taiwan to deviate from seeking what all agree on—namely, a peaceful resolution of the cross-strait problem.

Does this mean China is a threat to the United States and Japan? In terms of both intentions and military capabilities the answer is "no"—and will be for at least another decade. A policy of containment would therefore be unnecessary and dangerous. Thus, when China pressed Tokyo and Washington to explain whether Taiwan would be covered by the U.S–Japan Defense Guidelines in the summer of 1997, both allies answered honestly that they did not conduct the Guidelines review to cover Taiwan. At the same time, neither Washington nor Tokyo was prepared to say that the Guidelines and the U.S.–Japan alliance would remain unaffected should Beijing attempt to use force in the Taiwan Strait. In a sense, the U.S. and Japanese positions on the Guidelines application to Taiwan was an extension of the traditional U.S. policy toward Taiwan; that is, a position of strategic ambiguity (not saying what we would do if China attacked Taiwan) and tactical clarity (knowing that we have the capability to act if required by events). Any other position would have provoked either Taiwanese independence or Chinese ire.

The fact remains, however, that both Washington and Tokyo are concerned about China's future, while sharing the hope of many Chinese that China will successfully grapple with its massive domestic challenges. A tight bilateral alliance is therefore critical, not just as a hedge, but also as a backstop for our efforts to integrate China as a cooperative partner in the region's security and economic framework. When Beijing began criticizing the U.S.–Japan alliance, the first instinct of some officials in Washington was to back-pedal on the Guidelines, TMD, and other aspects of U.S.–Japan security cooperation. Some even spoke of China as the United States' "natural" and "strategic" partner in Asia, and with the 1998 Clinton-Jiang summit and the Asian financial crisis gave a general perception that China is now "more important" to the United States than Japan. It is shortsighted to see the U.S. relationships with Japan and China in zero-sum terms, however. The credibility of U.S. engagement of China—both domestically in the United States and in the region—depends on a firm strategic and political partnership with Japan. At the same time, the United States and Japan must continue the process of transparency established with the 1996 Joint Security Declaration. The Chinese side could make no *specific* criticisms about the contents of the Guidelines after receiving repeated briefings from U.S. and Japanese officials. The transparency of the process was a useful model to encourage the Chinese side to follow itself. Since Beijing's unease is over the larger strategic context of the U.S.–Japan alliance rather than the specifics of the Guidelines, it is now important to establish a trilateral process of dialogue with Beijing—beginning at the working level and possibly arriving at a trilateral summit in the years ahead.

The process of confidence-building and cooperation with China will be evolutionary, and transparency will not always bring immediate consensus. Beijing's second white paper on defense, issued in the summer of 1998, criticized bilateral alliances as destabilizing—the antithesis of the future spelled out by the United States and Japan in the 1996 Security Declaration. While the demise of alliances might serve longer-term Chinese ambitions for regional influence, it would actually be counter to China's own interests in regional stability. Thus the United States and Japan should seize on China's concerns, both genuine and rhetorical, in order to broaden the depth and breadth of trilateral consultation, and to gradually build a common vision of the future of regional security.

## Toward a Global Security Partnership

Engagement of China is only the most immediate area that requires close U.S.–Japan security cooperation. U.S. and Japanese common security interests also extend to the Persian Gulf, where the world's largest known oil resources exist, and to global issues such as nonproliferation. There will inevitably be areas where Tokyo and Washington take a different approach. In policy toward Burma and Cambodia, Japan has parted with the United States by focusing on stability and economic interests over human rights and democracy. In Iran, Japan has moved toward the Europeans in rejecting the harder-line U.S. approach (although the U.S. side has been looking closely at President Khatemi's attempts to ease U.S.–Iran tension). These policy differences can have a trickle-down effect that undermines the bilateral military-to-military relationship. In effect, Japanese divergence on high-profile foreign policy issues leads to questions about the value of the alliance relationship for those in the United States who are not focused on Asia.

The U.S.–Japan global security relationship must be put in perspective, however. Several points are in order. First, divergence with a close ally is hardly unique to Japan. The United States' traditional partnership with Great Britain faced numerous points of divergence, such as the Suez Canal crisis of 1956. Second, as the U.S.–U.K. partnership demonstrates, a foundation of close bilateral military-to-military cooperation is important to developing a broader security relationship. In that area, the United States and Japan are moving in the right direction. Third, despite doubts generated by the Asian financial crisis, Japan's ability to contribute to regional and international stability is increasing relative to that of the United States. The American unipolar moment will not last indefinitely, but there is little to suggest that Japan will challenge the status quo or push for multipolarity in the way China might. For that reason, Japan can contribute to a kind of "virtual unipolarity" well into the next century, if the United States is willing to share leadership and Japan is willing to share risk. The Clinton administration was therefore right to support an expansion of the U.N. Security Council to include Japan and Germany.

## The Long-Term Perspective

Thus far, our agenda for the future of the U.S.–Japan alliance has been premised on the current strategic environment. It would be a mistake at this stage to restructure the alliance or reduce U.S. capabilities *in anticipation* of the end of the North Korean threat; first, because that end may not come for some time; and second, because deterrence on the peninsula would be undermined by such moves. However, it is worth considering how U.S. presence and the U.S.–Japan alliance might be structured *after* the North Korean threat is gone and North–South reconciliation is well advanced.

If the peninsula ceases to be divided, much will depend on the process of unification. The strategic environment would be quite different depending on whether the United States, Japan, and China cooperate or compete for influence on the peninsula, and whether unification results from war or peaceful integration of the North. If the regional context for unification is generally cooperative, then the United States will most likely want to maintain alliances and a forward military presence in both Korea and Japan. In Japan, the Seventh Fleet would continue to have regional and global responsibilities and should be maintained. The size and position of the U.S. Marine and Air Force presence in Japan would depend on other factors, such as the revolution in military affairs and the nature of other forces in the region. It would be useful, however, to maintain some mobile ground presence in the region near the amphibious capabilities of the Seventh Fleet. Forces in South Korea would be significantly smaller, but for the first time would share a regional mission with U.S. forces in Japan (as opposed to its present singular mission of deterrence against North Korea). This confluence of the missions of the U.S.–Republic of Korea (ROK) and U.S–Japan alliances would necessitate stronger trilateral coordination, though a formal trilateral alliance is difficult to imagine in the foreseeable future.

It is unlikely that Tokyo would reject a continued U.S. military presence given the uncertain futures of China and the Korean Peninsula and Japanese interests in stability as far as the Gulf. However, as Lee Howell suggests, local political pressure could increase on U.S. bases, especially on Okinawa. There could be two solutions to this problem in the future. The first would be greater integration of U.S. and SDF bases. The second would be a more explicit recognition of the global roles and responsibilities of U.S. forces based in Japan. The Japanese government maintains a policy of prior consultation based on the artificial notion (introduced in Diet deliberations in the 1960s) that the scope of the U.S.–Japan Security Treaty extends only to the "Far East," an area from Taiwan to the Kuriles. Absent a direct North Korean threat, the Japanese side will have to give more explicit support for global U.S. deployments from Japan, based on Tokyo's shared global interests with the United States. Eventually, there will have to be further consolidation of U.S. bases, as regional security allows and local politics demand.

The nature of bilateral military cooperation could also change significantly in a post-unification environment. It is not unrealistic to imagine a future in which U.S. and Japanese forces operate together as far as the Gulf. It is easy to predict the public hue and cry should Japan's role in a future Gulf War be as limited and tardy as it was in the last one. Such military cooperation would be the logical extension of increasing bilateral cooperation and a recognition of Japanese global interests. After all,

Japanese dependency on Gulf oil is increasing dramatically relative to U.S. dependency. The scenario becomes more likely if U.S. and Japanese forces are cooperating as part of a joint multinational task force, under U.N. mandate, and including Australian, Korean, and even Chinese naval forces (though the latter would require a dramatically different Chinese view of collective security). The vision of U.N.-centered collective security animates many younger politicians in Japan and is implied in Ichiro Ozawa's *Blueprint for a New Japan*. If this new generation of leadership can build the trust and understanding with the rest of Asia necessary for such a role, the development would certainly be in U.S. interests.

Some have argued that multilateral security architectures must some day be established in Asia to replace the bilateral U.S. alliances and avoid confrontation with China. It is difficult to imagine how the transition of the Korean Peninsula could be handled peacefully without an effective Northeast Asian forum playing the role that the Conference on Security and Cooperation in Europe (CSCE) played during German unification. Functional multilateralism on specific issues such as energy or maritime cooperation will also play an increasingly important role, but the membership will likely vary depending on the subject (as demonstrated by the U.S.–Japan–ROK cooperation in Korean Peninsula Energy Development Organization [KEDO], for example). However, as important as multilateral dialogue and confidence-building are to Asia's future, they will not substitute for the stability provided by U.S. forward presence in the medium to long run. The most stable environment would be one in which bilateral military alliances work within a broader network of multilateral forums for confidence- and consensus-building in the region.

By placing contemporary and future policy questions within the historical context of the evolution of U.S.–Japan security cooperation, we hope to have demonstrated that the alliance requires continuous but incremental redefinition to survive. There will always be critics who see the stationing of U.S. forces on Japanese soil as unacceptable or traditionalists who will object to any changes in the existing patterns of bilateral security cooperation. Nevertheless, the diverse authors in this volume provide reasons for optimism that the majority of Americans and Japanese will continue to see a strong U.S.–Japan alliance as essential to each side's national interests, and that there will be support for further redefinition. As the reader considers how U.S. interests in Asia will be protected in the generations ahead, it is worth questioning whether there really are any good strategic choices preferable to a strong U.S.–Japan alliance. It is likely that we will want to further complement our alliance relationships with multilateral structures, to modernize our military-to-military relationship, or eventually to consolidate or integrate our forces in Japan. But it is difficult to imagine how U.S. leadership will be maintained in the 21st century without a close-knit and comprehensive U.S.–Japan alliance at the core of our Asia policy.

# Appendixes

# Appendix 1

# Alliance Chronology

**August 1945:** Japan surrenders.

**September 1945:** Japan signs the Instrument of Surrender, ending the Pacific War.

**June 1950:** Korean War begins (ends in July 1953). Japan provides minesweepers and repairs U.S. equipment.

**August 1950:** National Police Reserve Force Ordinance is promulgated and enforced.

**November 1950:** U.S. announces its seven principles for concluding the peace treaty with Japan.

**September 1951:** First U.S.–Japan Security Treaty is signed.

— Japan signs a peace treaty with forty-nine countries in San Francisco.

**April 1952:** U.S. occupation of Japan ends.

**August 1952:** National Safety Agency, renamed to JDA in 1954, is established.

**October 1952:** National Safety Force is formed.

**December 1953:** United States agrees to restore the Amami Islands to Japan.

**March 1954:** Japan and the United States sign the "Mutual Defense Assistance (MDA) Agreement."

**July 1954:** Japan Defense Agency (JDA) and Self-Defense Forces (SDF) are formed (relevant laws are passed in June).

**November 1954:** Prime Minister Yoshida and President Eisenhower announce their intent to work to maintain peace in Asia.

**December 1956:** Japan is admitted to the United Nations.

**May 1957:** Japan adopts the Basic Policy for National Defense.

**June 1957:** Japan releases its first defense buildup plan.

**August 1957:** Japan–U.S. Security Council is founded to review the U.S.–Japan Security Treaty.

**January 1960:** New U.S.–Japan Security Treaty is signed (comes into effect in June).

**February 1960:** Foreign Minister Fujiyama defines the "Far East" (Article VI of the Treaty) to be north of the Philippines, inclusive of Taiwan.

**July 1961:** Japan releases its second defense buildup plan.

**March 1967:** Japan releases its third defense buildup plan.

**April 1967:** Prime Minister Sato announces Three Principles on Arms Export.

**December 1967:** Prime Minister Sato announces Three Non-Nuclear Principles.

**January 1968:** A U.S. nuclear-powered aircraft carrier, the USS *Enterprise,* enters a Japanese port (Sasebo) for the first time.

**June 1968:** Ogasawara Islands are restored to Japan.

**July 1968:** President Nixon announces the "Guam Doctrine" (that U.S. allies have first responsibility to provide personnel for the purpose of self-defense).

**November 1969:** Prime Minister Sato and President Nixon issue a joint statement on Okinawa's return to Japan in 1972 and extension of the Security Treaty.

**June 1970:** The U.S.–Japan Security Treaty is renewed automatically. Fixed ten-year expiration period is dropped.

**October 1970:** Japan publishes its first Defense White Paper.

— Minister of State for Defense Nakasone announces draft for the fourth defense buildup plan, which doubled the defense budget from the level of the third defense buildup plan.

**June 1971:** Okinawa Defense Pact, requiring Japan to play a major role in the defense of Okinawa, and "Agreement on the Return of Okinawa" are signed.

**October 1971:** To reduce the American trade deficit with Japan, the JDA announces that Japan will double the amount of military equipment it buys from the United States in the next four-year defense buildup plan, from $500 million to $1 billion.

**January 1972:** Prime Minister Sato and President Nixon announce a joint declaration that Okinawa is returned to Japan in May 1972 and U.S. bases are reduced.

**February 1972:** Japan releases its fourth defense buildup plan.

**May 1972:** The United States returns Okinawa to Japan.

**June 1972:** Japan and the United States agree there is no need to revise the bilateral Security Treaty. Japan assures the United States it will use economic means to improve international conditions.

**July 1972:** President Nixon announces his plan to visit China (first "Nixon Shock").

**August 1972:** President Nixon announces to stop the gold-based dollar exchange system (the second "Nixon Shock").

**January 1973:** SCC agrees on the consolidation of U.S. bases in Japan (Kanto Program).

— The bilateral Security Consultative Group is established.

**February 1973:** Japan announces the "Peacetime Defense Capability" concept.

**January 1974:** In SCC meetings, the United States agrees to reduce its land holdings on Okinawa by 10 percent.

**November 1974:** Prime Minister Tanaka and President Ford issue a joint statement stressing the vital and lasting importance of the relationship to Asian security. Ford became first U.S. president to visit Japan.

**March 1975:** The Defense Study Group is established.

**September 1975:** The Defense Study Group issues a report "Thinking about National Security," which initiates the first NDPO.

**June 1976:** Japan's second Defense White Paper "Defense of Japan" is published (published annually hereafter).

**July 1976:** Security Consultative Committee (SCC) establishes Sub-Committee for Defense Cooperation (SDC).

**October 1976:** Japan adopts its NDPO.

**November 1976:** Japan adopts a cabinet resolution to set a GNP 1 percent ceiling on defense budget.

**March 1977:** Prime Minister Fukuda and President Carter issue a joint declaration affirming the importance of bilateral cooperation for the stability of the Asia Pacific.

**August 1977:** Japan's Study on Legal Problems with Regard to Emergency Situations begins.

**November 1978:** First U.S. Air Force–Japan Air Self-Defense Force (JASDF) joint training.

— The Guidelines for U.S.–Japan Defense Cooperation are announced.

**April 1979:** Comprehensive Security Study Group is established by Prime Minister Ohira.

**July 1979:** Japan announces the midterm defense plan for FY1980–1984.

**November 1979:** U.S.–Japan Eminent Persons Group is established to review state of the bilateral relations.

**February 1980:** JMSDF participates in Rim of the Pacific Exercises (RimPac) for the first time.

**July 1980:** Comprehensive Security Study Group issues a report which concludes that U.S. economic and military superiority is over and peace has to be maintained through burden-sharing. The report articulates Japan's security agenda, including U.S.–Japan relations, strengthening self-defense capability, relations with China and the Soviet Union, and security regarding energy and food.

**May 1981:** Former U.S. ambassador to Japan Edwin O. Reischauer admits the existence of a 1960 secret agreement between the United States and Japan allowing the U.S. Navy to carry nuclear arms in and out of Japan.

— Prime Minister Suzuki states that Japan will defend 1000 nautical miles of its sea-lanes.

**October 1981:** First U.S. Army–Japan Ground Self-Defense Force (JGSDF) joint training.

**February 1982:** First U.S. Army–JGSDF joint command post exercises take place.

**May 1982:** In accordance with the special measure law concerning the use of Japanese land by U.S. forces, the United States begins using public property within its bases and installations in Okinawa.

**January 1983:** Japan's cabinet approves its position regarding the transfer of military technologies to the United States.

— Prime Minister Nakasone and President Reagan issue a joint declaration affirming the bilateral alliance relationship. Nakasone refers to Japan as an "unsinkable aircraft carrier."

**June 1984:** First U.S. Navy–Japan Maritime Self-Defense Force (JMSDF) joint command post exercises.

**October 1984:** The results of the "Studies on Legal Problems with Regard to Emergency Situations," begun in 1977, are presented to the Diet (also in April 1984 and in September 1978).

**February 1986:** First U.S.–Japan joint command post exercises.

**May 1986:** Bill calling for the establishment of the Security Council of Japan becomes law.

**October 1986:** First U.S.–Japan joint field exercises take place.

**September 1987:** Japan approves first transfer of military technology to the United States.

**October 1987:** United States and Japan hold first meeting on Toshiba Machine Co., Ltd.'s violation of the agreement of the Coordinating Committee for Export Control to Communist Area (COCOM).

**November 1988:** United States and Japan sign MOU on Cooperation in the Development of the FS-X Weapon System.

**April 1990:** DoD "A Strategic Framework for the Asian Pacific Rim (EASI I)" announces three-stage reduction of U.S. forces from Asia.

**December 1990:** Japan releases midterm defense plan for FY1991–1995.

**January 1991:** "The Agreement Between Japan and the United States Concerning New Special Measures on Cost of Stationing of U.S. Forces in Japan" is signed (comes into effective April 1991 and is terminated March 1996).

**April 1991:** Japan sends minesweepers to the Persian Gulf.

**September 1991:** The aircraft carrier USS *Independence* replaces the USS *Midway* at Yokosuka.

**October 1991:** SDF personnel join chemical weapons inspection teams in Iraq for the first time.

**January 1992:** Prime Minister Miyazawa and President Bush announce "the Tokyo Declaration on Japan–U.S. Global Partnership."

**April 1992:** DoD issues "A Strategic Framework for the Asian Pacific Rim (East Asia Security Initiative II-EASI II)."

**June 1992:** Japan's Diet passes the International Peace Cooperation bill.

**December 1993:** U.S.–Japan TMD Working Group is established.

**July 1994:** Prime Minister Murayama (Japan Socialist Party) approves the constitutionality of SDF.

**August 1994:** Prime Minister's Advisory Group on Defense Issues (Higuchi Commission) releases "The Modality of the Security and Defense Capability of Japan," setting the parameters for post–Cold War defense policy.

**February 1995:** U.S. Department of Defense (DoD) issues "U.S. Strategic Security for the East Asia-Pacific Region (East Asia Strategy Report-EASR)," in which the United States announces its pledge to keep 100,000 troops in East Asia.

**September 1995:** Okinawan schoolgirl is raped by U.S. servicemen.

**November 1995:** Japan's revised National Defense Program Outline (NDPO) is approved.

**December 1995:** Japan releases midterm defense plan for FY1996–2000.

**April 1996:** ACSA for peacetime and international peace operations is signed.

— Prime Minister Hashimoto and President Clinton issue "the Japan–U.S. Joint Declaration on Security-Alliance for the 21st Century," reaffirming both countries' commitment to the bilateral security alliance established in the Treaty of Mutual Cooperation and Security Between Japan and the U.S. (Security Treaty). The two leaders agree to initiate a review of the 1978 Guidelines.

**July 1996:** Production Memorandum of Understanding (MOU) on F-2 (FS-X) is adopted.

**December 1996:** Special Action Committee on Okinawa (SACO) issues final report.

**April 1997:** The Parliament passes amendment to the Special Action Law Regarding the Use of Land Accompanied with the Enforcement of Agreement under Article 6 of the Treaty of Mutual Cooperation and Security between Japan and the United States Regarding Facilities and Areas and the Status of U.S. Forces in Japan. Over 70 percent of Diet members support this controversial extension of U.S. base leases on Okinawa.

**June 1997:** Interim report on the revision of the 1978 Guidelines issued.

**September 1997:** New Guidelines for U.S.–Japan Defense Cooperation issued.

**April 1998:** Acquisition and Cross-Servicing Agreement (ACSA) for situations in areas surrounding Japan is signed.

**August 1998:** North Korea launches a three stage ballistic missile, the Tacpo dong, over Japanese airspace.

**September 1998:** U.S. and Japanese governments agree at Security Sub-Committee (SSC) meeting to proceed with joint research on Theater Missile Defense (TMD).

**January 1999:** LDP forms coalition with Ozawa's Liberal Party to accelerate Guidelines legislation.

# Appendix 2

# Treaty of Mutual Cooperation and Security Between Japan and the United States

(Source: *American Foreign Policy: Current Documents, 1960*)
June 23, 1960

The United States of America and Japan,

Desiring to strengthen the bonds of peace and friendship traditionally existing between them, and to uphold the principles of democracy, individual liberty, and the rule of law,

Desiring further to encourage closer economic cooperation between them and to promote conditions of economic stability and well-being in their countries,

Reaffirming their faith in the purposes and principles of the Charter of the United Nations, and their desire to live in peace with all peoples and all governments,

Recognizing that they have the inherent right of individual or collective self-defense as affirmed in the Charter of the United Nations,

Considering that they have a common concern in the maintenance of international peace and security in the Far East,

Having resolved to conclude a treaty of mutual cooperation and security,

Therefore agree as follows:

ARTICLE I

The Parties undertake, as set forth in the Charter of the United Nations, to settle any international disputes in which they may be involved by peaceful means in such a manner that international peace and security and justice are not endangered and to refrain in their international relations from the threat or use of force against the territorial integrity or political independence of any state, or in any other manner inconsistent with the purposes of the United Nations.

The Parties will endeavor in concert with other peace-loving countries to strengthen the United Nations so that its mission of maintaining international peace and security may be discharged more effectively.

ARTICLE II

The Parties will contribute toward the further development of peaceful and friendly international relations by strengthening their free institutions, by bringing about a better understanding of the principles upon which these institutions are founded, and by promoting conditions of stability and well-being. They will seek to eliminate conflict in their international economic policies and will encourage economic collaboration between them.

ARTICLE III

The Parties, individually and in cooperation with each other, by means of continuous and effective self-help and mutual aid will maintain and develop, subject to their constitutional provisions, their capacities to resist armed attack.

ARTICLE IV

The Parties will consult together from time to time regarding the implementation of the Treaty, and, at the request of either Party, whenever the security of Japan or international peace and security in the Far East is threatened.

ARTICLE V

Each Party recognizes that an armed attack against either Party in the territories under the administration of Japan would be dangerous to its own peace and safety and declares that it would act to meet the common danger in accordance with its constitutional provisions and processes.

Any such armed attack and all measures taken as a result thereof shall be immediately reported to the Security Council of the United Nations in accordance with the provisions of Article 51 of the Charter. Such measures shall be terminated when the Security Council has taken the measures necessary to restore and maintain international peace and security.

ARTICLE VI

For the purposes of contributing to the security of Japan and the maintenance of international peace and security in the Far East, the United States of America is granted the use by its land, air and naval forces of facilities and areas in Japan.

The use of these facilities and areas as well as the status of United States armed forces in Japan shall be governed by a separate agreement, replacing the Administrative Agreement under Article III of the Security Treaty between the United States of America and Japan, signed at Tokyo on February 28, 1952, as amended, and by such other arrangements as may be agreed upon.

ARTICLE VII

This Treaty does not affect and should not be interpreted as affecting in any way the rights and obligations of the Parties under the Charter of the United Nations or the responsibility of the United Nations for the maintenance of international peace and security.

ARTICLE VIII

This Treaty shall be ratified by the United States of America and Japan in accordance with their respective constitutional processes and will enter into force on the date on which the instruments of ratification thereof have been exchanged by them in Tokyo.

ARTICLE IX

The Security Treaty between the United States of America and Japan signed at the city of San Francisco on September 8, 1951, shall expire upon the entering into force of this Treaty.

ARTICLE X

This Treaty shall remain in force until in the opinion of the Governments of the United States of America and Japan there shall have come into force such United Nations arrangements as will satisfactorily provide for the maintenance of international peace and security in the Japan area.

However, after the Treaty has been in force for ten years, either Party may give notice to the other Party of its intention to terminate the Treaty, in which case the Treaty shall terminate one year after such notice has been given.

# Appendix 3

# The Guidelines for U.S.–Japan Defense Cooperation

(Source: internet http://www.jda.go.jp)
September 23, 1997

## I. THE AIM OF THE GUIDELINES

The aim of these Guidelines is to create a solid basis for more effective and credible U.S.–Japan cooperation under normal circumstances, in case of an armed attack against Japan, and in situations in areas surrounding Japan. The Guidelines also provide a general framework and policy direction for the roles and missions of the two countries and ways of cooperation and coordination, both under normal circumstances and during contingencies.

## II. BASIC PREMISES AND PRINCIPLES

The Guidelines and programs under the Guidelines are consistent with the following basic premises and principles.

1. The rights and obligations under the Treaty of Mutual Cooperation and Security between the United States of America and Japan (the U.S.–Japan Security Treaty) and its related arrangements, as well as the fundamental framework of the U.S.–Japan alliance, will remain unchanged.

2. Japan will conduct all its actions within the limitations of its Constitution and in accordance with such basic positions as the maintenance of its exclusively defense-oriented policy and its three non-nuclear principles.

3. All actions taken by the United States and Japan will be consistent with basic principles of international law, including the peaceful settlement of disputes and sovereign equality, and relevant international agreements such as the Charter of the United Nations.

4. The Guidelines and programs under the Guidelines will not obligate either Government to take legislative, budgetary, or administrative measures. However, since the objective of the Guidelines and programs under the Guidelines is to establish an effective framework for bilateral cooperation, the two Governments are expected to reflect in an appropriate way the results of these efforts, based on their own judgments, in their specific policies and measures. All actions taken by Japan will be consistent with its laws and regulations then in effect.

## III. COOPERATION UNDER NORMAL CIRCUMSTANCES

Both Governments will firmly maintain existing U.S.–Japan security arrangements. Each Government will make efforts to maintain required defense postures. Japan will possess defense capability within the scope necessary for self-defense on the basis of the "National Defense Program Outline." In order to meet its commitments, the United States will maintain its nuclear deterrent capability, its forward deployed forces in the Asia-Pacific region, and other forces capable of reinforcing those forward deployed forces.

Both Governments, based on their respective policies, under normal circumstances will maintain close cooperation for the defense of Japan as well as for the creation of a more stable international security environment.

Both Governments will under normal circumstances enhance cooperation in a variety of areas. Examples include mutual support activities under the Agreement between the Government of Japan and the Government of the United States of America concerning Reciprocal Provision of Logistic Support, Supplies and Services between the Self-Defense Forces of Japan and the Armed Forces of the United States of America; the Mutual Defense Assistance Agreement between the Unites States of America and Japan; and their related arrangements.

### 1. Information Sharing and Policy Consultations

Recognizing that accurate information and sound analysis are at the foundation of security, the two Governments will increase information and intelligence sharing and the exchange of views on international situations of mutual interest, especially in the Asia-Pacific region. They will also continue close consultations on defense policies and military postures.

Such information sharing and policy consultations will be conducted at as many levels as possible and on the broadest range of subjects. This will be accomplished by taking advantage of all available opportunities, such as Security Consultative Committee (SCC) and Security Sub-Committee (SSC) meetings.

### 2. Various Types of Security Cooperation

Bilateral cooperation to promote regional and global activities in the field of security contributes to the creation of a more stable international security environment.

Recognizing the importance and significance of security dialogues and defense exchanges in the region, as well as international arms control and disarmament, the two Governments will promote such activities and cooperate as necessary.

When either or both Governments participate in United Nations peacekeeping operations or international humanitarian relief operations, the two sides will cooperate closely for mutual support as necessary. They will prepare procedures for cooperation in such areas as transportation, medical services, information sharing, and education and training.

When either or both Governments conduct emergency relief operations in response to requests from governments concerned or international organizations in the wake of large-scale disasters, they will cooperate closely with each other as necessary.

3. Bilateral Programs

Both Governments will conduct bilateral work, including bilateral defense planning in case of an armed attack against Japan, and mutual cooperation planning in situations in areas surrounding Japan. Such efforts will be made in a comprehensive mechanism involving relevant agencies of the respective Governments, and establish the foundation for bilateral cooperation.

Bilateral exercises and training will be enhanced in order not only to validate such bilateral work but also to enable smooth and effective responses by public and private entities of both countries, starting with U.S. Forces and the Self-Defense Forces. The two Governments will under normal circumstances establish a bilateral coordination mechanism involving relevant agencies to be operated during contingencies.

## IV. ACTIONS IN RESPONSE TO AN ARMED ATTACK AGAINST JAPAN

Bilateral actions in response to an armed attack against Japan remain a core aspect of U.S.–Japan defense cooperation.

When an armed attack against Japan is imminent, the two Governments will take steps to prevent further deterioration of the situation and make preparations necessary for the defense of Japan. When an armed attack against Japan takes place, the two Governments will conduct appropriate bilateral actions to repel it at the earliest possible stage.

1. When an Armed Attack against Japan Is Imminent

The two Governments will intensify information and intelligence sharing and policy consultations and initiate at an early stage the operation of a bilateral coordination mechanism. Cooperating as appropriate, they will make preparations necessary for ensuring coordinated responses according to the readiness stage selected by mutual agreement. Japan will establish and maintain the basis for U.S. reinforcements. As circumstances change, the two Governments will also increase intelligence gathering and surveillance, and will prepare to respond to activities which could develop into an armed attack against Japan.

The two Governments will make every effort, including diplomatic efforts, to prevent further deterioration of the situation.

Recognizing that a situation in areas surrounding Japan may develop into an armed attack against Japan, the two Governments will be mindful of the close interrelationship of the two requirements: preparations for the defense of Japan and responses to or preparations for situations in areas surrounding Japan.

2. When an Armed Attack against Japan Takes Place

(1) Principles for Coordinated Bilateral Actions

(a) Japan will have primary responsibility immediately to take action and to repel an armed attack against Japan as soon as possible. The United States will provide appropriate support to Japan. Such bilateral cooperation may vary according to the scale, type, phase, and other factors of the armed attack. This cooperation may include preparations for and execution of coordinated bilateral operations, steps to prevent further deterioration of the situation, surveillance, and intelligence sharing.

(b) In conducting bilateral operations, U.S. Forces and the Self-Defense Forces will employ their respective defense capabilities in a coordinated, timely, and effective manner. In doing this, they will conduct effective joint operations of their respective Forces' ground, maritime and air services. The Self-Defense Forces will primarily conduct defensive operations in Japanese territory and its surrounding waters and airspace, while U.S. Forces support Self-Defense Forces' operations. U.S. Forces will also conduct operations to supplement the capabilities of the Self-Defense Forces.

(c) The United States will introduce reinforcements in a timely manner, and Japan will establish and maintain the basis to facilitate these deployments.

(2) Concept of Operations

(a) Operations to Counter Air Attack against Japan

U.S. Forces and the Self-Defense Forces will bilaterally conduct operations to counter air attack against Japan.

The Self-Defense Forces will have primary responsibility for conducting operations for air defense.

U.S. Forces will support Self-Defense Forces' operations and conduct operations, including those which may involve the use of strike power, to supplement the capabilities of the Self-Defense Forces.

(b) Operations to Defend Surrounding Waters and to Protect Sea Lines of Communication

U.S. Forces and the Self-Defense Forces will bilaterally conduct operations for the defense of surrounding waters and for the protection of sea lines of communication.

The Self-Defense Forces will have primary responsibility for the protection of major ports and straits in Japan, for the protection of ships in surrounding waters, and for other operations.

U.S. Forces will support Self-Defense Forces' operations and conduct operations, including those which may provide additional mobility and strike power, to supplement the capabilities of the Self-Defense Forces.

(c) Operations to Counter Airborne and Seaborne Invasions of Japan
U.S. Forces and the Self-Defense Forces will bilaterally conduct operations to counter airborne and seaborne invasions of Japan.

The Self-Defense Forces will have primary responsibility for conducting operations to check and repel such invasions.

U.S. Forces will primarily conduct operations to supplement the capabilities of the Self-Defense Forces. The United States will introduce reinforcements at the earliest possible stage, according to the scale, type, and other factors of the invasion, and will support Self-Defense Forces' operations.

(d) Responses to Other Threats

(i) The Self-Defense Forces will have primary responsibility to check and repel guerrilla-commando type attacks or any other unconventional attacks involving military infiltration in Japanese territory at the earliest possible stage. They will cooperate and coordinate closely with relevant agencies, and will be supported in appropriate ways by U.S. Forces depending on the situation.

(ii) U.S. Forces and the Self-Defense Forces will cooperate and coordinate closely to respond to a ballistic missile attack. U.S. Forces will provide Japan with necessary intelligence, and consider, as necessary, the use of forces providing additional strike power.

(3) Activities and Requirements for Operations

(a) Command and Coordination
U.S. Forces and the Self-Defense Forces, in close cooperation, will take action through their respective command-and-control channels. To conduct effective bilateral operations, the two Forces will establish, in advance, procedures which include those to determine the division of roles and missions and to synchronize their operations.

(b) Bilateral Coordination Mechanism
Necessary coordination among the relevant agencies of the two Governments will be conducted through a bilateral coordination mechanism. In order to conduct effective bilateral operations, U.S. Forces and the Self-Defense Forces will closely coordinate operations, intelligence activities, and logistics support through this coordination mechanism, including use of a bilateral coordination center.

(c) Communication/Electronics

The two Governments will provide mutual support to ensure effective use of communications and electronics capabilities.

(d) Intelligence Activities

The two Governments will cooperate in intelligence activities in order to ensure effective bilateral operations. This will include coordination of requirements, collection, production, and dissemination of intelligence products. Each Government will be responsible for the security of shared intelligence.

(e) Logistics Support Activities

U.S. Forces and the Self-Defense Forces will conduct logistics support activities efficiently and properly in accordance with appropriate bilateral arrangements.

To improve the effectiveness of logistics and to alleviate functional shortfalls, the two Governments will undertake mutual support activities, making appropriate use of authorities and assets of central and local government agencies, as well as private sector assets. Particular attention will be paid to the following points in conducting such activities:

(i) Supply

The United States will support the acquisition of supplies for systems of U.S. origin while Japan will support the acquisition of supplies in Japan.

(ii) Transportation

The two Governments will closely cooperate in transportation operations, including airlift and sealift of supplies from the United States to Japan.

(iii) Maintenance

Japan will support the maintenance of U.S. Forces' equipment in Japan; the United States will support the maintenance of items of U.S. origin which are beyond Japanese maintenance capabilities. Maintenance support will include the technical training of maintenance personnel as required. Japan will also support U.S. Forces' requirement for salvage and recovery.

(iv) Facilities

Japan will, in case of need, provide additional facilities and areas in accordance with the U.S.–Japan Security Treaty and its related arrangements. If necessary for effective and efficient operations, U.S. Forces and the Self-Defense Forces will make bilateral use of Self-Defense Forces facilities and U.S. facilities and areas in accordance with the Treaty and its related arrangements.

(v) Medical Services

The two Governments will support each other in the area of medical services such as medical treatment and transportation of casualties.

## V. COOPERATION IN SITUATIONS IN AREAS SURROUNDING JAPAN THAT WILL HAVE AN IMPORTANT INFLUENCE ON JAPAN'S PEACE AND SECURITY (SITUATIONS IN AREAS SURROUNDING JAPAN)

Situations in areas surrounding Japan will have an important influence on Japan's peace and security. The concept, situations in areas surrounding Japan, is not geographical but situational. The two Governments will make every effort, including diplomatic measures, to prevent such situations from occurring. When the two Governments reach a common assessment of the state of each situation, they will effectively coordinate their activities. In responding to such situations, measures taken may differ depending on circumstances.

### 1. When a Situation in Areas Surrounding Japan Is Anticipated

When a situation in areas surrounding Japan is anticipated, the two Governments will intensify information and intelligence sharing and policy consultations, including efforts to reach a common assessment of the situation.

At the same time, they will make every effort, including diplomatic efforts, to prevent further deterioration of the situation, while initiating at an early stage the operation of a bilateral coordination mechanism, including use of a bilateral coordination center. Cooperating as appropriate, they will make preparations necessary for ensuring coordinated responses according to the readiness stage selected by mutual agreement. As circumstances change, they will also increase intelligence gathering and surveillance, and enhance their readiness to respond to the circumstances.

### 2. Responses to Situations in Areas Surrounding Japan

The two Governments will take appropriate measures, to include preventing further deterioration of situations, in response to situations in areas surrounding Japan. This will be done in accordance with the basic premises and principles listed in Section II above and based on their respective decisions. They will support each other as necessary in accordance with appropriate arrangements.

Functions and fields of cooperation and examples of items of cooperation are outlined below and listed in the Annex.

### 3. Cooperation in Activities Initiated by Either Government

Although either Government may conduct [the following] activities at its own discretion, bilateral cooperation will enhance their effectiveness.

#### (a) Relief Activities and Measures to Deal with Refugees

Each Government will conduct relief activities with the consent and cooperation of the authorities in the affected area. The two Governments will cooperate as necessary, taking into account their respective capabilities.

The two Governments will cooperate in dealing with refugees as necessary. When there is a flow of refugees into Japanese territory, Japan will decide how to respond and will have primary responsibility for dealing with the flow; the United States will provide appropriate support.

ANNEX

## EXAMPLES OF ITEMS OF COOPERATION FOR CONSIDERATION IN SITUATIONS IN AREAS SURROUNDING JAPAN

| Functions and Fields | | | Examples of Items of Cooperation |
|---|---|---|---|
| humanitarian activities | | | transportation of personnel and supplies to the affected area<br>medical services, communications, and transportation in the affected area ,<br>relief and transfer operations for refugees, provision of emergency materials to refugees |
| search and rescue | | | search and rescue operations at sea in areas surrounding Japan<br>information sharing on search and rescue |
| activities for ensuring the effectiveness of economic sanctions for the maintenance of international peace and stability | | | inspection of ships and related activities<br>information sharing |
| noncombatant evacuation operations | | | information sharing (requirements and capabilities)<br>use of Self-Defense Forces facilities and civilian ports and airports<br>customs, immigration, and quarantine upon entry into Japan<br>assistance in such matters as temporary accommodations, transportation, and medical services in Japan. |
| Japan's support for U.S. activities | use of facilities forces | | use of Self-Defense forces facilities and civilian ports and airports for supplies and other purposes<br>reservation of spaces for loading/unloading of personnel and materials and of storage areas at Self-Defense Forces facilities and civilian ports and airports<br>extension of operating hours for Self-Defense Forces facilities and civilian ports and airports<br>use of Self-Defense Forces airfields by U.S. aircraft<br>provision of training and exercise areas<br>construction of temporary structures inside U.S. facilities and areas |
| | rear area support | supply | provision of materials (except weapons and ammunition) and POL (petroleum, oil, and lubricants) to U.S. vessels and aircraft at Self-Defense Forces Facilities and civilian ports and airports<br>use of vehicles and cranes for transportation of materials, personnel, and POL<br>provision of materials (except weapons and ammunition) and POL to U.S. facilities and areas |
| | | transportation | land, sea, and air transportation inside Japan of materials, personnel, and POL<br>sea transportation to U.S. vessels on the high seas |

| Functions and Fields | | | Examples of Items of Cooperation |
|---|---|---|---|
| Japan's support for U.S. Forces activities | rear area support | maintenance | repair and maintenance of U.S. vessels, aircraft, and vehicles<br>provision of repair parts<br>temporary provision of tools and materials for maintenance |
| | | medical services | medical treatment of casualties inside Japan<br>provision of medical supply |
| | | security | security of U.S. facilities and areas including joint use facilities and areas<br>sea surveillance around U.S. facilities and areas<br>security of transportation routes inside Japan<br>information sharing on security situations in Japan |
| | | communications | provision of frequencies (including for satellite communications) and equipment for communications among relevant Japanese and U.S. agencies |
| | | others | support for port entry/exit by U.S. vessels<br>loading/unloading of materials at Self-Defense Forces facilities and civilian ports and airports<br>sewage disposal, water supply, and electricity inside U.S. facilities and areas<br>temporary increase of workers at U.S. facilities and areas |
| Japan-U.S. operational cooperation | surveillance | | intelligence sharing |
| | minesweeping | | minesweeping operations in Japanese territorial waters and on the high seas<br>information sharing |
| | sea and air space management | | maritime coordination in response to increased sea traffic around Japan<br>air traffic control and air space management in areas surrounding Japan |

(b) Search and Rescue

The two Governments will cooperate in search and rescue operations. Japan will conduct search and rescue operations in Japanese territory; and at sea around Japan, as distinguished from areas where combat operations are being conducted. When U.S. Forces are conducting operations, the United States will conduct search and rescue operations in and near the operational areas.

(c) Noncombatant Evacuation Operations

When the need arises for U.S. and Japanese noncombatants to be evacuated from a third country to a safe haven, each Government is responsible for evacuating its own nationals as well as for dealing with the authorities of the affected area. In stances in which each decides it is appropriate, the two Governments will coordinate in planning and cooperate in carrying out their evacuations, including for the securing of transportation means, transportation, and the use of facilities, using their respective capabilities in a mutually supplementary manner. If similar need arises for noncombatants other than of U.S. or Japanese nationality, the respective countries may consider extending, on their respective terms, evacuation assistance to third country nationals.

(d) Activities for Ensuring the Effectiveness of Economic Sanctions for the Maintenance of International Peace and Stability

Each Government will contribute to activities for ensuring the effectiveness of economic sanctions for the maintenance of international peace and stability. Such contributions will be made in accordance with each Government's own criteria.

Additionally, the two Governments will cooperate with each other as appropriate, taking into account their respective capabilities. Such cooperation includes information sharing and cooperation in inspection of ships based on United Nations Security Council Resolutions.

(2) Japan's Support for U.S. Forces Activities

(a) Use of Facilities

Based on the U.S.–Japan Security Treaty and its related arrangements, Japan will, in case of need, provide additional facilities and areas in a timely and appropriate manner, and ensure the temporary use by U.S. Forces of Self-Defense Forces facilities and civilian airports and ports.

(b) Rear Area Support

Japan will provide rear area support to those U.S. Forces that are conducting operations for the purpose of achieving the objectives of the U.S.–Japan Security Treaty. The primary aim of this rear area support is to enable U.S. Forces to use facilities and conduct operations in an effective manner. By its very nature, Japan's rear area support will be provided primarily in Japanese territory. It may also be provided on the high seas and international airspace around Japan, which are distinguished from areas where combat operations are being conducted.

In providing rear area support, Japan will make appropriate use of authorities and assets of the central and local government agencies, as well as private sector assets. The Self-Defense Forces, as appropriate, will provide such support consistent with their mission for the defense of Japan and the maintenance of public order.

(3) U.S.–Japan Operational Cooperation

As situations in areas surrounding Japan have an important influence on Japan's peace and security, the Self-Defense Forces will conduct such activities as intelligence gathering, surveillance, and minesweeping, to protect lives and property and to ensure navigational safety. U.S. Forces will conduct operations to restore the peace and security affected by situations in areas surrounding Japan.

With the involvement of relevant agencies, cooperation and coordination will significantly enhance the effectiveness of both forces' activities.

## VI. BILATERAL PROGRAMS FOR EFFECTIVE DEFENSE COOPERATION UNDER THE GUIDELINES

Effective bilateral defense cooperation under the Guidelines will require the United States and Japan to conduct consultative dialogue throughout the spectrum of security conditions: normal circumstances, an armed attack against Japan, and situations in areas surrounding Japan. Both sides must be well informed and coordinate at multiple levels to ensure successful bilateral defense cooperation. To accomplish this, the two Governments will strengthen their information and intelligence sharing and policy consultations by taking advantage of all available opportunities, including SCC and SSC meetings, and they will establish the following two mechanisms to facilitate consultations, coordinate policies, and coordinate operational functions.

First, the two Governments will develop a comprehensive mechanism for bilateral planning and the establishment of common standards and procedures, involving not only U.S. Forces and the Self-Defense Forces but also other relevant agencies of their respective Governments.

The two Governments will, as necessary, improve this comprehensive mechanism. The SCC will continue to play an important role for presenting policy direction to the work to be conducted by this mechanism. The SCC will be responsible for presenting directions, validating the progress of work, and issuing directives as necessary. The SDC will assist the SCC in bilateral work.

Second, the two Governments will also establish, under normal circumstances, a bilateral coordination mechanism that will include relevant agencies of the two countries for coordinating respective activities during contingencies.

1. Bilateral Work for Planning and Establishment of Common Standards and Procedures

Bilateral work listed below will be conducted in a comprehensive mechanism involving relevant agencies of the respective Governments in a deliberate and efficient manner. Progress and results of such work will be reported at significant milestones to the SCC and the SDC.

(1) Bilateral Defense Planning and Mutual Cooperation Planning

U.S. Forces and the Self-Defense Forces will conduct bilateral defense planning under normal circumstances to take coordinated actions smoothly and effectively in case of an armed attack against Japan. The two Governments will conduct mutual cooperation planning under normal circumstances to be able to respond smoothly and effectively to situations in areas surrounding Japan.

Bilateral defense planning and mutual cooperation planning will assume various possible situations, with the expectation that results of these efforts will be appropriately reflected in the plans of the two Governments. The two Governments will coordinate and adjust their plans in light of actual circumstances. The two Governments will be mindful that bilateral defense planning and mutual cooperation planning must be consistent so that appropriate responses will be ensured when a situation in areas surrounding Japan threatens to develop into an armed attack against Japan or when such a situation and an armed attack against Japan occur simultaneously.

(2) Establishment of Common Standards for Preparations

The two Governments will establish under normal circumstances common standards for preparations for the defense of Japan. These standards will address such matters as intelligence activities, unit activities, movements and logistics support in each readiness stage. When an armed attack against Japan is imminent, both Governments will agree to select a common readiness stage that will be reflected in the level of preparations for the defense of Japan by U.S. Forces, the Self-Defense Forces and other relevant agencies.

The two Governments will similarly establish common standards for preparations of cooperative measures in situations in areas surrounding Japan so that they may select a common readiness stage by mutual agreement.

(3) Establishment of Common Procedures

The two Governments will prepare in advance common procedures to ensure smooth and effective execution of coordinated U.S. Forces and Self-Defense Forces operations for the defense of Japan. These will include procedures for communications, transmission of target information, intelligence activities and logistics support, and prevention of fratricide. Common procedures will also include criteria for properly controlling respective unit operations. The two forces will take into account the importance of communications/electronics interoperability, and will determine in advance their mutual requirements.

2. Bilateral Coordination Mechanism

The two Governments will establish under normal circumstances a bilateral coordination mechanism involving relevant agencies of the two countries to coordinate respective activities in case of an armed attack against Japan and in situations in areas surrounding Japan.

Procedures for coordination will vary depending upon items to be coordinated and agencies to be involved. They may include coordination committee meetings, mutual dispatch of liaison officers, and designation of points of contacts. As part of such a bilateral coordination mechanism, U.S. Forces and the Self-Defense Forces will prepare under normal circumstances a bilateral coordination center with the necessary hardware and software in order to coordinate their respective activities.

VII. TIMELY AND APPROPRIATE REVIEW OF THE GUIDELINES

The two Governments will review the Guidelines in a timely and appropriate manner when changes in situations relevant to the U.S.–Japan security relationship occur and if deemed necessary in view of the circumstances at that time.

# Appendix 4a

# Special Action Committee on Okinawa (SACO) Final Report

(Source: *Defense of Japan, 1997*. Tokyo: Japan Defense Agency)
December 2, 1996

The Special Action Committee on Okinawa (SACO) was established in November 1995 by the Governments of the United States and Japan. The two Governments launched the SACO process to reduce the burden on the people of Okinawa and thereby strengthen the U.S.–Japan alliance.

The mandate and guidelines for the SACO process were set forth by the Governments of the United States and Japan at the outset of the joint endeavor. Both sides decided that the SACO would develop recommendations for the Security Consultative Committee (SCC) on ways to realign, consolidate and reduce U.S. facilities and areas, and adjust operational procedures of U.S. forces in Okinawa consistent with their respective obligations under the Treaty of Mutual Cooperation and Security and other related agreements. The work of the SACO was scheduled to conclude after one year.

The SCC which was held on April 15, 1996, approved the SACO Interim Report which included several significant initiatives, and instructed the SACO to complete and recommend plans with concrete implementation schedules by November 1996.

The SACO, together with the Joint Committee, has conducted a series of intensive and detailed discussions and developed concrete plans and measures to implement the recommendations set forth in the Interim Report.

Today, at the SCC, Secretary Perry, Ambassador Mondale, Minister Ikeda, and Minister Kyuma approved this SACO Final Report. The plans and measures included in this Final Report, when implemented, will reduce the impact of the activities of U.S. forces on communities in Okinawa. At the same time, these measures will fully maintain the capabilities and readiness of U.S. forces in Japan while addressing security and force protection requirements. Approximately 21 percent of the total acreage of the U.S. facilities and areas in Okinawa excluding joint use facilities and areas (approx. 5,002ha/12,361 acres) will be returned.

Upon approving the Final Report, the members of the SCC welcomed the successful conclusion of the year-long SACO process and underscored their strong resolve to continue joint efforts to ensure steady and prompt implementation of the plans and measures of the SACO Final Report. With this understanding, the SCC designated the Joint Committee as the primary forum for bilateral coordination in the implementation phase, where specific conditions for the completion of each item will be addressed. Coordination with local communities will take place as necessary.

The SCC also reaffirmed the commitment of the two governments to make every endeavor to deal with various issues related to the presence and status of U.S. forces, and to enhance mutual understanding between U.S. forces and local Japanese communities. In this respect, the SCC agreed that efforts to these ends should continue, primarily through coordination at the Joint Committee.

The members of the SCC agreed that the SCC itself and the Security Sub-Committee (SSC) would monitor such coordination at the Joint Committee as described above and provide guidance as appropriate. The SCC also instructed the SSC to seriously address the Okinawa-related issues as one of the most important subjects and regularly report back to the SCC on this subject.

In accordance with the April 1996 U.S.–Japan Joint Declaration on Security, the SCC emphasized the importance of close consultation on the international situation, defense policies and military postures, bilateral policy coordination and efforts towards a more peaceful and stable security environment in the Asia-Pacific region. The SCC instructed the SSC to pursue these goals and to address the Okinawa-related issues at the same time.

Return Land:

*Futenma Air Station (see below)*

*Northern Training Area*
Return major portion of the Northern Training Area (approx. 3,987ha/9,852 acres) and release U.S. joint use of certain reservoirs (approx. 159hr/393 acres) with the intention to finish the process by the end of March 2003 under the following conditions:

Provide land area (approx. 38ha/93 acres) and water area (approx. 121 ha/298 acres) with the intention to finish the process by the end of March 1998 in order to ensure access from the remaining Northern Training Area to the ocean.

Relocate helicopter landing zones from the areas to be returned to the remaining Northern Training Area.

*Aha Training Area*
Release U.S. joint use of Aha Training Area (approx. 480ha/1,185 acres) and release U.S. joint use of the water area (approx. 7,895ha/19,509 acres) with the

intention to finish the process by the end of March 1998 after land and water access areas from the Northern Training Area to the ocean are provided.

*Gimbaru Training Area*
Return Gimbaru Training Area (approx. 60ha/149 acres) with the intention to finish the process by the end of March 1998 after the helicopter landing zone is relocated to Kin Blue Beach Training Area, and the other facilities are relocated to Camp Hansen.

*Sobe Communication Site*
Return Sobe Communication Site (approx. 53ha/132 acres) with the intention to finish the process by the end of March 2001 after the antenna facilities and associated support facilities are relocated to Camp Hansen.

*Yomitan Auxiliary Airfield*
Return Yomitan Auxiliary Airfield (approx. 191ha/471 acres) with the intention to finish the process by the end of March 2001 after the parachute drop training is relocated to Ie Jima Auxiliary Airfield and Sobe Communication Site is relocated.

*Camp Kuwae*
Return most of Camp Kuwae (approx. 99ha/245 acres) with the intention to finish the process by the end of March 2008 after the Naval Hospital is relocated to Camp Zukeran and remaining facilities there are relocated to Camp Zukeran or other U.S. facilities and areas in Okinawa.

*Senaha Communication Station*
Return Senaha Communication Station (approx. 61ha/151 acres) with the intention to finish the process by the end of March 2001 after the antenna facilities and associated support facilities are relocated to Torii Communication Station. However, the microwave tower portion (approx. 0.1ha/0.3 acres) will be retained.

*Makiminato Service Area*
Return land adjacent to Route 58 (approx. 3ha/8 acres) in order to widen the Route, after the facilities which will be affected by the return are relocated within the remaining Makiminato Service Area.

*Naha Port*
Jointly continue best efforts to accelerate the return of Naha Port (approx. 57ha/140 acres) in connection to its relocation to the Urasoe Pier area (approx. 35ha/87 acres).

*Housing consolidation (Camp Kuwae and Camp Zukeran)*
Consolidate U.S. housing areas in Camp Kuwae and Camp Zukeran and return portions of land in housing areas there with the intention to finish the process by the end of March 2008 (approx. 83ha/206 acres at Camp Zukeran; in addition, approx. 35ha/85 acres at Camp Kuwae will be returned through housing consolidation. That land amount is included in the above entry on Camp Kuwae).

Adjust Training and Operational Procedures:

*Artillery live-fire training over Highway 104*
Terminate artillery live-fire training over Highway 104, with the exception of artillery firing required in the event of a crisis, after the training is relocated to maneuver areas on the mainland of Japan within Japanese Fiscal Year 1997.

*Parachute drop training*
Relocate parachute drop training to Ie Jima Auxiliary Airfield.

*Conditioning hikes on public roads*
Conditioning hikes on public roads have been terminated.

Implement Noise Reduction Initiatives:

*Aircraft noise abatement countermeasures at Kadena Air Base and Futenma Air Station*
Agreements on aircraft noise abatement countermeasures at Kadena Air Base and Futenma Air Station announced by the Joint Committee in March 1996 have been implemented.

*Transfer of KC-130 Hercules aircraft and AV-8 Harrier aircraft*
Transfer 12 KC-130 aircraft currently based at Futenma Air Station to Iwakuni Air Base after adequate facilities are provided. Transfer of 14 AV-8 aircraft from Iwakuni Air Base to the United States has been completed.

*Relocation of Navy aircraft and MC-130 operations at Kadena Air Base*
Relocate Navy aircraft operations and supporting facilities at Kadena Air Base from the Navy ramp to the other side of the major runways. The implementation schedules for these measures will be decided along with the implementation schedules for the development of additional facilities at Kadena Air Base necessary for the return of Futenma Air Station. Move the MC-130s at Kadena Air Base from the Navy ramp to the northwest corner of the major runways by the end of December 1996.

*Noise reduction baffles at Kadena Air Base*
Build new noise reduction baffles at the north side of Kadena Air Base with the intention to finish the process by the end of March 1998.

*Limitation of night flight training operations at Futenma Air Station*
Limit night flight training operations at Futenma Air Station to the maximum extent possible, consistent with the operational readiness of U.S. forces.

Improve Status of Forces Agreement Procedures:

*Accident reports*
Implement new Joint Committee agreement on procedures to provide investigation reports on U.S. military aircraft accidents announced on December 2, 1996.

In addition, as part of the U.S. forces' good neighbor policy, every effort will be made to insure timely notification of appropriate local officials, as well as the Government of Japan, of all major accidents involving U.S. forces' assets or facilities.

*Public exposure of Joint Committee agreements*
Seek greater public exposure of Joint Committee agreements.

*Visits to U.S. facilities and areas*
Implement the new procedures for authorizing visits to U.S. facilities and areas announced by the Joint Committee on December 2, 1996.

*Markings on U.S. forces official vehicles*
Implement the agreement on measures concerning markings on U.S. forces official vehicles. Numbered plates will be attached to all non-tactical U.S. forces vehicles by January 1997, and to all other U.S. forces vehicles by October 1997.

*Supplemental automobile insurance*
Education programs for automobile insurance have been expanded. Additionally, on its own initiative, the United States has further elected to have all personnel under the SOFA obtain supplemental auto insurance beginning in January 1997.

*Payment for claims*
Make joint efforts to improve payment procedures concerning claims under paragraph 6, Article XVIII of the SOFA in the following manner:

Requests for advance payments will be expeditiously processed and evaluated by both Governments utilizing their respective procedures. Whenever warranted under U.S. laws and regulatory guidance, advance payment will be accomplished as rapidly as possible.

A new system will be introduced by the end of March 1998, by which Japanese authorities will make available to claimants no-interest loans, as appropriate, in advance of the final adjudication of claims by U.S. authorities.

In the past there have been only a very few cases where payment by the U.S. Government did not satisfy the full amount awarded by a final court judgment. Should such a case occur in the future, the Government of Japan will endeavor to make payment to the claimant, as appropriate, in order to address the difference in amount.

*Quarantine procedures*
Implement the updated agreement on quarantine procedures announced by the Joint Committee on December 2, 1996.

*Removal of unexploded ordnance in Camp Hansen*
Continue to use USMC procedures for removing unexploded ordnance in Camp Hansen, which are equivalent to those applied to ranges of the U.S. forces in the United States.

*Continue efforts to improve the SOFA procedures in the Joint Committee*

# Appendix 4b

# The SACO Final Report on Futenma Air Station

(Source: internet http://www.nttls.co.jp/infomofa/ju/security/96saco2.html)
December 2, 1996

**1. Introduction**

a. At the Security Consultative Committee (SCC) held on December 2, 1996, Minister Ikeda, Minister Kyuma, Secretary Perry, and Ambassador Mondale reaffirmed their commitment to the Special Action Committee on Okinawa (SACO) Interim Report of April 15, 1996 and the Status Report of September 19, 1996. Based on the SACO Interim Report, both Governments have been working to determine a suitable option for the return of Futenma Air Station and the relocation of its assets to other facilities and areas in Okinawa, while maintaining the airfield's critical military functions and capabilities. The Status Report called for the Special Working Group on Futenma to examine three specific alternatives: (1) incorporate the heliport into Kadena Air Base; (2) construct a heliport at Camp Schwab; and (3) develop and construct a sea-based facility (SBF).

b. On December 2, 1996, the SCC approved the SACO recommendation to pursue the SBF option. Compared to the other two options, the SBF is judged to be the best option in terms of enhanced safety and quality of life for the Okinawan people while maintaining operational capabilities of U.S. forces. In addition, the SBF can function as a fixed facility during its use as a military base and can also be removed when no longer necessary.

c. The SCC will establish a bilateral U.S.–Japan working group under the supervision of the Security Sub-Committee (SSC) entitled the Futenma Implementation Group (FIG), to be supported by a team of technical experts. The FIG, working with the Joint Committee, will develop a plan for implementation no later than December 1997. Upon SCC approval of this plan, the FIG, working with the Joint Committee, will oversee design, construction, testing, and transfer of assets. Throughout this process, the FIG will periodically report to the SSC on the status of its work.

## 2. Decisions of the SCC

a. Pursue construction of a SBF to absorb most of the helicopter operational functions of Futenma Air Station. This facility will be approximately 1,500 meters long, and will support the majority of Futenma Air Station's flying operations, including an Instrument Flight Rules (IFR)-capable runway (approximately 1,300 meters long), direct air operations support, and indirect support infrastructure such as headquarters, maintenance, logistics, quality-of-life functions, and base operating support. The SBF will be designed to support basing of helicopter assets, and will also be able to support short-field aircraft operations.

b. Transfer 12 KC-130 aircraft to Iwakuni Air Base. Construct facilities at this base to ensure that associated infrastructure is available to support these aircraft and their missions.

c. Develop additional facilities at Kadena Air base to support aircraft, maintenance, and logistics operations which are currently available at Futenma Air Station but are not relocated to the SBF or Iwakuni Air Base.

d. Study the emergency and contingency use of alternate facilities which may be needed in the event of a crisis. This is necessary because the transfer of functions from Futenma Air Station to the SBF will reduce operational flexibility currently available.

e. Return Futenma Air Station within the next five to seven years, after adequate replacement facilities are completed and operational.

## 3. Guiding Principles

a. Futenma Air Station's critical military functions and capabilities will be maintained and will continue to operate at current readiness levels throughout the transfer of personnel and equipment and the relocation of facilities.

b. To the greatest extent possible, Futenma Air Station's operations and activities will be transferred to the SBF. Operational capabilities and contingency planning flexibility which cannot be supported by the shorter runway of the SBF (such as strategic airlift, logistics, emergency alternate divert, and contingency throughput) must be fully supported elsewhere. Those facilities unable to be located on the SBF, due to operational, cost, or quality-of-life considerations, will be located on existing U.S. facilities and areas.

c. The SBF will be located off the east coast of the main island of Okinawa, and is expected to be connected to land by a pier or causeway. Selection of the location will take into account operational requirements, air-space and sea-lane deconfliction, fishing access, environmental compatibility, economic effects, noise abatement, survivability, security, and convenient, acceptable personnel access to other U.S. military facilities and housing.

d. The design of the SBF will incorporate adequate measures to ensure platform, aircraft, equipment, and personnel survivability against severe weather and ocean conditions; corrosion control treatment and prevention for the SBF and all equipment located on the SBF; safety; and platform security. Support will include reliable and secure fuel supply, electrical power, fresh water, and other utilities and consumables. Additionally, the facility will be fully self-supporting for short-period contingency/emergency operations.

e. The Government of Japan will provide the SBF and other relocation facilities for the use of U.S. forces, in accordance with the U.S.–Japan Treaty of Mutual Cooperation and Security and the Status of Forces Agreement. The two Governments will further consider all aspects of life-cycle costs as part of the design/acquisition decision.

f. The Government of Japan will continue to keep the people of Okinawa informed of the progress of this plan, including concept, location, and schedules of implementation.

**4. Possible Sea-Based Facility Construction Methods**

Studies have been conducted by a "Technical Support Group" comprised of Government engineers under the guidance of a "Technical Advisory Group" comprised of university professors and other experts outside the Government. These studies suggested that all three construction methods mentioned below are technically feasible.

a. Pile-Supported Pier Type (using floating modules)—supported by a number of steel columns fixed to the sea bed.

b. Pontoon Type—platform consisting of steel pontoon type units, installed in a calm sea protected by a breakwater.

c. Semi-Submersible Type—platform at a wave-free height, supported by buoyancy of the lower structure submerged under the sea.

**5. The Next Steps**

a. The FIG will recommend a candidate SBF area to the SCC as soon as possible and formulate a detailed implementation plan no later than December 1997. This plan will include completion of the following items: concept development and definition of operational requirements, technology performance specifications and construction method, site survey, environmental analysis, and final concept and site selection.

b. The FIG will establish phases and schedules to achieve operational capabilities at each location, including facility design, construction, installation of required components, validation tests and suitability demonstrations, and transfer of operations to the new facility.

c. The FIG will conduct periodic reviews and make decisions at significant milestones concerning SBF program feasibility.

# Appendix 5

# U.S.–Japan Joint Declaration on Security: Alliance for the 21st Century

(Source: *Defense of Japan, 1997*. Tokyo: Japan Defense Agency)
April 17, 1996

1. Today, the President and the Prime Minister celebrated one of the most successful bilateral relationships in history. The leaders took pride in the profound and positive contribution this relationship has made to world peace and regional stability and prosperity. The strong Alliance between the United States and Japan helped ensure peace and security in the Asia-Pacific region during the Cold War. Our Alliance continues to underlie the dynamic economic growth in this region. The two leaders agreed that the future security and prosperity of both the United States and Japan are tied inextricably to the future of the Asia-Pacific region.

The benefits of peace and prosperity that spring from the Alliance are due not only to the commitments of the two governments, but also to the contributions of the American and Japanese people who have shared the burden of securing freedom and democracy. The President and the Prime Minister expressed their profound gratitude to those who sustain the Alliance, especially those Japanese communities that host U.S. forces, and those Americans who, far from home, devote themselves to the defense of peace and freedom.

2. For more than a year, the two governments conducted an intensive review of the evolving political and security environment of the Asia-Pacific region and of various aspects of the U.S.–Japan security relationship. On the basis of this review, the President and the Prime Minister reaffirmed their commitment to the profound common values that guide our national policies: the maintenance of freedom, the pursuit of democracy, and respect for human rights. They agreed that the foundations for our cooperation remain firm, and that this partnership will remain vital in the twenty-first century.

## THE REGIONAL OUTLOOK

3. Since the end of the Cold War, the possibility of global armed conflict has receded. The last few years have seen expanded political and security dialogue among countries of the region. Respect for democratic principles is growing. Prosperity is more widespread than at any other time in history, and we are witnessing the emergence of an Asia-Pacific community. The Asia-Pacific region has become the most dynamic area of the globe.

At the same time, instability and uncertainty persist in the region. Tensions continue on the Korean Peninsula. There are still heavy concentrations of military force, including nuclear arsenals. Unresolved territorial disputes, potential regional conflicts, and the proliferation of weapons of mass destruction and their means of delivery all constitute sources of instability.

## THE U.S.–JAPAN ALLIANCE AND THE TREATY OF MUTUAL COOPERATION AND SECURITY

4. The President and the Prime Minister underscored the importance of promoting stability in this region and dealing with the security challenges facing both countries. In this regard, the President and the Prime Minister reiterated the significant value of the Alliance between the United States and Japan. They reaffirmed that the U.S.–Japan security relationship, based on the Treaty of Mutual Cooperation and Security between the United States of America and Japan, remains the cornerstone for achieving common security objectives, and for maintaining a stable and prosperous environment for the Asia-Pacific region as we enter the twenty-first century.

(a) The Prime Minister confirmed Japan's fundamental defense policy as articulated in its new National Defense Program Outline adopted in November 1995, which underscored that the Japanese defense capabilities should play appropriate roles in the security environment after the Cold War. The President and the Prime Minister agreed that the most effective framework for the defense of Japan is close defense cooperation between the two countries. This cooperation is based on a combination of appropriate defense capabilities for the Self-Defense Forces of Japan and the U.S.–Japan security arrangements. The leaders again confirmed that U.S. deterrence under the Treaty of Mutual Cooperation and Security remains the guarantee for Japan's security.

(b) The President and the Prime Minister agreed that continued U.S. military presence is also essential for preserving peace and stability in the Asia-Pacific region. The leaders shared the common recognition that the U.S.–Japan security relationship forms an essential pillar which supports the positive regional engagement of the United States. The President emphasized the U.S. commitment to the defense of Japan as well as to peace and stability in the Asia-Pacific region. He noted that there has been some adjustment of U.S. forces in the Asia-Pacific region since the end of the Cold War. On the basis of a thorough assessment, the United States reaffirmed that meeting its commitments in the prevailing security environment requires the maintenance of its current force structure of about 100,000 forward deployed military personnel in the region, including about the current level in Japan.

(c) The Prime Minister welcomed the U.S. determination to remain a stable and steadfast presence in the region. He reconfirmed that Japan would continue appropriate contributions for the maintenance of U.S. forces in Japan, such as through the provision of facilities and areas in accordance with the Treaty of Mutual Cooperation and Security and Host Nation Support. The President expressed U.S. appreciation for Japan's contributions, and welcomed the conclusion of the new Special Measures Agreement which provides financial support for U.S. forces stationed in Japan.

## BILATERAL COOPERATION UNDER THE U.S.–JAPAN SECURITY RELATIONSHIP

5. The President and the Prime Minister, with the objective of enhancing the credibility of this vital security relationship, agreed to undertake efforts to advance cooperation in the following areas.

(a) Recognizing that close bilateral defense cooperation is a central element of the U.S.–Japan alliance, both governments agreed that continued close consultation is essential. Both governments will further enhance the exchange of information and views on the international situation, in particular the Asia-Pacific region. At the same time, in response to the changes which may arise in the international security environment, both governments will continue to consult closely on defense policies and military postures, including the U.S. force structure in Japan, which will best meet their requirements.

(b) The President and the Prime Minister agreed to initiate a review of the 1978 Guidelines for Japan–U.S. Defense Cooperation to build upon the close working relationship already established between Japan and the United States. The two leaders agreed on the necessity to promote bilateral policy coordination, including studies on bilateral cooperation in dealing with situations that may emerge in the areas surrounding Japan and which will have an important influence on the peace and security of Japan.

(c) The President and the Prime Minister welcomed the April 15, 1996 signature of the Agreement Between the Government of the United States of America and the Government of Japan Concerning Reciprocal Provision of Logistic Support, Supplies and Services Between the Armed Forces of the United States of America and the Self-Defense Forces of Japan and expressed their hope that this Agreement will further promote the bilateral cooperative relationship.

(d) Noting the importance of interoperability in all facets of cooperation between the U.S. forces and Self-Defense Forces of Japan, the two governments will enhance mutual exchange in the areas of technology and equipment, including bilateral cooperative research and development of equipment such as the support fighter.

(e) The two governments recognized that the proliferation of weapons of mass destruction and their means of delivery has important implications for their common security. They will work together to prevent proliferation and will continue to cooperate in the ongoing study on ballistic missile defense.

6. The President and the Prime Minister recognized that the broad support and understanding of the Japanese people are indispensable for the smooth stationing of U.S. forces in Japan, which is the core element of the U.S.–Japan security arrangements. The two leaders agreed that both governments will make every effort to deal with various issues related to the presence and status of U.S. forces. They also agreed to make further efforts to enhance mutual understanding between U.S. forces and local Japanese communities.

In particular, with respect to Okinawa, where U.S. facilities and areas are highly concentrated, the President and the Prime Minister reconfirmed their determination to carry out steps to consolidate, realign, and reduce U.S. facilities and areas consistent with the objectives of the Treaty of Mutual Cooperation and Security. In this respect, the two leaders took satisfaction in the significant progress which has been made so far through the Special Action Committee on Okinawa (SACO), and welcomed the far-reaching measures outlined in the SACO Interim Report of April 15, 1996. They expressed their firm commitment to achieve a successful conclusion of the SACO process by November 1996.

## REGIONAL COOPERATION

7. The President and the Prime Minister agreed that the two governments will jointly and individually strive to achieve a more peaceful and stable security environment in the Asia-Pacific region. In this regard, the two leaders recognized that the engagement of the United States in the region, supported by the U.S.–Japan security relationship, constitutes the foundation for such efforts.

The two leaders stressed the importance of peaceful resolution of problems in the region. They emphasized that it is extremely important for the stability and prosperity of the region that China play a positive and constructive role, and, in this context, stressed the interest of both countries in furthering cooperation with China. Russia's ongoing process of reform contributes to regional and global stability, and merits continued encouragement and cooperation. The leaders also stated that full normalization of Japan-Russia relations based on the Tokyo Declaration is important to peace and stability in the Asia-Pacific region. They noted also that stability on the Korean Peninsula is vitally important to the United States and Japan and reaffirmed that both countries will continue to make every effort in this regard, in close cooperation with the Republic of Korea.

The President and the Prime Minister reaffirmed that the two governments will continue working jointly and with other countries in the region to further develop multilateral regional security dialogues and cooperation mechanisms such as the ASEAN Regional Forum, and eventually, security dialogues regarding Northeast Asia.

## GLOBAL COOPERATION

8. The President and the Prime Minister recognized that the Treaty of Mutual Cooperation and Security is the core of the U.S.–Japan alliance, and underlies the mutual confidence that constitutes the foundation for bilateral cooperation on global issues.

The President and the Prime Minister agreed that the two governments will strengthen their cooperation in support of the United Nations and other international organizations through activities such as peacekeeping and humanitarian relief operations.

Both governments will coordinate their policies and cooperate on issues such as arms control and disarmament, including acceleration of the Comprehensive Test Ban Treaty (CTBT) negotiations and the prevention of the proliferation of weapons of mass destruction and their means of delivery. The two leaders agreed that cooperation in the United Nations and APEC, and on issues such as the North Korean nuclear problem, the Middle East peace process, and the peace implementation process in the former Yugoslavia, helps to build the kind of world that promotes our shared interests and values.

## CONCLUSION

9. In concluding, the President and the Prime Minister agreed that the three legs of the U.S.–Japan relationship—security, political, and economic—are based on shared values and interests and rest on the mutual confidence embodied in the Treaty of Mutual Cooperation and Security. The President and the Prime Minister reaffirmed their strong determination, on the eve of the twenty-first century, to build on the successful history of security cooperation and to work hand-in-hand to secure peace and prosperity for future generations.

# Appendix 6a

# National Defense Program Outline in and after FY1996 (Tentative Unofficial Translation)

(Source: internet http://www.jda.go.jp)
November 28, 1995

I. Purpose

In order to preserve its independence and peace, Japan, under its Constitution, has been making efforts to secure stability in the international community through diplomatic activities including efforts to prevent and settle conflicts, to establish a sound basis for security through domestic political stability, to maintain firmly the Japan–U.S. security arrangements and to build up appropriate defense capabilities.

In 1976, under those policies, Japan formulated the National Defense Program Outline (adopted by the National Defense Council and by the Cabinet on October 29, 1976, hereinafter cited as "the Outline"). The Outline was drafted on the premise that the international situation, in which efforts for stabilization were being continued, the international political structure of the surrounding regions and Japan's own domestic situation would not undergo any major changes for some time and judging that the existence of the Japan–U.S. Security Arrangements would continue to play a major role in maintaining the stability of international relations. Since then, Japan has developed its defense capability according to "the Outline," and the steady defense efforts, in conjunction with the existence of the Japan–U.S. Security Arrangements and the efforts made to ensure the smooth and effective implementation of these arrangements, have both prevented any aggressions against Japan and contributed to the maintenance of peace and stability in the surrounding region.

Herein, a new set of guidelines for Japan's defense capability is laid forth, taking into consideration that almost two decades have passed since the adoption of "the Outline," that during this time the international situation has undergone significant changes, including the demise of the structure of the military confrontation between East and West, led respectively by the Soviet Union and the United States, brought on by the end of the Cold War; and that expectations for the role of the Self-Defense Forces have been increased in such functions as providing aid in cases of large-scale disasters and contributing to building a more stable security environment through participation in international peace cooperation activities, in addition to their principal mission of defending Japan.

Japan, abiding by its Constitution, following the guidelines set forth herein and paying due attention to enhancing the credibility of the Japan–U.S. Security Arrangements, will strive to ensure its own national defense and contribute to the peace and stability of the international community by appropriately upgrading, maintaining, and operating its defense capability.

II. International Situation

The following trends in the international situation were considered in the drafting of these new guidelines.

With the end of the Cold War, which led to the demise of the structure of military confrontation between East and West, backed by overwhelming military capabilities, the possibility of a global armed conflict has become remote in today's international community. At the same time, various unresolved territorial issues remain, and confrontations rooted in religious and ethnic differences have emerged more prominently. Complicated and diverse regional conflicts have been taking place. Furthermore, new kinds of dangers, such as the proliferation of weapons of mass destruction, including nuclear arms and of missiles, are on the increase. Thus, unpredictability and uncertainty persist in the international community.

On the other hand, as interdependence among nations intensifies, efforts are under way in various areas, such as political and economic spheres, to promote international cooperation and to further stabilize international relations. An emphasis has been placed on preventing destabilizing factors from escalating into serious international problems. In the area of security, continued progress is being made in arms control and disarmament, based on agreements between the United States and Russia and within Europe. Efforts are also being made toward enhancing regional security frameworks, expanding multilateral and bilateral dialogues and promoting the role of the United Nations.

Major countries are making active efforts to reorganize and streamline their military capabilities, which used to be aimed at countering large-scale aggression, and taking account of their respective strategic environments, to secure adequate capability to properly respond to regional conflicts and other various situations. These efforts constitute important factors toward the establishment of a more stable security environment, in combination with the initiatives based on international cooperation, including those launched by the United Nations. In this context, the United States, with its great power, continues to play a significant role for world peace and stability.

In the areas surrounding Japan, the end of the Cold War and the collapse of the Soviet Union have brought about a reduction of the military force level and changes in the military posture in Far East Russia. At the same time, there still remain large-scale military capabilities, including nuclear arsenals, and many countries in the region are expanding or modernizing their military capabilities mainly against the background of their economic development. There remain uncertainty and unpredictability, such as continued tensions on the Korean Peninsula, and a stable security environment has not been fully established. Under these circumstances, the possibility of a situation in this region, which could seriously affect the security of Japan, cannot be excluded. At the same time, various activities are being pursued to deepen cooperative relations among nations and to achieve regional stability, such as promotion of bilateral dialogues and search for a regional security framework.

The close cooperative relationship between Japan and the United States, based on the Japan–U.S. Security Arrangements, will help to create a stable security environment, provide the foundation for securing the engagement of the United States and the U.S. military presence which are necessary for peace and stability in this region, and thus will continue to play a key role for the security of Japan, as well as the stability of the international community.

## III. Security of Japan and Roles of Defense Capabilities

### *Security of Japan and the basic defense policy*

Japan, under its Constitution, while promoting diplomatic efforts and establishing a sound basis for security through domestic political stability, has moderately built up its defense capability on its own initiative, in accordance with the fundamental principles of maintaining an exclusively defense-oriented policy, not becoming a military power that might pose a threat to other countries, upholding civilian control, adhering to the three non-nuclear principles, and maintaining firmly the Japan–U.S. Security Arrangements. Japan is determined to maintain those basic defense policies.

### *Defense capability as it ought to be*

Japan has built its defense capability in accordance with "the Outline," which incorporates the concept of a basic and standard defense capability, defined as possessing the minimum necessary defense capability for an independent nation so that it would not become a source of instability in the surrounding region by creating a vacuum of power rather than building a capability directly linked to a military threat to Japan. The defense capability defined in "the Outline" aims to possess the assorted functions required for national defense, while retaining a balanced posture in terms of organization and deployment, including logistical support. This capability was derived from relevant factors such as the strategic environment, geographical characteristics, and other aspects of Japan's position.

It is considered appropriate that Japan continue to adhere fundamentally to this concept of a basic and standard defense capability based on a recognition that various efforts for the stabilization of international relations will continue to be pursued, while there remain uncertainty and unpredictability in the international situation, and that the Japan–U.S. Security Arrangements will continue to play a key role for the security of Japan and for the peace and stability in the surrounding region of Japan.

At the same time, in terms of the defense capability which Japan should maintain, it is necessary to review the specific content so as to seek the most efficient and appropriate capability, taking into account the reduction of military force level and changes in military posture of some of Japan's neighboring countries following the end of the Cold War, as well as the diversification of situations that should be addressed from the security point of view, including the outbreak of regional conflicts and the proliferation of weapons of mass destruction. This review also needs to reflect such factors as recent advances in science and technology, a decreasing population of young people and increasingly severe economic and fiscal conditions.

Furthermore, while the principal mission of the Self-Defense Forces continues to be the defense of Japan, the Self-Defense Forces, taking into account changes in domestic and international circumstances and Japan's position in the international community, will also have to be prepared for various situations such as large-scale disasters which can have a significant impact on our highly developed and diversified society and play an appropriate role in a timely manner in the Government's active efforts to establish a more stable security environment.

From this perspective, it is appropriate that Japan's defense capability be restructed, both in scale and functions, by streamlining, making it more efficient and compact, as well as enhancing necessary functions and making qualitative improvements to be able to effectively respond to a variety of situations and simultaneously ensure the appropriate flexibility to smoothly deal with the development of the situations.

*Japan–U.S. security arrangements*

The security arrangements with the United States are indispensable to Japan's security and will also continue to play a key role in achieving peace and stability in the surrounding region of Japan and establishing a more stable security environment.

From this perspective, in order to enhance the credibility of the Japan–U.S. Security Arrangements and ensure their effective implementation, it is necessary to make efforts (1) to promote exchange of information and policy consultation, (2) to establish an effective posture for cooperation in operational areas including joint studies, exercises and training, as well as enhancement of mutual support in those areas, (3) to enhance broad mutual exchange in the areas of equipment and technology, and (4) to implement various measures to facilitate smooth and effective stationing of U.S. forces in Japan.

Additionally, this close cooperative bilateral relationship, based on the Japan–U.S. Security Arrangements, facilitates Japanese efforts for peace and stability of the international community, including promotion of regional multilateral security dialogues and cooperation, as well as support for various United Nations activities.

*Role of defense capability*

It is necessary that the role of Japan's defense capability be appropriately fulfilled in the respective areas described below in accordance with the aforementioned concepts.

(1) National defense
Prevent aggressions against Japan together with the Japan–U.S. Security Arrangements, by possessing a defense capability of an appropriate scale which includes the functions required for defense, consistent with Japan's geographical characteristics, taking account of the military capabilities of neighboring countries by ensuring a posture to fully utilize the capability and by clearly showing the nation's will to defend their own country.

Against the threat of nuclear weapons, rely on the U.S. nuclear deterrent, while working actively on international efforts for realistic and steady nuclear disarmament aiming at a world free from the nuclear weapons.

Should indirect aggression—or any unlawful military activity which might lead to aggression against this nation—occur, take immediate responsive action in order to settle the situation at an early stage.

Should direct aggression occur, take immediate responsive action by conducting an integrated and systematic operation of its defense capabilities, in appropriate cooperation with the United States, in order to repel such aggression at the earliest possible stage.

(2) Response to large-scale disasters and various other situations
In case of large-scale disasters, disasters caused by acts of terrorism or other situations which require the protection of lives or assets, and, for example, upon request for assistance from related organizations, take necessary measures in an appropriate and timely manner, including provisions of disaster relief, in close cooperation with related organizations, thereby contributing to public welfare.

Should a situation arise in the areas surrounding Japan, which will have an important influence on national peace and security, take appropriate response in accordance with the Constitution and relevant laws and regulations, by properly supporting the United Nations activities when needed, and by ensuring the smooth and effective implementation of the Japan–U.S. Security Arrangements.

(3) Contribution to creation of a more stable security environment
Contribute to efforts for international peace through participation in international peace cooperation activities, and contribute to promotion of international cooperation through participation in international disaster relief activities.

Continue to promote security dialogues and exchanges among defense authorities to enhance mutual confidence with countries, including neighboring states.

Cooperate with efforts of the United Nations and other international organizations in the areas of arms control and disarmament for the purpose of preventing the proliferation of weapons of mass destruction and missiles, as well as controlling and regulating conventional weapons, including land-mines.

IV. Contents of Japan's Defense Capability

As the basis for fulfilling the roles for defense capability outlined in section III, the Ground, Maritime and Air Self-Defense Forces will maintain structures as described in paragraph 1, and assume the postures suggested in paragraphs 2 and 3.

*Ground, Maritime and Air Self-Defense Force structures*

(1) Ground Self-Defense Force (GSDF)
The GSDF, in order to be capable of rapid and effective systematic defense operations from the outset of aggression in any part of Japan, must deploy its divisions and brigades in a balanced manner that conforms to Japan's geographical and other characteristics.

The GSDF must possess at least one functional unit of each of the various types of forces used mainly for mobile operations.

The GSDF must possess ground-to-air missile units capable of undertaking the air defense of divisions and other units, as well as vital areas.

The GSDF, in order to maintain a high level of proficiency and to rapidly counter aggressions and other situations, must, in principle, staff its units with regular Self-Defense Personnel, while, when organizing, some units may be staffed by Self-Defense Force Reserves personnel capable of being quickly mobilized.

(2) Maritime Self-Defense Force (MSDF)
The MSDF must possess one fleet escort force as a mobile operating ship unit in order to quickly respond to aggressive action and such situations at sea. The fleet escort force must be able to maintain at least one escort flotilla on alert at all times.

The MSDF must possess, as ship units assigned to coastal surveillance and defense, at least one escort ship division in each specified sea district.

The MSDF must maintain submarine units, patrol helicopter and minesweeping units, providing the capability for surveillance and defense missions as well as minesweeping at important harbors and straits as necessary.

The MSDF must maintain fixed-wing patrol aircraft units to provide a capability for surveillance, patrol, and other operations in nearby seas.

(3) Air Self-Defense Force (ASDF)
The ASDF must possess aircraft control and warning units capable of vigilance and surveillance throughout Japanese airspace on a continuous basis, as well as performing warning and control functions as necessary.

The ASDF must possess fighter units and ground-to-air missile units for air defense to provide the capability of maintaining continuous alert, to take immediate and appropriate steps against violations of Japan's territorial airspace and air incursions.

The ASDF must possess units capable of engaging in the interdiction of airborne or amphibious landing invasions and air support for land forces as necessary.

The ASDF must possess units capable of effective operational supports including air reconnaissance, air transportation, and other operations as necessary.

*Necessary postures to be maintained*

In maintaining the following postures, special attention must be paid to achieving joint and integrated operations among each Self-Defense Force through enhancement of the Joint Staff Council's function and to promoting integrated cooperative relationships with related organizations so that the Self-Defense Forces can quickly and effectively carry out their missions.

(1) Setup for countering aggressions or similar situations
In the case of direct aggression, Japan's defense structure must be able to respond immediately in accordance with the type and scale of the aggression, and exert its capability effectively by integrating its assorted defense functions and by maintaining and enhancing the credibility of the Japan–U.S. Security Arrangements through various bilateral studies, joint exercises and training.

Japan's defense structure must be capable of responding immediately and taking appropriate actions, should an indirect act of aggression or unlawful military action occur.

Japan's defense structure must be capable of taking immediate and appropriate actions to cope with aircraft invading or threatening to invade its territorial airspace.

(2) Setup of disaster-relief operations
Japan's defense structure must be capable of taking timely and appropriate disaster relief activities in any area of Japan in response to large-scale disasters or other situations which require protection of lives and assets.

(3) Setup of international peace cooperation activities and others
The Self-Defense Forces must be capable of participating in international peace cooperation activities and international disaster relief activities in a timely and appropriate manner to contribute to the maintenance of peace and stability in the international community.

(4) Setup of warning, intelligence, and command and communication
Japan's defense structure must be capable of conducting warning and surveillance on a continuous basis to detect any changes in circumstances as soon as possible, so as to utilize this information for quick decision-making. It must be capable of high-level intelligence gathering and analysis, including strategic intelligence, through possession of diversified intelligence-gathering means and mechanisms, and highly able intelligence specialists.

Additionally, it must possess a sophisticated command and communication capability and be able to quickly and effectively conduct integrated defense operations from a joint perspective.

(5) Setup of logistic support
Japan's defense structure must be capable of carrying out necessary functions in each area of logistic support, such as transportation, search and rescue, supply, maintenance and medical and sanitary affairs, so that responses to various situations can be effectively conducted.

(6) Setup of personnel affairs, and education and training
Japan's defense structure must be capable of exerting its full potential as an organization by forming an appropriate personnel structure, maintaining strict discipline, and being composed of individuals with high morale and capability and broad perspective. For training personnel, it is necessary to promote personnel exchange programs within the Self-Defense Forces, as well as with other ministries and the private sector. It must be capable of recruiting, treating, educating and training its personnel in appropriate ways, while paying attention to the smooth execution of international peace cooperation activities.

*Maintenance of flexible defense capability*

As a result of the revision of the scale and functions of Japan's defense capability, Japan's defense structure must possess adequate flexibility, so that smooth response can be made to changing situations by maintaining education and training sections, personnel and equipment which require long training or acquisition time periods and by retaining high readiness Self-Defense Force Reservists.

The specific scales of key organizations and equipment are given in the attachment.

## V. Points of Note in Upgrading, Maintaining and Operating Defense Capability

The following points should be noted in upgrading, maintaining and operating the defense capabilities in accordance with the outlines described in Section IV including the structure of each of the Self-Defense Forces.

Decisions on major items in annual defense improvement programs will be submitted to the Security Council.

(1) The upgrading, maintenance and operation of Japan's defense capability will be conducted in harmony with other national policies, taking into account economic, fiscal and other situations. In light of the increasingly tight fiscal situation, special attention will be given to making appropriate budgetary allocations from a medium- and long-term perspective, so that Japan's defense capability can smoothly and thoroughly carry out its functions as a whole.

(2) Necessary steps will be taken to promote the effective maintenance and improvement, as well as the smooth consolidation and reduction of defense facilities, with the close cooperation of relevant local governments, and to facilitate further harmonization with surrounding areas.

(3) Equipment acquisition programs will be effectively implemented with overall consideration of such factors as speedy emergency resupply, easier education and training requirement and cost effectiveness, including future obligatory expenditures accompanying the introduction of equipment, and with special attention on developing a procurement and supply mechanism which helps reduce procurement costs.

Attention will also be given to maintaining defense production and technology foundations through appropriate promotion of domestic productions.

(4) Efforts will be made to enhance technical research and development that contributes to maintaining and improving the qualitative level of Japan's defense capability to keep up with technological advances.

If such an important change of situations occurs in the future that it is considered necessary to reexamine Japan's defense capability, another review will he initiated based on the circumstances at that time.

# Appendix 6b

# Scales of Procurement

| | | 1995 NDPO | 1976 NDPO |
|---|---|---|---|
| GSDF | Self-Defense Personnel | 160,000 | 180,000 |
| | Regular Personnel | 145,000 | |
| | Ready Reserve Personnel | 15,000 | |
| | Major Units | | |
| | Regionally Deployed Units | 8 Divisions<br>6 Brigades | 12 Divisions<br>2 Combined Brigades |
| | Mobile Operation Units | 1 Armored Division<br>1 Airborne Brigade<br>1 Helicopter Brigade | 1 Armored Division<br>1 Airborne Brigade<br>1 Helicopter Brigade |
| | Ground-to-Air Missile Units | 8 Anti-aircraft Artillery Groups | 8 Anti-aircraft Artillery Groups |
| | Main Equipment | | |
| | Battle Tanks | Approx. 900 | Approx. 1,200 |
| | Artillery | Approx. 900 | Approx. 1,000 |
| MSDF | Major Units | | |
| | Destroyer Units (for Mobile Operations) | 4 Flotillas | 4 Flotillas |
| | Destroyer Units (Regional District Units) | 7 Divisions | 10 Divisions |
| | Submarine Units | 6 Divisions | 6 Divisions |
| | Minesweeping Units | 1 Flotilla | 2 Flotillas |
| | Land-based Patrol Aircraft Units | 13 Squadrons | 16 Squadrons |

| (continued) | | 1995 NDPO | 1976 NDPO |
|---|---|---|---|
| | Main Equipment | | |
| | Destroyers | Approx. 50 | Approx. 60 |
| | Submarines | 16 | 16 |
| | Combat Aircraft | Approx. 170 | Approx. 220 |
| ASDF | Major Units | | |
| | Aircraft Control and Warning Units | 8 Groups<br>20 Squadrons<br>1 Squadron (Airborne Early Warning Squadron) | 28 Groups |
| | Interceptor Units | 9 Squadrons | 10 Squadrons |
| | Support Fighter Units | 3 Squadrons | 3 Squadrons |
| | Air Reconnaissance Units | 1 Squadron | 1 Squadron |
| | Air Transport Units | 3 Squadrons | 3 Squadrons |
| | Ground-to-Air Missile Units | 6 Groups | 6 Groups |
| | Main Equipment | | |
| | Combat Aircraft | Approx. 400 | Approx. 430 |
| | Fighters (included in Combat Aircraft) | Approx. 300 | Approx. 350 |

# Appendix 7

# The Three Principles on Arms Export

(Source: *Defense of Japan, 1997*. Tokyo: Japan Defense Agency)

Export of arms needs license of the minister of international trade and industry pursuant to the Foreign Exchange and Foreign Trade Control Law (1949 Law No. 228) and the Export Trade Control Law (1949 Cabinet Order 378).

**1. The Three Principles on Arms Export**

On April 21, 1967, then prime minister Eisaku Sato declared the three principles during a House of Representatives Audit Committee meeting.

(summary)

The principles provide that arms export to the following countries shall not be permitted:

1. Communist bloc countries;
2. Countries to which the export of arms is prohibited under United Nations resolutions;
3. Countries which are actually involved in or likely to become involved in international conflicts.

**2. The Unified Government View of Arms Export**

On February 27, 1976, then prime minister Takeo Miki announced the government's view during a House of Representatives' Budget Committee meeting.

(full text)

*1. Government policy*

With regard to the export of "arms," the government, from the standpoint of Japan as a pacifist country, has always been dealing with the problem of arms export in a cautious manner in order to prevent that from furthering international conflict. The government will continue to deal with the matter pursuant to the following policy and will not promote arms export.

1. The export of "arms" to areas subject to the three principles on arms export shall be prohibited.
2. The export of "arms" to other areas which are not subject to the three principles shall be restrained in line with the spirit of the Constitution and Foreign Exchange and Foreign Trade Control Law.
3. Equipment related to arms production (export Trade Control Order, Separate Table 1, Section No. 109, etc.) shall be treated in the same category as "arms."

2. *Definition of "arms."*

The term "arms" is used in laws and ordinances or in terms of application, and its definition should be interpreted in accordance with the effect of the law.

1. "Arms" in the Three Principles on Arms Export are what military forces directly use for combating and specifically mean "arms" that match definitions stated in sections from No. 197 to No. 205 in the separate table 1 for the Export Trade Control Order.
2. "Arms" under the Self-Defense Forces Law are interpreted as "firearms, explosives, swords and other machines, equipment and devices aimed at killing and injuring people or destroying things as means of armed struggle." Such things as destroyers, fighters and tanks that move, intrinsically carrying firearms, etc., for the purposes of directly killing and injuring people or destroying things as means of armed struggle, are considered "arms."

(Note: Due to partial revision of the Export Trade Control Law, "the paragraph 109" in (3) of (1) and "the paragraphs from 197 to 205" in (1) of (2) have been changed to "the paragraph 1.")

### 3. The Resolution as to the Problem of Arms Export and Others

Adopted at a House of Representatives plenary session on March 20, 1981, and also at a House of Councilors plenary session on March 30, 1981.

(full text)

Parliament has resolved that: Our country, from the standpoint of the Japanese constitutional idea for a pacifist nation, has been dealing with the export of arms in a cautious manner on the basis of the Three Principles of Arms Export and the unified government view of 1976.

It is regrettable, however, that there lately appeared instances which contravened the stated government policy. The government, therefore, should take effective measures, including institutional improvement, while dealing with the export of arms in strict fairness and with prudence.

# Appendix 8

# Statement of Chief Cabinet Secretary on Transfer of Military Technologies to the United States

(Source: *Defense of Japan, 1997.* Tokyo: Japan Defense Agency)
January 14, 1983

Since June 1981, the Japanese Government has received requests from the U.S. Government for exchange of defense-related technologies. After careful studies on the transfer to the U.S. of "military technologies" as a part of such exchange, the Japanese Government has reached the following conclusion, which was approved by the Cabinet meeting today:

1. Under the Japan–U.S. security arrangement, the United States and Japan, in cooperation with each other, are to maintain and develop their respective capacities to resist armed attack. In improving its defense capabilities, Japan has been benefiting from various kinds of cooperation extended by the United States, including transfer of U.S. technologies to Japan. In view of the new situation which has been brought about by, among other things, the recent advance of technology in Japan, it has become extremely important for Japan to reciprocate in the exchange of defense-related technologies in order to ensure the effective operation of the Japan–U.S. Security Treaty and its related agreements, which provide for and envisage mutual cooperation between Japan and the United States in the field of defense, and contribute to peace and security of Japan and in the Far East.

2. The Japanese Government has so far dealt with the question of arms export (including transfer of "military technologies") in accordance with the Three Principles on Arms Export and the Government Policy Guideline on Arms Export. In view of the foregoing, however, the Japanese Government has decided to respond positively to the U.S. request for exchange of defense-

related technologies and to open a way for the transfer to the United States of "military technologies" (including arms which are necessary to make such transfer effective) as a part of the technology exchange with the United States mentioned above; such transfer of "military technologies" will not be subject to the Three Principles on Arms Export. The implementation of such transfer will be made within the framework of the relevant provisions of the MDA Agreement. In this manner, the fundamental objective of refraining from aggravating international disputes, which Japan upholds as a nation committed to peace and on which the Three Principles are based, will be secured.

3. The Japanese Government will continue to maintain, basically, the Three Principles on Arms Export and to respect the spirit of the Diet Resolution on arms export adopted in March 1981.

# Appendix 9

# Three Non-Nuclear Principles

(Source: Glenn D. Hook, *Militarization and Demilitarization in Contemporary Japan*. New York: Routledge, 1996, p. 46. Also Peter J. Katzenstein and Nobuo Okawara, *Japan's National Security and Policy Responses in a Changing World*. Ithaca, NY: Cornell University Press, 1993, p. 165)

In 1967 the administration of Prime Minister Eisaku Sato was the first to articulate the three non-nuclear principles:

*Japan will not manufacture, possess, or allow introduction of nuclear weapons into Japan.*

(Additional source: John Endicott, *Japan's Nuclear Option: Political, Technical, and Strategic Factors*. New York: Praeger, 1975)

Sato's three non-nuclear principles were incorporated into a Diet Resolution on November 11, 1971 as part of an agreement between the Liberal Democratic Party (LDP) and opposition parties to resolve misgivings about the Okinawa Reversion Agreement. (The LDP, Komeito and Democratic Socialist Parties voted. The Japan Socialist Party and the Communist Party abstained.)

# Appendix 10

# Japan's Initial Defense Budget

(Source: *Bouei Hand Book, 1997*. Tokyo: Asagumo Shinbunsha)

| Year | Total Budget (Billion Yen) | % of GNP |
|---|---|---|
| 1977 | 1690.6 | 0.88 |
| 1978 | 1901.0 | 0.9 |
| 1979 | 2094.5 | 0.9 |
| 1980 | 2230.2 | 0.9 |
| 1981 | 2400.0 | 0.91 |
| 1982 | 2586.1 | 0.93 |
| 1983 | 2754.2 | 0.98 |
| 1984 | 2934.6 | 0.99 |
| 1985 | 3137.1 | 0.997 |
| 1986 | 3343.5 | 0.993 |
| 1987 | 3517.4 | 1.004 |
| 1988 | 3700.3 | 1.013 |
| 1989 | 3919.8 | 1.006 |
| 1990 | 4159.3 | 0.997 |
| 1991 | 4386.0 | 0.954 |
| 1992 | 4551.8 | 0.941 |
| 1993 | 4640.6 | 0.937 |
| 1994 | 4683.5 | 0.948 |
| 1995 | 4723.6 | 0.949 |
| 1996 | 4845.5 | 0.968 |
| 1997 | 4941.4 | 0.946 |
| 1998 | 4929.0 | 0.936 |

*Note:* The FY1997 budget does not include the cost for SACO-related projects, which account for 6.1 billion yen.

# Appendix 11
## Major Fora for U.S.–Japan Consultations on Security

| Consultative Forum | Japanese Side | U.S. Side | Purpose | Legal Basis |
|---|---|---|---|---|
| Security Consultative Committee (SCC) | Minister for Foreign Affairs<br>Minister of State for Defense | Secretary of State<br>Secretary of Defense (Note 1) | Study of matters which would promote understanding between the Japanese and U.S. governments and contribute to the strengthening of cooperative relations in the areas of security, and that form the basis of security and are related to security | Established on the basis of letters exchanged between Prime Minister of Japan and U.S. Secretary of State Jan. 19, 1960, in accordance with Article IV of Security Treaty |
| Security Subcommittee | Participants are not specified (Note 2) | Participants are not specified (Note 2) | Exchange of views on security issues of common concern to the U.S. and Japan | Article IV of Security Treaty |
| Security Consultative Group | Deputy Vice Minister of Foreign Affairs and Director General North American Affairs Bureau Ministry of Foreign Affairs, Director General | Minister and Counselor at U.S. Embassy, Commander and Chief of Staff of U.S. Forces in Japan, and others | Consultation and coordination concerning operation of Security Treaty and related arrangements | Established on the basis of the agreement reached between Minister for Foreign Affairs and U.S. Ambassador to Japan, Jan. 19, |

| | | | | |
|---|---|---|---|---|
| | Defense Facilities Administration Agency, Director General Defense Policy Bureau Defense Agency, Chairman of Joint Staff Council, and others | | | 1973, in accordance with Article IV of Security Treaty |
| Subcommittee for Defense Cooperation (SDC) | Director General American Affairs Bureau Ministry of Foreign Affairs, Director General Defense Policy Bureau Defense Agency, Chairman of Joint Staff Council, and others | Assistant Secretary of State, Assistant Secretary of Defense, Representatives from U.S. Embassy, U.S. Forces in Japan, and Joint Staff USPACOM | Study and consideration of consultative measures between Japan and the U.S., including guideline to ensure consistent joint responses covering the activities of SDF and USFJ in emergencies | Established on July 8, 1976, as a sub-entity under the Japan–U.S. Security Consultative Committee in its 16th meeting. Reconstituted in June 1996 at Japan–U.S. vice-ministerial consultation |
| Japan–U.S. Joint Committee | Director General North American Affairs Bureau Ministry of Foreign Affairs, Director General Defense Facilities Administration Agency, and others | Chief of Staff of U.S. Forces in Japan, Minister and Counselor at U.S. Embassy, and others | Consultation concerning implementations of Status of Forces Agreement | Article XXV of Status of Forces Agreement |

Note 1: The U.S. side was headed by the U.S. ambassador to Japan and the commander in chief of the U.S. Pacific Command before December 26, 1990.

Note 2: Meetings are held from time to time between working-level officials of the two governments, such as officials corresponding in rank to vice-minister or undersecretary.

(Source: *Defense of Japan, 1997.* Tokyo: Japan Defense Agency)

# About the Authors

THOMAS U. BERGER is an Assistant Professor in the Political Science Department of Johns Hopkins University. He is the author of *Culture of Antimilitarism: National Security in Germany and Japan* and has written extensively on national security, immigration, and political culture.

MICHAEL CHINWORTH is Senior Analyst for Technology Assessments at Litton Industries' Information System Group. He served as Senior Analyst for Asian Technology at TASC, Inc. He was Director of Research of the M.I.T. Japan Program at the Massachusetts Institute of Technology. Mr. Chinworth received his M.A. from the Johns Hopkins School of Advanced International Studies.

PATRICK M. CRONIN is Director of Research and Studies at United States Institute of Peace. He previously served as Deputy Director of the Institute for National Security Studies, National Defense University, where he was simultaneously Director of Research. Dr. Cronin received his Ph.D. from Oxford University.

ANNE M. DIXON is an Associate at Booz, Allen & Hamilton, Inc., where she specializes in strategy and planning. She was formerly on the research staff of the Center for Naval Analyses. Ms. Dixon received her M.A. from the Johns Hopkins School of Advanced International Studies.

PAUL S. GIARRA is Senior Analyst at Science Applications International Corporation, where he analyzes Asian strategic, economic, political, and security issues. He retired from the U.S. Navy and served as Senior Country Director for Japan in the Office of the Secretary of Defense. Mr. Giarra is also a technical advisor for Universal Studios.

MICHAEL J. GREEN is Olin Fellow for Asian Security Studies at the Council on Foreign Relations. He is also acting director of the Edwin O. Reischauer Center for East Asian Studies at the Johns Hopkins University School of Advanced International Studies and a consultant to the Office of the Secretary of Defense. Dr. Green received his Ph.D. from the Johns Hopkins School of Advanced International Studies.

W. LEE HOWELL is Deputy Director of Corporate Programs and Policy Planning at the Japan Society. He served as a Fellow at the Center for Strategic and International Studies. Mr. Howell received his LL.M. in International Legal Studies from the Washington College of Law at American University and his J.D. from the Widener University School of Law.

ROBERT A. MANNING is Senior Fellow and Director of Asia Studies at the Council on Foreign Relations. He served as Advisor for Policy to the Assistant Secretary for East Asian and Pacific Affairs, Department of State, and was an advisor to the Office of the Secretary of Defense.

MIKE M. MOCHIZUKI is Senior Fellow in the Foreign Policy Studies Program at the Brookings Institution. He previously was Co-Director of the Center for Asia-Pacific Policy at RAND, Associate Professor of International Relations at the University of Southern California, and Assistant Professor of Political Science at Yale University. Dr. Mochizuki received his Ph.D. from Harvard University.

AKIHISA NAGASHIMA is a Research Associate for Asian Security Studies at the Council on Foreign Relations. He previously served as Chief of Staff to Representative Nobuteru Ishihara (LDP, Tokyo). Mr. Nagashima received his LL.M. from Keio University, Tokyo, and his M.A. from the Johns Hopkins School of Advanced International Studies.

JAMES J. PRZYSTUP is Senior Fellow at the Institute for National Security Studies, National Defense University. He served as Director of the Asian Studies Center at the Heritage Foundation, and previously was on the Policy Planning Staff at the Department of State and in the Office of the Secretary of Defense. Dr. Przystup received his Ph.D. in diplomatic history from the University of Chicago.

GREGG A. RUBINSTEIN is Director of GAR Associates and is associated with the aerospace industry. He previously worked on U.S.–Japan security and economic relations at the Departments of State and Defense, as well as the U.S. Embassy in Tokyo. Mr. Rubinstein was educated at the University of Chicago, Columbia, and Sophia University, Tokyo.

RICHARD J. SAMUELS is Ford International Professor of Political Science at the Massachusetts Institute of Technology, where he also is Founding Director of the M.I.T. Japan Program. He served as vice-chairman of the Committee on Japan of the National Research Council. His most recent book, *Rich Nation, Strong Army: National Security and the Technological Transformation of Japan* published by Cornell University Press, won the John Whitney Hall Prize of the Association for Asian Studies.

SHEILA A. SMITH is an Assistant Professor in the Department of International Relations at Boston University. At the time of this book's publication she was on leave at the University of Ryukyus, Okinawa, conducting research on the local protest of U.S. military bases. Dr. Smith received her Ph.D. in Political Science from Columbia University.

LAURA STONE is a foreign service officer with the Department of State and served previously as an analyst with the Bureau of Intelligence and Research at the Department.

CHRISTOPHER P. TWOMEY is a doctoral candidate in the Department of Political Science at the Massachusetts Institute of Technology. He has served as a consultant to RAND and previously worked at the University of California's Institute on Global Conflict and Cooperation as Policy Researcher for Asia.

# Index

CPSIA information can be obtained at www.ICGtesting.com
233736LV00001B/1/A

9 780876 092491